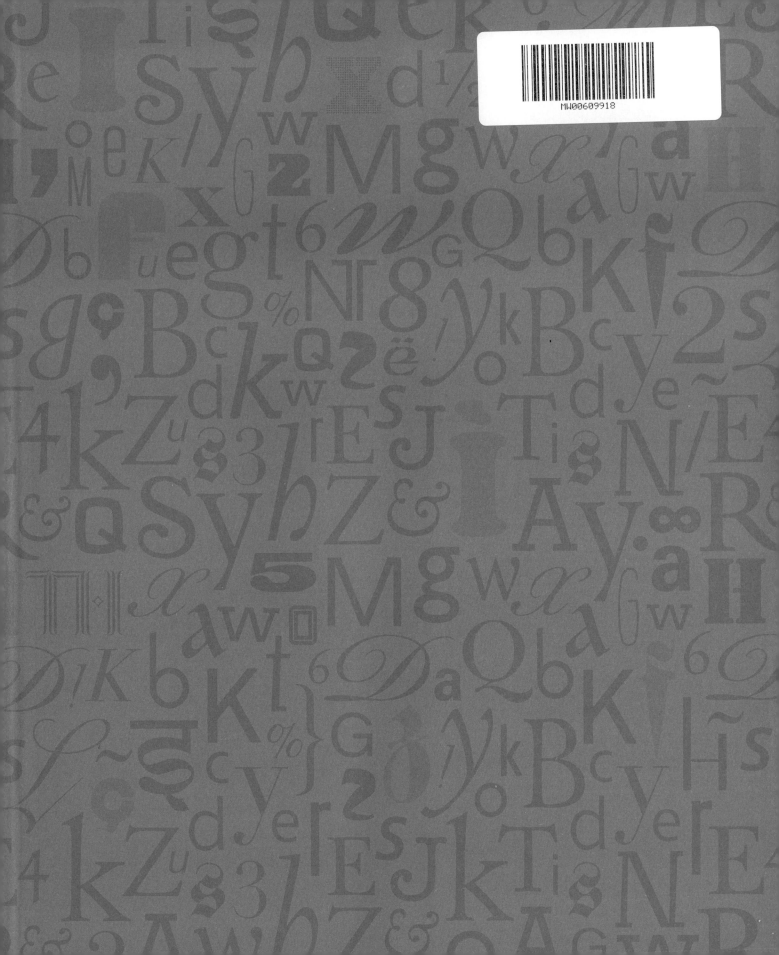

Typography Referenced

A Comprehensive Visual Guide
to the Language, History, and
Practice of Typography

ROCKPORT

First published in the United States of America by
Rockport Publishers, a member of
Quayside Publishing Group
100 Cummings Center
Suite 406-L
Beverly, MA 01915-6101
Telephone: (978) 282-9590
Fax: (978) 283-2742
www.rockpub.com

Library of Congress Cataloging-in-Publication Data is available

ISBN: 978-1-59253-702-0

Digital edition published in 2012
eISBN: 978-1-61058-205-6

10   9   8   7   6   5   4   3   2   1

Design
Donald Partyka

Layout and Production
Paula Daneze and Cathie Yun

Cover Design
Donald Partyka

Typography
This book is typeset in Tiempos by Kris Sowersby/Klim Type Foundry
Cover Typography: The cover is typeset in LaPolice, a revival of the
Romain du Roi by François Rappo/b+p swiss typefaces

Printed in China

Typography
Referenced

A Comprehensive Visual Guide to
the Language, History, and
Practice of Typography

Allan Haley, Richard Poulin, Jason Tselentis
Tony Seddon, Gerry Leonidas, Ina Saltz, Kathryn Henderson
with Tyler Alterman

Rockport Publishers
100 Cummings Center, Suite 406L
Beverly, MA 01915

rockpub.com • rockpaperink.com

Contents

} Introduction

Wrapping Paper:
Linotype Didot, Braille,
and sign language,
MOD/Michael Osborne
Design, United States

The history of type development has seen many exciting eras. The invention of moveable type, for instance, revolutionized our world, allowing the transmittal and sharing of knowledge, raising the level of the world's literacy, and enabling civilization to progress and prosper. And today we find ourselves in an unprecedented era of typographic fervor and productivity. Technological developments, principally the ubiquity of computers, the availability of sophisticated software, and Internet connectivity, have raised even the average person's awareness about the power of typography. In 2007, the TV game show *Jeopardy!* had "Fonts" as a category, with Bodoni and Helvetica among the answers. Popular magazines such as the *Atlantic*, *GQ*, *New Yorker*, and the *New York Times Magazine* have published significant articles about typographic topics that once would have been considered too esoteric for mainstream media. Network television shows and public radio programs have interviewed type designers. For the first time in history, the lay public has an appreciation for and an understanding of good typography.

Today, hundreds of colleges and universities worldwide teach courses about typography and even type design. There is a virtual army of enthusiastic young people devoted to the pursuit of typographic knowledge, excellence of typographic design, and type design. Prominent type designers are sought after as speakers and teachers; some have even attained rock star status.

Type is no longer the invisible servant of design, but rather recognized as design of the highest order. Typography is a subject of fierce debate and even controversy. Its passionate base celebrates and covets its innate complexity and characteristics. Typography conferences—formerly dry and scholarly— have become must-attend events, entertaining revels, even. Type-centric game shows and typographic "performance art" have appeared on the scene as inventive expressions of typography's enormous appeal.

Dare we venture a guess as to the number of readily available, downloadable, relatively inexpensive typefaces offered by a profusion of foundries, some with as few as a couple fonts, some with thousands? At this writing, that number surely tops 200,000. That's an astonishing number when we consider that only a few short years ago the figure was likely in the tens of thousands, with many fewer just prior to that. The tools—namely, software—for sophisticated and fully functional digital typeface design have themselves become easier to use and more affordable, and the means for distribution of digital fonts is only a click away.

O Y A C

v V v V q Q m M

e E a A r R t T

r R g G i I p P

w W u U x X z Z

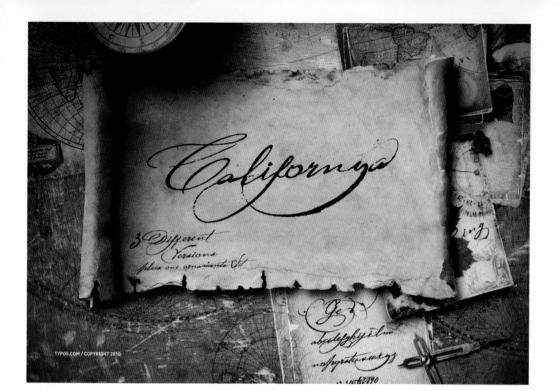

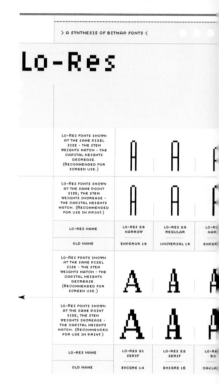

There are now many books devoted to the art, design, practice, resources, and teachings of typography. Because of that, there is an even greater need than ever for a book like this, an all-in-one comprehensive reference guide to all things typographic. We intend for this book to be a broad, authoritative, complete resource of typographic knowledge.

While many typography books contain wonderfully deep, scholarly, and essential material (more about these later), each has its own point of view, its own strengths and weaknesses, and inclusions and omissions. There is no single volume with it all, presented in an easy-to-navigate and accessible format. While *Typography, Referenced* covers every area of typography, it provides breadth rather than depth, for typography is a wonderfully dense and rich topic. For depth, we cite additional sources as needed.

As *Typography, Referenced* came into being, the book *An Incomplete Education* by Judy Jones and William Wilson (published by Ballantine Books in 1987) came to mind. The concept

of this hefty volume was astonishingly ambitious: To encompass and explicate the whole of science, philosophy, religion, political science, music, art, world history, psychology, economics, film, and American studies. In short, 10,000 years of culture in one fell swoop, or everything an "educated" person should know. Its aim was to provide key pieces of information, banishing those embarrassing gaps caused by missed educational opportunities or a lack of retention of what had once been learned.

We hope this book emulates the latter idea, as a single sourcebook in which practitioners and the average person alike can find every aspect of typography, with resources and guides for further research. *Typography, Referenced*, like *An Incomplete Education*, strives for breadth and inclusiveness, to cover the essential knowledge of the complex subject of typography, everything that a "typographically educated" person should know.

This book contains the basic foundations and core concepts of what constitutes

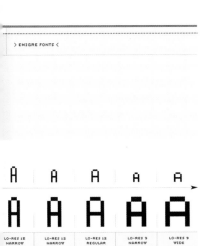

FOUNTAIN PRESENTS

ORBE

QUÍRON & GRIFOS

PERANTE GIGANTES E MONSTRUOSOS

DISCOBOLO

SERÃO ESFERAS, ORBES OU GLOBOS?

RETUMBAR

PARA TODOS SAUDAR DE MANSINHO

From left to right:
Californya I by German Olaya,
Lo-Res 1 by Zuzana Licko,
and Orbe I by Rui Abreu

typography and typographic design, delineating and defining type-specific language, terms, ideas, principles, and processes. It begins with the invention of moveable type and chronicles the entire history of typography, including the future of type on the Web, mobile devices, tablets, and beyond. It provides essential biographies of prominent type designers and their influence on contemporary design, as well as those designers shaping typography's future. It includes type specimens documenting the contributions of significant and classic type designs.

And *Typography, Referenced* incorporates all sources of typography and typographic design:

- Type foundries throughout the world
- Type-specific publications and books
- Online resources and blogs, which provide an ongoing and lively discourse about typographic topics
- Organizations that archive, acknowledge, support, and celebrate typographic achievements
- Institutions offering specialized type education
- Institutions that document, curate, collect, and preserve typographic heritage

In short, *Typography, Referenced* serves as a comprehensive source of information and inspiration by documenting and chronicling the scope of essential typographic knowledge and design from the beginnings of moveable type to the present golden age of typography.

Typography has entered the mainstream. Its devotees and acolytes have never been more visible, more active in the field, or more passionate. Given the vast scope of the current typographic landscape, this seems the perfect time for this particular volume about typography, one that aims to fill a void, find its place in many personal and public libraries, and serve as a springboard for the continued celebration and practice of the typographic arts.

—*Ina Saltz*

Type History and Timeline

By Allan Haley with Kathryn Henderson

**The history of type dates back to the ancient Greeks.
Here's a look at that timeline, from its start through 2010.**

Greek lapidary letters

Roman monumental capitals

Fifth Century BCE

Greek lapidary letters, letters carved into hard surfaces, were one of the first formal uses of Western letterforms. The Greeks adopted the Phoenician alphabet for their own needs, and as a result, changed several letters and created the foundation for Western writing.

Second Century BCE

Roman lapidary letters exemplified transitional letterforms from ancient Greek to the more modern Roman shapes and proportions.

First Century BCE

Roman monumental capitals are the foundation for Western type design, as well as the ancestor of all serif typefaces

Fourth and Fifth Centuries CE

This time period saw square capitals, formal hand-written letters that evolved from Roman monumental capitals.

Eighth through Eleventh Centuries

Thanks to Charlemagne, Carolingian minuscule became the basis for the standard **lowercase** (332) alphabet.

Te a quartana liberatū gaudeo:itēq; Pyliā.ego dum naues & cætera pa⁄
rant excurro i Pompeianū.Vectieno ueli gratias q; studiosus sit:si que⁄
quā nactus fueris qui pferat litteras:des ate q̄ discedimus.Vale.

OOmmodū ad te dederā litteras de pluribus rebus :cū ad me bene
nane Dionysius fuerit:ego quidé non mō placabilé me præbuis⁄
sé:sed totū remisissé si uenisset qua méte tu ad me scripseras.Erat eim
sic in tuis litteris quas Arpini accæperā eū uentu₷ : factu₷q; quod ego

Nicolas Jenson 1470

Fourteenth and Fifteenth Centuries

Although he did not invent movable type, the printing press, or printing ink, nor was he even the first person to print with metal type, **Johannes Gutenberg** (1394–1468) did create the art of typography. Gutenberg synthesized all existing devices into an economical and practical product. His adjustable mold, for example, enabled one letterform model produced by a designer to be replicated thousands of times. Gutenberg then took these products and combined them into works of typographic art that, more than 500 years later, are still considered some of the best ever produced.

Nicolas Jenson (77) (1420–1480) was one of the first printers to cut and use fonts based on Roman rather than northern European Fraktur letterform. Revivals of his type include William Morris's Golden Type, and the very successful Jenson Oldstyle first released in 1893 by American Type Founders.

Another fifteenth-century notable, **William Caxton** (1421–1491), a man credited with introducing to England the craft of printing with movable type, was first a successful businessman and government official before beginning his typographic career. He printed one of the first commercial advertisements, a poster that extolled the products and services of his shop.

The earliest fonts Caxton used came from mainland Europe, but once he established his business, he convinced a noted Flemish calligrapher to change professions to typeface designer and to move to England to produce type fonts. Caxton eventually had eight fonts produced for his press, most in the **Blackletter** (192) style of northern Germany, and one of which is generally considered the ancestor to Old English types still used today.

In 1450, the Gutenberg Bible was printed. This was the first important book printed in moveable type. In 1476, Caxton set up his printing business in the Almonry of Westminster Abbey.

Around the same time, the great Italian printer and type founder **Aldus Manutius** (78) (1450–1515) commissioned font designer **Francesco Griffo** (76) to create several typefaces, the most important of which is now revived under the name **Bembo** (155). The basis for the typeface was first used in Pietro Bembo's book *de Aetna*, printed in 1495 by Manutius in a font designed by Griffo. (Interestingly, Griffo only designed a **lowercase** [332] for the project, with the caps pulled from an existing font.) This became a model followed by **Claude Garamond** (74), as well as the ancestor of many seventeenth-century European types.

Also, Manutius and Griffo are generally credited with inventing italic type as a means to produce inexpensive books. The former is true, but not the latter; Manutius never produced an inexpensive book in his life. He created italic type as a "marketing tool" to help sell his books to well-off scholars and government officials who wrote in a similar style.

Granjon

Aa Bb Cc Dd Ee Ff Gg Hh Ii Jj Kk Ll Mm Nn
Oo Pp Qq Rr Ss Tt Uu Vv Ww Xx Yy Zz
abcdefghijklmnopqrstuvwxyz

Sixteenth Century

Garamond (74) (1500–1567) was the most distinguished type designer of his time, perhaps of the entire Renaissance period. A true typographic innovator, he was instrumental in the adoption of Roman typeface designs in France as a replacement for the commonly used Gothic, or **blackletter** (192), fonts. In 1530, his first Roman type appeared in *Paraphrais in Elgantiarum Libros Laurentii Vallae*. He also was one of the first type designers to create obliqued capitals to complement an italic **lowercase** (332).

Though Garamond's designs were exceptionally popular for a long time (the **Helvetica** [176] of their day), they did not, however, enjoy uninterrupted popularity. After a time, new French designs and styles created by English, Dutch, and Italian foundries began to replace Garamond's type as the design of choice among printers. Not until the beginning of the **twentieth century** (18) did new versions of Garamond style begin to appear again in print shops.

The work of **Robert Granjon** (75) (1513–1589) is closely associated with Garamond. Active from 1545 to 1589, Granjon is credited with introducing italic type form as a complement to the roman faces popular at the time. His work provided the models for **Plantin** and **Times New Roman** (165), as well as **Matthew Carter's** (85) Galliard. The face that bears his name, however, is based on a design by Garamond.

Type designer **Jean Jannon** (76) (1580–1658) created the typeface on which most modern Garamond revivals are based. Jannon worked more than 80 years after Garamond, and was the first to release revivals of the earlier Frenchman's work.

Seventeenth and Eighteenth Centuries

During this period, English gunsmith-turned-type-designer **William Caslon I** (72) (1692–1766) founded the Caslon Type Foundry. He was one of the few wealthy type designers. His work, based on earlier Dutch designs, does not possess irreproachable perfection like that of **Bodoni** (156) or **Baskerville** (154). Caslon's strength as a type designer was not in his ability to create flawless letters, but to create a font that when set in a block of text copy appeared perfect in spite of the vagaries and individuality of each letterform.

The first modern revivals of Caslon's work came out in the United States under the name Old Style. When American Type Founders (ATF) was formed in 1892, this design later became Caslon 471. After that came many succeeding ATF Caslons all based on Caslon's work: Monotype Caslon, Adobe Caslon, and even ITC Caslon. His surviving punches now reside in the St Bride Printing Library in London.

When **John Baskerville** (70) (1706–1775) first endeavored to create fonts of type, he found that printing technology of the day did not allow him to print as he wished. As a result, he explored, changed, and improved virtually all aspects of the printing process. He made his own printing press, a vastly improved version over others of the period; he developed his own ink, which even today is difficult to match for darkness and richness; and he invented the hot-pressing process to create smooth paper stock, even having a small mill built on his property to produce paper that met his standards.

Today Baskerville's "unpopular" type is one of the most popular and most frequently used serif typestyles. It is represented in essentially every type library, and can be reproduced on practically every kind of imaging device.

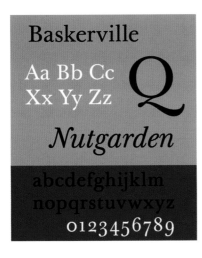

Also during the eighteenth century, French printer and type designer **Pierre Simon Fournier** (73) (1712–1768) was working. His work predated that of **Giambattista Bodoni** (71) (1740–1813) and is the foundation for much of Bodoni's first typeface designs; Monotype Fournier and Barbou are based on Fournier's work, as is Dwiggins Electra.

In 1734, **Caslon's** (72) types were first shown. Although based on Dutch old style weights and proportions, his font became the first great British type and set the standard for all that followed. It is said that just as Shakespeare gave England a national theater, Caslon gave the country a national typeface.

After the introduction of Caslon's fonts came Bodoni's work. The typography and type designs Bodoni created are still regarded as among the most refined and elegant ever produced. But he did have the luxury of almost limitless time, money, and effort to spend on his projects. Bodoni worked for the Duke of Parma, and outside of the occasional royal commission, only worked on projects of his choosing.

Bodoni's type was the result of an evolutionary process. The first fonts he used were **Old Style** (54) designs purchased from **Fournier** (73), and his first own fonts relied heavily on the Fournier type. Over many years, however, Bodoni's design style changed to the Modern with which we are familiar today. Interestingly, when Bodoni's style changed, he would simply recut specific letters for existing fonts to make them current.

This designer was one of history's mostly prolific creators of type. He was a demanding and exacting typographer who wanted to use exactly the size and proportion of type that best suited his needs. As a result, he created hundreds of fonts—all in the Bodoni style. An 1840 inventory of his output showed more than 25,000 punches and more than 50,000 matrices (letter molds).

When Bodoni was just twenty years old, in 1760, the Industrial Revolution began. This set the stage for advances in graphic design production. In 1762, **Baskerville** (154) typeface was first used. Baskerville's fonts bridged the gap between the Old Style designs produced during the Renaissance and the moderns created by **Firmin Didot** (73) (1764–1836) and Bodoni.

Early Nineteenth Century

Early in this century, Lord Stanhope invented the first printing press made of all cast-iron parts, requiring one-tenth the manual labor and doubling the possible paper size. A few years later, in 1816, William Caslon IV, the great, great grandson of *the* **William Caslon** (72), designed the first sans serif font, creating the English serifed design. Many claim that the design for this sans is based on the Greek lapidary letters of the fifth century. Note how close they also look to the caps found in faces such as **Futura** (174) and ITC Avant Garde Gothic.

In 1818, **Bodoni's** (71) *Manuale* (completed by his wife after his death) showed the quintessential modern type. Today, there are hundreds of **Bodoni** (156) revival designs based on those shown in this benchmark of typography. Three years later, in 1821, Italienne—one of the first commercially popular advertising display designs—was first used. Because serifs are heavier than main character strokes, this style of type has been called a reversed Egyptian.

The 1840s saw some important typography milestones. In the early part of the decade, Edward Binn's *The Anatomy of Sleep*, the first book typeset by a mechanical typesetting machine, published in London. In 1844, R. Besley & Co. Type Founders released **Clarendon** (58) as a heavy face to accompany standard text composition in directories and dictionaries. Clarendon became popular as an advertising display face, eventually copied by other foundries.

Bodoni

Aa Qq Rr
Aa Qq Rr
a
HORATII
abcdefghijklm
nopqrstuvwxyz
0123456789

Clarendon

Aa Ee Rr
Aa Ee Rr
Q
Anatomy
abcdefghijklm
nopqrstuvwxyz
0123456789

MANUALE

TIPOGRAFICO

DEL CAVALIERE

GIAMBATTISTA BODONI

———

VOLUME PRIMO.

PARMA

PRESSO LA VEDOVA

MDCCCXVIII.

1816

Bodoni

Mid to Late Nineteenth Century

Frederic Goudy (90) (1865–1947) was one of America's most prolific and well-known type designers, displaying originality and technical skill. He created more diverse typefaces than any designer before him. (**Morris Fuller Benton** [81] [1872–1948] may have created a larger and more divergent library, but also had a staff of designers to help him with his task.) Goudy was self-taught and didn't begin designing until age thirty.

As a designer and printer, Goudy developed a distinctive personal style. Early on he learned that even the most beautiful typefaces were doomed to failure unless they had a good marketing program. As a result, this man used his typefaces in specimen books and promotional material that were both exceptional graphic designs and compelling marketing vehicles. In addition, Goudy was his own best spokesperson. It is a testament to his ability that so many of his designs are still in active use.

Benton, on the other hand, is the unknown father of U.S. type design. He was the person behind American Type Founders' (ATF) type development program for more than thirty-five years. Benton is responsible for novelty designs such as Broadway, Tower, and Wedding, sans serifs such as Alternate Gothic, **Franklin Gothic** (172), and **News Gothic** (179), and mainstay advertising faces such as Century Oldstyle, Stymie, and the **Cheltenham** (186) family. He also created the first modern revival of **Bodoni's** (71) work and developed the quintessential **legibility** (330) face in Century Schoolbook—and this is only a sampling of his prodigious work.

For many years, ATF had the greatest offering of typefaces in the world—

Rudolf Koch, 1924

an offering that Benton essentially built. Outside the United States during this period, Emil Rudolf Weiss (1875–1943), **Rudolf Koch** (93) (1876–1934), **Lucian Bernhard** (82) (1885–1972), and **Paul Renner** (98) (1878–1956) began designing type.

A leading German typographer, designer, and calligrapher, Weiss was associated with the Bauer foundry in the **1930s** (21) and **1940s** (22).

Koch was primarily a calligrapher and teacher, but his association with the Klingspor type foundry in Germany provided the opportunity for a number of his designs to become type fonts. Most famous for his sans serif design, **Kabel** (177), he is also responsible for several other typefaces that have been made into digital type fonts. His calligraphic Locarno has been enlarged into a much bigger family than he anticipated, and Neuland is available from several sources. Other faces by Koch include Holla, Jessen, Marathon, Offenbach, Steel, and Wallau.

Bernhard was a character. He never owned an automobile, radio, television, or virtually

Kabel

Cooper Black

Aa Bb Cc Xx Yy Zz Coolidge

abcdefghijklm nopqrstuvwxyz 0123456789

1922

any other electrical appliance. He was an avid tango dancer and world-class admirer (an enlightened society might use harsher words) of women. He also was fond of telling tales about himself—such as how he ran away from home because he was hopelessly in love with the bareback rider—charming stories that likely stretched the truth more than a little.

He began designing typefaces as a young man in Germany, with his first cut in 1910. From then on, he designed a typeface a year until he came to the United States in 1922 to work with ATF, for which he produced thirteen types. Many of his typefaces are still available, among them Bernhard Cursive, Bernhard Gothic, Bernhard Tango, and Bernhard Fashion. Unfortunately, a few such as Bernhard Booklet, Bernhard Brushscript, and Lucian are not.

Renner created the first modern, **geometric** (62) sans serif face: **Futura** (174). Although not a member of the Bauhaus, Renner shared its ideals and believed that a modern typeface should express modern models, rather than revivals of previous designs. His original renderings for Futura's **lowercase** (332) were much more experiential and geometric in character than those finally released by the Bauer foundry.

Primarily a lettering artist and graphic designer, American **Oswald Bruce Cooper** (86) (1879–1940) is also responsible for designing a number of advertising **display typefaces** (213). He patterned all his type designs after his hand lettering. A student of **Goudy** (90), Cooper shunned the limelight, becoming famous in his time

almost in spite of himself. As his fame in graphic arts, copy writing, and advertising spread, Barnhart Brothers & Spindler foundry approached him to produce type designs. Creating more than a dozen families of type, Cooper persisted in thinking of himself as a "just" a lettering artist.

His best-known typeface, Cooper Black, has been called a design for farsighted printers and nearsighted readers. Recently there has been a revival of several of his designs, the more important of which are Oz Handicraft from **Bitstream** (124), as well as Ozwald and Highlander from **International Typeface Corporation** (128).

Another U.S. graphic, typographic, and book designer, **William Addison Dwiggins** (87) (1880–1956) came about during this period. Dwiggins's self-imposed challenge in all his type designs was to create beautiful and utilitarian typefaces for machine composition. In fact, this challenge became the catalyst for Dwiggins to begin his career in type design. He once wrote an article in the trade press complaining about a lack of acceptable Gothic typefaces available for **Linotype** (129) composition. Upon seeing the article, Chauncey Griffith, the director of typography at Mergenthaler Linotype, wrote Dwiggins a letter that said, in essence, "If you think you're so good, let's see you draw a Gothic." Dwiggins accepted the challenge, which began a twenty-seven-year association between Mergenthaler Linotype and the designer. For Mergenthaler Linotype, Dwiggins designed Caledonia, Eldorado, Electra, Falcon, and Metro.

1935

Elektra

Strange case of Dr. JEKYLL and Mr. HYDE. *Robert Louis Stevenson.* With illustrations by W. A. DWIGGINS.

RANDOM HOUSE · NEW YORK 1929

William A. Dwiggins, 1929

Elektra

Aa Bb Cc Dd Ee Ff Gg Hh Ii Jj Kk Ll Mm Nn Oo Pp Qq Rr Ss Tt Uu Vv Ww Xx Yy Zz

Nineteenth-century Birthdays

Tolbert Lanston (1844–1913) American inventor of the Monotype hot-metal composition system

Ottmar Mergenthaler (1845–1899) German inventor of the Linotype machine

Frederic Goudy (1865–1947) American typeface designer

Morris Fuller Benton (1872–1948) American typeface designer who headed American Type Founders' (ATF) type development program for thirty-five years

Emil Rudolf Weiss (1875–1943) German type designer

Rudolf Koch (1876–1934) German type designer most famous for his sans serif design Kabel

Paul Renner (1878–1956) German type designer who created Futura, the first modern, geometric sans serif face

Oswald Bruce Cooper (1879–1940) American lettering artist and graphic designer

William Addison Dwiggins (1880–1956) American graphic, typographic, and book designer

Eric Gill (1882–1940) English sculptor, stonecutter, artist, and type designer who created Gill Sans

Victor Hammer (1882–1967) Australian designer who created American Uncial

Lucian Bernhard (1885–1972) German type designer who came to the United States in 1922 to work with ATF

Stanley Morison (1889–1967) English typographical advisor to the Monotype Corporation for more than twenty-five years

Jan van Krimpen (1892–1957) Dutch type designer and book typographer

Georg Trump (1895–1985) German teacher of graphic design and type designer primarily associated with the Weber foundry

Charles Peignot (1897–1983) French director of Deberny & Peignot for fifty years

Robert Hunter Middleton (1898–1985), American type director for Ludlow Company type foundry for fifty years

1898

Akzidenz-Grotesk	Antiqua
Aa Ee Rr	Aa Qq Rr
Aa Ee Rr	**Aa Qq Rr**
Buchdruck	*Heirloom*
abcdefghijklm nopqrstuvwxyz 0123456789	abcdefghijklm nopqrstuvwxy 0123456789

Late Nineteenth and Early Twentieth Centuries

In 1892, **American Type Founders** (ATF) was founded as a consortium of twenty-three individual type foundries. The late 1800s saw an intense demand for type, but the type business was in turmoil, with too many competing type foundries each designing, manufacturing, marketing, and distributing their own fonts. Out of this atmosphere grew ATF, founded as a venture to improve business margins and restore stability to the type industry. Not only did the consortium meet its commercial goals, but the design community benefited from the monumental outpouring of exceptional type designs it produced. In its most prolific years between 1900 and 1935, ATF built the foundation of U.S. type design.

Also during this time period, Lanston Monotype Machine Company was founded in Washington, D.C. It released its first typeface, Modern Condensed, in 1896. Ottmar Mergenthaler designed the Blower Linotype, first installed at the *New York Herald Tribune*. And in 1898, **H. Berthold AG** (126) released **Akzidenz Grotesk** (170), the great-grandparent of **Helvetica** (176). It did yeoman's duty as what was then called a "jobbing face" until the late **1930s** (21), when the **geometric** (62) sans serif designs took over. Revival of Akzidenz Grotesk came at the hands of **Max Miedinger** (96) in 1957.

Several type influencers—some designers, some not—came onto the scene during this time as well:

Eric Gill

Eric Gill (1882–1940) was an English sculptor, stonecutter, artist, and type designer. His most important work—and his only sans—is **Gill Sans** (175). His other designs include Joanna, Perpetua, and Pilgrim.

A true iconoclast, Gill was well known for his radical political beliefs and sexual adventures. Through his friendship with **Stanley Morison** (97) and Beatrice Warde, often called the First Lady of Typography, Gill first began to design type. Morison felt Gill's background would give the stonecutter an understanding of the construction and purpose of serifs, and so he commissioned Gill's first face, Perpetua. Gill also designed Gill Sans at the request of Morison. The goal for Gill Sans was to provide **Monotype** (125) an alternative design to the many **geometric** (62) sans serif faces being released in Europe at the time. While not a geometric design like its competition, Gill's sans became the most popular serifless type in the United Kingdom.

Gill Sans Italic

1928

Stanley Morison

Though not a type designer, lettering artist, or calligrapher, Stanley Morison (1889–1967) was one of the most influential figures in modern British typography. As typographical advisor to the **Monotype Corporation** (125) for several decades, he was responsible for the release of such classic designs as **Rockwell** (190), **Gill Sans** (175), Perpetua, Albertus, and perhaps his most successful face, **Times New Roman** (165). In addition to new type styles, Morison also sponsored a series of typeface revivals—**Bembo** (155), **Baskerville** (154), Ehrhardt, Fournier, and Walbaum—unequaled in Britain or Europe.

Although rarely referenced in books on typographic history, another of Morison's contributions was his avid support of Beatrice Warde. Morison was Warde's friend, lover, and, perhaps most importantly, mentor. He provided her the opportunity and guidance to excel as a typographic historian, publicist, and passionate advocate for the printing arts.

Victor Hammer

Type designer Victor Hammer (1882–1967) created American Uncial, his most famous design, in 1943. Born in Australia, Hammer acquired a reputation for craftsmanship as a designer, punchcutter, and printer in Italy. He immigrated to the United States where he became a fine arts professor at Wells College in Aurora, New York. This is where he cut the punches for Uncial.

Jan van Krimpen

Jan van Krimpen (1892–1957) was a good type designer and one of the greatest book typographers of the **twentieth century** (18). His first and most successful type design was Lutetia, which he drew for the prestigious Netherlands printing house of Enschedé en Zonen. Other faces by Van Krimpen include Cancelleresca Bastarda, Romanée, Romulus, Spectrum, and Van Dijck.

Georg Trump

Georg Trump (1895–1985) was a teacher of graphic design and type designer primarily associated with Germany's Weber foundry. He released his most important design, Trump Mediaeval, in 1954. He also drew the typefaces City, Delphin, Schadow Antiqua, and **Codex** (350).

Charles Peignot

Director of Deberny & Peignot for nearly fifty years, Charles Peignot (1897–1983) stayed closely involved in the creation of all new faces emanating from his foundry. He commissioned the poster artist A. M. Cassandre to create the typeface that bears his name, Peignot. He also led the cause for typeface copyright protection and helped found the **Association Typographique Internationale** (354).

Robert Hunter Middleton

Type director for Ludlow Company type foundry for almost fifty years, Robert Hunter Middleton (1898–1985) devoted almost his entire professional life to that company. By the time he retired, Middleton had created almost 100 typefaces, among them Radiant, Stellar, Karnak, and Record Gothic.

Beatrice Warde

Although she never drew a typeface, Beatrice Warde (1900–1969) was vital to modern typographic history. As **Monotype's** (125) director of publicity, she was the passion behind Monotype's typographical efforts during its most important years from 1925 into the **1950s** (22). She's often dubbed the First Lady of Typography: In addition to creating marketing programs, she was an educator, historian, typographer, and the moving force behind **Eric Gill's** (89) designs of **Gill Sans** (175) and Perpetua.

Jan Tschichold

In the early part of this century, Jan Tschichold (1902–1974) revolutionized typography by almost single-handedly making asymmetric (226) typographic arrangement the style of choice for young designers. For many years, Tschichold created posters, book covers, advertisements, and even letterheads that showcased quintessential examples of asymmetric design. His work not only created a new typographic genre, but it also served as the benchmark for those who followed in his footsteps.

In addition to being a teacher, typographer, book designer, and rebel, Tschichold also designed typeface. **Sabon** (164), a typographic tour de force, is the face that established Tschichold's reputation as a type designer.

Early Twentieth-Century Birthdays

Beatrice Warde (1900–1969) American, known as the First Lady of Typography

Jan Tschichold (1902–1974) German teacher, typographer, book designer, and typeface designer

Warren Chappell (1904–1991) American type designer and typographic scholar

Roger Excoffon (1910–1983) French graphic and type designer

Max Miedinger (1910–1980) Swiss designer

Freeman (Jerry) Craw (1917–) American graphic and type designer

Tony Stan (1917–1988) American who designed, among others, ITC Berkeley Old Style, ITC Garamond, ITC Century, and ITC Cheltenham

Herb Lubalin (1918–1981) American designer whose creative graphic design and typographic handling broke new ground

Hermann Zapf (1918–) German typeface designer

Aldo Novarese (1920–1998) Italian type designer

Aaron Burns (1922–1991) American, cofounder of International Typeface Corporation

Ed Benguiat (1927–) American designer who has drawn more than 600 typefaces

Adrian Frutiger (1928–) Swiss graphic designer and typographer

Franklin Gothic

Aa Ee Rr
Aa Ee Rr
a

Wigglesworth

**abcdefghijklm
nopqrstuvwxyz
0123456789**

Century Schoolbook

Aa Qq Rr
Aa Qq Rr
a

Run, run, run!

abcdefghijklm
nopqrstuvwxyz
0123456789

Goudy Old Style

Aa Qq Rr
Aa Qq Rr
a

Adirondacks

abcdefghijklm
nopqrstuvwxyz
0123456789

Twentieth Century

In the beginning part of the century:

- Benton created Century Expanded (1900) based on Century, the typeface cut by his father, Linn Boyd Benton, in collaboration with Theodore Low DeVinne for *Century Magazine*. The objective for Century was a darker, more readable typeface than the type being used and one that could accommodate the magazine's two-column format. Century Expanded is a wider version of the magazine typeface.

- ATF released Franklin Gothic (1905). Named after Benjamin Franklin and originally issued in just one weight, the Franklin Gothic family eventually expanded to include several designs.

- Benton added Century Oldstyle to the Century family (1906), considered an exceptionally successful melding of Century typeface and Old Style design traits. Although almost ninety years old, it is still one of the most frequently used serif designs for advertising typography.

- The year 1915 brought the release of Century Schoolbook, a design the result of Benton's research into vision and reading comprehension. It was conceived and widely used for setting children's schoolbooks. The face also served as the foundation for the many legibility types that followed.

- Goudy released Goudy Oldstyle (1915), his most consistently popular typeface, but a design with which he was not completely satisfied.

- ATF released its first modern revival of Garamond (1917).

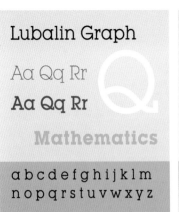

Warren Chappell

American type designer and typographic scholar Warren Chappell (1904–1991) studied under **Rudolf Koch** (93) in Germany and created typefaces for both American and European foundries. His works include Trajanus, Lydian, and Lydian Cursive.

Roger Excoffon

French graphic and type designer Roger Excoffon (1910–1983) created, among other faces, Mistral in 1953 and Antique Olive in the **1960s** (24). The latter was always popular in its country of origin, but did not enjoy success outside of France until Compugraphic Corporation released and heavily promoted the face in the late **1970s** (25).

Tony Stan

A prolific New York letter and type designer affiliated with Photo-Lettering, Inc. and **International Typeface Corporation** (128), Tony Stan (1917–1988) created or adapted a number of typefaces. His designs include, among others, ITC Berkeley Old Style, ITC Garamond, ITC Century, and ITC Cheltenham.

Freeman (Jerry) Craw

American graphic and type designer Freeman (Jerry) Craw (1917–) created both metal and phototype faces, among them Craw Clarendon, Craw Modern, and Ad Lib. For several years, he was vice president and art director of Tri-Arts Press during which he was responsible for some of the United States' most eloquent printed material.

Herb Lubalin

In the **1960s** (24) and **1970s** (25), the creative graphic design and typographic handling of American designer Herb Lubalin (1918–1981) broke new ground. At the same time, it set the standard for graphic communication that much of the graphic design community emulated. He designed logotypes, posters, magazines, advertising, packaging, books, stationery, and collateral promotional materials. In addition, Lubalin cofounded ITC and created more than 200 alphabets. He was responsible for such typefaces as ITC Lubalin Graph and ITC Ronda, and codesigned ITC Avant Garde Gothic with Tom Carnese.

Hermann Zapf

One of the **twentieth century's** (18) most important and prolific typeface designers, Hermann Zapf (1918–) has created such universally acclaimed typefaces as Optima, Palatino, Melior, ITC Zapf Chancery, Zapfino, and ITC Zapf Dingbats. He began his career with the D. Stempel AG foundry in West Germany after World War II. After leaving Stempel in 1956, Zapf created typefaces for foundries such as **H. Berthold AG** (126), **Linotype** (129), and ITC, in addition to many exclusive designs for private and corporate use. Zapf is also probably the world's most famous and successful calligrapher.

Aldo Novarese

Italian type designer Aldo Novarese (1920–1998) created a variety of text and display designs. Early in his career, he was associated with Turin's Nebiolo type foundry and created faces primarily in conjunction with Alessandro Butti, among them Augustea and Microgramma (which later became Eurostile when he added **lowercase** [332]). Later in his career, Novarese developed several faces that became ITC designs, including ITC Novarese (his most successful), ITC Symbol, and ITC Mixage.

Aaron Burns

Although Aaron Burns (1922–1991) was not a type designer, his contribution to the typographic world is as significant as many of the most important and well-known typeface creators. Burns founded **International Typeface Corporation** (128), which released more than 600 original and revival typeface designs and gave many type designers a first opportunity to create a commercial typeface design.

Kabel

Aa Qq Rr
Aa Qq Rr

Daylight

a b c d e f g h i j k l m
n o p q r s t u v w x y z
0123456789

Gill Sans

Aa Qq Rr
Aa Qq Rr

COLLEGIUM

a b c d e f g h i j k l m
n o p q r s t u v w x y z
0123456789

Futura

Aa Qq Rr
Aa Qq Rr

Zuführung

a b c d e f g h i j k l m
n o p q r s t u v w x y z
0 1 2 3 4 5 6 7 8 9

Bembo

Aa Ee Rr
Aa Ee Rr

VESUVIUS

a b c d e f g h i j k l m
n o p q r s t u v w x y z
0 1 2 3 4 5 6 7 8 9

Frutiger

Aa Ee Rr
Aa Ee Rr

Accès aux avions

a b c d e f g h i j k l m
n o p q r s t u v w x y z
0123456789

1920s

- In 1927, Klingspor type foundry released the **geometric** (62) sans **Kabel** (177), named for the Transatlantic Cable and designed by **Rudolf Koch** (93).

- **Monotype** (125) released **Gill Sans** (175) in 1928. Commissioned by **Stanley Morison** (97) for Monotype, this **Eric Gill** (89) design aimed to recover sales being lost to the new German **geometric** (62) sans. Gill Sans is not, however, a true geometric face; most of its character designs and proportions derive from classical serif designs.

- A year later saw the release of **Futura** (174). Drawn by **Paul Renner** (98), this was the first modern **geometric** (62) sans influenced by the Herbert Bayer's Universal typeface and the Bauhaus design philosophy. Futura became the benchmark design for modern sans, forcing virtually every type foundry to create its own version.

- In 1929, **Monotype** (125) release **Bembo** (155), the **twentieth-century** (18) version of a typeface designed by **Francesco Griffo** (76) for **Aldus Manutius** (78). Monotype released the design as part of **Stanley Morison's** (97) typeface revival program.

- That same year, D. Stempel AG foundry put out **Memphis** (188), the first twentieth-century **slab serif** (59) design. The similarities between this and **Futura** (174) are obvious. Almost every type supplier now has its slab serif version of Memphis, plus many completely original designs, as a result of this font's success.

Ed Benguiat

Ed Benguiat (1927–) has drawn more than 600 typefaces, possibly more than any other type designer. He has designed faces for ITC, Photo-Lettering, Inc., and a variety of corporate clients. He has revived old metal faces such as ITC Souvenir, ITC Bookman, and Sara Bernhardt, and has drawn new and original designs such as Charisma, ITC Panache, and Spectra.

Adrian Frutiger

Contemporary Swiss graphic designer and typographer Adrian Frutiger (1928–) is one of the most important type designers of the post–World War period. He began his work as an apprentice to a printer and studied woodcutting and calligraphy before launching his type design career. Deberny & Peignot asked him to adapt **Futura** (174), but he found it too geometric. Instead, he chose to create a large type family with matching weights; thus, **Univers** (181) was born. He also created a number of other popular typefaces: Egyptienne, **Serifa** (191), OCR-B, and the face used at the Charles De Gaulle Airport in France, now known as **Frutiger** (173).

Times Roman

Aa Ee Rr *a*

Aa Ee Rr

Publisher

abcdefghijklm
nopqrstuvwxyz
0123456789

BoltBold

Aa Qq Rr Q

Yy Ee Tt

Kryton

abcdefghijklm
nopqrstuvwxyz
0123456789

1930s

The first year of this decade saw the release of Metro, the only sans serif type **William Addison Dwiggins** (87) designed. Although originally intended for newspaper headline copy, this face became popular for a variety of advertising display applications. A face with more humanity than **Helvetica** (176) or **Univers** (181), less obvious overtones than **Gill Sans** (175), and just a hint of **art deco** (66) panache, Metro is unlike most other sans.

Two years later, **Times Roman** (165) arrived, commissioned by the *Times* (London) newspaper. **Stanley Morison** (97) supervised the design and provided the original Plantin specimens used to draw the face. He also appointed the designer, Victor Lardent, an artist on the *Times* staff.

During the second half of the 1930s, DIN 1451 was released. It was a realist sans serif typeface widely used for traffic, administration, and business applications, established by the German standards body Deutsches Institut für Normung as a standard typeface for German signage. Ludlow Company foundry released its stressed sans Radiant in 1938. It was intended to express the modern spirit of the 1930s while breaking away from previous sans serifs' geometric proportions and monotone weight. And Mergenthaler Linotype released Caledonia.

Birthdays of the 1930s

Friedrich Poppl (1932–1982)
German type designer who worked primarily for the H. Berthold AG foundry

Leslie Usherwood (1932–1983)
Canadian who founded Typsettra, Ltd. in Toronto and created Caxton, ITC Usherwood, and Flange

Matthew Carter (1937–)
American who cofounded Bitstream

Tom Carnese, (1939–)
American best known for his collaborations with Herb Lubalin at ITC who created or helped create a number of popular fonts, including ITC Avant Garde Gothic, ITC Bolt Bold, and ITC Pioneer

Memphis 1929

Amerigo

Aa Qq Rr
Yy Ee Tt
Americana **Q**

abcdefghijklm
nopqrstuvwxyz
0123456789

Stone Sans

Aa Ee Rr
Aa Ee Rr
Chariot **Q**

abcdefghijklm
nopqrstuvwxyz
0123456789

Birthdays of the 1940s

Gerard Unger (1942–)
Dutch type designer who has drawn
several faces for the Enschedé type
foundry in The Netherlands and Dr-Inf
Rudolf Hell in Germany

Colin Brignall (1945–)
British type designer and director of
type development at Letraset who
designed Corinthian, Edwardian,
Italia, Revue, Romic, and Retro

Sumner Stone (1945–)
American type designer and former
director of typographic development
for Adobe Systems

David Quay (1947–)
British type designer who drew ITC
Quay Sans, and more recently Coptek,
La Bamba, and Lambada for Letraset

Erik Spiekermann (1947–)
German type and graphic designer
who designed faces such as ITC
Officina, FF Meta, FF Info, Lo Type,
and Berliner Grotesk

1940s

In 1941, IBM announced its Electromatic Model 04 electric typewriter, featuring proportional spacing. Seven years later, Mergenthaler Linotype released **Trade Gothic** (180), and then René Higonnet and Louis Moyroud invented the Lithomat in France.

The Lithomat was the first successful phototypesetting machine. Later models called Lumitype could print more than 28,000 characters per hour.

1950s

In the 1950s, under the direction of Edouard Hoffmann, the Haas foundry asked **Max Miedinger** (96) of Zurich, Switzerland, to update Haas Grotesk, a version of Berthold's **Akzidenz Grotesk** (170). His creation, New Haas Grotesque—rechristened **Helvetica** (176) in honor of its country of origin—was released in 1957. The typeface has supplanted **Futura** (174) as the world's most widely used typeface. Miedinger released only three variants; several designers have added other styles and weights. Also in the early part of the 1950s, Mergenthaler Linotype released Palatino.

By the middle of the decade, the first phototypesetting machine was placed in a commercial business, Trump Mediaeval was released, and the Courier Monospaced typeface debuted. Howard "Bud" Kettler designed the monospaced (fixed-width or nonproportional) **slab serif** (59) typeface to resemble the output from a strike-on typewriter.

In 1958, Optima—**Hermann Zapf's** (107) favorite typeface—was released. (He used it to set his own wedding invitation.) While not the first, Optima has become the benchmark for all stressed, or **calligraphic** (64), sans serif typefaces. Optima italic also was one of the first typefaces created using the aid of mechanical distortion system. The roman was photographically obliqued as a starting point for the design by the New York typography studio of Photo-Lettering, Inc.

1958

Optima
Aa Qq Rr
Aa Qq Rr
MEMORIAL **a**

abcdefghijklm
nopqrstuvwxyz
0123456789

Courier

Aa Ee Qq
Aa Ee Qq

Think.

abcdefghijklm
nopqrstuvwxyz
0123456789

Helvetica

Aa Ee Rr
Aa Ee Rr

Kunsthalle

abcdefghijklm
nopqrstuvwxyz
0123456789

Palatino

Aa Bb Cc Dd Ee Ff
Gg Hh Ii Jj Kk Ll
Mm Nn Oo Pp Qq
Rr Ss Tt Uu Vv
Ww Xx Yy Zz

*abcdefghijklmn
opqrstuvwxyz*

1234567890

Lucida Sans

Aa Ee Rr
Aa Ee Rr

Informatica

abcdefghijklm
nopqrstuvwxyz
0123456789

LITHOS PRO

AA QQ RR
AA QQ RR

ΠΑΡΘΕΝΩΝΑΣ

ABCDEFGHIJKLM
NOPQRSTUVWZYZ
0123456789

1962

Eurostile

Aa Ee Rr
Aa Ee Rr

Proletariat

abcdefghijklm
nopqrstuvwxyz
0123456789

Sabon

Aa Ee Rr
Aa Ee Rr

Rapture

abcdefghijklm
nopqrstuvwxyz
0123456789

Birthdays of the Late Twentieth Century

Zuzana Licko (1961–) Czechoslovakian designer who immigrated to the United States in 1968

Jonathan Hoefler (1970–) American typeface designer who established The Hoefler Type Foundry (now Hoefler & Frere-Jones)

Tobias Frere-Jones (1970–) American type designer

Christian Schwartz (1977–) American type designer who partnered with Paul Barnes to form Commercial Type, a digital type foundry based in London and New York

1960s

Zuzana Licko (94) (1961–) is a Czechoslovakian designer who immigrated to the United States in 1968. Licko first created type designs for the publication *Emigre*, but because the young design community loved her designs, the faces eventually became commercial fonts. Her more successful faces include Matrix and Variex.

In 1962, Nebiolo foundry released Eurostile, a **square sans** (63) that was first a cap-only face. Later **Aldo Novarese** (98) drew **lowercase** (332) characters to complement the earlier designs on which he had collaborated with A. Butti, and the face was reissued and renamed Microgramma.

Shortly thereafter, **Linotype** (129) and **Monotype** (125) released **Sabon** (164), created by **Jan Tschichold** (105). This was a collaboration between the two to create a face concurrently available as hand-set and machine-set metal type, as well as photo type fonts. The roman is based on a **Garamond** (162) design, the italic on a **Granjon** (75) font.

In 1968, Compugraphic Corporation, the company that made low-cost photo-typesetting a practical reality, entered the phototypesetting machinery market. A year later, **Herb Lubalin** (95), Aaron Burns, and Photo-Lettering, Inc., founded ITC. Lubalin and Burns would provide new typeface designs and the marketing to make them successful; Photo-Lettering, Inc., would supply the technical know-how to produce artwork that would serve as production tools for phototype font development.

Avant Guarde Gothic
Aa Ee Rr
Aa Ee Rr
Moderist
abcdefghijklm
nopqrstuvwxyz
0123456789

Souvenir
Aa Ee Rr
Aa Ee Rr
Friendly
abcdefghijklm
nopqrstuvwxyz
0123456789

1970s

The year 1970 experienced the release of ITC Avant Garde Gothic and ITC Souvenir. ITC Avant Garde Gothic was ITC's first typeface, initially drawn by **Herb Lubalin** (95) as the logo and headline face for *Avant Garde* magazine. With the help of Photo-Lettering, Inc., the design was later converted to a text and display font. (Look at the caps in this face, then go back and look at the fifth-century BCE Greek lapidary type.)

That year, ITC also released the typeface designers love to hate, ITC Souvenir. Originally developed by **Morris Fuller Benton** (81) for atf in 1918, **Ed Benguiat** (80) revived the basic design, enlarged the family, and created the first italic variants. One year later, in 1971, Gary Starkweather at Xerox PARC invented the laser printer by modifying a Xerox copier.

In the mid- and late-1970s, ITC released Korinna and Galliard. The former was based on a turn-of-the-century **Berthold** (126) design updated and revived by Benguiat. **Matthew Carter** (85) designed the latter— based on a sixteenth-century design by **Robert Granjon** (75)—for **Linotype** (129), but later licensed it to ITC in 1982. In between these two releases, IBM introduced the IBM 3800, the first commercially available laser printer for use with its mainframes.

Avant Garde

Korinna
Aa Ee Rr
Aa Ee Rr
Casanova
abcdefghijklm
nopqrstuvwxyz
0123456789

Galliard
Aa Ee Rr
Aa Ee Rr
Blubber
abcdefghijklm
nopqrstuvwxyz
0123456789

1987

Charter

Hoefler Text

Aa Ee Rr
Aa Ee Rr
a
Pictorial

abcdefghijklm
nopqrstuvwxyz
0123456789

Comic Sans

Aa Bb Cc
Aa Bb Cc
a
Kidz Korner

abcdefghijklm
nopqrstuvwxyz
0123456789

Georgia

Aa Qq Rr
Aa Qq Rr
a
Bobwhite

abcdefghijklm
nopqrstuvwxyz
0123456789

Verdana

Aa Ee Rr
Aa Ee Rr
a
Sylvestris

abcdefghijklm
nopqrstuvwxyz
0123456789

1980s

In the 1980s, the Internet was invented.

In 1981, **Matthew Carter** (85) (1937–) and **Mike Parker** (1929–) founded **Bitstream** (124) to design and market type in digital form. The son of a printing historian, Carter is considered one of the founders of electronic type. He and Parker designed Bell Centennial for **Linotype** (129) and ITC Galliard. Bitstream Charter is the first of his new designs; he continues to work on new designs now. He also cofounded Carter & Cone Type, Inc., with Cherie Cone. A few of Carter's other designs include **Snell Roundhand** (205), Skia, Mantinia, Miller, and Charter.

In 1982, John Warnock and Chuck Gerschke founded **Adobe Systems** (124). In 1983, Adobe PostScript was announced, one of the three most important technological advancements in typographic history (the first being Gutenberg's invention of the adjustable mold, the second the Higonnet–Moyroud phototypesetting machine). It opened up digital typesetting and created what's now called the Desktop Publishing Revolution. That same year, ITC released ITC Berkeley Old Style, a revival of **Goudy's** (90) University of California Oldstyle.

During the **1980s**, Paul Brainerd, who founded Aldus Corporation, introduced PageMaker, the first widely used WYSIWIG (What You See is What You Get) page layout program for personal computers, and **David Berlow** (82) and Roger Black formed the Boston-based foundry **The Font Bureau, Inc.** (127). American typeface designer **Jonathan Hoefler** (92) (1970–) established The Hoefler Type Foundry— now **Hoefler & Frere-Jones** (132), a digital type foundry in New York that Hoefler shares with fellow type designer **Tobias Frere-Jones** (87) (1970–).

Georgia

1990s

ITC released Tekton in 1990, possibly the ITC Souvenir of this decade. It was designed by David Siegel for **Adobe Systems** (124) and based on the hand lettering of D. K. Ching, a Seattle architect. The following year, Adobe introduced the Portable Document Format—what's today commonly called PDF—to aid in the transfer of documents across platforms. Apple introduced its TrueType to compete with Adobe's PostScript.

Every other year in the 1990s but 1995 saw important milestones:

- 1992: The first Adobe Multiple Masters font was released. Multiple Master technology enables the type designer to create master designs at each end of one or more predetermined design axes. The graphic designer can then interpolate, or generate intermediate variations, between the master designs on demand.

- 1993: Apple announced TrueType GX, fonts heralded as "smart fonts" that can automatically insert ligatures, alternate character, and swash letters, in addition to providing the graphic designer with automatic optical alignment and other typographic refinements. Also, the first weights of the Interstate typeface were released.

- 1994: Comic Sans by Vincent Connare was released.

- 1996: Apple announced OpenType. Built on its predecessor, TrueType, it retained the basic structure but also added many intricate data structures for prescribing typographic behavior. Microsoft also made available Georgia and Verdana typefaces.

- 1997: Microsoft supported Embeddable OpenType (known as EOT) as a propriety format for Internet Explorer web fonts. No other browser companies jumped on the bandwagon.

- 1998: Agfa Corporation acquired Monotype Typography. Also, the first TypeCon Conference took place over Halloween weekend in Westborough, Massachusetts.

- 1999: ITC published the last issue of *U&lc*, its journal of typography. The journal had a cult following when it was published as a tabloid. That same year, Microsoft and eBook pioneers NuvoMedia and SoftBook Press hosted the first review of a draft specification for electronic book devices. And Adobe released InDesign.

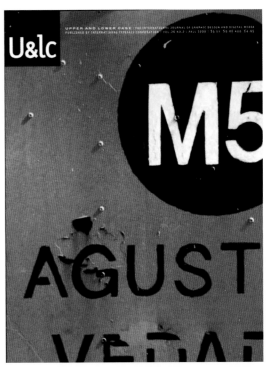

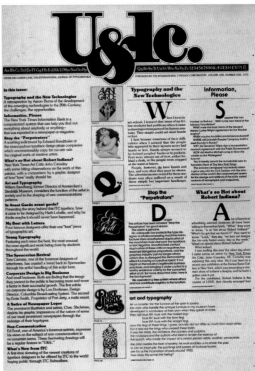

U&lc was ITC's journal of typography.

Gotham

Aa Ee Rr
Aa Ee Rr a

Vernacular

abcdefghijklm
nopqrstuvwxyz
0123456789

2000s

In 2000 and 2001, Agfa purchased the ITC type library and created Agfa Monotype, a merger of Agfa Typographic Systems and Monotype Typography. The Gotham typeface family, by **Tobias Frere-Jones** (87), was released. Apple introduced Mac OS X 10.0 code named Cheetah. Harvey R. Ball, who created the cultural and typographic iconic drawing of a smiling face on a yellow background, passed away.

In the middle part of the decade, Apple announced its intention to sell fonts online—but decided to sell music instead. The U.S. State Department issued a decree banning Courier from all official correspondence, replacing it with **Times New Roman** (165). People stopped caring about "grunge" fonts. And American type designer **Christian Schwartz** (100) (1977–) partnered with Paul Barnes to form Commercial Type, a digital type foundry based in London and New York.

Toward the second half of the 1990s, *Emigre* magazine stopped publishing after more than twenty-one years, and Monotype Imaging acquired **Linotype GmbH** (129).

Stag Family by Christian Schwartz

Meet the cast:
ABCD EFGHIJK LMNOP QRSTUV WXYZ
Now see the movie:
Helvetica
A documentary film by Gary Hustwit

Helvetica the movie was released in 2007.

The final issue of *Emigre* magazine.

In 2007:

- EOT submitted to World Wide Web Consortium as a public format for Web fonts.

- Monotype Imaging begins trading as "TYPE" on the Nasdaq Global Market Exchange.

- *Helvetica* the movie was released.

- Microsoft released Calibri, Cambria, Candara, Consolas, Constantia, and Corbel fonts as part of Vista OS to replace, among others, Arial and Times New Roman.

- Sweden's *Post- och Inrikes Tidningar* newspaper, the world's oldest still in circulation, dropped its print edition, publishing only online.

In 2009:

- Swedish furniture giant IKEA swapped its signature branding typeface, **Futura** (174), for the more Web-friendly Verdana, leading design fans to unleash a frenzy of hate email. Web fonts became commercially viable. The following year, **Matthew Carter** (85) won the MacArthur Foundation (genius) grant. The Gap logo was redesigned using **Helvetica** (176), outraging the design community. The clothing company reverted back to its original logo.

Calibri

Aa Bb Cc Dd Ee Ff Gg Hh Ii Jj Kk Ll Mm Nn Oo
Pp Qq Rr Ss Tt Uu Vv Ww Xx Yy Zz

abcdefghijklmnopqrstuvwxyz

Erin McLaughlin's Katari typeface combines a strong engagement with the writing of Devanagari, translating a pen-inspired structure into an incised style with both text and display variants.

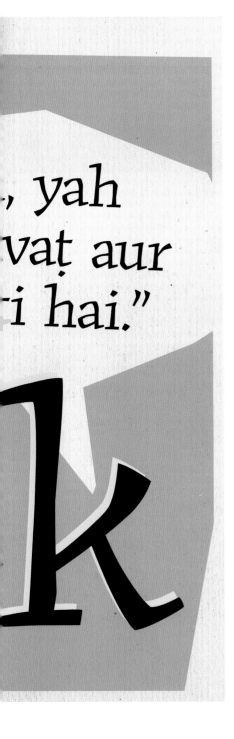

Type Design and Development

By Gerry Leonidas

Years ago we stopped trying to count how many typefaces are in circulation, but the market is growing: Digital type foundries are flourishing (as evident in the foundries chapter on page 122), specialist design courses are thriving (for more information, turn to the "Schools of Typography" chapter on page 346), and ever more designers want to publish their own typefaces.

The retail market is pushing the envelope in many areas. **Text typefaces** (212) are expanding to include many weights and widths and are increasingly refined in catering for detail typography. **Display typefaces** (213) are extending beyond simple forms to experiments in typographic textures and alternate glyphs. At the other end, corporate branding now demands typefaces that can be deployed across several markets and in a wide range of environments. The internationalization of publications and brands for products and services is redefining our ideas of what is a typeface family, extending across scripts.

More visibly, the explosion of smart phones, eBook readers, and tablets bring typefaces to the foreground of the design process. As less-than-forgiving surfaces with constant dimensions replace format, color fidelity, and material properties, typefaces and typography emerge as the dominant ways to distinguish one publication from the next. The recent maturity of Web fonts not only enables this process but hints at the next big thing: typefaces for browser-based texts. Although it isn't yet widely understood, we are gradually moving toward an environment in which brands and publications are primarily personal, local, and portable. Well-designed, **readable** (330) typefaces that convey strong identities sit at the center of this process.

In many ways, the type market has never been so healthy. New rendering technologies and new scenarios for using texts increase the demand for new typefaces, and by implication, the demand for designers, font engineers, and the many professionals who manage and develop the market. But the skills to make a mark in this industry are also becoming more refined and extensive. It takes years of practice to reach an international level of competence, but a good grasp of the basic principles makes the first steps easier. That's what we'll provide in this chapter.

The Past as Inspiration

Typeface design is personal and social at the same time. It sits at the intersection of a designer's desire for identity and originality, the demands of the moment, and the conventions shared by the intended audience. The designer also needs to take into account the constraints of the type-making and typesetting technology, the characteristics of the rendering process (whether printing or illuminating), and the past responses to similar conditions by countless designers. A good visual history of past designs is an essential element of every designer's toolkit.

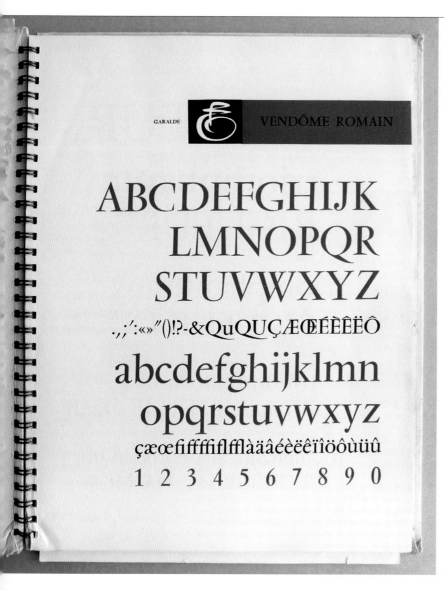

GARALDE · VENDÔME ROMAIN

ABCDEFGHIJK
LMNOPQR
STUVWXYZ
.,;':«»"()!?-&QuQUÇÆŒÉÈÊËÔ
abcdefghijklmn
opqrstuvwxyz
çæœfifffffiflfflàäâéèëêïíöôùüû
1 2 3 4 5 6 7 8 9 0

Until recently, the divide between **display** (213) and **text typefaces** (212) was wide: Text typefaces were often designed with clear references to historical forms and quite separate from display types. They also had long shelf lives. The few exceptions, usually sans serif families such as **Univers** (181) or **Futura** (174), targeted specific markets. Type histories tended to focus only on text typefaces for books, often downplaying the contribution of sans serifs to typographic design, ignoring display type and non-Latin scripts. Not until 1970 did we begin to see narratives with wider scope that considered the full range of print production, from small ephemera to broadside posters, newspapers to lectern bibles.

Today we tell a richer story of typeface, looking at the development of styles in response to document types, the effect of technology, market forces, and the interplay between cultural movements and typeface design. Old books and specimens enrich our understanding, provide inspiration, and protect us from reinventing the wheel.

A page from a 1958 Fonderie Olive specimen showing François Ganeau's Vendome Romain, an inspired interpretation of the Garamond style.

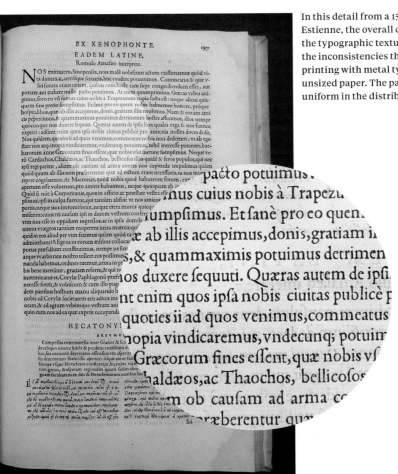

In this detail from a 1570 book by Henri Estienne, the overall consistency of the typographic texture overcomes the inconsistencies that result from printing with metal type on damp, unsized paper. The paragraph is uniform in the distribution of black.

A typical Modern typeface by Firmin Didot from an 1832 pamphlet. The high contrast and strong features require generous line spacing and reward good presswork.

HYMNE A LA VERTU.

Vertu, qui forces l'homme à vaincre la nature,
O le premier des biens qu'il doive conquérir,
C'est pour toi que la Grèce, heureuse de souffrir,
Supporte avec constance un labeur sans mesure,
Et pour ta beauté sainte, ò Vierge noble et pure,
    Voit ses enfants mourir.

Tant il est beau le fruit inaltérable
Dont tu séduis les ames des héros !
Tant pour les Grecs ce fruit est préférable
A la naissance, à l'or, au doux repos !

Jusqu'à toi se frayant un sentier difficile,
Les deux fils de Léda, sans redouter la mort,
Te forçaient, noble proie, en ton céleste asyle ;
Ils imitaient Alcide : et, par un même effort,
Pour toi le grand Ajax et le divin Achille
    Virent le sombre bord.

Letters, Lines, and Paragraphs

Although we can look at typefaces within the framework of classification systems, it is better to examine them in the context in which we see them on the page, so to speak. Traditional systems categorize typefaces by features such as angle of **contrast** (230), rate of modulation, and shape of serifs. (This partly explains why sans serifs were not classified with the same degree of analysis.) But if we look at typefaces in use, we see that many letter features distort or become less important to overall impression. The darkness of a block of text, the visual reinforcement of horizontal and vertical axes,

the distribution of space within and between letters, the length of ascenders and descenders, and the **line spacing** (335) become the dominant features. The typeface's overall texture becomes less important than the individual features. The presence or absence of complementary styles and weights within the paragraph and the editorial structure of the text determine our reading strategy.

Typeface design never happens in a vacuum. The designer acknowledges the wider historical and cultural environments in which a typeface sits and must respect the users'

expectations. This does not mean that a designer should not push the envelope and surprise users, but to do this well it's important to know what is considered conventional and acceptable—conventions that change over time and across geography, demographics, and document types, and according to the specifics of document use. A good designer is at least a social observer, decoding the culture of visual communication. A great designer is a social commentator, adding a layer of interpretation and response.

This is a detail from one of the many sketches in the development of Antonio Cavedoni's Enquire. The typeface is typical of contemporary designs that question the conventions of stress angles for modulated typefaces. At the bottom is the regular weight of a near-final design.

▶ Michael Hochleitner's award-winning typeface Ingeborg revisits Modern conventions with originality and humor. The typeface is refined and discreetly playful in the regular, but extends beyond the historical model in its much more fluid italic. In addition, the extreme weights integrate influences from later in the nineteenth century.

The Language of Letters

Typeface design, type design, or font design? Letter or glyph? Letterform, perhaps? Designers often use terms interchangeably, but it is helpful to have a good grasp of the nuances, if only because they reveal different aspects of the design process.

Think of a word. A sequence of letters should spring to mind. Write that sequence on a sheet of paper and these letters assume a concrete form made manually: They have been translated into letterforms. Any representations of letters made manually, regardless of the tool and the scale, are letterforms. Their maker controls their sequence and size and knows the dimensions and properties of the surface on which they are rendered. A hasty shopping list, Trajan's column, John Downer's brush-made signs. They're all meaningful collections of letterforms.

On the other hand, any representation of letters intended for mechanical reproduction is a collection of typeforms. The sequence in which a user places them and the size he or she will use remains unknown at the time of their making. Their maker also cannot predict the specifics of their rendering environment. Crucially, typeforms represent formal relationships in two dimensions rather than a specific way of capturing and rendering a shape. In other words, a **Univers** (181) **lowercase** (332) *a* is a Univers lowercase *a* regardless of the type-making and typesetting technology. Although there are differences in the visible forms produced with handset, hot-metal, and digital type, for example, the differences reflect the influence of the encoding and rendering technology. In other words, a typeface is a snapshot of the designer's intentions for a collection of typeforms.

To use these shapes in a specific typesetting environment, the typeforms get converted into glyphs (the term for digital formats), precise encodings in a machine-readable language enriched with information about the space surrounding the shape, its relationship to other glyphs, and its behavior. This machine-specific implementation of a typeface is called a font. To return to our Univers example, the typeface can be represented by a **Linotype** (129) matrix or bits in an OpenType font, but the essence of the design survives, hopefully with fidelity to the designer's intentions. Typeface design and font making are nominally sequential processes, even if design today closely interweaves typeface design and font production. One person may embody both roles, but often the typeface designer and font maker are separate members of the same team.

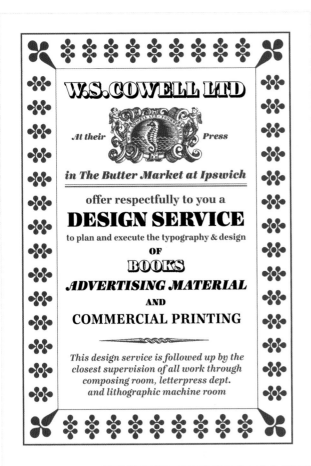

A spread using Futura by Bauer for the North American market, showing sample designs—a typical way to promote typefaces. The generous use of white space around the heavier forms emphasizes the texture and reinforces the range of weights in the family. These constructed styles offer less room for experimentation and have survived for decades as workhorses of display typesetting.

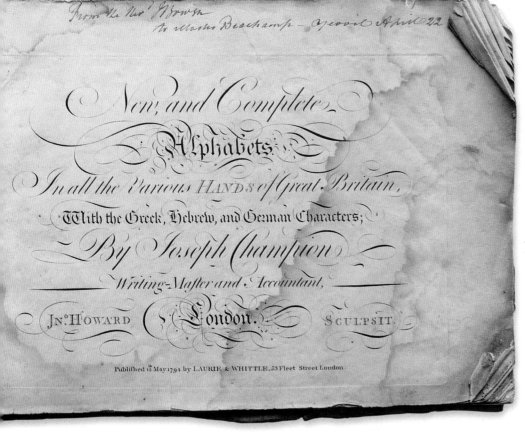

Joseph Champion's 1794 writing manual demonstrates the various styles of writing with a steel pen and the skill of the engraver. The wide range of alternate letterforms in such examples is one inspiration for contemporary typefaces.

Tools and Concepts

Typeforms are inextricably linked to writing. Not calligraphy, the craft of exploring expression with hand-rendered forms, but writing in the widest possible sense, from graffiti to a hasty "back in five minutes" sign to the most elaborate piece of public lettering. These forms determine the fundamental relationships between strokes and empty space at the heart of typeface design. On top of these, the designer adds a layer of interpretation and elaboration, making unknown combinations of typeforms with consistent texture and adding stylistic cues. Even the most constructed of typefaces hints at the underlying rhythm of manual mark-making.

Type design involves abstraction. A type designer imagines an idealized shape captured with type-making technology, then typeset and rendered on material or screen. Part of a type designer's skill includes capitalizing on the potential of these technologies, while at the same time understanding their limitations and their effect on the final forms. Producing the same typeface for different sizes and for a range of technologies is impossible without separating the reference model for a typeface, often designed first with pencil and paper, and each implementation with its specific properties (usually relating to rendering limitations, character set restrictions, etc.).

Technologies for which the type designer works directly on the final rendering size (foundry type, hot-metal type, some photo typefaces, and Bitmap typefaces, etc.) have a direct connection between the designer's specification and the outcome. Even there, however, the technology imposes a degree of abstraction. Early foundry type often has pen-like strokes, yet punchcutters would often employ counterpunches to form consistent negative spaces, carving separately the outside of

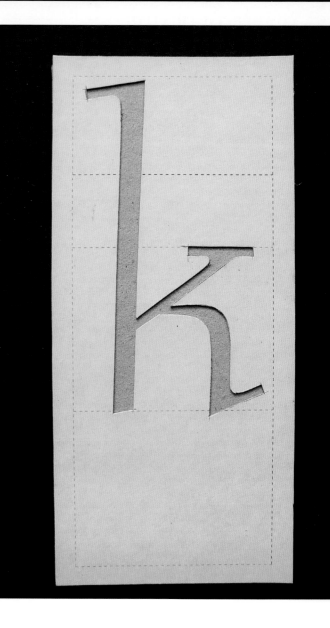

A card template cut by Jim Rimmer for his typeface Stern. The gentle tapering of the downstroke survived Rimmer's use of a pantograph to reduce the shape onto a brass matrix. Though Rimmer sketched the outline in pencil before cutting the shape, the result echoes a single stroke with a pen that modulates width through rotation or pressure.

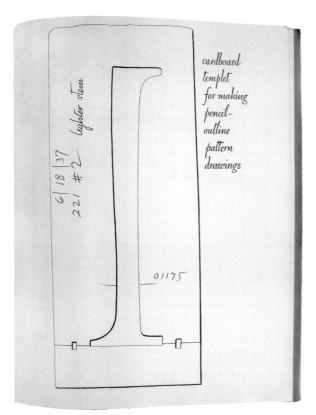

This sketch of a template cut in card by William Addison Dwiggins in his 1940 monograph *WAD to RR* showed a technique that allowed Dwiggins to combine the fluency of hand-rendered curves with the facility to repeat the shape in letters with similar strokes. The process suggests an element of modularization, but one reserved for main strokes only.

This series of nibs cut by Tim Holloway appear in the angle required for Indian penmanship, in which the stroke modulation is the reverse of that for Latin. These nibs were used to produce sketches that formed the basis for a Devanagari typeface from a major typeface foundry. The roots of all scripts are influenced by the interface of the writing tool, the pen-holding technique, and the writing surface. Although smooth paper is now ubiquitous, the characteristics of palm leaves and other such substrates still echo in typographic forms.

Wood letters, like other carved or dug-out forms, are largely agnostic as to the style of letters on their face. The letter-maker is imagining a shape written, designed, or constructed, and transfers this onto the face of the block. The stylistic cues survive longer than the original tools and techniques for letter making, perpetuated through the longevity of the format and the demand for the style.

the stroke. Hot-metal type making operations would use brass patterns, specially made French curves, and other methods of storing shapes. Throughout the hot-metal and phototypesetting eras, shapes were captured as engineering drawings, each letter several inches high, at scales that had little to do with the specific tool's movements. The arrival of platform-independent digital type stored without reference to the rendering size pushed further this separation between the model for a typeface and the specific shape of its rendered forms.

When designing a script typeface, the designer can reference written forms directly, modifying for output size and rendering. Most typefaces, however, depart from written form shapes. To ensure a typeface's consistency, the designer must develop a mental model of a tool. This may imitate the behavior of a writing tool, but may include mark-making and movement quite unlike anything possible to render with a real tool. An invented tool

that, for example, makes incised vertical strokes and pen-like bowls can become the basis for a wide range of styles, ensuring consistency without the limitations of a specific tool. This approach is especially pertinent in scales for which the limits of manual tools do not offer useful guidelines, such as typefaces in very small sizes. In those extremes a tool model might mark the counters and space between elements as much as the strokes.

It also does not hinder the generation of large, consistent families even without directly related elements. A light condensed, for example, can belong to the same family as a wide extra bold when the modulation, the joins between vertical strokes and curves, and the shape of instrokes and outstrokes are similar. Imagined tools are particularly helpful when a design abandons the organic shapes that reference pens, nibs, brushes, and other existing tools for entirely constructed shapes, treatments of the strokes that hint at perspective, or surface effects.

at cfr

In Eben Sorkin's Arrotino, the baseline outstrokes of the *a* and *e* are similar but not identical. The same treatment in the top outstrokes of the *c, f,* and *r* ensures a consistent typeface that retains a hint of written irregularity and balanced terminals. This is particularly noticeable in the *r*, which has a shorter arm, placing the terminal close to the strong top half-serif.

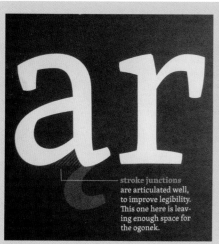

a r
c

stroke junctions are articulated well, to improve legibility. This one here is leaving enough space for the ogonek.

This detail from a poster by Type-Together on David Březina's Skolar shows a typical hybrid typeface. The bowl of the *a* and the bottom serifs have organic modulation, but the top serifs are typical of constructed elements. Some of the details get lost in smaller sizes and lower resolutions such as footnote text, but the overall low contrast helps maintain texture.

To understand the conventions for weight distribution and modularization, hold two pencils tied together and write slowly with the pencil angle unchanged. The resulting shapes will have, for the Latin script mainly, the stress and modulation typical of the traditional western style. Abstracted from the specific "nib" dimensions, this method can help answer questions such as where to place the thick strokes in extreme widths.

This spread from *Emigre* 19, designed by Laurie Haycock Makela, exemplifies the sea change in type making and typesetting brought by platform-independent font formats and object-based layout. Although seen initially as a place for experimentation and new thinking on design, *Emigre* also functioned as a mirror to preconceptions. Barry Deck's Template Gothic is typical of an approach questioning the means of type making with roots all the way back to Wim Crouwel's 1967 proposal for a new style of typefaces.

NO SIGN NO FORM NO WORD NO GOD

I was cranky and dehydrated. It was the morning after the party--the party of a thousand meaningless typefaces and dead-end discourses--I just didn't feel like getting up and making anything.

Can't make anything out of aesthetic and philosophical fallout. Can't find anything new in the black hole of Post-Modernism. The chattering, so-called "layering" of vacant meanings and the little type-tick fetishes that make graphic designers speak non-sense to each other just made me want to leave the party.

After prolonged theoretical dry-heaving, I made this piece within a month of arriving at Cranbrook: No form begins with an academic rejection of Modernism. No word is what I get if I call on literary theory to tell the story. No sign is what I'm left with as Deconstructivism steals the meaning from my experience and cuts it into little pieces. No god is the endpoint of confusion and doubt in the Post-Modern world.

This philosophical/emotional polemic poured lava-like over the studio discourse. My colleagues responded with equally direct language: from Kathleen Palmer's "Comprehend the Divine," a huge piece soaked in Christian ideology, to Scott Makela's muscular command to "Select Your Network" with the word "Your" digitally sifted into the back of a black man's neck. My own piece was a photograph of an excited, engorged clitoris called "Response of the Vulva."

The point is: consider an image of the smallest thing, the central thing, the only thing you know as authentic experience. Start there and be direct. Perfection doesn't count.

Laurie Haycock Makela, June 1991.

From a Letter to a Typeface

It is not too difficult to design one letter or even a few. But to design a full alphabet, a designer must balance complementary and contrasting features across a large character set. Making sure that range of shapes combines to form a unified whole is the first step toward a new typeface. This underlying homogeneity distinguishes typefaces from lettering and allows integration of unique features that impart personality and style while maintaining **readability** (330).

Where to start? Many designers think of some variation of "hamburgefons" (a typical test word used by type foundries) when starting a new typeface. But which of those letters to attempt first? Ideally, a designer works with a small set of letters that allows for the rapid development of ideas while embodying a wide range of strokes to give an impression of the face's more distinctive features.

The details here depend on a number of factors, not least of which is the designer's experience and skill and whether he or she is making an entirely original design or one inspired by an existing typeface. Sketching the *n* and the *o* alone is not enough to give a good idea of where the typeface will end up.

Sequences such as *a f g n p r s t, a b d e g h i n o y*, and *a g h m n o p* are well documented as starting sequences; they allow rapid development of a new typeface. An experienced designer might start with only *a e h n t*, or even *b a n d*.

A new designer might try the letters *a d e h i n o s* (or the word "adhesion" for ease) to get started. The letters offer a good compromise: It's a small enough set for the designer to change direction quickly, but it's large enough to offer a good balance of typeface-wide features and style in text settings. Letters such as *f g k*, which are relatively unique, are omitted, as are the diagonals *(k v w x y z)*, which share strong features among themselves, but not with the other letters.

Here is a sequence of basic strokes identified by Dwiggins for his typeface Falcon: long and short downstrokes, a top joining stroke, and clockwise and counter-clockwise bowls. From these five basic strokes, the designer can easily develop twelve to fifteen letters depending on the design's homogeneity. The remaining letters either have diagonal strokes or unique features that allow the designer to refine the style.

These are four stages in the early development of Neel Kshetrimayum's Frijky. The first drawings show main strokes that are too light, leading to light gray paragraphs. In the next few versions the strokes gain weight and the curves become less pointed. The highlighted terminals start as inconsistent outstrokes, but soon change to relatively safe slab serif shapes. The terminals of the fourth version balance a range of shapes with enough presence to emphasize the baseline.

Design by Team

There has been a gradual return to typeface design as a team enterprise, drawing on the expertise of a group rather than an individual. This concept is not new: Typeface design in the hot-metal and phototype eras was very much a team product. But just as the digital, platform-independent formats enabled designers to function outside of a heavy engineering world as sole traders, so it enabled the explosion of character sets and families to unprecedented levels. The necessary skills and the sheer volume of work required for text and branding typefaces have driven a growth of mid-size foundries where people with complementary skills collaborate on a single product. The corollary is a rise in the need for documentation and explanation to a community of fellows. The short-lived "creative hermit" model is giving way to new work modes.

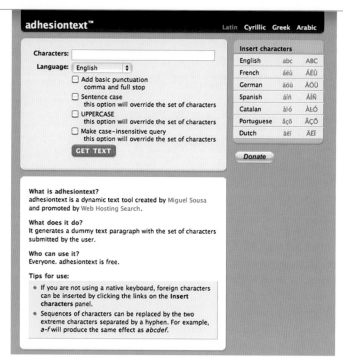

Miguel Sousa's text generator grew out of the need to source test texts for incomplete character sets. The tool allows designers to test the feel of their typeface as it develops across many languages, with texts that imitate real context as closely as possible. Adhesiontext.com is one of a growing range of online typeface design tools.

Most of the typeface drawings that museums, archives, and collections have show x-heights at anything from a couple inches (or centimeters) to around ten inches (25 cm) high, depending on their ultimate purpose. Designing on a computer screen requires a similarly large zoom factor. In **display typefaces** (213), this often reflects the rendering scale to allow the designer to grasp how the typeforms will look. But typefaces rendered at text sizes demand that the designer understands how design decisions translate across scales. This is one of the trickiest challenges for new designers.

Understanding how to make shapes at one scale behave a particular way in another scale is not straightforward. Readers look at words, lines, or paragraphs of typeset text, but a designer makes changes only to a single character. Imagining how a small change in a single letter will affect a whole paragraph is not an innate skill, but rather one learned through experience.

Most designers use interpolation, for example, the Multiple Master tools built in the widely used font-design application Fontlab, to develop and fine-tune designs. This works for anything from fairly basic proportions to fine details. Although interpolation can be a powerful tool, its effectiveness depends on the quality of the fonts at the extremes and the span the interpolation covers for each parameter. (For example, it is easier to obtain good results if interpolating within a relatively narrow range, rather than between extreme weights or widths.)

La vignette représente l'interieur d'une chambre,
La vignette représente l'interieur d'une cham
La vignette représente l'interieur d'une cha
La vignette représente l'interieur d'une ch

Typeface designers may use interpolation to produce closely matched versions of typefaces optimized for specific purposes, such as Adobe's Arno Pro, which ships with five optical sizes (small text [for captions], regular, subhead, and display). Four of these appear here as green outlines; for comparison, the black outline is the bold. Once the basic interpolation is done, the designer often returns to the outlines to improve details for intermediate styles. Setting the four variants at the same size highlights the weight and spacing differences.

représente
représente
représente
représente

Another use of interpolation involves the development of grades, which allow the designer to fine-tune the fit of a typeface to specific presses. Here the widths of the different styles remain identical to avoid the need to reflow text based on grade selection.

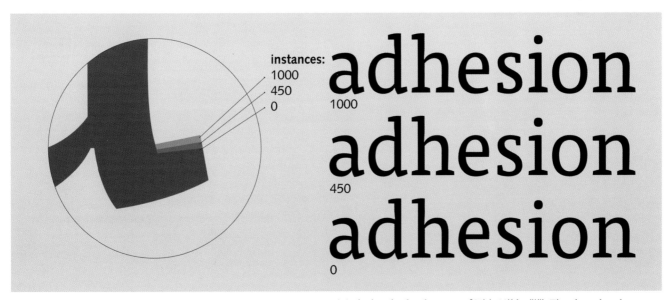

instances:
1000
450
0

adhesion
1000
adhesion
450
adhesion
0

Trials during the development of Mitja Miklavčič's Tisa show that the two extremes share basic dimensions. Just the weight of the outstrokes changes. The same approach was used to fine-tune many aspects of the typeface.

Rendering Environment

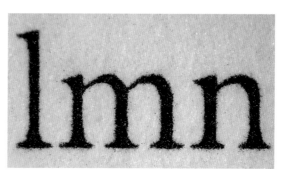

Three letters from 9-point Minion Pro, printed on a 600 dpi laser printer, photographed under a microscope. In comparison with the original outlines (left) the laser printer introduced inconsistencies of width in the vertical strokes, as well as in serifs and terminals. Although the resolution of laser printers is generally higher, this level of detail is comparable to many print-on-demand services.

The rendering environment (the test design application's display of type) plays an important role in the connection between the appearance of paragraphs and specific design choices. Type design applications may allow the designer to zoom in until a detail fills the whole screen, but this precludes the display of a whole paragraph. Zoom out to allow multiple lines of text on the screen, and the low resolution renders the details too fuzzy to judge. But printouts are also unreliable: Postscript version, toner level, paper quality and orientation, and many other factors influence the quality of laser output.

Instead, get printouts from different printers. Some type designers sneak lines of type on the margins of print jobs (or even place small advertisements in their own typeface) to get an idea of how the typeface performs in offset conditions. Here's a tip: Process black is generally lighter than laser toner, and a typeface may look washed out on offset.

For many years, a limit of 256 characters per font hampered digital typefaces, as did a need to ship in linked styles of four: regular, italic, bold, and bold italic. Most foundries have now expanded their character sets to include coverage for Latin script and are extending into other scripts, driven mostly by branding demand. But the most interesting developments are in regard to thinking about typeface families.

The establishment of OpenType and the support of wide families by page-layout applications allowed designers to rethink what constitutes a family. Traditional, individually bought typefaces were often developed to meet specific user needs. For example, a family like Monotype's Grotesque had several widths and weights for the upright styles, but only two inclined ones. The different styles have strong differences, and some weights seem reworked from standalone typefaces, but the family hangs together well because the individual styles work for their intended purpose. Although the completeness of a **Univers**-like (181) system is appealing, it irons out a designer's interpretation of a style for small sizes, display weights, and even alternate styles within the text styles.

At the same time, a family based on small weight increments can help publications such as magazines that need to combine different typefaces for headings, straplines, main text, captions, pull quotes, etc. The ability to select something a little heavier or lighter can make the difference between using a typeface or not. The profusion of typeface families with many weights near the middle of the range (regular, book, medium, semi-bold, etc.) is a welcome development in the past decade.

Testing the Design

The process of typeface design is, in essence, a reductive refinement of details. First ideas are just sketches that offer starting points followed by a clear methodology of structured changes, reviews, testing—and repetition of the whole process. The designer's attention progresses in ever-decreasing scales of focus:

- First, paragraph-level values on the overall density of a design
- Next, fundamental interplay of space and main strokes
- Third, elements within a typeface that ensure consistency and homogeneity
- Finally, elements that impart individuality and character

At the heart of this process is a question-filled dialogue: What are the conditions of use for the new design? How will the success of the design be evaluated?

The wider the typeface family, the deeper the need to test conclusively, not only with documents that highlight the typeface's qualities, but also with documents that approximate a wide range of possible uses. Even very tight briefs (as in the case of typefaces for corporate clients) can generate an extremely broad range of uses—scenarios that may even change after typeface delivery.

But good designers also understand the constraints of their testing environment. Ironically, the screen is gradually becoming an area of better control than print. Standardized tests to check the quality of type rendering on screen are increasingly published online for developers and designers to use. But the limitations of laser printers, the range of quality in digital printers, and the loss of wet proofs for offset complicate testing.

Emilie Rigaud's Coline combines a relatively restrained regular and bold, with an informal upright style, an upright italic with an associated light version, and an extra bold that pushes the style to its extreme.

Monotype Grotesque, a reference historical sans family with an incomplete family, works well for a wide range of documents.

* *

« Animated Lasagne »

Moot & Mutable

№ 63 Rue des Beaux Arts

* *

† βεβαια γυναίκα †

Je t'aime, moi non plus

drizzledrop queens

* *

ANGLE OF STRESS

hhh nnn

HEIGHT OF JUNCTION

THREE POINT JUNCTIONS AND CURVES

CONCAVE   CONVEX CONCAVE

ROUNDED   FACETED   POINTED

hhh nnn

CONVEX   CONCAVE

Aoife Mooney's Magnimo employs both an upright italic and an inclined one. There is a careful mix of features across the three styles to ensure that all combinations hang together well. Depending on the text to be set and the document's tone, the designer can choose a more or less discreet secondary style or employ all three instead of using an extra weight for differentiation.

Mathieu Reguer's plan for the Cassius family demonstrates the separation between text styles and display weights: The text variants are interpolated, but the extra bold and light need to be drawn separately to maximize effect. Note also the beginning of the extension into a second script, starting at the main text weight.

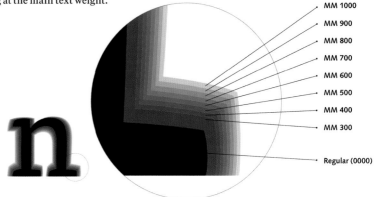

MM 1000
MM 900
MM 800
MM 700
MM 600
MM 500
MM 400
MM 300

Regular (0000)

A study of a typeface's possible weight variants can be extremely helpful for publications such as magazines that need to combine different typefaces for headings, straplines, main text, captions, pull quotes, and so on.

Space Matters

Punchcutters and letter cutters know firsthand that the most important element in a typeface is the space between letters. Readers are terrible at identifying specific widths along a line of text but extremely adept at picking out inconsistencies. Within the space of a few words, a designer can establish the typeface's basic rhythm; with small variations of basic dimensions and spacing a typeface can appear normal or impart the impression of a wider or narrower variant. This basic pattern greatly affects **readability** (330) of the typeface, even more so than the details of the dark shapes themselves.

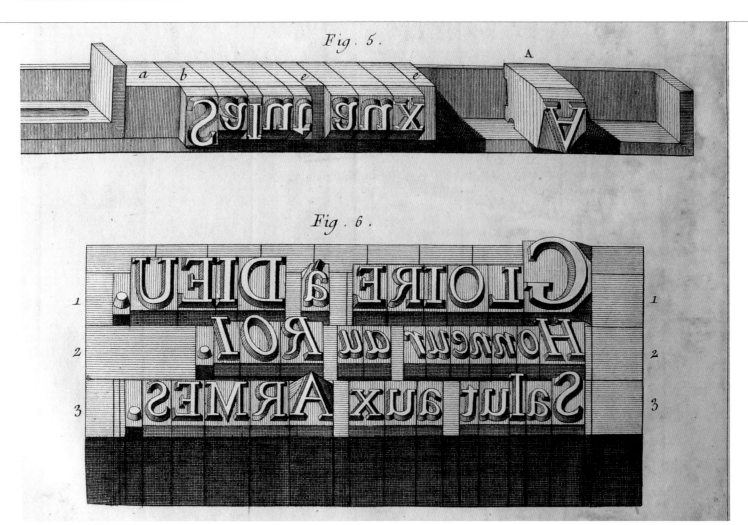

A detail from the *Encyclopedie* of 1754 shows composed foundry type. Even though digital type is disembodied, the same basic measurements apply. Studying good quality typesetting for hand-set type can help a designer discover how much is possible to achieve with good spacing (before the application of kerning). The middle row italics are offset on the body, an approach many digital typeface designers today use.

Although **display typefaces** (213) are relatively straightforward to space, spacing **text typefaces** (212) can be extremely time-consuming. It is not easy to describe how in a few sentences, but careful examination of good examples points to one basic rule and a fundamental set of relationships. Here's the rule: The optimum average space between typeforms depends on the relationship of the vertical-stroke width and the width of the counters in two-stroke forms (such as the *n* and *b*), modified by the optical size for which the typeface is intended. Outside a relatively narrow range, the x-height in relation to the width of the stroke is also a factor. We can easily imagine a system of interlocking ratios that change with the modification of one of these variables.

Of course, this approach does not directly answer how much space to leave between letters; it only indicates a series of relationships. The trick is to remember that a text typeface is spaced for paragraphs, not individual letter combinations. In other words, the designer should aim for a specific density in the texture. Well-spaced paragraphs tend to have a minimum of a stroke width's **white space** (228) between round letters and proportionately more between straight ones.

L A Vignette repréſente l'intérieur d'une chambre, dans laquelle ſont les caſſes, & pluſieurs compoſiteurs occupés à compoſer. Cette chambre communique à une ſeconde piece dans laquelle ſont les preſſes ; elle ſera repréſentée dans une des planches ſuivantes. On voit dans le fond du tableau la porte qui communique à cet attelier, & différentes tablettes ſur leſquelles ſont placés les caſſeaux des différents caraĉteres dont une Imprimerie doit être aſſortie. Au-deſſous de ces tablettes ſont des armoires qui contiennent des paquets de lettre, vignettes, & les différentes garnitures & uſtenſiles dont l'Imprimerie doit être fournie. On voit auſſi près le plancher les différentes cordes ſur leſquelles on étend le papier imprimé pour le faire ſécher.

L A Vignette repréſente l'intérieur d'une chambre, dans laquelle ſont les caſſes, & pluſieurs compoſiteurs occupés à compoſer. Cette chambre communique à une ſeconde piece dans laquelle ſont les preſſes ; elle ſera repréſentée dans une des planches ſuivantes. On voit dans le fond du tableau la porte qui communique à cet attelier, & différentes tablettes ſur leſquelles ſont placés les caſſeaux des différents caraĉteres dont une Imprimerie doit être aſſortie. Au-deſſous de ces tablettes ſont des armoires qui contiennent des paquets de lettre, vignettes, & les différentes garnitures & uſtenſiles dont l'Imprimerie doit être fournie. On voit auſſi près le plancher les différentes cordes ſur leſquelles on étend le papier imprimé pour le paire ſécher.

L A Vignette repréſente l'intérieur d'une chambre, dans laquelle ſont les caſſes, & pluſieurs compoſiteurs occupés à compoſer. Cette chambre communique à une ſeconde piece dans laquelle ſont les preſſes ; elle ſera repréſentée dans une des planches ſuivantes. On voit dans le fond du tableau la porte qui communique à cet attelier, & différentes tablettes ſur leſquelles ſont placés les caſſeaux des différents caraĉteres dont une Imprimerie doit être aſſortie. Au-deſſous de ces tablettes ſont des armoires qui contiennent des paquets de lettre, vignettes, & les différentes garnitures & uſtenſiles dont l'Imprimerie doit être fournie. On voit auſſi près le plancher les différentes cordes ſur leſquelles on étend le papier imprimé pour le paire ſécher.

A well-spaced paragraph of foundry type, from the *Encyclopedie* of 1754 demonstrates how an even typographic texture makes a text readable even with variations in the density of some letters, the horizontal alignment on the x-height, and inconsistent inking or pressure. In the digital versions, the top paragraph is spaced to exactly match the letterpress example, and the bottom one makes full use of InDesign's composer and spacing tools. The differences in texture are modest. Both paragraphs have some rivers of white. If anything, the lower paragraph is slightly more cramped and overcompresses the space around punctuation. The metal type preserves the minimum amount of space to the left and right of letters, whereas the digital version overcompresses some spaces.

Character Expansion

This drawing for the Linotype VIP system from 1976 shows a typeface still in use in other formats developed by a team of designers. The type-making process and the costs associated mean that drawings such as this encapsulate significant knowledge about the typographic script.

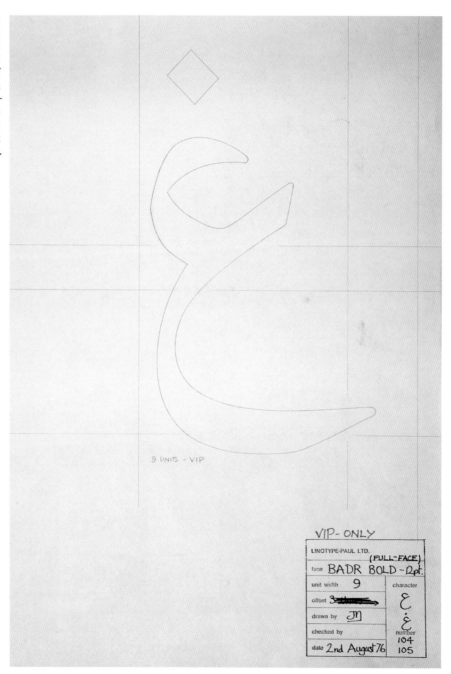

9 UNITS - VIP

VIP- ONLY

LINOTYPE-PAUL LTD.
(FULL-FACE)
face BADR BOLD -12pt.

unit width 9	character
offset 3	ع
drawn by JM	غ
checked by	number
date 2nd August 76	104 105

The demand for typefaces with extended character sets has been growing steadily for many years. Operating systems and application interfaces must be capable of displaying many languages. That and the internationalization of publications as well as brands for products and services means larger typeface character sets. Today, a typical custom typeface for a big brand may easily extend to several thousand characters and span five or more scripts.

Typefaces bundled with operating systems and applications and custom typefaces for brands are expected to cover more than one script—and often three or more. The current minimum for international brands covers the wider European region: Cyrillic, Greek, and extended Latin. Increasingly character sets also cover Arabic, Hebrew, and Indian scripts.

Typeface design is linked to the limitations of the typesetting environment. Most subsets of the Latin script (simple, alphabetic, left-to-right models) do not push the limits of a system based on a simple structure of sequential rectangular units. But this approach is strained by multiple diacritics and collapses when the shapes do not fit in boxes or change shape in algorithmically complicated ways. As a result, typesetting systems have had to be adapted, extended, and even rewritten to accommodate the complexities of non-Latin scripts. Although designers do design Latin typefaces with typesetting technology in mind, in many cases of non-Latin scripts, they have had to modify their designs quite drastically just to get the shapes to render.

In general, non-Latin scripts do not have the full profusion in styles that arises from a competitive publications market, as well as a culture of constant text production. (It's no surprise that the language of display typography first developed in nineteenth-century Britain during the Industrial Revolution.) This is gradually changing, largely under the pressure of international branding and localized publications. We are beginning to see rapid growth in new typefaces for non-Latin scripts, and a growing interest by typeface designers.

Διασκέδαση – Η Αβάνα είναι γεμάτη bars και clubs με live μουσική για πολύ χορό. Τα πιο γνωστά συγκροτήματα της πόλης εναλλάσσουν τις εμφανίσεις τους στα πιο φημισμένα clubs της πόλης: το Casa de la Musica de Centro Habana (Calle Galiano, entre Neptuno y Concordia, 78624165), το Casa de la Musica de Miramar (Calle 20, esquina 35, Playa, 72040447), το Salon Piano Bar «Delirio Habanero» (Teatro Nacional de Cuba, Paseo, esquina 39, Plaza de la Revolucion, 78790710) και το Cafe Cantante Mi Habana (Teatro Nacional de Cuba, Paseo, esquina 39, Plaza de la Revolucion, 78790710). Πολύ δημοφιλείς είναι οι Van Van, Paulito FG και Isaac Delgado. Απόλυτο must είναι το υπαίθριο Cabaret Tropicana (Calle 72, Marianao, 7170010), το παλιότερο και πιο θρυλικό cabaret show της Αβάνας.

The Capucine family by Alice Savoie integrates Latin and Greek text in magazines without disrupting the texture of the paragraph. Despite this, the typeforms for each script are developed with sensitivity and do not appear derivative.

Three typeforms from the Markant typeface exemplify how similar proportions and features can be integrated within the constraints of each writing model (italic and upright Latin and Greek).

hqﬀﬁﬂﬃ ﬃﬄﬅﬆ﬇﬈

﬉﬊﬋﬌﬍﬎ ﬏﬐﬑﬒ﬓﬔﬕ

1958ﬖ

ﬗ ﬘ ﬙ ﬚

﬛ ﬜ יִ ﬞ

This is the italic style from Khajag Apelian's Arek typeface, a new Armenian and Latin design and one of the first to introduce a more flowing style to the Armenian italic, hinting at the scope of typographic invention possible in non-Latin scripts.

Non-native Speakers

Can a non-native speaker design a typeface for a language? A typeface arises in response to a client's brief, which taps into wider design problems.

For example, many of the conventions surrounding newspapers apply regardless of the market; the constraints on the typographic specification can be deduced from the general qualities of the script and the language. Can the typeface include hyphenation? How long are the words and sentences? With what range of word lengths? What is the editorial practice in the region in terms of article structure, levels of **hierarchy** (222), and headline composition?

Only after establishing the typographic environment can we examine the written forms of the language and the tools that have determined the key shapes. In this matter most scripts other than the Latin (and to some degree Cyrillic) maintain a close relationship between writing and typographic forms. Writing exercises and a structural analysis of examples can help the designer develop a feel for the script before reading the words. More importantly, when working with a language or alphabet that is not his or her own, analysis of the script's structure and the relationship between mark-making tools and typeforms can help the designer to develop criteria for evaluating quality.

Typographic history is well populated with designers excelling in the design of scripts they could not read. Encouraging students to address the complicated design problems inherent in non-Latin scripts is not only a way of enriching the global typographic environment, but also is a superb means of producing designers who can tackle a higher level of difficulty in any aspect of their design.

Titus Nemeth's Aisha typeface is a new Arabic that draws on North African influences and traditions. This area has been relatively ignored by recent developments, but promises a wealth of material that can inform new designs.

Familiar Shapes, New Interpretations

A typeface is a product of the applied arts: It embodies functionality and usability and has intrinsic value through its utilization. On the most basic level, it allows encoding of textual meaning, but on a higher level it allows expression of values such as association, style, identity, differentiation, and beauty. This is the least tangible aspect of a typeface, but the one that most motivates designers.

Excellence in typeface design can be difficult to identify without the perspective of long-term review. Typefaces can become prominent because they embody a strong brand well or capture the moment in terms of their visual style. Typefaces for important publications or services are typical of the first kind (think **Cheltenham** [186] for the *New York Times* headlines, for example) and Excoffon's Mistral of the second. Other typefaces may become successful through their wide use, even as designers complain about their ubiquity. (**Times** [165] is a great example. It has become, arguably, a meta-typeface, existing in countless versions and adaptations, but its typographic feel is instantly recognizable worldwide.) But a capacity for discovery and invention characterize the field of typeface design.

L'art du livre & l'écriture du xvᵉ siècle

vibrant

a soft breeze and the harvest moon

fiery brilliance

It was at that moment, under the stars, that he proposed

Nuits St Georges

Arabesque Nᵒ 2, Claude Debussy

ein zauberhafter Abend

dignité

hues of aureolin & violet flooded the room

characteristic

Tom Grace's Givry is a fresh take on the *bâtarde flamande* from the fifteenth century. This black-letter is lesser known than other heavy, pen-written styles of the period but is typographically more interesting for the potential of its flowing strokes.

Typeface designers have proven extremely resourceful in their search for new typographic forms. Four areas seem to encompass these efforts.

1. Designers enter a dialog with typographic history. There are still many underexplored sources of inspiration in old type specimens and in the challenge of updating older styles to contemporary needs (for example, the recent spate of Modern typefaces).

2. New technology is informing typographic design and opens up possibilities. The profusion of typefaces exploring glyph substitution is the most visible example.

3. Questioning of genres and the design process waters down the distinctions of historical classifications and introduces hybrid forms into the mainstream.

4. The challenge of developing new typefaces for non-Latin scripts can serve a widening set of typographic conditions (for example, typefaces for multiple levels of emphasis in scripts that had, until recently, only a few typefaces at their disposal).

Depending on the brief and the language in which a typeface is expressed, there is more or less room for pushing the envelope of the acceptable. But in all cases there is room for offering new interpretations on familiar shapes.

Sutturah

Bombtrack
The Brutal Charade
The thirst of the Power Drones
Shucklah
Radically poetic
We gotta take the power back
Degree 189

Octavio Pardo-Virto's Sutturah pushes the limits of how much a flowing style can be combined with an extra bold stroke. The joining strokes and deep cuts hint at a three-dimensionality that can be exploited with interesting effects.

Type Classification and Identification

By Allan Haley

Most typefaces fall into one of three basic groups: those with serifs (little feet and tails), those without serifs, and scripts (designed to look like cursive handwriting). Many more definitive classification systems have been developed, some with more than 100 different categories.

A classification system can help identify and combine various typefaces. Though three categories may be inadequate, hundreds become self-defeating. Here we present fifteen groups of type styles, listed in chronological order of their appearance. In all likelihood, larger systems would break down into subdivisions of these.

Blaze
Script
Calligraphic

Young Baroque
Script
Formal

Clarendon
Serif
Clarendon

Centaur
Serif
Old Style

Nadianne
Script
Casual

Gill Sans
Sans Serif
Humanist

Electra
Serif
Transitional

Bodoni
Serif
Neoclassical/Didone

Silica
Serif
Slab

Élan
Serif
Glyphic

Helvetica
Sans Serif
Grotesque

Eurostile
Sans Serif
Square

Futura
Sans Serif
Transitional

Cresci Rotunda
Script
Blackletter/Lombardic

Raphael
Ornamental
Art Nouveau

Serif **Old Style**

These are the first Roman types, faces originally created between the **late- fifteenth century** (9) and **mid- eighteenth century** (10) or patterned after typefaces originally designed during this period.

The axis of curved strokes normally inclines to the left in these designs, so that weight stress falls at approximately eight o'clock and two o'clock. The **contrast** (230) in character stroke weight is not dramatic, and hairlines tend to be on the heavy side. Some versions, such as the earlier Venetian Old Style designs, are distinguished by the diagonal cross stroke of the **lowercase** (332) *e*. Serifs are almost always bracketed in Old Style designs and head serifs are often angled.

e Bembo

Head serifs are angled.

Some versions have a diagonal cross stroke of the lowercase *e*.

Contrast in stroke weight is not dramatic.

Hairlines tend to be on the heavy side.

Serifs are bracketed.

Weight stress falls at two o'clock and eight o'clock.

Berkeley Oldstyle

Legacy Serif   Centaur

Weidemann

Serif Transitional

The English printer and typographer **John Baskerville** (70) established the style for these typefaces in the middle of the **eighteenth century** (10). His work with calendared paper and improved printing methods (both of which he developed) allowed for the reproduction of much finer character strokes and the maintenance of subtler character shapes.

While the axis of curve strokes can be inclined in Transitional designs, they generally have a vertical stress. Weight **contrast** (230) is more pronounced than in **Old Style** (54) designs. Serifs are still bracketed and head serifs are oblique. These typefaces represent the transition between Old Style and **Neoclassical** (56) designs, and incorporate some characteristics of each.

Head serifs
are oblique.

Baskerville

Weight contrast is
more pronounced
than in Old
Style designs.

Serifs are
bracketed.

Axis of curve
strokes have a
vertical stress.

Americana

Bulmer Electra

Perpetua

Serif Neoclassical/Didone

These are typefaces created during the **late eighteenth century** (10), or their direct descendants. The work of **Giambattista Bodoni** (71) epitomizes this type style. When first released, these typefaces were called Classical designs. Early on, however, it became apparent that rather than updated versions of classic type styles, these were altogether new designs. As a result, their classification name was changed to Modern. Because they are no longer modern today, they are also classified as Neoclassical or Didone.

Contrast (230) between thick and thin strokes is abrupt and dramatic here. The axis of curved strokes is vertical, with little or no bracketing. In many cases, stroke terminals are ball shapes rather than the reflection of a broad pen. These tend to be highly mannered designs, which are obviously constructed.

a Bodoni

In many cases, stroke terminals are ball shapes.

Contrast between thick and thin strokes is abrupt and dramatic.

Axis of curved strokes is vertical, with little or no bracketing.

Arepo | Fenice

Modern No. 216

Walbaum

Serif **Glyphic**

Typefaces in this category tend to reflect lapidary inscriptions rather than pen-drawn text. **Contrast** (230) in stroke weight is usually minimal, and the axis of curved strokes tends to be vertical. The distinguishing feature of these typefaces is the triangular-shaped serif design, or a flaring of the character strokes at termination. Some type classification systems break down this one category into two groups: Glyphic and Latin. Latins are faces with strict triangular-shaped serifs.

Albertus

Triangular-shaped serif design.

Minimum contrast in stroke weight.

Vertical axis of curved strokes.

Élan | Cartier Book

Friz Quadrata

Quorum

Serif Clarendon

As the name implies, these are typefaces patterned after the Clarendon type styles first released in the **mid nineteenth century** (13). Clarendons were designed as boldfaces to accompany text composition. Their stroke **contrast** (230) is slight and serifs tend to be short to medium length. Many of these designs were later released as **display types** (213). More obvious character stroke weight and serifs longer than earlier designs mark more current interpretations of this style.

Accolade

Slight stroke contrast

Short- to medium-length serifs

Bookman

Charter

Clarendon

Nimrod

Serif **Slab**

Slab serif typefaces became popular in the **nineteenth century** (13) as advertising display designs. These typefaces have very heavy serifs with little or no bracketing. Generally, changes in stroke weight are imperceptible. Many view slab serif type styles as sans serif designs with the simple addition of heavy (stroke weight) serifs.

Very heavy serifs with little or no bracketing

Rockwell

Generally imperceptible changes in stroke weight

Lubalin Graph

Officina Serif

Silica

Egyptian Slate

Soho

Sans Serif Grotesque

These are the first commercially popular sans serif typefaces. **Contrast** (230) in stroke weight is most apparent in these styles, there is a slight "squared" quality to many of the curves, and several designs have the bowl-and-loop **lowercase** (332) *g* common to roman types. In some cases the *R* has a curled leg and the *G* usually has a spur.

Some modern sans serif designs derive from the first Grotesques, but are more refined in form. Stroke contrast is less pronounced than earlier designs, and much of the squareness in curved strokes is also lost. Typically the most obvious distinguishing characteristic of these faces is their single-bowl *g* and more monotone weight stress.

g Helvetica

Obvious contrast
in stroke weight

Bowl-and-loop
lowercase *g* in
many designs

Slight "squared"
quality to many
of the curves

Bureau Grotesque

Franklin Gothic

News Gothic   Univers

Sans Serif Humanist

These are based on the proportions of roman inscriptional letters. In many cases, **contrast** (230) in stroke weight is also readily apparent. Many claim that these are the most **legible** (330) in terms of character design and most easily read in terms of typography of the sans serif typefaces. They also most closely match the design characteristics and proportions of serif types. Many of these typefaces display a strong **calligraphic** (64) influence.

Goudy Sans

Readily apparent contrast in stroke weight

Strong, apparent calligraphic influence

Based on the proportions of roman inscriptional letters

Frutiger | Gill Sans

Mentor Sans

Stone Humanistic

Sans Serif Geometric

Simple geometric shapes heavily influence the construction of these typefaces. Strokes appear like strict monolines, and seemingly perfect geometric forms make up the character shapes. Geometric sans tend to be less readable (330) than Grotesques (60).

o | Futura

Seemingly perfect geometric forms make up character shapes.

Strokes appear as strict monolines.

Simple geometric shapes

Avant Garde Gothic

Avenir | **Bauhaus** | Kabel

Harmonia Sans

Sans Serif **Square**

These designs, generally based on **Grotesque** (60) character traits and proportions, have a definite and at times dramatic squaring of normally curved strokes. They usually have more latitude in character spacing than their sans serif cousins, and tend to be limited to display designs.

Phenix American

Definite squaring
of normally
curved strokes

Condensed
typeface

Cachet | Eurostile

Felbridge

Neo Sans | Smart Sans

Script Formal

Bickham Script

Script Casual

Brush Script

Script Calligraphic

Belltrap

These typefaces derive from seventeenth-century (10) formal writing styles. Many characters have strokes that join them to other letters.

Elegy

Helinda Rook

Mahogany Script

Young Baroque

These script typefaces intentionally look informal or quickly drawn. Often they appear drawn with a brush. Typically, character strokes connect one letter to the next.

Limehouse Script

Nadianne

Freestyle Script

Studio Script

These script faces mimic calligraphy. They can be connecting or nonconnecting in design. Many appear written with a flat-tipped writing instrument.

Blaze

Mistral

Riptide

Vivaldi

Script Blackletter/Lombardic

LOMBARDIC CAPITALS

**Ornamental Antiques,
Art Nouveau, and Art Deco**

BUCKEROO

Ornamental Decorative

Aftershock

These typefaces look like manuscript lettering prior to the invention of movable type.

Agincourt **Cresci Rotunda**

Goudy Text **Monmouth**

These typefaces and their revivals were used for display applications between the mid 1800s and early 1900s. They have a distinct feeling of time and place.

Parisian **Raphael** **Virgin Roman**

BEESKNEES **ROSEWOOD**

These typefaces defy simple pigeonholing. They can look like letters cut from stencil or decorated with flowers, or can appear three-dimensional. Some use unorthodox letter shapes and proportions to achieve distinctive and dramatic results.

MO FUNKY FRESH **Tremor**

Airstream **WacWakOoops!**

Type Designers

By Richard Poulin

In simple terms, type designers design type. Due to the specialized requirements of producing and designing typefaces, practitioners at this discipline's beginning were far and few between. Even at the start of the postindustrial revolution, type design occurred in relatively few locations, undertaken by a small group of individuals.

During the **twentieth century** (18), type design was realized in many forms. Some designers worked alone, others collaborated yet still retained independent control of their ultimate work. These collaborations frequently occurred between designers in different cities and even different countries. In the early 1900s, most type designers worked for large companies or foundries; during the later part of the century, this became more and more the exception.

Advances in twentieth-century technology, an ever-growing demand for new typefaces, and access to the Internet have increased the public's need and desire for new and innovative type design. Contemporary type designers have had a tremendous influence on the current state of this discipline. Today, notable practitioners span all ages, cultures, and countries.

Peter Bilák, Fedra Multiscript, 2001

abcdefghijkl

mnopqrstuvw

xyz ABCDEFG

HIJKLMNOPQ

RSTUVWXYZ

1234567890

£&/()'-,. ◣ ⬅

Dark on light letterform

Pre-twentieth Century

*John Baskerville, Giambattista Bodoni, William Caslon,
Firmin Didot, Pierre Simon Fournier, Claude Garamond,
Philippe Grandjean, Robert Granjon, Francesco Griffo,
Jean Jannon, Nicolas Jenson, Aldus Manutius*

John Baskerville

British, 1706–1775
Typeface: *Baskerville (1757)*

Born in Worcestershire, England, John Baskerville moved to Birmingham in 1725 where he began working as a writing and cutting master of gravestone inscriptions. Baskerville was cranky, vain, and scornful of convention. His peers disapproved of him, his type, and his printing. Baskerville was also an iconoclast of the first order. He lived with a woman for sixteen years before marrying her (something not unheard of in eighteenth-century England, but also not something approved of by eighteenth-century society). He also had a lifetime aversion to Christianity, even going so far as to build a mausoleum on his property for his burial.

Almost no one liked Baskerville's fonts or printing; his work was truly created out of love for the craft. In the truest sense of the word, Baskerville was an amateur. Freedom from paying customers, however, provided him an advantage: He could take as much time and be as demanding as he wanted. Lack of paying clients also provided Baskerville the opportunity to experiment with practically every aspect of type founding and printing.

In 1750, he set up his first printing press and soon realized that existing typefaces, substandard printing inks, and the technical limitations of the eighteenth-century printing press prevented him from meeting his own high

P. VIRGILII MARONIS

BUCOLICA

ECLOGA I. cui nomen *TITYRUS.*

MELIBOEUS, TITYRUS.

TITYRE, tu patulæ recubans sub tegmine fagi
Silveſtrem tenui Muſam meditaris avena:
Nos patriæ fines, et dulcia linquimus arva;
Nos patriam fugimus: tu, Tityre, lentus in umbra
5 Formoſam reſonare doces Amaryllida ſilvas.
  T. O Meliboee, Deus nobis hæc otia fecit:
Namque erit ille mihi ſemper Deus: illius aram
Sæpe tener noſtris ab ovilibus imbuet agnus.
Ille meas errare boves, ut cernis, et ipſum
10 Ludere, quæ vellem, calamo permiſit agreſti.
  M. Non equidem invideo; miror magis: undique totis
Uſque adeo turbatur agris. en ipſe capellas
Protenus æger ago: hanc etiam vix, Tityre, duco:
Hic inter denſas corylos modo namque gemellos,
15 Spem gregis, ah! filice in nuda connixa reliquit.
Sæpe malum hoc nobis, fi mens non læva fuiſſet,
De cœlo tactas memini prædicere quercus:
Sæpe finiſtra cava prædixit ab ilice cornix.
Sed tamen, iſte Deus qui fit, da, Tityre, nobis.
20   *T.* Urbem, quam dicunt Romam, Meliboee, putavi
Stultus ego huic noſtræ fimilem, quo ſæpe folemus
Paſtores ovium teneros depellere fœtus.
Sic canibus catulos fimiles, fic matribus hœdos
              A   Noram;

Virgil, 1757

book-production standards. Up to this point, printed type lacked clarity and definition. The spread of ink on paper created heavier, softer letterforms than their metal type counterparts. Baskerville modified his printing press to reproduce a lighter typographic impression, used denser and more concentrated inks for enhanced **contrast** (230) and clarity, and introduced the use of hot-pressed "calendared" or wove paper that had a harder, crisper, less absorbent surface not previously available.

These innovations provided him with finer results in the printing process, as well as a more pronounced visual contrast on the printed page (this became an inherent characteristic of his typefaces, too).

While Baskerville contributed significantly to eighteenth-century printing, he also was a true innovator in designing type. His typeface, Baskerville, possesses sharp, vertical proportions with stark contrasts between their thick and thin strokes. It is one of the few eighteenth-century

typefaces successfully adapted to accommodate a wide range of technological advances. It remains one of the most attractive and **legible** (330) of all **text typefaces** (212).

His attention to fine detail and perfectionism to typographic nuances carried over into his romans, italics, large-scale capitals, small capitals, and **Old Style** (54) numerals. It's also noticeable in his unorthodox use of judicious leading and letterspacing. While the typeface Baskerville remains one of the most distinctive

and legible **Transitional** (55) typefaces ever designed, most British printers continued to use Old Style or Garalde typefaces such as **Garamond** (162) throughout the eighteenth and nineteenth centuries. The typeface Baskerville was largely forgotten until **Bruce Rogers** (99) rediscovered it in 1917 and prompted several revivals.

Giambattista Bodoni

Italian, 1740–1813
Typeface: *Bodoni* (1798)

In the **late eighteenth century** (10), Giambattista Bodoni was one of the most renowned punchcutters, type designers, and printers in Europe, as well as the creator of one of the first Modern or **Didone** (56) typefaces. Born in 1740 in the northern Italian city of Turin, he was the son of a printer. At age eighteen, he worked as a compositor for Propaganda Fide in Rome and then became director of the Duke of Parma's press at the age of twenty-eight.

Typefaces created during the same time period by designers **Pierre Simon Fournier** (73) and **Firmin Didot** (73) influenced Bodoni's work. He used them as his primary references in developing his typeface, Bodoni, in 1798. It was one of the first Modern typefaces to exhibit extreme **contrasts** (230) of light and

dark in its thick and thin strokes, as well as have a vertical stress and razor-sharp serifs with unsupported brackets. During his lifetime, Bodoni also designed numerous script typefaces.

This designer documented his philosophy and principles of typography in his *Manuale Tipografico*, which reveals his innovative use of large-scale type, generous **white space** (228) on the page, and minimal page ornamentation. Bodoni's typography and type designs are still regarded as among the most refined and elegant ever produced. He created hundreds of fonts—all in the Bodoni style. An 1840 inventory of his output showed more than 25,000 punches and more than 50,000 matrices.

Bodoni, 1816

Caslon, 1734

William Caslon

British, 1692–1766
Typeface: *Caslon* (1725)

William Caslon was well known in eighteenth-century Great Britian for designing typefaces that had crisp, upright characters. He was the first British type designer of any renown, responsible for ending British printers' dependence on using imported Dutch and French typefaces that had dominated printing and publishing throughout the seventeenth century (10).

Born in Worcestershire, England, Caslon began his career as an engraver before becoming interested in punchcutting and type design in 1722. His first roman typeface, the Pica Roman (circa 1725), was closely based on a Dutch typeface. His subsequent typefaces included Caslon English, Small Pica No. 1, Long Primer No. 2, and the celebrated Great Primer Roman. He was one of the first type designers to publish a specimen sheet illustrating almost the full range of his roman typefaces.

Caslon's typefaces marked the end of the **Old Style** (54) or Garalde era and for more than 200 years became the standard roman for most printers in Great Britain. William Caslon was undeniably the most important member of the Caslon family due to his contributions to typeface design, but the Caslon family continued in the type foundry business until 1938 as the Stephenson Blake & Co. Foundry.

Firmin Didot

French, 1764–1836
Typeface: *Didot (1784)*

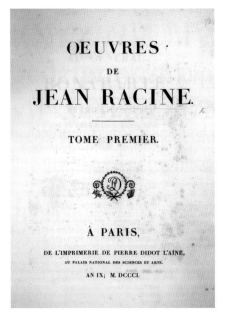

Didot, 1801

The Didot family of Paris was involved in every aspect of publishing, printing, type design, punchcutting, and paper manufacturing during the late-eighteenth and early-nineteenth centuries. Firmin Didot, grandson of the founder, is historically known as the most important member of this family because he is commonly thought to have produced the first Modern typeface.

In 1783, at the age of nineteen, Didot took control of his father's type foundry. The following year, he produced the first Modern typeface characterized by thin, slab-like, unbracketed serifs, a marked vertical stress, and an abrupt transition from thick to thin strokes. During this same time period, the Didots began reproducing these typographic details for the first time by using wove paper and an improved printing press. As a result of these developments, **Didot** (161) became the prevalent book type used throughout France during the **nineteenth century** (12). It is still in use today.

Pierre Simon Fournier

French, 1712–1768
Typefaces: *Fournier (1742)*, *Narcissus (1745)*

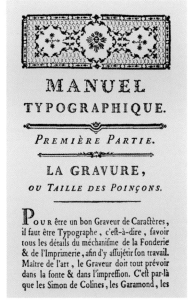

Fournier, 1766

Pierre Simon Fournier, also known as Fournier le jeune, was the youngest son of the Fournier printing family. At an early age, he developed an interest in engraving woodblocks and large capitals before moving on to punchcutting and type design.

In 1736, he established his own foundry in Paris, where he cut and designed more than 147 typefaces and typographical ornaments, and developed the idea of the type family. In 1737, he published the first version of his standardized system of type measurement—the point—and in 1742, published his first type specimen book.

Fournier's typefaces were influenced by the Romain du Roi cut by **Philippe Grandjean** (75) in 1702 and by the narrow proportioned letterforms predominantly used at that time by printers and publishers in Holland and Germany. Fournier designed one of the first early **Transitional** (55) typefaces, St. Auguston Ordinaire, which served as the model for Monotype's Fournier released in 1925.

Claude Garamond

French, 1500–1567
Typefaces: *Garamond* (circa 1530), *Grecs du Roi* (circa 1549), *Granjon* (1561)

Claude Garamond was the first to sell fonts of his type to others as a business. He also was the first designer to create typefaces, cut punches (used to make letter molds), and sell the type produced from the punches. Unfortunately, though many bought and used his fonts, Garamond had little lasting financial success in this business. In fact, when he died, he owned little more than his punches, and shortly after his death his widow was forced to sell even those. Thus began the time-honored tradition of type designers creating beautiful tools for others to use profitably.

On the plus side, Garamond *was* the most distinguished type designer of his time, perhaps of the entire Renaissance period. He worked with several punchcutters before starting a career of his own in the early 1520s in Paris. He designed many roman typefaces, including two italics, and a full set of chancery Greeks.

In the late 1520s, French printer and classical scholar Robert Estienne commissioned Garamond to cut typefaces for several publications, including the 1530 edition of *Paraphrasis* by Erasmus. Following the positive reception and success of Garamond's roman typeface, which he based on one designed by **Aldus Manutius** (78) for a 1455 edition of *de Aetna*, Garamond was asked by King Francois I of France to design a Greek typeface for his exclusive use, now known as Grecs du Roi.

By the end of the **sixteenth century** (10) Garamond's roman typeface had become the standard European style. It was still in use 200 years later. In the beginning of the **twentieth century** (16), new versions of **Garamond** (162) style begin to appear again in print shops.

Garamond, 1549

Philippe Grandjean

French, 1666–1714
Typeface: *Romain du Roi* *(1705)*

Une description historique & allégorique aurait accompagné les dessins, & chaque page de la description devait être entourée d'un cadre différent, également composé & gravé par Cochin. Au bas de chaque description se trouverait un cul-de-lampe allégorique.

Romain du Roi, 1705

The Romain du Roi designed by Philippe Grandjean in 1705 marked a significant development in typography history: It was the first new typographic development that diverged from the **Old Style** (54) typefaces prevalent throughout Europe during this time period. Therefore it's identified as the first **Transitional** (55) typeface.

Philippe Grandjean de Fouchy was born in 1666. As a young man in Paris, he visited a printing office by chance, which led him to design a set of type capitals. A member of the Royal Court saw Grandjean's early attempts, recommended him to Louis XIV, and subsequently, Grandjean started working for the Imprimerie Royale.

In 1692, Louis XIV appointed a committee to draw up plans for a new typeface that would become the exclusive property of the Imprimerie Royale. The committee studied typefaces then in current use, historical manuscripts, and geometric principles. The outcome of this extensive study became the typeface Romain du Roi translated as the "King's Roman." Grandjean was assigned to cut this new typeface, which took him eight years from 1694 until 1702, and ultimately established his reputation.

Grandjean's Romain du Roi remained popular throughout the **eighteenth century** (10), and despite its protection under the King's law, was extensively copied, most notably by **Pierre Simon Fournier** (73) and **Firmin Didot** (73).

Robert Granjon

French, 1513–1589
Typeface: *Parnagon de Granjon* *(circa 1550)*

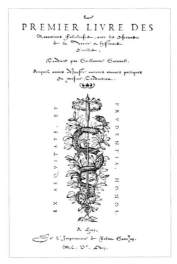

Granjon, 1558

Robert Granjon was a French punchcutter and type designer who, during the course of his career, worked in Paris, Lyon (France), Antwerp (Belgium), Frankfurt, and Rome. He designed many Renaissance and Mannerist Romans, italics, Greeks, a Cyrillic, Hebrews, and the first successful Arabic typeface.

His most notable contribution to typeface design was his italic type, Parnagon de Granjon, which possessed a greater slant angle, slanted roman capitals, and a reduced weight. These characteristics, as well as an extreme **contrast** (230) between its thick and thin strokes, gave it a beautiful appearance but sacrificed **legibility** (330) and **readability** (330). Nevertheless, Granjon's italic was the primary influence for italic typeface design until revival of the Arrighi model in 1920. (Arrighi's italic typeface [circa 1527] derived from Renaissance Italian handwritten scripts known as *cursiva humanistica*.) **Matthew Carter** (85) based his typeface Galliard primarily on the historical forms of Granjon's romans and italics.

Francesco Griffo

Italian, unknown–1518
Typefaces:
Bembo (1495),
Poliphilus (1499),
Griffo Classico (1501)

Griffo
Italics,
1501

Francesco Griffo was a Bolognese punchcutter who worked mostly in Venice. **Aldus Manutius** (78) commissioned him to design several typefaces, the most important of which is now revived under the name **Bembo** (155). The basis for the typeface came from Pietro Bembo's *de Aetna*, printed by Manutius in a font Griffo designed.

Griffo also created several romans, three italics (discussed below), four Greeks, and a Hebrew. Though we don't know what happened to his original punches or matrices—none of them survived—printers and type designers have reconstructed the majority of his letterforms by looking at printed books in which his type appeared. Examples include Giovanni Mardersteig's Griffo type, an exact replica of one of Griffo's fonts; Monotype's Bembo Roman, also loosely based on this same font; and Monotype's Poliphilus, a reproduction of the same **lowercase** (332) with slightly different caps.

Manutius and Griffo generally get credit for the invention of italic type. It made its first appearance in a 1501 edition of *Virgil* based on a script used by the Papal Chancery. Griffo also designed two other italics, one for the printer Geronimo Soncino for his book *Petrarch* of 1503, and one for himself. Griffo used the latter when, after Manutius's death, he published small editions on his own in his native Bologna. Though the pair had a successful idea, later designers followed other models for their italics.

Jean Jannon

French, 1580–1658
Typefaces: *Jannon Antiqua,*
Sarabande (1621)

Jannon, 1642

French punchcutter, type designer, and printer Jean Jannon was born in 1580 in Sedan, a northern province of France. Jannon studied and trained in Paris with Robert Estienne, a French classical scholar and printer. He first worked as a punchcutter and printer at the Protestant Academy in Sedan, where in 1621 he developed his first type specimen, Caractères de l'Université.

Subsequently, Jean Jannon's roman typefaces were used by the Imprimirie Royal and in an edition of Cardinal Richelieu's memoirs in 1642. These typefaces are considered the first Baroque typefaces.

Because of his religious beliefs as a Protestant, Jannon continually got into trouble with the Catholic government of France. On one such occasion, the government confiscated his fonts. These eventually found their way into the French National Printing Office, where they remained in obscurity for more than 200 years. In the **twentieth century** (18), they were mistakenly used as a basis for the first revival of **Garamond's** (74) type.

Nicolas Jenson

French, 1420–1480

Beniuolentiam autem a perfonis ducimus:aut a caufis accipimus:fed perfonarum non eft:ut pleriq; crediderint:triplex ratio:ex litigatore:& aduerfario:& iudice.Nam exordium duci nonnunq̃ etiã ab actore cau/ fæ fol&:q̃q̃ enim pauciora de fe ipfo dicit:& parcius:plurimũ tamé ad oĩa momenti eft in hoc pofitũ:fi uir bonus creditur:fic enĩ continget: ut nõ ftudium aduocati uideatur afferre:fed pene teftis fidem.Quare in primis exiftimetur ueniffe ad agendum ductus officio uel cognatio/

Jenson, 1471

Jenson, 1480

Nicolas Jenson studied punch-cutting, printing, and typography in Mainz, the German birthplace of typography, before establishing his own press in Venice. He was one of the first printers to use type based on the traditional roman letter model rather than the dark Gothic type found in earlier German printed books. His early roman letterforms have strong vertical stems, and the transition from thick to thin reflects the path of a broad-nibbed pen.

Born in France's northeastern district of Sommevoire in 1420, Jenson initially apprenticed in the Paris Mint before being promoted to master of the mint in Tours. In 1458, Charles VII sent him to Mainz to learn more about the new invention of printing. His roman type, first used in 1470 in Eusebius's *De Praeparatio Evangelica*, was designed specifically to typographic ideals and in rejection of prevalent manuscript models. From 1470 until his death in 1480, Jenson lived and worked in Venice.

This designer's roman greatly influenced printing and typography during its revival in the **late-nineteenth** (16) and **twentieth centuries** (16). Those typefaces modeled after his include **Bruce Rogers's** (99) Montaigne (1902), Morris's Golden (1980), and **Robert Slimbach's** (101) Adobe Jenson (1995).

Aldus Manutius

Italian, 1449–1515

Aldus Manutius was born in 1449 in the Duchy of Sermoneta. He spent his early career working for Alberto Pio, the Count of Capri, but left for Venice in 1489 to pursue his dream of publishing Greek classics in their original Greek. He released his first publication in 1484.

The early typefaces of this prolific Renaissance printer and publisher and his punchcutter **Francesco Griffo** (76) greatly improved on earlier **Jenson** (77) types. Manutius commissioned Griffo to design several typefaces, the most important of which is now revived under the name **Bembo** (155). The basis for the typeface first appeared in Pietro Bembo's *de Aetna*, printed by Manutius in a font designed by Griffo.

Because of the attractiveness and **legibility** (330) of these typefaces, they became the publishing models for the next 250 years. Manutius and Griffo typically get credit for the invention of italic type, which made its first appearance in a 1501 edition of *Virgil*.

Per laquale cosa, principiai poscia ragioneuolmente suspicare & credere peruenuto nella uastissima Hercynia silua. Et quiui altro non essere che latibuli de nocente fere, & cauernicole de noxii animali & de seuiente belue. Et percio cum maximo terriculo dubitaua, di essere sencia alcuna defensa, & sencia auederme dilaniato da setoso & dentato Apro, Quale Charidemo, ouero da furente, & famato Vro, Ouero da sibillante serpe & da fremendi lupi incursanti miseramente dimembrabondo lurcare uedesse le carne mie. Dicio dubitãdo ispagurito, Iui proposi (damnata qua lunque pigredine) piu non dimorare, & de trouare exito & euadere gli occorrenti pericoli, & de solicitare gli gia sospesi & disordinati passi, spesse fiate negli radiconi da terra scoperti cespitãdo, de qui, & de li peruagabon do errante, hora ad lato dextro, & mo al sinistro, tal hora retrogrado, & tal fiata antigrado, inscio & oue non sapendo meare, peruenuto in Salto & dumeto & senticoso loco tutto gransiato dalle frasche, & da spinosi prunuli, & da lintractabile fructo la facia offensa. Et per gli mucronati carde ti, & altri spini lacerata la toga & ritinuta impediua pigritando la tentata fuga. Oltra questo non uedendo delle amaestreuole pedate indicio alcuno, ne tritulo di semita, non mediocremente diffuso & dubioso, piu solicitamente acceleraua. Si che per gli celeri passi, si per el meridionale æsto quale per el moto corporale facto calido, tutto de sudore humefacto el fredo

Poliphilli, 1499

NARRA QVIVI LA DIVA POLIA LA NOBILE ET
ANTIQVA ORIGINE SVA. ET COMO PER LI PREDE
CESSORI SVI TRIVISIO FVE EDIFICATO. ET DI QVEL
LA GENTE LELIA ORIVNDA. ET PER QVALE MO-
DO DISAVEDVTA ET INSCIA DISCONCIAMENTE
SE INAMOROE DI LEI IL SVO DILECTO POLIPHILO.

Manutius, 1499

Twentieth Century to the Present

Otl Aicher, Jonathan Barnbrook, Ed Benguiat, Morris Fuller Benton, David Berlow, Lucian Bernhard, Charles Bigelow, Peter Bilak, Neville Brody, Margaret Calvert, Matthew Carter, Oswald Bruce Cooper, Willem Hendrik Crouwel, William Addison Dwiggins, Tobias Frere-Jones, Adrian Frutiger, Eric Gill, Frederic Goudy, Luc(as) de Groot, Jonathan Hoefler, Rudolf Koch, Zuzana Licko, Herb Lubalin, Martin Majoor, Max Miedinger, James Montalbano, Stanley Morison, Aldo Novarese, Paul Renner, Bruce Rogers, Christian Schwartz, Robert Slimbach, Fred Smeijers, Erik Spiekermann, Sumner Stone, Jan Tschichold, Carol Twombly, Gerard Unger, Jürgen Weltin, Hermann Zapf

Otl Aicher

German, 1922–1991
Typefaces: *Traffic (1974)*, *Rotis (1988)*

Otl Aicher was born in Ulm, Germany, in 1922, the same place where he established his own design studio in 1948. He studied sculpture at the Munich Academy of Fine Arts and was a founding member of the school Hochschule für Gestaltung in Ulm.

He was a type designer, graphic designer, author, and teacher who gained worldwide recognition during the post–World War II period for his identity programs for international corporations such as Braun (1954) and Lufthansa (1960), as well as for his pictogram system for the 1972 Olympic Games in Munich.

Aicher designed the typeface Traffic, which was used in the public transport systems in Munich and at the Munich Airport. But his best-known typeface, Rotis, combined elements of serif, semi-serif, sans serif, and semi-sans serif. Aicher produced Rotis in four weights—light, roman, bold, and black—with related italics for light and roman.

Jonathan Barnbrook

British, 1966–
Typefaces: *Exocet (1990)*, *Mason (1991)*,
Mason Sans, *Mason Serif (1992)*,
Bastard, *Delux*, *Draylon*, *Drone*, *Nixon Script*,
Nylon, *Patriot*, *Prototype*, *Prozac (1995)*,
Apocalypso, *False Idol (1997)*, *Newspeak (1998)*,
Echelon, *Moron (2000)*, *Melancholia (2001)*, *Coma (2002)*,
Priori (2003), *Tourette (2003, with Marcus Leis Allion)*,
Expletive Script (2004, with Allion),
Infidel, *Shock & Awe (2004)*,
State Machine (2004, with Allion), *Bourgeois (2005)*,
Doublethink (2006, with Allion), *Sarcasti (2007)*,
Hopeless Diamond, *Regime (2009, with Allion)*

Jonathan Barnbrook is a British typographer and graphic
designer. Born in Luton in 1966, Barnbrook studied at
Central Saint Martins College of Art & Design from 1985 to
1988 and at the Royal College of Art from 1988 to 1990.

Initial recognition for his typographic work came
for his cover art for David Bowie's 2002 album *Heathen*,
which featured the debut of Barnbrook's Priori typeface.
Barnbrook has worked with London's why not associates,
and in 1990 started freelancing as a designer. In 1996, he
launched his own digital type foundry, Virus.

Other well-known typefaces designed by Barnbrook,
such as Exocet, False Idol, Infidel, and Mason, have emotional and controversial titles reflecting the style and
themes found in most of his work.

Ed Benguiat

American, 1927–
Typefaces: *Charisma (1969)*, *Souvenir (1972)*,
Korinna (1974, with Victor Caruso), *Tiffany (1974)*,
Bauhaus (1975, with Caruso), *Bookman (1975)*,
Benguiat (1978), *Benguiat Gothic (1979)*,
Barcelona (1981), *Modern No. 216 (1982)*,
Panache (1988), *Edwardian Script (1994)*

 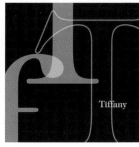

Ed Benguiat is a prolific calligrapher and type designer
with more than 600 typefaces to his name. He played
a critical role in establishing **International Typeface
Corporation (ITC)** (128), the first independent licensing
company for type designers, with his first ITC typeface,
Souvenir. He was vice president of ITC and worked with
Herb Lubalin (95) on the influential *U&lc* magazine.

Benguiat attended the Workshop School of Advertising
Art and studied calligraphy under Arnold Bank and Paul
Standard, both in New York City. After he left his job as
associate art director of *Esquire* magazine in 1953, he
opened his own design studio. In 1962, he joined Photo-
Lettering, Inc., as its typographic design director.

In addition to typeface design, he has created logotypes
for the *New York Times, Playboy, Reader's Digest, Sports
Illustrated, Esquire, Photoplay, McCall's,* and *Look*.

In 1990, Benguiat received the Gold Medal from the
Type Directors Club (355) and the prestigious Frederic W.
Goudy Award in Typography from **Rochester Institute of
Technology** (349). That same year, he was inducted into
the New York Art Directors Hall of Fame.

Morris Fuller Benton

American, 1872–1948
Typefaces: *Academy* (1896), *Cloister* (1897),
Century Expanded (1900), *Engravers Old Style*,
Linotext, *Marriage*, *Wedding* (1901),
Alternate Gothic, *Franklin Gothic* (1903),
Bold Antique, *Cheltenham* (1904),
Linoscript (1905), *Century Old Style* (1906),
Clearface (1907), *Clear Gothic*, *Commercial Script*,
Lightline Gothic, *News Gothic* (1908),
Hobo (1910), *Souvenir* (1914),
Century Schoolbook (1919),
Canterbury Old Style (1926), *Broadway* (1927),
Bulmer, *Chic*, *Modernique*, *Novel Gothic*,
Parisian (1928), *Louvaine* (1929),
Bank Gothic, *Piranesi* (1930), *Stymie* (1931),
American Text, *Raleigh Gothic* (1932),
Agency, *Agency Gothic*, *Eagle* (1933),
Benton, *Tower* (1934), *Phoenix* (1935), *Empire* (1937)

Benton, 1935

Benton, 1934

Morris Fuller Benton is known as the most prolific type designer in U.S. history and for making enormous contributions to type design development in the first half of the **twentieth century** (16). Benton's father, Linn Boyd Benton, was the first director of the American Type Founders (ATF) design department. There the younger Benton became his father's assistant and learned every aspect of type founding and design.

He was the director of the ATF design department from 1900 to 1937. During his tenure, Benton designed 221 typefaces, ranging from historic revivals and original typefaces to his large family of **Grotesque** (60) sans serifs known as Gothics, plus eighteen variations on the typeface **Century** (159), including the popular Century Schoolbook. Benton also worked closely with his contemporary at ATF, Henry Lewis Bullen, collector of the company's famous type library and mentor of type publicist and scholar Beatrice Warde.

David Berlow

American, 1955–
Typefaces: *Belizio* (1988),
Grot, *Millennium* (1989), *Numskill* (1990),
Phaistos (1991), *Vernacular* (1992),
Berlin Sans, *Gra*,
Meyer Two, *Moderno* (1994),
Esperanto, *Hitech*, *Nature*, *Online
Gothic*, *Throhand*, *Truth*, *Zenobia* (1995),
Charcoal, *Rhode*, *Techno* (1997),
Gadget (1998)

Born in Boston, Massachusetts, in 1955,
David Berlow studied art history at
the University of Wisconsin–Madison.
From 1978 to 1982, he worked as a type
designer for Mergenthaler, **Linotype** (129),
D. Stempel AG, and Haas type
foundries. In 1982, he started as a type
designer for the newly formed
digital type foundry **Bitstream** (124).

Seven years later, in 1989, Berlow
opened the type foundry **The Font
Bureau, Inc.** (127) with Roger Black, a
former art director for *Rolling Stone*. To
date, The Font Bureau has produced
more than 300 new and revised typefaces and logotypes for clients such as
the *Chicago Tribune*, the *Wall Street
Journal*, *Entertainment Weekly*, *Newsweek*, *Esquire*, *Rolling Stone*, and Hewlett
Packard, as well as OEM fonts for Apple
Computer, Microsoft, and ITC. The Font
Bureau's entire retail library is made
up of mostly original type designs and
includes more than 500 typefaces.

Lucian Bernhard

German, 1885–1972
Typefaces: *Bernhard Antiqua*, *Bernhard Fraktur* (1912),
Bernhard Privat (1919), *Bernhard Brushscript*,
Bernhard Cursive Madonna, *Bernhard Schönschrift*, *Lucian* (1925),
Bernhard Bold Condensed (1926), *Bernhard Handschrift* (1928),
Bernhard Fashion, *Bernhard Gothic* (1929), *Lilli*, *Negro* (1930),
Bernhard Booklet (1932), *Bernhard Tango* (1934),
Bernhard Modern (1937), *Bernhard Tango Swash Capitals* (1939)

Bernhard Modern

Bernhard Gothic

Lucian Bernhard (a.k.a. Emil
Kahn) was a German graphic
designer, type designer, teacher,
interior designer, and fine
artist during the first half
of the **twentieth century**
(16). He was born in 1883 in
Stuttgart, Germany. Though
he studied briefly at the
Akademie in Munich, he was
largely self-taught. In 1901,
he moved to Berlin, where
he became a poster designer
and magazine art director.

Bernhard was influential
in creating two distinctive
twentieth-century design styles,
namely *Plakatstil* (or "Poster
Style"), which relied on reductive
imagery and flat color, and
Sachplakat (or "Object Poster"),
which simplified the image
to the object being advertised

and its brand name. Both
of these styles appear in his
renowned work for Stiller shoes,
Manoli cigarettes, and Priester
matches. He also designed
several roman typefaces
distinguished by their long
extenders. These were primarily
cut and cast by American
Type Founders and Bauer.

From 1920 until 1923 when he
immigrated to the United States,
Bernhard taught at the Akademie
der Künste in Berlin. In 1928,
he started the Contempora
Studio with artists Rockwell
Kent, Paul Poiret, Bruno Paul,
and Erich Mendelsohn. There
he worked as a graphic artist
and interior designer. Between
1930 and his death in 1972,
Bernhard worked primarily
as a painter and sculptor.

Charles Bigelow

American, 1945–
Typefaces: *Leviathan (1979)*, *Lucida (1984)*,
Chicago, *Geneva (1991)*, *Wingdings (1993)*

Charles Bigelow is a type historian, educator, and
type designer. He was born in Detroit, Michigan
in 1945 and attended **Cranbrook Academy of Art** (349)
from 1957 to 1963. In 1982, Bigelow became one of
the few graphic designers to receive a MacArthur
Foundation Prize Fellowship. He also received the
Frederic W. Goudy Award in Typography from
Rochester Institute of Technology (349).

Bigelow's accomplishments are extensive, including
establishing Stanford University's digital typography
master's program. He and Kris Holmes cofounded the
Bigelow & Holmes foundry and designed the Wingdings
and Lucida type families, the latter of which is one
of the first fonts to optimize typography for output on
the lower resolution printers of personal computers.
This duo also created some of the first TrueType
fonts, including Apple's city fonts—Chicago, Geneva,
Monaco, New York—Apple Chancery, and the
ubiquitous Microsoft Wingdings font.

Bigelow taught type design, typography, and the
history and theory of writing at Stanford University
from 1982 until 1997. In 2006, RIT's School of Print Media
named him the Melbert B. Cary Distinguished Professor.

Peter Bilak

Czechoslovokian, 1973–
Typefaces: *Craft (1994)*,
Atlanta, *Champollion*, *Holy Cow (1995)*,
Masterpiece (1996), *Orbital (1997)*,
Eureka (1998), *Fedra Sans (2001)*,
Fedra Serif (2003), *Greta Text (2007)*,
History (2008), *Fedra Mono*, *Irma (2009)*

Greta Grande, 2007

Peter Bilak was born in 1973 in what was then
Czechoslovakia. Today, he is a graphic and typeface
designer based in The Hague, The Netherlands.

He started the type foundry **Typotheque** (139) in 1999
and the Indian Type Foundry in 2009. Bilak teaches
postgraduate typeface design at the **Royal Academy
of Art** (347) in The Hague and lectures widely about
graphic design and typography. He also contributes
regularly to international publications including *Print*,
Eye, *Items*, *tipoGrafica*, and *Idea*.

In 2000, Bilak and Stuart Bailey cofounded *Dot Dot
Dot* magazine, which they coedited until 2007.

Neville Brody

British, 1957–
Typefaces: *Industria, Insignia* (1989), *Arcadia* (1990), *Blur, Typeface 6 & 7,* (1991), *Gothic, Pop, Typeface 4* (1992), *Dome, Harlem, Tokyo, World* (1993), *Autotrace, Dirty* (1994), *Meta Subnormal* (1995, with Erik Spiekermann)

Renowned British graphic designer, art director, and typographer Neville Brody gained public acclaim in the early **1980s** (26) with his highly innovative approach to typography.

Brody was born in London in 1957 and attended the London College of Printing and Hornsey College of Art. His early work included experimental and revolutionary combinations of typographic expression for magazines such as the *Face* and *Arena*, as well as for independent music labels and artists such as Cabaret Voltaire and Depeche Mode.

In 1988, two volumes about his work became the world's best-selling graphic design book, and an accompanying exhibition of his designs at the Victoria and Albert Museum drew more than 40,000 visitors before it moved around Europe and Japan. In 1991, Brody started the design consultancy Research Studios, the type foundry Fontworks, and Fuse, a regularly published collection of experimental typefaces continually challenging the boundaries between editorial, graphic, and type design.

In 2011, Brody was named the new head of the communication art and design department at London's Royal College of Art.

Margaret Calvert

South African, 1936–
Typefaces: *Transport* (1963), *Calvert* (1980), *A 26* (1994), *New Rail* (2009, with Henrik Kubel)

Jesmond Station sign, 1981

BAA Signs, 1964

BAA Type, 1964

Matthew Carter

British, 1937–
Typefaces: *Auriga*, *Cascade Script* (1965),
Freehand 471, *Snell Roundhand* (1966), **Dutch 811** (1970),
Gando Ronde (1970, with Hans Jorg Hunziker),
Olympian (1970), *Shelley Script* (1972),
CRT Gothic (1974), *Video* (1977),
Bell Centennial, *Galliard* (1978), **V&A Titling** (1979),
Charter (1987), *Elephant* (1992),
Mantinia, *Sophia* (1993), **Big Caslon**, *Skia* (1994),
Alisal, *Tahoma*, *Walker*, *Wilson Greek* (1995),
Georgia, *Verdana* (1996), *Miller*, **Big Figgins** (1997),
Manutius, *Rocky* (1998),
Monticello (2002), **Carter Sans** (2010)

Galliard

Centennial

Margaret Calvert was born in South Africa in 1936. In 1950, she and her family immigrated to the United Kingdom, where she studied illustration at Chelsea School of Art and typography at the Central School of Arts and Crafts. Her former tutor, Jock Kinneir, then asked her to assist him in designing the sign system for Gatwick Airport.

During the **1960s** (24), Calvert again collaborated with Kinneir on the typography and design of Great Britain's comprehensive road-sign system, which included creating the typeface Transport and several pictograms. In addition, Calvert has designed integrated lettering and sign systems for British rail, British airports, and the Tyne and Wear Metro. In 1981, **Monotype** (125) released Calvert, an Egyptian typeface originally designed for the Tyne and Wear Metro and later adapted for the Royal College of Art.

Previously, Calvert was the chairperson of the communication art and design department at London's Royal College of Art, as well as a fellow of the **University of the Arts** (348), London, and an honorary doctor of the University of Brighton.

Matthew Carter is an English-born American type designer, punchcutter, and scholar based in Cambridge, Massachusetts.

He is the son of Harry Carter, a printing historian and the archivist for Oxford University Press. In 1956, Carter spent a year studying the traditional crafts of type design and type founding with Jan van Krimpen's assistant, the punchcutter P. H. Raidische at the **Enschedé Font Foundry** (131) in Holland.

For the past fifty years, Carter has designed and made type in every possible medium, from metal to film and digital. Prior to starting his own digital type foundry, Carter & Cone Type, Inc., with Cherie Cone in 1991, he worked for Mergenthaler Linotype and **Bitstream** (124).

He received the Chrysler Award for Innovation in Design, the **Type Directors Club** (355) Medal and the **American Institute of Graphic Arts** (354) Medal. In 1981, London's Royal Society of Arts elected him a Royal Designer for Industry. Carter was named a MacArthur Foundation Fellow in 2011.

Oswald Bruce Cooper

American, 1879–1940
Typefaces: *Oz Poster*, *Packard* (1913),
Cooper Old Style (1919), *Cooper Black* (1920),
Maiandra (circa 1924), *Pompeian Cursive* (1927),
Cooper Fullface, *Ozwald* (1928),
Highlander (circa 1930), *Oz Brush* (1930)

Oswald Bruce Cooper was born in 1879 in Mount Gilead, Ohio. He left his hometown at a young age to become a printer's apprentice and to study illustration at the Frank Holme School of Illustration in Chicago.

It was at the Holme School that Cooper befriended his lettering instructor, **Frederic Goudy** (90). He soon became part of Goudy's circle of artists and designers, including Will Ransom and **William Addison Dwiggins** (87). The same year, Cooper formed a creative partnership with Fred Bertsch—aptly named Bertsch & Cooper—designing general typography, newspaper advertisements, and layouts for books and magazines, with Cooper specializing as a hand-lettering artist. In 1913, he achieved his first notable success with lettering he designed for the Packard Motor Company. He subsequently received a design patent and released the lettering as the typeface Packard by American Type Founders.

To supplement lettering and layout services, Bertsch & Cooper added typesetting in 1914. Shortly after that, Cooper designed Cooper Black, the first typeface with rounded serifs that started the **twentieth-century** (16) trend for ultra bold typefaces. It was an immediate success and became one of the most popular typefaces in the United States during the **1920s** (20) and **1930s** (21). He created a companion italic in 1924.

Willem Hendrik Crouwel

Dutch, 1928–
Typefaces: *Vormgevers* (1962), *Edgar Fernhout* (1964), *New Alphabet* (1967), *Gridnik* (1974), *Fodor* (1977)

Willem Hendrik Crouwel (also known as Wim) is a Dutch graphic designer, type designer, and educator. He was born in Groningen, The Netherlands, in 1928, and studied fine arts at the Academie Minerva there from 1947 until 1949. He also studied typography at Amsterdam's Gerrit Rietveld Academie.

In 1963, he cofounded the design studio Total Design (currently known as Total Identity) with graphic designers Benno Wissing, Friso Kramer, and the Schwarz brothers. In 1967, Crouwel designed the typeface New Alphabet, a font that embraces the limitations of cathode ray tube technology and therefore only uses horizontal and vertical strokes.

Throughout his career, Crouwel has also been dedicated to design education. He taught design at the Royal Academy of Art (Akademie Voor Kunst en Vormgeving St. Joost or AKV|St. Joost), at the Gerrit Rietveld Academie, in Delft University of Technology's department of industrial design, and at Erasmus University Rotterdam.

From 1985 to 1993, he was director of the Museum Boijmans Van Beuningen in Rotterdam. In 2009, Crouwel received the Gerrit Noordzij Prize from the **Royal Academy of Art** (347), The Hague, for extraordinary contributions to the fields of type design, typography, and type education.

William Addison Dwiggins

American, 1880–1956
Typefaces: *Metro, Geometric 415* (1929),
Elante, Electra, Transitional 521 (1935), *Caledonia* (1938),
Winchester (1944), *Eldorado* (1953), *Falcon* (1961)

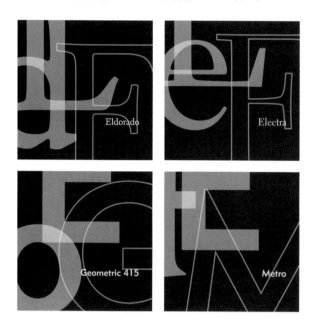

William Addison Dwiggins was born in 1880 in Cambridge, Ohio. At nineteen, he studied lettering with **Frederic Goudy** (90) at the Frank Holme School of Illustration in Chicago.

Dwiggins pursued a diverse career that included illustration, calligraphy, printing, advertising, and book design. After working as a freelance designer, he was appointed acting director of Harvard University Press in 1917, and in 1919, founded the Society of Calligraphers in Boston.

At age forty-four, he began designing typefaces exclusively for the **Linotype** (129) machine and at the invitation of Mergenthaler Linotype. His first typeface was a sans serif, Metro. His best-known typeface, Caledonia, combines characteristics of the Scotch Romans and the typeface Bulmer designed by William Martin. In the **1930s** (21) and **1940s** (22), Dwiggins created the typographic house style for publisher Alfred Knopf in New York City. In 1929, the **American Institute of Graphic Arts** (354) awarded Dwiggins his profession's highest honor, the AIGA medal.

Tobias Frere-Jones

American, 1970–
Typefaces: *Dolores, Nobel* (1991),
Archipelago, Garage Gothic (1992),
*Cafeteria, Epitaph, Interstate, Reactor,
Reiner Script, Stereo* (1993),
Armada, Fibonacci, Hightower, Niagara (1994),
Asphalt, Citadel, Microphone, Pilsner (1995),
Whitney (1996), *Griffith Gothic, Phemister* (1997),
Grand Central, Welo Script (1998), *Gotham, Retina* (2000),
Nitro, Surveyor (2001), *Exchange, Idlewild* (2002),
Dulcet, Monarch (2003), *Argosy, Tungsten* (2004)

Tobias Frere-Jones is a prolific type designer and teacher, and the director of typography at **Hoefler & Frere-Jones** (132), a prominent type foundry in New York City.

After completing his studies at the **Rhode Island School of Design** (349) in 1992, he joined **The Font Bureau, Inc.** (127) in Boston as a senior designer. During his seven-year tenure there, he created some of the foundry's best-known typefaces, including Interstate.

Frere-Jones left The Font Bureau in 1999 to return to New York City, where he began working with **Jonathan Hoefler** (92). In the past decade-plus, he has designed more than 500 typefaces for publications, institutions, and corporate clients including the *Wall Street Journal, Martha Stewart Living, GQ, Esquire,* the *New York Times,* and the *Boston Globe.*

He joined the faculty of the **Yale School of Art** (349) in 1996, where he continues to teach graduate-level typeface design courses. In 2006, Frere-Jones became the first American to receive the Gerrit Noordzij Prize, presented by the **Royal Academy of Art** (347), The Hague in honor of his unique contribution to type design, typography, and type education.

Adrian Frutiger

Swiss, 1928–
Typefaces: *Phoebus* (1953),
Formal Script, *Ondine*, *President* (1954),
Egyptienne (1955), *Meridien*, *Univers* (1957),
Opera (1959), *Apollo* (1962),
Serifa (1967), *OCR-A*, *OCR-B* (1968),
Iridium (1972), *Frutiger* (1976), *Glypha* (1979),
Breughel, *Icone*, *Versailles* (1982),
Janson (1985), *Centennial* (1986),
Avenir (1988), *Westside* (1989),
Herculaneum (1990), *Vectora* (1991),
Pompeijana, *Rusticana* (1992), *Nami* (2006)

Adrian Frutiger is one of the greatest typographers and typeface designers of the **twentieth century** (16). He created more than 175 typefaces, many of which have become notable fonts, including **Univers** (181) and **Frutiger** (173). He also was one of the first type designers to create type for film and photocomposition.

Frutiger was born in Switzerland in 1928 near Interlaken and apprenticed as a compositor to a local printer. From 1948 to 1951, he was a student at the Kunstgewerbeschule, where he was studied graphic design, calligraphy, wood engraving, and sculpture. Following his studies, he relocated to Paris, where he worked at the renowned Deberny & Peignot type foundry until 1962, the year he started his own graphic design studio in Arcueil, a Paris suburb.

He has taught typography and illustration at **École Estienne** (347) and École nationale superieure des Arts Décoratifs in Paris. In 1986, Frutiger received the Gutenberg Prize for Technical and Aesthetic Achievement in Type.

Univers, 1957

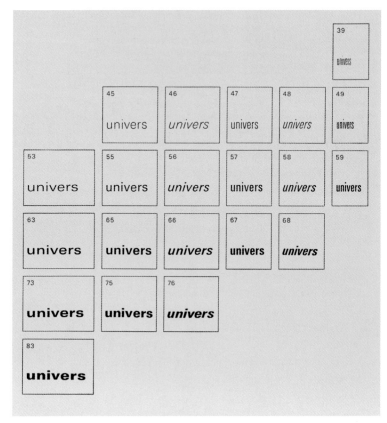

Univers, 1957

Eric Gill

British, 1882–1940
Typefaces: *Gill Sans*, *Perpetua* (1928), *Golden Cockerel*, *Solus* (1929), *Joanna* (1931), *Aries* (1932), *Jubilee*, *Pilgrim* (1934)

THE GOLDEN COCKEREL PRESS SPRING 1930

Golden Cockerel, 1929

Eric Gill was a prominent British letter cutter, sculptor, wood engraver, and type designer. He was born in 1882 in Brighton and studied at the Chichester Art School before becoming an apprentice to a London architect. While working in London, he attended classes taught by British calligrapher Edward Johnston at the Central School of Arts and Crafts, launching him into a career as a stonecutter and letterer.

Gill designed his first typeface, Perpetua, in 1928 for **Stanley Morison** (97), typographic advisor for **Monotype Corporation** (125). Perpetua takes it name from the first book in which it was used (in its first size), *The Passion of Perpetua and Felicity*. The original italic, cut in 1930, was called Felicity, but is not the same as the Perpetua italic finally released.

Gill Sans (175), designed during the same time period and for Morison, was conceived as a text face, in comparison to New Johnston designed by Edward Johnston, specifically developed for the London Metro sign system, and the many **geometric** (62) sans serif faces being released in Europe at the time.

In 1935, Gill became an Associate of the Royal Institute of British Architects and an Associate of the Royal Academy of Art. In 1936, Gill was part of the first group of individuals to receive the title "Royal Designer of Industry."

Frederic Goudy

American, 1865–1947
Typefaces: Camelot *(1896),* **DeVinne** *(1898),*
Copperplate Gothic *(1901),* **Pabst** *(1902),*
Powell *(1903),* **Kennerley** *(1911),* **Forum** *(1912),*
Goudy, Goudy Old Style *(1915),* **National Oldstyle** *(1916),*
Hadriano *(1918),* **Garamont** *(1921),* **Cushing Antique,**
Deepdene *(1927),* **Kaatskill, Remington Typewriter** *(1929),*
Mediaeval, Truesdell *(1930),*
Village *(1932),* **Bertham** *(1936),* **Friar** *(1937),*
Berkeley Oldstyle, Californian *(1938),* **Bulmer** *(1939)*

GOUDY MEDIAEVAL
Drawings begun Aug. 19, 16 pt. finished Sept. 15, 1930
A NEW TYPE is here presented, which, judged by
pragmatic standards, may not meet the approval of those
critics who demand in their types the elimination of any
atavistic tendency. Quite obviously it cannot be judged fairly by the advertising compositor or the job printer, nor must
unassuming legibility be made its first criterion. At one
time books were entirely written out by hand, but the qualities that made the writing charming defy completely successful reproduction in types. Goudy Mediæval presents
a face that in its lower case borrows the freedom of the pen
of the Renaissance. Its capitals however, owe less to the
pen-hands since they are more or less composites of mon-
astic ms. & painted Lombardic forms. The designer hopes
nevertheless, that his capitals will be found in accord with

Mediaeval, 1930

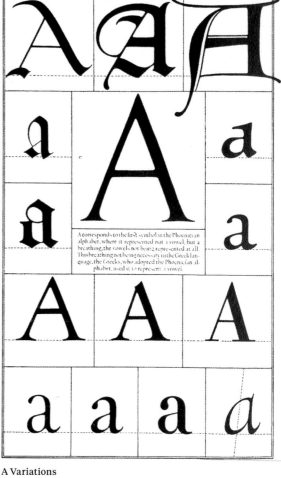

A Variations

Frederic Goudy was one of the most prolific U.S. type designers of the **twentieth
century (16)**. By his own account, he
designed 123 faces (though he counted
each italic as a separate typeface).

Goudy, born in Bloomington, Illinois, in 1865, was interested in type at an
early age. He held several jobs in various
cities before founding a printing business, the Booklet Press, in Chicago in
1895. Renamed the Camelot Press, he
printed the journal *American Cap-Book*
before selling his interest a year later. In
his next successful endeavor, he sold a set
of capitals of his own design to the Bruce
Type Foundry in Boston, which encouraged him to become a freelance lettering
artist. He also taught lettering and design
at the Frank Holme School of Illustration.
In 1903, Goudy started The Village Press
in partnership with Will Ransom in Park
Ridge, Illinois.

Goudy's breakthrough with type
design came in 1911 when he designed
Kennerley Old Style for the publisher
Mitchell Kennerley. He set up the Village
Letter Foundry to cast and sell Kennerley and a titling font, Forum. These two
typefaces established his reputation
and became particularly popular in the
United Kingdom. Subsequently, American Type Founders commissioned Goudy
to design a typeface, resulting in Goudy
Old Style, regarded by many critics as
one of his finest designs. In 1920, with
forty types to his name, Goudy became
Lanston Monotype's appointed art
adviser; in this capacity, he worked on
the revival Garamont.

As one of his final influences on the
type-design world, Goudy wrote about
type and the origins of his work in his
book *A Half Century of Type Design and
Typography: 1895–1945*, completed when
he was nearly eighty years old.

Luc(as) de Groot

Dutch, 1963–
**Typefaces: *Folha Serif*, *Jesus Loves You All*, *Nebulae*,
TheMix, *TheSans*, *TheSerif*, *Thesis* (1994),
TheSansMonospace, *TheSansTypewriter* (1996),
Corpid III, *Spiegel* (1997), *Taz* (2000), *Sun* (2001),
Punten (2002), *Tazzer* (2006), *Floris* (2007),
Calibri, *Consolas*, *Qua* (2008), *TheAntiqua* (2010)**

Shocking!
Compact broadsheet
DAILY
Yesterdays forecast
Above the fold:

SOFT HYPHEN HUNTING IS NOW ON
MANY BIG Jackdaws quickly zipped over the fox pen. My grandfather picks up quartz and valuable onyx jewels. Mix Zapf with Veljovic and get quirky Beziers. Oozing quivering jelly fish expectorated by mad hawk. Pack my box with five dozen liquor jugs! Playing jazz vibe chords quickly excites my wife. Six big devils from Japan quickly forgot how to waltz. Six leopards move their quick jaws in frenzy. The job of wax

Taz, 2000

Ampersand conference
AGENDA
Open Doors ∿ **Round Tables**
Конференция
stage
Ετήσιος συνδιάσκεψη
Speed Geeking
Scientific ∿ *Society*

TheSans, 1994

Born in Noordwijkerhout, The Netherlands, Luc(as) de Groot is a Berlin-based Dutch type designer, graphic designer, educator, and head of the type foundries Font-Fabrik and **LucasFonts** (132). He is widely known for the popular and large font family, Thesis (TheSans, TheSerif, TheMix, TheSansMono, and TheAntiqua), and Corpid (also known as AgroSans).

He also has designed custom fonts for prestigious international publications and newspapers such as *Folha de S. Paulo* (Brazil), *Le Monde* (France), *Metro* (the free, international paper), and *Der Spiegel* (Germany), as well as for international corporations including Sun Microsystems, Bell South, Heineken, Siemens, and Miele. De Groot designed two font families for Microsoft: the monospaced font family Consolas, a new alternative to Courier, and Calibri, a new default typeface for Microsoft Word.

In addition, de Groot is a member of the design faculty of the University of Applied Sciences in Potsdam, Germany.

De zingende Premier
Convicted
6500 cheer yesterday
Het grote fashion nummer:
Trend
Fear for 360 suburbs
Survey: Not acceptable!
Tatort Küche
Former chairman finds new way

Floris, 2007

SAFE CONDITION SIGN
Wayfinding
Do not feed the animals!
Маршрутный щиток
exterior
Baby on board
→*Information system*←
οδοδείκτης
Guide the public

TheMix, 1994

Jonathan Hoefler

American, 1970–
Typefaces: *Egiziano Filigree* (1989),
Bodoni Grazia**, **Champion Gothic (1990),
Gestalt**, **Hoefler**, **Ideal Sans**, **Mazarin**, **Requiem**, **Ziggurat (1991),
Didot (1992), ***Acropolis**, **Fetish**, **Leviathan**, **Quantico**, **Saracen*** (1993),
Knockout**, **Troubadour (1994), ***Jupiter**, **Pavisse*** (1995),
Giant**, **New Amsterdam**, **Plainsong**, **Verlag (1996), ***Radio City*** (1998),
Cyclone**, **Deluxe**, **Mercury**, **Topaz (2000), ***Ideal Sans*** (2011)

Jonathan Hoefler is a typeface designer and type historian who specializes in designing original typefaces. He established Hoefler Type Foundry in 1989.

Named one of the forty most influential designers in America by *I.D. Magazine,* his work includes award-winning original typeface designs for *Rolling Stone, Harper's Bazaar,* the *New York Times Magazine, Sports Illustrated,* and *Esquire.* His institutional clients range from the Solomon R. Guggenheim Museum in New York City to the rock band They Might Be Giants.

Hoefler's best known work is the Hoefler Text family of typefaces, designed for Apple Computer, Inc., and now part of the Macintosh operating system. His work has been exhibited internationally and is included in the permanent collection of the Smithsonian's Cooper-Hewitt, National Design Museum in New York City.

In 1999, he teamed up with **Tobias Frere-Jones** (87) and the pair's foundry became known as **Hoefler & Frere-Jones** (132). In 2002, the **Association Typographique Internationale** (354) presented Hoefler with its most prestigious award, the Prix Charles Peignot for outstanding contributions to type design.

Rudolf Koch

German, 1876–1934
Typefaces: *Deutsche Schrift*, *Neu Deutsch* *(1909),*
Fruhling *(1913),* ***Maximillian Antiqua*** *(1914),*
Zierfraktur *(1919),* ***Koch Antiqua*, *Locarno*, *Xmas*** *(1922),*
Neuland*, *Schmale Anzeigenfraktur *(1923),* ***Banco*,**
Klingspor Schrift*, *Wilhelm Klingspor Gotisch *(1925),*
Jessen *(1926),* ***Geometric 231*, *Kabel*** *(1927),*
Offenbach *(1928),* ***Zeppelin*** *(1929),* ***Wallau*** *(1930),*
Marathon*, *Prisma *(1931),* ***Holla*** *(1932),* ***Neufraktur*** *(1933),*
Claudius *(1937),* ***Steel*** *(1939)*

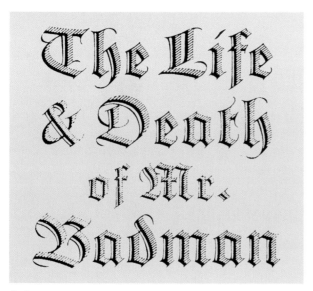

Koch, 1921

Koch, 1910

Born in Nuremberg, Germany, Rudolf Koch was the son of a sculptor. He apprenticed in a metal foundry, attended evening classes at the Art School, and left the foundry before completing his apprenticeship. Returning to Nuremberg, he trained as a teacher and then in 1898, found work as a designer in Leipzig.

At the age of thirty, Koch began a long, fruitful position as a type designer in a small type founders firm at Offenbach. The company was Rudhardsche Giesserei, later internationally known as the Klingspor type foundry. Shortly after joining Klingspor, Koch designed his first typeface, Deutsche Schrift, a bold **blackletter** (192).

As with all his typefaces, he experimented with hand-drawn letters using a broad pen. He drew the same letters again and again until every letter was perfect, the type ready to cut.

First came Neuland in 1923, a family of convex-shaped capitals reminiscent of German Expressionist woodcut lettering. He then designed Wilhelm, Klingspor Schrift, and Jesson, which he cut himself, a simplified blackletter with Romanized capitals, created originally for the *Four Gospels* printed by Klingspor, one of the seminal publications that reflects this approach to typography.

One of the most respected designers and teachers of his day, Koch was first and foremost a calligrapher; all types he designed but one developed from his calligraphic forms. "Lettering," he once said, "gives me the purest and greatest pleasure, and on countless occasions, it has been to me what a song is to a singer."

Zuzana Licko

Czechoslovakian, 1961–
Typefaces: *Low-Res* (1985),
Emigre, Emperor, Matrix, Modula Sans,
Oakland, Universal (1986), *Modula Serif* (1988),
Lunatix, Oblong, Senator, Variex (1989), *Citizen,*
Elektrix, Totally Glyphic, Totally Gothic, Triplex (1990),
Journal (1991), *Quartet* (1992), *Narly* (1993),
Dogma, Whirligig (1994), *Base, Soda Script* (1995),
Mrs. Eaves (1996), *Filosophia, Hypnopaedia* (1997),
Tarzana (1998), *Solex* (2000), *Fairplex* (2002),
Puzzler (2005), *Mr. Eaves* (2009)

Cahuenga

Zuzana Licko is the cofounder of the **Emigre, Inc.** (94) foundry and influential journal *Emigre* magazine, together with her husband Rudy VanderLans. She was born in 1961 in what was Bratislava, Czechoslovakia, and immigrated to the United States in 1968. She graduated with a degree in graphic communications from the University of California, Berkeley, in 1984.

In the **mid-1980s** (26), personal computers and low-resolution printers put the tools of typography in the hands of a broader public. In 1985, Licko began designing typefaces that exploited the rough grain of early desktop systems. While other digital fonts imposed the coarse grid of screen displays and dot-matrix printers onto traditional typographic forms, Licko's embraced the language of digital equipment. At the time, she and VanderLans called themselves "new primitives" and pioneers of a new technological dawn.

She also produced historical revivals alongside her experimental digital display faces. Licko's typeface Mrs. Eaves, inspired by the eighteenth-century typefaces of **John Baskerville** (70) (and named after his mistress and housekeeper Sarah Eaves) became one of the most popular typefaces during the **1990s** (27).

(WEDNESDAY, JULY 20, 1989, 3:00 PM, LOMPA PRINTING, ALBANY, CALIFORNIA, USA.)

... *RICK:* This is gonna jog to the head anyway, so we're gonna be trimming a half inch off. Did you allow for that? *RUDY:* I did, sort of. All this background stuff will be totally incomprehensible once it's bound like this. The only things that matter on this small booklet are these lines of type. *RICK:* It's printed on a twentyfive thirtyeight sheet. Last time we probably never changed the setup on the lips, so we wound up with a short lip. *ELIZABETH:* So if we're doing twentyfive thirtyeight, and I got a half inch head trim on the film that is provided, does that mean I have to guillotine cut, or do you want me to take that stuff ... *RICK:* No, we want everything with a half inch head trim, even if you have to do a new rule out. *ELIZABETH:* OK that's fine. *RICK:* Then we should lay everything out and get proper lip from front to back. *ELIZABETH:* Now what about eh... going to take some trim on the folder? *RICK:* Let's see. It's eleven and a quarter, that's twentytwo and a half, out of twentyfive, that's two and a half inches split between front and back. If you want one and one ... one half ... *ELIZABETH:* Can you run that through the Müller? *RICK:* Yes. *ELIZABETH:* I thought it was one and one eight. *RICK:* We'll have to doublecheck that. How about this letterpress insert? We can run this through the Müller without a problem. We'll put the cover on ... or is that too big? We should marry these two inside signatures first and then put it back on. We can combine it inside piece. Actually it depends on what that letterpress piece looks like. *RUDY:* It's printed on a ten by thirteen inch sheet. They'll have a three and a half inch flap and it will be die cut in the shape of a house on its side. *RICK:* Do we have a half inch head trim? *RUDY:* No, an eight. You want a half inch? It hasn't been printed yet. We can still change it. *RICK:* Well, the rest of the book has a half inch. *RUDY:* OK we'll get you a half inch trim. *RICK:* It's either that or we can try and float it in the center. I can float it into the very center of the book...

Senator et al, 1989

Herb Lubalin

American, 1918–1981
Typefaces: *Avant Garde Gothic* (1970, with Tom Carnase), *Ronda* (1970), *Lubalin Graph* (1974), *Serif Gothic* (1974, with Tony DiSpigna)

In post–World War II United States, few designers or typographers were more charismatic and influential than Herb Lubalin. Born in New York City, Lubalin attended **Cooper Union** (349), graduating in 1939.

As a young art director, he worked at Sudler & Hennessey for more than ten years before starting his own design firm, Herb Lubalin Inc., in 1964. His partnership with Aaron Burns and Edward Rondthaler created **International Typeface Corporation (ITC)** (128), which in its heyday became the world's largest typeface supplier. Today it is **Monotype Imaging Company** (125).

Lubalin also founded and designed the magazine *U&lc* for ITC, which was distributed worldwide. As an editorial designer, he was in charge of the *Saturday Evening Post*, *Eros* (1962), *Fact* (1967), and *Avant Garde* (1968), which led him to design a type family with the same name. In 1977, Lubalin was inducted into the New York Art Directors Hall of Fame and in 1981, earned his profession's highest honor, the **American Institute of Graphic Arts** (354) Medal.

Martin Majoor

Dutch, 1960–
Typefaces: *Scala* (1990), *Scala Sans* (1993), *Seria* (2000), *Nexus* (2004)

Martin Majoor is a Dutch graphic designer and type designer trained at the School of Fine Art in Arnhem, Denmark. He has been designing type since the **mid-1980s** (26).

In 1986, he started working as a typographic designer in the research and development department at Océ-Netherlands, where he did research on screen fonts and worked on the production of digital typefaces for laser printers.

After working at the Vredenburg Music Centre in Utrecht (for which he designed the typeface Scala), Majoor became an independent type designer and book typographer in Arnhem in 1990. Since then, he has designed several type families and numerous books and covers.

Majoor now works as a type designer and graphic designer in Arnhem and Warsaw.

Max Miedinger

Swiss, 1910–1980
**Typefaces: *Pro Arte* (1954), *Helvetica* (1956),
Monospace 821, *Neue Haas Grotesk* (1957),
Horizontal (1964)**

Max Miedinger was born in 1910 in Zurich, Switzerland. Between 1926 and 1930, Miedinger trained as a typesetter and attended evening classes at the Kunstgewerbeschule.

In the early **1950s** (22), he became an in-house type designer with Haas Type Foundry in Münchenstein, Switzerland. He designed his most famous typeface, **Helvetica** (176), in 1956; it is still the most widely used sans serif in the world.

It was at the Haas where Edouard Hoffmann asked Miedinger to adapt the foundry's existing Haas Grotesk to accommodate current taste. Haas Grotesk had its origins in nineteenth-century German work such as Berthold's Akzidenz Grotesk. The new typeface, created from Miedinger's china-ink drawings, was a new design in its own right rather than one with minor modifications, as had been the original plan. Neue Haas Grotesk, as it was then called, proved extremely popular. When D. Stempel AG in Germany released the typeface in 1957, the foundry called it Helvetica—the traditional Latin name for "Switzerland," to capitalize on the increasing popularity of Swiss typography. Although Helvetica was not planned as a diverse family of weights like that of **Adrian Frutiger's** (88) **Univers** (181), several designers have added to it during the past thirty years. These additional weights are available on most typesetting systems.

Two of Miedinger's other typefaces, Pro Arte, a revival of a nineteenth-century poster typeface, and Horizontal, a heavy, square, titling face, were atypical in terms of his style and approach.

James Montalbano

American, 1953–
**Typefaces: *Orbon* (1995), *Freddo* (1996), *Nora* (1997),
Clearview (2004), *Moraine* (2010), *Trilon* (2011)**

Living Social, 2010

James Montalbano's professional career began as a public school graphic arts teacher in New York City. Following graduate studies in technology education, he studied lettering with **Ed Benguiat** (80), and began working as a graphic designer and art director at various type foundries and trade publications.

In 1990, he formed Terminal Design, Inc., and began to concentrate on lettering and typeface design. He has created custom typeface designs for editorial, corporate, government, and publishing clients including **International Typeface Corporation** (128), Warner Music, The American Medical Association, *Vanity Fair, Vogue, Men's Vogue, Gourmet, Mademoiselle, Details, Glamour, Fortune*, Scribner, J. C. Penney, AT&T, and MillerCoors. In 2001, he completed a new family of typefaces for the U. S. National Park Service, and for the past few years he has been involved with Meeker & Associates in the development of the Clearview type system for text, display, roadway, and an interior guide sign program.

Montalbano has taught typography and type design at the **Pratt Institute** (349), **Parsons The New School for Design** (349), and the **School of Visual Arts** (349) in New York City.

Stanley Morison

British, 1889–1967
Typefaces: *Blado* (1923), *Gill Sans* (1928), *Bembo* (1929),
Perpetua (1932), *Times New Roman* (1932)

Stanley Morison was a British graphic designer, printing historian, and major influence on the reform of typographic standards used in the printing industry during the **early twentieth century** (16).

Born in 1896 in Wanstead, Essex, England, Morrison was self-taught, having left school at a young age after his father abandoned the family. In 1918, he became design supervisor at Pelican Press and then held a similar position at Cloister Press before becoming an editorial assistant at *The Imprint* magazine in 1923. In 1925, he was appointed Cambridge University Press typographic adviser, and he published a book, *First Principles of Typography*, in 1928.

From 1923 to 1967, Morison was typographic advisor to the **Monotype Corporation** (125), where he commissioned **Eric Gill** (89) to design **Gill Sans** (175) (1928) and **Perpetua** (1932). He was a founding member of the Fleuron Society dedicated to typographical matters (a fleuron is a typographical flower or ornament) and also functioned as the Society's editor for its journal, *The Fleuron*, from 1925 to 1930. Morison was also typographic advisor to the *Times* of London newspaper from 1929 to 1960. In 1932, the paper commissioned him to produce an easy-to-read typeface. **Times New Roman** (165), developed with graphic artist Victor Lardent, was introduced in 1932 and subsequently issued commercially by Monotype in 1933.

In 1960, Morison was elected a Royal Designer for Industry by the British Royal Society of Arts honoring individuals who have achieved "sustained excellence in aesthetic and efficient design for industry."

8.16 Stanley Morison, Times New Roman Typeface, 1932.

Morison, 1932

Aldo Novarese

Italian, 1920–1998
**Typefaces: *Athenaeum* (1945), *Patrizia* (1950),
Augustea, *Fluidum* (1951), *MicrExpanded* (1952),
Fontanesi (1954), *Egizio*, *Juliet*, *Ritmo* (1955),
Garaldus (1956), *Slogan* (1957), *Belizio*, *Recta* (1958),
Estro (1961), *Eurostile*, *Square 721* (1962),
Formal 436 (1966), *Metropol* (1967), *Stop* (1971),
Sprint (1974), *Geometric 885* (1976), *Lapidar* (1977),
Fenice, *Justus Fraktur*, *Novarese* (1980),
Colossalis, *Symbol* (1984), *Mixage* (1985), *Arbiter* (1989),
Central, *Nadianne* (1998), *Press Gothic* (2007)**

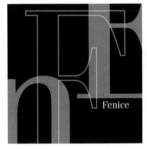

Fenice   Microgramma

Aldo Novarese was one of the modern era's most prolific
type designers. Born in Italy in 1920, he attended the
Turin School of Printing, where he studied woodcarving,
etching, and lithography. Following a brief period working
as a graphic arts teacher, he joined the Nebiolo type
foundry, where he ultimately became the foundry's art
director in 1952.

He collaborated with Alessandro Butti on many
of his early typeface designs. These include Augustea
and MicrExpanded, which, with the addition of its
lowercase (332), became Eurostile in 1962. The **Garamond-**
based (162) Garaldus takes its name from a category
in the Vox system of type classification. In 1980, Novarese
designed the type that bears his name, Novarese, for
the Haas foundry. Novarese is also well known as the
author of *Alfabeta*, a book about the origins and evolution
of typefaces in history.

Paul Renner

German, 1878–1956
**Typefaces: *Futura* (1927), *Plak* (1928),
Renner Grotesk (1936), *Ballade* (1937),
Renner Antiqua (1939)**

Futura, 1927   Advertisement, 1927

Paul Renner was a German typographer, graphic designer,
and teacher best known as the designer of **Futura** (174), a
groundbreaking typographic landmark of modernist form
still popular today.

During the **1920s** (20) and **1930s** (21), he was a
prominent member of the Deutscher Werkbund (German
Work Federation) while creating his first book designs
for various Munich-based publishers. As an author,
he fashioned a new set of guidelines for balanced book
design in his books *Typografie als Kunst* (translated
"Typography as Art") and *Die Kunst der Typographie*
(translated as "The Art of Typography").

Renner established the Meisterschule fur Deutchlands
Buchdrucher (Advanced School of German Bookprinting)
in Munich and recruited fellow type designers **Georg
Trump** and **Jan Tschichold** (105) to teach there. In 1933,
Tschichold was removed from his post and interned by
the Nazis for "subversive typography," and four years later,
in 1937, Renner himself was forced to resign.

Bruce Rogers

American, 1870–1957
Typefaces: *Brimmer (1901),*
Montaigne (1902), Riverside Modern (1904),
Centaur (1914), Metropolitan (1928)

Born in Linnwood, Indiana, in 1870, Bruce Rogers was an American graphic and type designer considered by some the greatest book designer of the **twentieth century** (16). He was known for a classical approach to typography and page layout and for dismissing modernism.

After completing his studies at Purdue University, Rogers worked as an artist for the *Indianapolis News*. During this same time period, he became interested in publishing and producing fine books, so he moved to Boston, where he worked as a freelance designer for Louis Prang & Co. It was here that he cut one of his first typefaces, Montaigne, a Venetian-style design named for the earliest book in which it appeared, a 1903 limited edition of *The Essays of Montaigne*.

In 1912, Rogers moved to New York City where he worked both as a freelance designer and as house designer for the Metropolitan Museum of Art. During his tenure at the museum, he designed his most famous typeface, **Centaur** (158), for the 1915 limited edition of Maurice de Guérin's *The Centaur*. In subsequent years, Rogers worked extensively as a typographic advisor and book designer for Mount Vernon Press, Harvard University Press, **Monotype Corporation** (125), and Oxford University Press.

THE BANQUET OF PLATO

APOLLODORUS. I think that the subject of your inquiries is still fresh in my memory; for yesterday, as I chanced to be returning home from Phaleros, one of my acquaintance, seeing me before him, called out to me from a distance, jokingly, 'Apollodorus, you Phalerian, will you not wait a minute?'—I waited for him, and as soon as he overtook me, 'I have just been looking for you, Apollodorus,' he said, 'for I wish to hear what those discussions were on Love, which took place at the party, when Agathon, Socrates, Alcibiades, and some others met at supper. Some one who heard it from Phœnix, the son of Philip, told me that you could give a full account, but he could relate nothing distinctly him-

Rogers, 1915

Christian Schwartz

American, 1977–
Typefaces: *Flywheel* (1992), *Atlas, Elroy* (1993), *Hairspray* (1994), *Morticia, Zombie* (1995), *Fritz* (1997),
Casa Latino (1999), *Pennsylvania* (2000), *Loz Feliz, Simian* (2001), *Bau, Harrison, Neutra* (2002),
Amplitude, Eero, Houston (2003), *Symantec* (2003, with Conor Mangat), *Unit* (2003, with Erik Spiekermann),
Bosch (2004, with Spiekermann), *Farnham* (2004), *Guardian Egyptian* (2004, with Paul Barnes),
Popular (2004), *Deutsche Bahn* (2005, with Spiekermann), *Oxide, Stag* (2005), *Local Gothic* (2006),
Luxury (2006, with Dino Sanchez), *Giorgio* (2008), *Neutra Slab* (2009)

Capaoni, designed with Paul Barnes, 2010
Commissioned by *Entertainment Weekly*

Giorgio, 2007; Giorgio Sans, 2009
Commissioned by *T, The New York Times Style Magazine*
Published by Commercial Type

From Bach to Led Zeppelin, music has always had a powerful emotional pull for critic **Nick Coleman**. But since he lost hearing in one ear, listening is agony and his favourite artists no longer move him. Will the magic ever return?

Guardian Egyptian, designed with Paul Barnes, 2004
Commissioned by *The Guardian*

Amplitude, 2003
Published by Font Bureau

ESB Titling and Sans, designed with Paul Barnes, 2007
Commissioned by Two Twelve Associates

Unit Slab, designed with Kris Sowersby and Erik Spiekermann, 2009
Published by FontFont

Graphik, 2009
Published by Commercial Type

Neutraface, 2003; Neutraface Slab, designed with Kai Bernau and Susana Carvalho, 2009
Published by House Industries

Christian Schwartz was born in 1977 and grew up in a small town in New Hampshire. He graduated from Carnegie Mellon University in 1999 with a degree in communication design and spent three months as the in-house type designer at MetaDesign Berlin. He then joined **The Font Bureau, Inc.** (127) in 2000, as a member of its full-time design staff.

In 2001, Schwartz formed orange italic (with product designer Dino Sanchez) and Schwartzco, Inc. He is also a partner in the type foundry Commercial Type with the London-based designer, Paul Barnes. In addition to his work for The Font Bureau, Inc., he has designed fonts for **Emigre** (127), **FontShop** (140), and **House Industries** (128) (including the popular Neutra family, based on the work of modernist architect Richard Neutra), as well as proprietary designs for corporations and publications including Bosch, Deutsche Bank, *Esquire,* the *New York Times,* the *Houston Chronicle,* and the *Guardian.*

The New York **Type Directors Club** (355), the Smithsonian's Cooper Hewitt, National Design Museum in New York City, and the **International Society of Typographic Designers** (355) have all honored his typographic work. Schwartz also received the prestigious Prix Charles Peignot in 2007 from the **Association Typographique Internationale** (354).

Robert Slimbach

American, 1956–
Typefaces: *Slimbach* (1987), *Adobe Garamond*, *Giovanni*, *Utopia* (1989), *Minion* (1990),
Myriad (1990, with Carol Twombly), *Poetica* (1992), *Calfisch*, *Sanvito* (1993),
Adobe Jenson (1995), *Cronos*, *Kepler* (1996), *Warnock* (2000), *Brioso* (2002), *Arno* (2007)

Robert Slimbach is a prolific type designer who has worked at **Adobe Systems** (124) since 1987. His digital typefaces have been recognized for design excellence worldwide, most notably the rarely awarded Prix Charles Peignot from the **Association Typographique Internationale** (354).

Slimbach was born in Evanston, Illinois, in 1956 and spent the majority of his childhood in southern California. After completing college, he quickly developed an interest in graphic design and typography while running a small silkscreen printing business producing posters and greeting cards.

Following a two-year stint at Autologic Incorporated, he developed and designed the fonts ITC Slimbach and ITC Giovanni for **International Typeface Corporation** (128) in New York City.

In 1987, Slimbach joined Adobe Systems, where he has concentrated primarily on designing typefaces for digital technology and drawing inspiration from classical sources. During his tenure there, Slimbach has designed many new fonts for the Adobe Originals Program. His own roman script calligraphy formed the basis for his typeface Brioso. Though Slimbach has not produced as many typefaces recently, he has taken full advantage of the new linguistic and typographic capabilities offered by the OpenType format, which now provides the post-2000 type designer with a much broader range of glyphs and optical sizes within any given typeface.

Fred Smeijers

Dutch, 1961–
Typefaces: *Renard* (1992),
Quadraat (1997), **Quadraat Sans** (2000),
Fresco, Sansa (2001),
Arnhem, Custodia (2002), **Monitor** (2005),
Eva (2006), **Ludwig** (2009)

Quadraat, 1997

Sansa, 2001

Arnhem, 2002

Born in Eindhoven in 1961, Fred Smeijers is a Dutch type designer, graphic designer, author, and educator.

He studied at the Academie voor Beeldende Kunsten in Arnhem from 1980 to 1985. From 1987 to 1991, he worked at Océ Nederland (a Dutch manufacturer of printing and photocopying equipment) as the company's typographic advisor, designing digital typefaces for early laser printers. In 2002, he started the digital type foundry, OurType, with Rudy Geeraerts. As the foundry's creative director, he has designed numerous typefaces including FF Quadraat and Renard. He also has designed wordmarks and custom typefaces for clients such as Philips, Canon, and TomTom.

Smeijers is a professor of digital typography at the **Hochschule fur Grafik und Buchkunst** (347) in Leipzig, Germany and at the **Royal Academy of Art** (347) in The Hague, The Netherlands. He also authored *Counterpunch* (1996) and *Type Now* (2003), both published by Hyphen Press in London. In 2000, Smeijers received the Gerrit Noordzij Prize, the highest honor awarded by The Royal Academy of Art, for his innovations in type design and his outstanding contributions to type education.

Erik Spiekermann

German, 1947–
Typefaces: *Berliner Grotesk* (1979), *LoType* (1980), *Officina Serif* (1990),
Meta (1991), *Info* (1996), *Govan* (2001), *Unit* (2003, with Christian Schwartz),
Bosch (2004, with Schwartz), *Deutsche Bahn* (2005, with Schwartz), *Meta Serif* (2007)

Erik Spiekermann is an accomplished type designer, graphic designer, and typographic consultant. A native of Hanover, Germany, he spent five years working and lecturing in London and now lives in Berlin.

From 1967 to 1971, Spiekermann studied art history in Berlin's Free University and ran a printing and metal type business from his basement. In 1973, he moved to London, where he lectured at the London College of Communication (formerly called the London College of Printing) and worked as a freelance designer.

In 1979, he returned to Germany and founded Meta-Design, which grew into Germany's largest design firm with more than 200 employees.

Spiekermann is also a principal of the **FontShop** (127; 140), a company dedicated to selling high-quality PostScript fonts from all major manufacturers. In addition, FontShop, through its subsidiary FontFont, creates and promotes new fonts from up-and-coming designers and publishes the quarterly, disc-only magazine *Fuse*.

The FontFont library also includes several of Spiekermann's own typeface designs, including FF Meta, identified as "the Helvetica of the '90s" and one of the most popular typefaces in the world. Another of his typefaces, ITC Officina, is widely used in Web design. FF Info, his latest, is used for the navigation system of a major European airport.

Spiekermann frequently writes about type and typography, including his book *Stop Stealing Sheep & Find Out How Type Works*, published by Adobe Press. He holds an honorary professorship at the Academy of Arts in Bremen, Germany, and teaches workshops at design schools around the world.

In 2007, the Royal Society of Arts in London made Spiekermann an Honorary Royal Designer for Industry. In 2009, the European Union awarded him Ambassador for the European Year of Creativity and Innovation, and in 2011, the Federal Republic of Germany presented him with a lifetime achievement award.

Sumner Stone

American, 1945–

Typefaces: *Stone* (1987), *Ends Means Mends* (1992), *Stone Print* (1992), *Cycles* (1993), *Silica* (1993), *Arepo* (1996), *Basalt* (1998), *Leaves & Straw* (2003), *Magma* (2004), *Munc* (2005), *Tuff* (2009)

Arepo Pencil, 1996

Basalt, 1998

Munc typeface with leaves and straw ornaments, 2005

Sumner Stone created the Stone type family or "clan" (as he calls it), which is composed of four matched types: Stone Serif, Stone Sans, Stone Informal, and Stone Humanist Sans.

Following his undergraduate degree in sociology and an introductory course in calligraphy taught by Lloyd Reynolds at Reed College in Portland, Oregon, Stone worked as a lettering artist for Hallmark Cards. He then opened his own design studio in Sonoma, California, and earned an M.A. in mathematics from Sonoma State University.

After working as director of typography at Autologic in Newbury Park, CA, and Camex in Boston, Massachusetts, he joined **Adobe Systems** (124) in 1984 as its first director of typography. There he conceived and implemented Adobe's typographic program including the Adobe Originals, participated in the development of Adobe's hinting and font editing software, conceived and initiated the technology called Multiple Masters, and was responsible for licensing the first PostScript typefaces from Japan.

In 1990, Stone established Stone Type Foundry Inc., now located in Rumsey, California. The foundry produces and markets Stone's typeface designs, which include a wide range of styles. Its first release was Stone Print designed for the text of *Print* magazine. The foundry's repertoire now includes both historical revivals such as the prize-winning ITC Bodoni, and the extensive Magma super-family which in 2010 was selected by *Print* magazine as one of the ten typefaces of the decade.

Jan Tschichold

German, 1902–1974
**Typefaces: *Transito* (1930), *Zeus* (1931),
Saskia (1932), *Sabon* (1964)**

Jan Tschichold was one of the most controversial and influential graphic designers and typographers of the **twentieth century** (16). He was born in Leipzig, Germany, in 1902. As a teenager, he studied calligraphy, typography, and engraving, and continued his formal studies at the Academy for Graphic Arts and Book Trades in Leipzig and at the School of Arts & Crafts in Dresden.

Following a visit to the Weimar Bauhaus exhibition in 1923, he immediately became an advocate of "new typography," which celebrated abstract modernist principles such as **asymmetrical** (226) layouts and sans serif typefaces. Years later, he became as well known for denouncing these ideals and returning to traditional principles. Tschichold began his teaching career at the Leipzig Academy, and from 1926 to 1933, he taught at the German School for Master Printers in Munich.

He designed several typefaces during the **1920s** (20) and **1930s** (21) in Germany; however most of them were lost during World War II. He designed his well-known typeface, **Sabon** (164), in the early **1960s** (24). It remains widely used today.

In 1958, the **American Institute of Graphic Arts** (354) in New York presented him with its highest honor, the AIGA Medal, and in 1965, the Royal Society of Arts in London made him the first Honorary Royal Designer for Industry.

Carol Twombly

American, 1959–
**Typefaces: *Mirarae* (1984),
Adobe Caslon, *Charlemagne*, *Lithos*, *Trajan* (1990),
Myriad (1992, with Robert Slimbach), *Viva* (1993),
Nueva (1994), *Chapparal* (2000)**

Carol Twombly studied graphic design and architecture at the **Rhode Island School of Design** (349) where she first became interested in letterforms and type design. She subsequently received a master's degree from Stanford University in the digital typography graduate department under **Charles Bigelow** (83), and later joined his firm, Bigelow & Holmes.

In 1984, Twombly won first prize from the Morisawa Typeface Design Competition for her Latin typeface Mirarae, which **Bitstream** (124) subsequently produced. From 1988 to 1999, she worked as a staff designer at **Adobe Systems** (124) developing some of the most widely recognized digital fonts of the **twentieth century** (16), including Lithos (based on inscribed Greek lettering), Trajan (based on Roman capital letters found on the Trajan column), and Myriad (designed with fellow Adobe Systems designer, **Robert Slimbach** [101]).

Twombly retired from Adobe in 1999 to pursue other design interests including textile and jewelry design.

Gerard Unger

Dutch, 1942–
**Typefaces: *Demos* (1976), *Praxis* (1977),
Hollander (1983), *Flora* (1984),
Swift (1985), *Amerigo* (1986), *Argo* (1991),
Oranda (1992), *Gulliver* (1993),
ANWB-fonts (1997), *Capitolium* (1998),
Paradox (1999), *Coranto* (2000),
Vesta (2001), *Capitolium News* (2006)**

Born in Arnhem in 1942, Gerard Unger is a Dutch type designer, graphic designer, and educator. He studied at the Gerrit Rietveld Academie in Amsterdam, then worked at Total Design, Prad, and Joh. Enschedé. Since 1975, he has worked independently in Bussum, The Netherlands.

Unger also teaches graphic design and typography at the Gerrit Rietveld Academie in Amsterdam, for the **University of Reading's** (348) department of typography and graphic communication in the United Kingdom, and at The Netherlands's University of Leiden.

He has designed typefaces for the Dutch highway sign system and the Amsterdam Metro. His newspaper typeface, Gulliver (1993), is familiar to millions of readers as it is the typeface used in both *USA Today* and several international publications and newspapers, including Germany's *Stuttgarter Zeitung*.

Unger has received numerous recognitions and awards, including the H. N. Werkman Prize in 1984, the Maurits Enschedé Prize in 1991, and the Society for Typographic Arts Typography Awards in 2009.

Jürgen Weltin

German, 1969–
Typefaces: *Finnegan* (1997), *Yellow* (2001), *Balega* (2002), *Agilita* (2006), *Mantika* (2010)

Agilita, 2006

Jürgen Weltin was born in Constance, Germany, in 1969. Before beginning his formal studies in graphic design at the Technical College in Würzburg, Germany, he worked at a local publishing house. During this same time period, he apprenticed at Stankowski + Duschek and studied at the Bournemouth & Poole College of Art and Design in Dorset, United Kingdom.

Weltin joined Freda Sack and David Quay's The Foundry in 1997, where he worked on type development projects, including Foundry Gridnik and Foundry Form. He received a D&AD Silver Award in 1999 for his typeface design for the British Telecommunications's Yellow Pages directory.

Hermann Zapf

Germany, 1918–
**Typefaces: *Michelangelo, Palatino, Sistina* (1950), *Melior* (1952), *Saphir, Virtuosa* (1953),
Aldus, Kompakt, Mergenthaler Antiqua (1954), *Optima* (1958), *Hunt Roman* (1962), *Jeanette* (1967), *Firenze* (1968),
Textura, Venture (1969), *Hallmark Uncial* (1970), *Medici Script, Missouri* (1971), *Crown, Scriptura* (1972),
Orion (1974), *Comenius Antiqua, Marconi, Noris Script, Zapf, Zapf International* (1976), *Edison, Zapf Dingbats* (1978),
Zapf Chancery (1979), *Vario* (1982), *Aurelia, Euler* (1983), *Zapf Renaissance Antiqua* (1987), *Zapfino* (1998)**

Hermann Zapf was born in Nuremberg, Germany, in 1918. He is a master calligrapher, artist, educator, and one of the most prolific type designers of the **twentieth century** (16). He has created more than 175 typefaces for metal type foundries, photo compositors, and digital foundries. Two of his most renowned typefaces are Palatino and Optima. The latter, which he called a "serifless roman," was inspired by inscriptional lettering he had seen in Florence. It still remains extremely popular with calligraphers and stone carvers.

A self-taught type and book designer since 1938, Zapf has worked for D. Stempel AG, Mergenthaler Linotype Company, **H. Berthold AG** (126), Hell Digiset, Hallmark Cards, and **International Typeface Corporation** (128). In 1977, he became a professor of typographic computer programming at the **Rochester Institute of Technology** (349) in New York.

Zapf has received numerous awards for his typographic work including the 1989 Gold Medal at the International Buchkunst-Ausetllung in Leipzig, the Frederic W. Goudy Award in Typography from RIT in 1969, and the Gutenberg Prize for technical and aesthetic achievement in type in 1974. He was also made an Honorary Royal Designer for Industry in London in 1989.

In 2010, Zapf was awarded the Order of Merit of the Federal Republic of Germany.

Twenty First Century— A New Breed

Rui Abreu, Veronika Burian, Pilar Cano, Eric Chan, Joshua Darden, Tomi Haaparanta, Stefan Hattenbach, Jessica Hische, Chester Jenkins, German Olaya, Eric Olson, Alejandro Paul, José Scaglione, Kris Sowersby, Fabian Widmer, Stefan Willerstorfer, Luke Williams

Rui Abreu

Portuguese, 1979–
Typefaces: *Cifra* (2006), *Catacumba*, *Gesta* (2009), *Foral*, *Orbe*, *Tirana* (2010)

SHE IS NOT DOING ANY WORK
On morning I delightedly watched him outwit the boss
DISTINGUISH
All documents must be kept on you USB-memory stick at all times!
Blue Friday
SALUTE
For walks we prefer the narrow and winding lane
425 happy workers
Established

Foral 3, 2010

MAXILAR SUPERIOR 12 CÚBITOS
TRAPEZÓIDE
MATERIAL OSTEOLÓGICO
∼
EXUMADOS
METAMORFOSE TELÚRICA
ALEGORIA FUNERÁRIA
PORTO

Catacumba 2, 2009

Rui Abreu is a Portuguese type designer. He studied graphic design at Faculdade de Belas Artes da Universidade de Porto, graduating in 2003. Since then, he has worked as an interactive media designer in several design firms and advertising agencies, along with his independent type design work. In 2008, he launched R:Typography, a showcase to promote his own work.

THE MERRY TALE OF
↬LITTLE JOHN↫
YEOMAN
BREWED BY THE FAT FRIAR
TUCK
BEER • CERVEJAS
ROBIN.HOOD@SHERWOODFOREST.ORG
REWARD
✠£.37.452.900✠
BARNSDALE

Orbe 3, 2010

Veronika Burian

Czechoslovakian, 1973–
Typefaces: *Maiola* (2004), ***Ronnia*** (2004, with José Scaglione),
Foco (2006, with Fabio Luz Haag),
Karmina (2006, with Scaglione), **Crete**, **Tondo** (2007), **Athelas** (2008),
Bree (2008, with Scaglione), **Adelle** (2009, with Scaglione)

Bree, 2008

Athelas, 2008

Maiola, 2004

Veronika Burian was born in Prague in 1973. In 1980, she moved to Munich, where she studied industrial design at the University of Applied Sciences. Before completing her studies, she worked as a product designer at Gregerpauschitz in Vienna.

In 2000, she joined the team of Japanese designer Makio Hasuike in Milan, where her interests shifted from product design to graphic design and typography. Her decision to focus exclusively on type design developed through her collaboration with Italian design company Leftloft on the exhibition *italic 1.0* at the **Association Typographique Internationale** (354) and teaching at the Politecnico di Milano.

In 2003, she completed her master of arts in typeface design with distinction at the **University of Reading** (348), United Kingdom, where she started designing the typeface Maiola. In 2004, Maiola earned the **Type Directors Club** (355) Certificate of Excellence and in 2005 became part of the traveling exhibition *e-a-t*. She worked as a type designer at Dalton Maag in London until 2007, when she moved to Boulder, Colorado.

Burian currently lives and works in Prague, where she dedicates her time fully to **TypeTogether** (137), an independent type foundry that she cofounded with **José Scaglione** (118).

Pilar Cano

Czechoslovakian, 1978–
Typefaces: *Edita* (2009), *Techari* (2010)

Pilar Cano is a typeface designer from Barcelona, which is also the place where she earned her first degree in graphic design. During this period, she also studied at Lahti Polytechnic (in Finland), where she started to consider becoming a type designer.

In 2006, she graduated from the typeface design master's program at the **University of Reading** (348) in the United Kingdom. Since that time, she has worked as a freelance graphic and type designer, participated in several international typographic exhibitions, and lectured worldwide. Currently, Cano works at Dalton Maag in London as a type designer.

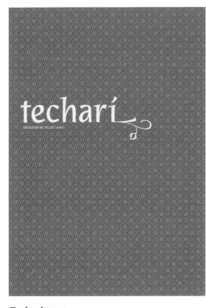

Techari, 2010

EDITA 2006–2009

Regular | *Italic*
Bold | ***Bold italic***
Small text | *Small text italic*

Distributed by Typetogether

Edita is a gentle typeface, humanistic in concept yet with a contemporary feel, where softness and fluidity play a very important role. This can be seen especially in its italics, which are loosely based on handwriting.

This book typeface family is a book typeface, versatile enough to be used in many other contexts, from novels to promotion material.

Edita's large character set, covering most languages which use Latin script, and styles give the designer the possibility to work with a big typographic palette, allowing complex typesetting with several levels of information.

This is further enhanced by the two optically corrected weights Edita Small and Small Italic. They have been particularly designed for their use in very small type sizes, such as in captions and notes. They differ in having a slightly bigger x-height, heavier stems, reduced contrast, and carefully drawn ink-traps to ensure legibility at sizes as small as 5 pt. Additionally, their extenders are shorter to save space which allows text to be set with tighter leading.

«Edita has long extenders and requires a *generous* leading»

EDITA small text has *less* contrasted letterforms, shorter extenders and a taller x-height!

BOLD has less space between letters and is slightly *taller* *

Edita, 2009

Eric Chan

Chinese, birth year unknown

Eric Chan is a graphic designer and corporate identity consultant based in Hong Kong. Following completion of his graphic design studies at The Hong Kong Polytechnic and The First Institute of Art & Design in 1981, he worked at Hill & Knowlton, Leo Burnett, and Bates Hong Kong before starting his own design consultancy in 1991.

Numerous professional organizations, publications, and institutions worldwide have recognized his work. In 2007, Chan was named one of Hong Kong's top ten outstanding designers.

Antalis

Joshua Darden

American, 1979–
Typefaces: *Locus* *(1993, with Timothy Freight),*
Omnes *(2006),* ***Corundum***, ***Jubilat*** *(2007),*
Birra Stout *(2008)*

Joshua Darden is a native of Los Angeles
who published his first typeface at the age of
fifteen. He spent the next ten years working
on the development and production of
typefaces before starting his own studio and
foundry, **Darden Studio** (130), in 2004.

He has taught type design and the history
of type at **Parsons The New School for Design**
(349) and at the **School of Visual Arts** (349),
both in New York City.

EXTRA LIGHT — Platforms *Bookcase*

LIGHT — Formerly *Gondolas*

REGULAR — Strafford *Combine*

MEDIUM — **Talfourd** *Paradox*

BOLD — **Majestic** *Relishes*

BLACK — **Develop** *Directly*

Jubilat, 2007

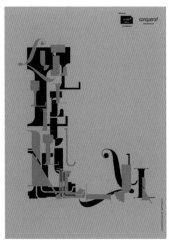

Tomi Haaparanta

Finnish, 1967–
Typefaces: *Talmud, Temporal, Tension, Testament,*
Torus, Tyrant (1998), *Caxton Script, Tantalus, Target, Teebone,*
Terylene, Tictac Toe, Tonic, Tummy, Vektori, War (1999),
Aged, Task, Torino (2000), *Tangerine, Tee Franklin Heavy,*
Teethreedee, Twinkle (2001), *That* (2002), *Story 20, Tale 20, Tale 40,*
Teebrush Paint (2003), *Suomi Script, Tang, Tubby, Tyke* (2004),
Pannartz, Tetra, Tomism (2005), *Suomi Sans* (2006),
Suomi Hand Script (2008), *Explosion, Giro, Kaapeli, Suomi Slab Serif,*
Taffee, Tailor, Taint, Talbot, Tame, Televisio, Ticketbook, Tink,
Titillation, Tobacco, Tonsure Script (2009),
Cider Script, Steelworks, Taste, Telltale, Tempest, Thud,
Tide Script, Tournedot, Tristan (2010)

Tomi Haaparanta was born in Helsinki, Finland, in 1967. He studied graphic design at the University of Industrial Arts in Helsinki and at the National College of Art and Design in Dublin, where he discovered type design during a short course held by Phil Baines. Haaparanta has worked as an art director for several design and advertising agencies. He has been designing typefaces since 1990. Haaparanta has also taught type design at the University of Industrial Arts in Helsinki since 2007. In 2004, he started the Suomi Type Foundry. Linotype (129), Monotype (125), International Typeface Corporation (128), T.26 (129), and PSY/OPS (135) also distribute Haaparanta's fonts.

Kaapeli, 2009

Suomi Logotype, 2004

Stefan Hattenbach

Swedish, 1961–
Typefaces: *Hattrick, Lunda Modern,*
New Global, Pomodoro,
Remontoire, Stylish (1999),
Oxtail (2000), *Montessori* (2001),
Luminance, Sophisto, Stalemate (2003),
Delicato (2004), *Anziano, Tarocco* (2006),
Brasserie, Euroglory,
Expansion, Omegaard (2007),
Graficz (2008), *Replay* (2010)

The well-tempered
chocolatiers
ELDER STATESMAN LIES
Global warming
How to make a good musical stiff!

WALKING ALL OVER THE WORLD
December 21st 2012 might be the end
New Mexican Tools
VOLUME 1 / ISSUE 3 / MAY 2009 / € 7.50
The right answer
thankfully has more than one soloution…

Replay 2, 2010

Stefan Hattenbach, born in 1961, is an art director and graphic designer specializing in typography and branding. He has managed his own design studio since 1986 and has provided a dynamic balance of experimental and traditional work for clients such as Greenpeace, Amnesty International, Telisa, and H&M (Hennes & Mauritz). Mac Rhino Fonts distributes Hattenbach's fonts.

Jessica Hische

American, 1984–
Typeface: *Buttermilk* (2009)

IT'S (AS YOU CAN SEE) A BOLD SCRIPT THAT WOULD BE JUST PERFECT FOR MAGAZINE HEADLINES, BOOK TITLE TYPE, HOLIDAY CARDS, INITIAL CAPS, YOU NAME IT. THERE ARE SOME PRETTY STELLAR NUMERALS AND A HUGE ARRAY OF LIGATURES TO HELP YOU SET IT BEAUTIFULLY AND EASILY.

ABCDEFGHI
JKLMNOPQR
STUVWXYZ

abcdefghijklmnopqrst
uvwxyz

No. 0123456789

AND MORE!

Buttermilk 1, 2009

Birds

Snowflake

Jessica Hische is a graphic designer and illustrator located in Brooklyn, New York. She graduated from Tyler School of Art in 2006 with a graphic design degree then worked for Headcase Design in Philadelphia. Next she became senior designer at design firm Louise Fili, Ltd, in New York. While at Fili, Hische developed freelance relationships with clients including Tiffany & Co. and the *New York Times*.

In September 2009, Hische left Louise Fili, Ltd, to pursue freelancing full time. Several design and illustration publications have featured Hische's work including *Communication Arts, Print, How, Graphis, American Illustration,* and *ILLO.* She's also been designated an up-and-coming designer to watch, picked as one of *STEP Magazine*'s top twenty-five emerging artists, as one of *Print Magazine*'s (352) New Visual Artists for 2009, and dubbed a New York Art Directors Club "Young Gun."

Chester Jenkins

Canadian, 1971–
Typefaces: *Apex Sans (2003, with Rick Valicenti),* *Apex Serif (2003),* *Mavis (2005), Galaxie Cassiopeia (2006), Galaxie Polaris (2008), Galaxie Copernicus (2009, with Kris Sowersby)*

Chester Jenkins was born in Montreal. He is a type designer, publisher, and cofounder of the cooperative foundry Village, with Tracy Jenkins. He studied graphic design at College Dawson in Montreal, and has spent the past fifteen years working in his hometown, as well as in London, Utrecht (The Netherlands), Chicago, and New York.

Jenkins has published several retail typeface families that are used worldwide by a range of clients including CBS Sports and the United Nations. He has created custom typefaces for the National Football League, Condé Nast, and the *New York Times Magazine*, as well as collaborated with Rick Valicenti of the design firm Thirst on several typefaces.

Since 2003, he has been developing typefaces in the OpenType format, taking advantage of OT's multilingual Unicose support and its stylistic potential. Jenkins's recent work outside the Latin alphabet includes Cyrillic, Greek, and Hebrew scripts, work he plans to incorporate into future editions of his published types.

German Olaya

Colombian, 1979–
Typefaces: *Chato Band, Foodshow, Kab, Mosketa, Soda (2004), Esso (2005), Fango, Fructosa, Uncle Typewriter, Yexivela (2007), Californya (2010)*

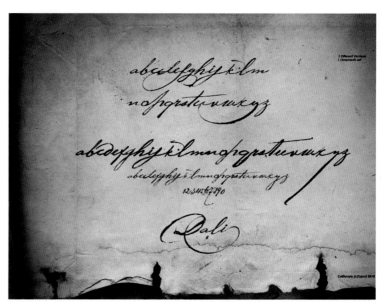

Californya 2, 2010

German Olaya was born in Bogotá, Colombia, in 1979. He started his career as a type designer in 1998 when he purchased his first copy of Fontographer, software for font designers. He subsequently started his own website, www.typo5.com, where he currently showcases his own type designs and graphic experiments—which have brought him worldwide recognition. Olaya's celebrated work appears in all types of media, including magazines, books, publications, and films, and on music labels, television, and snowboards.

Eric Olson

American, 1974–
Typefaces: Kettler, Maple (2002),
Linqua, Locator (2003),
Finderplace, Klavika, Stratum (2004),
Bryant, Fig (2005), **Seravek** (2007),
Anchor (2010)

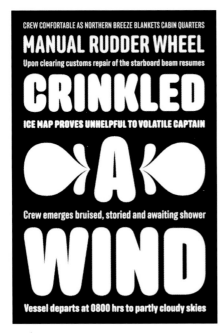

Anchor, 2010

Seravek, 2007

Klavika, 2004

Eric Olson is a typeface designer, founder, and partner at Process Type Foundry. He attended the University of Minnesota, where he earned a degree in graphic design. Since 2002, Olson has taught typography at Minneapolis College of Art and Design.

In recent years, he has focused his attention primarily on client-related work for Chevrolet, the *New York Times Magazine*, Thomson Reuters, and Walker Art Center. Numerous design publications have featured his work, including *Eye, Print, HOW Magazine* (351), *Metropolis Magazine*, and *STEP Magazine*.

Alejandro Paul

Argentinean, 1972–
**Typefaces: *Reflex* (2002),
*Downtempo, Latinaires,
Mosaico, Tierra* (2003),
*Cuisine, Dr. Carbfred,
Dr. Sugiyama, Grover,
Grover Slab, Herr Von
Muellerhoff, Miss Le Gatees,
Mr. Canfield, Mr. Dafoe,
Mr. Keningbeck,
Mr. Lackbones, Mr. Rafkin,
Mr. Saint-Delafield,
Mr. Sheffield, Mr. Shepards,
Mr. Sopkin, Mr. Von Eckley,
Mrs. Blackfort,
Politica* (2004),
*Buffet Script, Ministry Script,
Mousse Script,
Suave Script* (2005),
*Affair, Feel Script, Forma,
Miss Blaker, Miss Fitzpatrick,
Miss Lankfort,
Miss Robertson,
Miss Stephens, Monsieur La
Doulaise, Mr. Bedfort,
Mr. Benedict, Mr. Donaldson,
Piel Script, Salto Alto* (2006),
Candy Script (2007),
*Burgues Script, Calgary
Script, Compendium, Kewl
Script, Sugar Pie* (2008),
Adios Script, Semilla (2009),
Brownstone, Fan Script (2010)

Brownstone, 2010

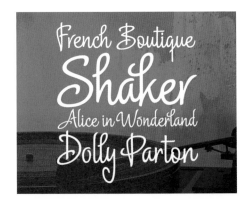

Delight Script, 2006

Alejandro Paul is one of the founders of the **Sudtipos** (136) project, the first Argentinean type foundry collective (whose other members include Ariel Garofalo, Claudio Pousada, and Diego Giaccone).

Paul taught graphic design and typography at the Universidad de Buenos Aires from 1996 until 2004 and has worked as an art director in Argentinean studios handling corporate brands such as Arcor, Proctor & Gamble, SC Johnson, Danone, and others.

In 2003, he began designing fonts and lettering for several packaging agencies, creating some of his best-known work to date. In 2006, he presented at TMDG06, the largest Latin American graphic design event attended by more than 4,000 designers, and he has been invited to speak at design and typography conferences in Portugal, Germany, Chile, Brazil, Ecuador, Uruguay, Mexico, Canada, and the United States. His work has been featured in *STEP Inside Design*, **Creative Review** (351), *Print, Computer Arts, Visual, Creative Arts,* and *Novum*. In 2009, Paul received his second **Type Directors Club** (355) award for his typeface Adios Script.

Piel, 2006

José Scaglione

Argentinean, 1974–
Typefaces: *Ronnia* *(2004, with Veronika Burian),*
Karmina *(2006, with Burian),*
Athelas *(2008),* ***Bree*** *(2008, with Burian),*
Adelle *(2009, with Burian)*

Adelle, 2009

Karmina, 2006

Bibliophiles

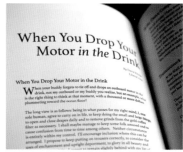

PNCA 1

José Scaglione is an Argentinean graphic and multimedia designer. He was born in Rosario, Argentina, where he studied undergraduate graphic design and postgraduate studies in multimedia. Scaglione graduated from the master's program in typeface design at the **University of Reading** (348) in the United Kingdom.

Since 1995, he has had his own design studio, where he manages editorial design, branding, and typographic projects. Scaglione cofounded Vision Media Design Studio in Argentina, as well as Multiplicity Advertising and The Prepaid Press in the United States. In 2006, he cofounded with **Veronika Burian** (109) the font label **TypeTogether** (137).

Scaglione is an adjunct professor at the Visual Communications Institute of Rosario where he teaches design for the Internet.

Kris Sowersby

New Zealander, 1981–
**Typefaces: *Feijoa*, *National* (2007), *Newzald* (2008), *Karbon* (2009),
Founders Grotesk, *Tiempos* (2010)**

Founders Grotesk C, 2010

Karbon, 2009

Kris Sowersby's typefaces reflect a striking integration of historical and contemporary visual references. He studied graphic design at the Wanganui School of Design, where he graduated in 2003. In 2005, he started the Klim Type Foundry based in Wellington, New Zealand. He released his first typeface, Feijoa, internationally in 2007. The **Type Directors Club (355)** in New York recognized Sowersby's second typeface, National, as well as his subsequent Serrano and Hardys typefaces for design excellence in 2008.

Sowersby has designed custom and retail typefaces including FF Meta Serif, the seriffed sibling of the renowned typeface FF Meta.

His international reputation for typeface design has lead to work with and for leading contemporary typographers and designers such as DNA Design, **House Industries (128)**, **Chester Jenkins (114)**, **Christian Schwartz (100)**, **Erik Spiekermann (103)**, and Pentagram. The Klim Type Foundry markets its typefaces exclusively through Village. In 2010, Sowersby was named a "Young Gun," a title from the New York Art Directors Club that honors "creative professionals who let loose their imaginations, shattering conventions and breaking boundaries with a dash of brilliance and personal flair."

Fabian Widmer

Swiss, 1981–
Typefaces: *Accore*, *Carrosserie* (2010)

· ALTERNATE GLYPHS ·

Carrosserie, 2010

Fabian Widmer was born in Zurich, Switzerland, in 1981. He studied type design and typography at the **Basel School of Design (348)**. After working for two years as a typographer, he launched his own type design studio in 2008 together with Dominique Bossener. The pair's studio, Letterwerk, is based in Zurich and Berlin.

Stefan Willerstorfer

Austrian, 1979–
Typeface: *Accorde* (2010)

el periódico global en español

posti ottaa keväällä käyttöön pakettiautomaatit

Qualifikation

wie wir in 20 Jahren fliegen werden

ice lagoon ticket

une grève dans le port de Marseille bloque l'activité pétrolière

MEISTER DER INSZENIERUNG

Milliarden

Accorde, 2010

un eurogol dell'olandese

Mähdrescher

sun protection factor 20

Ligue des champions : revivez le quart de finale retour Bordeaux–Lyon

Squadra Azzura

designers are looking forward to using this typeface

Reykjavík

andererseits sollte man bedenken, dass derzeit durchaus Bedarf besteht

dopo l'eliminazione

place à l'autoconsommation électrique

Vollmilch

Accorde, 2010

Acorde
a corporate design typeface

ACORDE REGULAR
Acorde is a reliable workhorse for large, demanding design projects. It was designed to be perfectly suited to all different sizes, from small continuous text to large headlines and big signage. The typeface's name is derived AaBbCcDdEeFfGgHhIiJjKkLl 01234567890 ABCDEF 012345

ACORDE ITALIC
Acorde is a reliable workhorse for large, demanding design projects. It was designed to be perfectly suited to all different sizes, from small continuous text to large headlines and big signage. The typeface's name is derived AaBbCcDdEeFfGgHhIiJjKkLl 01234567890 ABCDEF 012345

suitable for all sizes from small text to headlines and big signage

humanist sans

14 styles with 925 glyphs per font

Acorde's characterful details are found within all styles

workhorse
unique appearance

ACORDE MEDIUM + MEDIUM ITALIC
Acorde is a humanist sans serif with noticeable diagonal contrast and shows clear influences of the broad nib pen, especially in the Italics. Acorde's characterful details

ACORDE SEMIBOLD + SEMIBOLD ITALIC
Acorde is a humanist sans serif with noticeable diagonal contrast and shows clear *influences of the broad nib pen, especially in the Italics*. Acorde's characterful

ACORDE BOLD + BOLD ITALIC
Acorde is a humanist sans serif with noticeable diagonal contrast and shows clear *influences of the broad nib pen, especially in the Italics*. Acorde's characterful

Regular	Italic
Medium	*Medium Italic*
Semibold	*Semibold Italic*
Bold	***Bold Italic***
Extrabold	***Extrabold Italic***
Black	***Black Italic***
Extrablack	***Extrablack Italic***

→ www.willerstorfer.com

Accorde, 2010

Stefan Willerstorfer was born in Vienna in 1979 and studied in Austria, The Netherlands, and the United Kingdom. He completed a master's degree in design at the **Royal Academy of Art** (347) in The Hague. Subsequently, he completed a master's degree in information design at **University of Reading** (348) in the United Kingdom.

In 2010, he started the Willerstorfer Font Foundry and released the type family Accorde as the foundry's first. That same year, he received the Joseph Binder Award; in 2011, the Japan Typography Association awarded him the Grand Prize of Applied Typography.

Willerstorfer works as an independent design consultant focusing on areas for which typography plays a major role—information, editorial, and corporate design. Since 2009, he has been a professor of design and typography at the Höhere Graphische Bundeslehranstalt in Vienna.

Territories

Mise En Place

And Sometimes Y

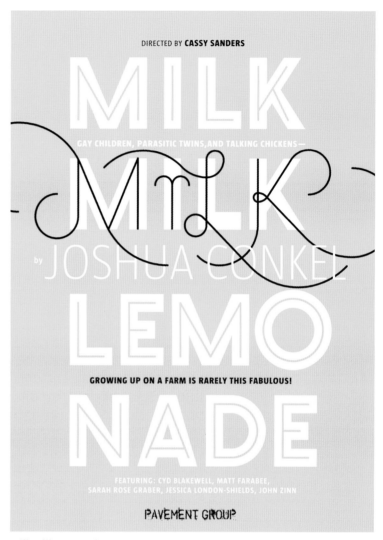

Milk Milk Lemonade

Luke Williams

American, 1986–

Luke Williams, who is currently based in Chicago, is a graphic designer and typographer. He completed his studies at the **Maryland Institute College of Art** (349) in 2009, earning a bachelor's degree in graphic design. Since then, he worked for design studios such as Pentagram as well as for companies such as Under Armour before opening his own studio. Williams's work has been published internationally in design publications, annuals, and books.

Type Foundries

By Kathryn Henderson with Ina Saltz

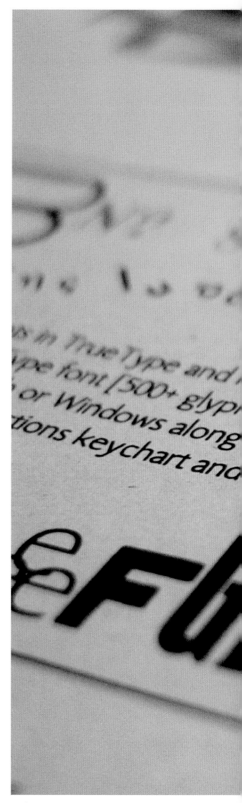

This section is devoted to an essential part of the design process: the type foundry. Foundries are vital because they design and distribute typefaces. The word "foundry" comes from the era when type was made of metal, but the term has survived the various technological transitions and continues to be used in the age of digital type.

Originally, foundries manufactured and distributed wood and metal type for **Linotype** (129) machines and other line casting or mechanical typesetting machines. But today, most foundries are digital type foundries that supply digital typefaces in various formats including TrueType and OpenType. There are three main types of foundries: Mega foundries (multifunctional commercial foundries),

large foundries (prolific partnerships and collaborations), and independent foundries (small-scale but significant foundries that may consist of one or a few designers). This stratification is arbitrary in terms of size and business structure, but it is made in an attempt to explain the complexity of conducting the business of type in a world in which readers consume on a wide variety of media.

Some of the largest and best-known foundries include **Adobe** (124), **Bitstream** (124), and **Monotype Imaging** (125). Across the globe there are hundreds, if not thousands of type foundries. This list is just a small cross section of some of the more notable and successful foundries in operation today. We've also included retailers/distributors, which are suppliers but not designers of fonts.

Dada1, P22 Type Foundry

stScript formats plus one
with unique features for
with easy to follow instal-
cense agreement

Mega Foundries

Mega Foundries (the large commercial foundries that design, sell, and distribute typefaces) may also hold trademarks for typeface names and market proprietary font-related software. They may be a division of a corporation or owned by a parent company. Some of the most notable mega foundries are now defunct, such as American Type Founders (ATF) created in 1892 by the merger of twenty-three type foundries (now subsumed by **Monotype Imaging** [125]). The mega foundries that today dominate the typography marketplace have either adapted to or driven the new technologies in typographic development.

Adobe

www.adobe.com

John Warnock and Charles Geschke founded the San Jose, California–based Adobe Systems in 1982. Since its inception, the company has been a major player in both the desktop publishing and design industries.

From 1984 until 1991, **Sumner Stone** (104) served as Adobe's director of typography. He licensed the company's initial range of fonts from **Linotype** (129) and International Typography Corporation type libraries. To respond to the growing need for fonts, Stone started the Adobe Originals program in 1989. With help from designers such as **Robert Slimbach** (101) and **Carol Twombly** (105), the program has released many original designs, including Minion, Lithos, and Myriad, plus revivals of classic typefaces such as **Garamond** (162) and **Caslon** (157).

In addition to typography, Adobe's best-known contributions to creative industries have been its PostScript graphics—developed in the **mid 1980s** (26) and implemented by Apple for the company's laser printers—the PDF file format, and Adobe's range of creative programs including such flagships as Illustrator, InDesign, and Photoshop.

Bitstream, Inc.

www.bitstream.com

In 1981, a group of typographic professionals including **Matthew Carter** (85) and Mike Parker founded Bitstream, Inc., the first company to create fonts for digital type-setting. The founders anticipated a major shift in the publishing industry, from phototypesetting to computer-based publishing. They shared the philosophy that the industry needed a vendor that specialized in creating fonts to work on any device and in any format.

The Marlborough, Massachusetts–based company digitized classic typefaces by using each font's earliest type specimens to inform the development of its digital version. One of Bitstream's best-known typefaces is Swiss 721 BT, a **Helvetica** (176) clone developed for use digitally.

In addition to Helvetica, the foundry offers more than 1,000 fonts including, among others, Bitstream's original, digitized versions of **Times New Roman** (165) and Courier. Bitstream also has developed font technologies such as TrueDoc, WebFont, and Font Fusion, and owns the online type retailer **MyFonts** (141), www.myfonts.com, which currently offers more than 62,000 fonts from 500 different foundries.

www.monotypeimaging.com

BEMBO™ ROMAN
A classical text typeface inspired by
the typefaces used by ALDUS MANUTIUS in 1495
Popular *for* Fine Printing
HISTORICAL MODELS
from the Italian Renaissance

Bembo

GILL SANS®
classic & contemporary
DESIGNED IN 1928 FOR MONOTYPE
and helped define the humanist sans serif genre
A Typeface Family Based on the
LETTERING OF EDWARD JOHNSTON

Gill Sans

The Monotype Corporation was an independent British company that manufactured hardware and developed type for its printing machines, including the Monophoto and the LaserComp. Since those days, the company has gone through acquisitions, including a purchase by the IPA Group that resulted in a split between the hardware and type divisions and lead to the formation of the type company, Monotype Typography.

In 1998, Agfa acquired Monotype Typography, integrating it into its operations to form the Afga-Monotype Corporation. In 2004, TA Associates purchased the company and renamed it Monotype Imaging, Inc.

Today, Monotype Imaging owns Linotype (129), **International Typeface Corporation** (128), and various font distributors such as **AscenderFonts** (140) (www.ascenderfonts.com) and Font.com (www.font.com), which offers more than 100,000 font products. In addition to retail fonts, Monotype also specializes in custom fonts for branding agencies and corporations. Some of Monotype's most popular typefaces include **Bembo** (155), **Times New Roman** (165), **Gill Sans** (175), and Arial.

Large Foundries

There are small differences between mega foundries and large foundries. Like the former, large foundries also hold trademarks for the most common typefaces and produce a great number of typefaces, though not to the same extent.

H. Berthold AG

www.bertholdtypes.com

Hermann Berthold founded the H. Berthold AG foundry in 1858 in Berlin. The foundry's best-known font is **Akzidenz Grotesk** (170), which it released in 1896. By 1918 the foundry had become one of the largest in the world, with offices throughout Europe.

In 1950, Günter Gerhard Lange began working with the company and in addition to designing typefaces, he oversaw the revivals of classic faces such as **Baskerville** (154), **Bodoni** (156), and **Garamond** (162). In addition to typefaces, Berthold also developed proprietary typesetting equipment such as the phototypesetting machine, the Diatype, and the Diatronic.

In 1993 H. Berthold AG ceased operations due to financial troubles. In 1997 Chicago-based Berthold Types acquired all of the copyrights, trademarks, and design rights associated with Berthold Exklusiv Collection, which consists of more than 800 typefaces including the fonts Block, City, and Quadra 57. Lange acted as an artistic consultant for the company until his death in 2008.

Elsner+Flake

www.elsner-flake.com

In 1986, after ten years of designing type and digitizing fonts and logos, Veronika Elsner and Günther Flake founded Elsner+Flake design studio. The company, based in Hamburg, Germany, aims to produce a continuously growing library of digital fonts.

Currently Elsner+Flake supplies more than 2,500 fonts worldwide, most of which are not electronically modified and were designed with particular attention to detail (for example, complete **kerning** [334] tables, individually designed accents, and Old Style numerals). Some of the foundry's more popular typefaces include Petras Script, TV Nord, and Bank Sans Caps.

Emigre, Inc.

www.emigre.com

Emigre Inc., founded in 1984 by husband-and-wife duo **Zuzana Licko** (94) and Rudy VanderLans, is a type foundry, publisher, and distributor of software based in Sacramento, California. Licko designed the foundry's first fonts for its type journal, *Emigre* magazine, a font the foundry offered to the publication's readers.

Over the years, *Emigre* transformed from a vehicle to showcase the foundry's typefaces into a graphic design journal exploring the discipline's various facets. The journal folded in 2005 after publishing for twenty-one years. Today, the foundry holds more than 300 original typeface designs including Mrs. Eaves, Mr. Eaves, Brothers, and Democratica.

Emigre Catalog

The Font Bureau, Inc.

www.fontbureau.com

Publication designer and consultant Roger Black and designer **David Berlow** (82) founded The Font Bureau in 1989. In addition to the founders, notable type designers such as **Tobias Frere-Jones** (87) and Cyrus Highsmith have also produced designs for the foundry.

The Font Bureau primarily serves the typographic needs of microcomputer-based magazine and newspaper publishers. To date, the foundry has designed more than 2,000 fonts for 300-plus publications.

Mr. Eaves

FSI/FontShop

www.fontshop.com

FF Scala

Designers **Neville Brody** (84) and **Erik Spiekermann** (103) founded FontShop in 1990 in Berlin. Today, the foundry is one of the world's largest manufacturers of digital typefaces. FSI has published thousands of fonts under the FontFont label including FF Meta, FF Scala, and FF Trixie. FontFont also features fonts from type designers such as **David Berlow** (82), Erik van Blokland, and **Tobias Frere-Jones** (87), as well as many up-and-coming designers.

House Industries

www.houseind.com

House Industries, based in Wilmington, Delaware, was established in 1993 by Andy Cruz and Rich Roat. The founders characterize themselves not just as developers of type design, but also as developers of the idea *behind* the design, by creating products such as shirts, books, and other objects inspired by their work. Some of their most notable typefaces include Neutraface, Eames, and Chalet. The foundry's fonts appear on billboards, greeting cards, logos, and in mainstream media.

International Typeface Corporation

www.ITCfonts.com

ITC Elegy

More than thirty-five years ago, type designers **Herb Lubalin** (95), Aaron Burns, and Edward Rondthaler, the principal founder of Photo-Lettering, Inc., founded the International Typeface Corporation (ITC) with the intention of supplying typefaces to industry professionals. Today, ITC, owned by **Monotype Imaging** (125), is known for its expansive classic font collection, including Avant Garde Gothic, **Bodoni** (156), and **Kabel** (177). Recently ITC also expanded its library to include more contemporary fonts including display and illustrative types such as Deelirious. Currently the foundry represents more than 1,650 typefaces.

Linotype

www.linotype.com

Klint

a superfamily of 30 typefaces

SUSHI LOUNGE

Futurism

El premio Nobel en Microbiologia

RASTERSYSTEM

Flashmob at Hydepark

Celebrating 40 years of Apollo XI

The first issue of our magazine is now available

Klint

Linotype, originally a manufacturer of typesetters used by newspaper and general printers, began developing fonts exclusively for its own equipment. The company eventually became the standard in typesetting and font development.

Not until the **1980s** (26) did Linotype make its fonts available for use on other equipment, such as **Adobe Systems** (124). The foundry granted Adobe permission to produce some of its most famous fonts in the digital PostScript Type 1 format, making them universally available. Some of Linotype's most famous typefaces include **Frutiger** (173), Optima, **Helvetica** (176), **Univers** (181), and Palatino. Currently, **Monotype Imaging** (125) owns the company.

T.26

www.t26.com

In 1994, Carlos Segura founded T.26, a digital type foundry based in Chicago and established to further the design, promotion, and distribution of type designs, as well as promote the integration of typography into graphic design, fine art, and popular culture. Today, the foundry offers fonts from more than 200 designers, equaling more than 3,000 individual type designs from 978 families. Some of most notable fonts from T.26 include Flux, Vinyl, and Leger.

URW++

www.urwpp.de/english/home.html

Neuestadt/Filo/Hair

URW++ is a Hamburg, Germany–based foundry that specializes in developing software products and custom type for corporations and productions, in addition to supplying a range of retail fonts, both original and licensed. Unlike other foundries, URW++ offers a comprehensive list of non-Latin fonts including Greek, Hebrew, and Arabic. Some of its most notable fonts include Filo Pro, Neustadt, and Cutoff Pro.

Independent Foundries

Independent foundries are much smaller than large and mega foundries and are usually made up of a small collective or an individual who is not commercially backed and operates with a low overhead.

Chank, Co.

www.chank.com

Minneapolis, Minnesota–based Chank is run by font designer Chank Diesel. In 1992, while working as creative director for the alternative music magazine, *Cake*, Diesel began designing typefaces. Just five years later, he was being profiled in the *Wall Street Journal*. His foundry develops custom fonts for retail and corporate clients, as well as free experimental fonts. Chank focuses on fun, playful fonts that the foundry believes a variety of users can access.

Club Type

www.clubtype.co.uk

Designer Adrian Williams founded the United Kingdom–based type foundry, Club Type, in 1985. Williams began his type career in 1969 converting well-known metal typefaces designed for phototypesetting devices. He has continued to develop as technology has, digitizing typefaces for contemporary systems. His ability to create versatile typefaces has led to custom fonts for corporate branding and identities such as Renault and Foster's Lager. Club Type offers a small but well-crafted collection of typefaces including Bulldog, Congress Sans, and Monkton.

Darden Studio

www.dardenstudio.com

**Sigur Rós
TAMIROFF
bristles & whiskers
HOW WE ARE
POLAR BEAR CLUB
HEDAYA
WHY?
WEATHERBOX
1517 - 1979**
Birra

Joshua Darden (111) founded the Brooklyn, New York–based type foundry, The Darden Studio, in 2004. The foundry focuses on creating new typefaces and lettering for various clients including publications, institutions, and corporations. It advertises a holistic approach to design, integrating other areas of interest such as painting, metalworking, and writing into daily activities. The foundry's type library includes the best-selling typefaces Omnes, Freight, and Jubilat.

The Enschedé Font Foundry

www.teff.nl

Peter Matthias Noordzij founded The Enschedé Font Foundry in 1991 as an extension of the printing house and type manufacturer, Enschedé, which was established in The Netherlands in 1703. The foundry continues the tradition of designing and manufacturing high-quality type for retail and commissioned custom projects. Notable typefaces include Trinité, Lexicon, and Ruse.

Exljbris Font Foundry

www.exljbris.com

Dutch designer Jos Buivenga founded The Netherlands–based foundry, Exljbris, in 2004 after years of designing typefaces for his personal use and posting them online for free. In 2008 he released Museo, which became an instant success and pushed him to make the SWITCH to full-time type designer. Buivenga's most notable fonts include Geotica, Calluna, and Museo.

Calluna

Museo Slab

FontHaus

www.fonthaus.com

FontHaus

FontHaus, founded in 1990 by Mark Solsburg, was the first independent font retailer in the United States and one of the first to sell and distribute fonts online. The retailer distributes more than 75,000 fonts for major font foundries such as **Adobe** (124), **Bitstream** (124), **The Font Bureau, Inc.** (127), **International Typeface Corporation** (128), **Monotype** (125), **URW++** (129), and many others. It also supplies fonts to numerous media companies, advertising agencies, designers, and corporations worldwide.

Fonthead

www.fonthead.com

Ethan and Lisa Dunham founded Fonthead in 1994. Over the years the Wilmington, Delaware–based foundry has built a solid library made up of a range of original contemporary fonts. Many of Fonthead's fonts have appeared on posters and websites and in books and other various applications. Some of its best-selling typefaces include Drawzing, ClickBits, and Tachyon.

Hoefler & Frere-Jones

www.typography.com

Jonathan Hoefler (92) and **Tobias Frere-Jones** (87) began working together in 1999 after Frere-Jones left **Font Bureau** (127). To date the duo has designed more than 500 typefaces, including personal work and collaborations through their foundry, Hoefler & Frere-Jones.

The foundry's typefaces have been used in almost every format, including newspapers, magazines, and museums, with clientele including the *Wall Street Journal*, *Martha Stewart Living*, Nike, Pentagram, *GQ*, *Esquire*, *Business 2.0*, the *New York Times*, and the *New York Times Magazine*.

LetterPerfect

www.letterspace.com

LetterPerfect, founded in 1986 by lettering artist Garrett Boge, supplies more than fifty unique typeface designs for both Macintosh and Windows platforms.

The foundry has two distinctive lines: Viva la Font and Legacy of Letters. The Viva la Font library consists of script and display faces such as Destijl and Longhand. Legacy of Letters, a collaboration with fellow lettering artist Paul Shaw, focuses on type designs based on lettering models from historical periods such as Kolo, Donatello, and Old Claude.

Lineto

www.lineto.com

Cornel Windlin and Stephan Müller founded Lineto in 1993. In 1998 the Switzerland-based company set up Lineto.com (www.lineto.com) as an electronic way to distribute its typefaces, as well as other designers' work. All of Lineto's typefaces are sold exclusively through its website, except for earlier work—aptly called "Lineto Legacy"—still sold through FontFont. Some of Lineto's notable work includes Le Corbusier, Valentine, and Cobra.

LucasFonts

www.lucasfonts.com

Dutch designer **Luc(as) de Groot** (91), who also founded Berlin-based FontFabrik, www.fontfabrik.com, founded LucasFonts in Berlin in 2000. The foundry specializes in creating original and custom quality typefaces with extended type families—supplied to encourage experimentation—as well as in redesigning existing fonts. Notable typefaces include Thesis, TheSans, and TheSerif.

Mark Simonson

www.marksimonson.com

Coquette

Proxima Nova

Mark Simonson started his own foundry in 2000 after spending more than twenty years working as an illustrator and designer at places like Minnesota Public Radio and Rivertown Trading Company, and more than eight years designing typefaces and licensing them to FontHaus (131). His current library contains more than 100 original typefaces for sale, including Proxima Nova, Mostra Nuova, and Coquette. His fonts have been used for book covers and environmental graphics, in magazines, and for a variety of other applications.

Steve Mehallo

www.mehallo.com

Designer, illustrator, and educator Steve Mehallo specializes in brand strategies, logo development, and custom fonts. He has been working in the design industry since the late 1980s (26). Mehallo originally started designing fonts for his own use. Today, he runs the Steve Mehallo type foundry and has supplied fonts to numerous companies including Monotype (125), TiVo, Pacific Bell, and Nike. Some of his foundry's most notable fonts include Jeanne Moderno, Alta California, and Chandler 42.

Nick's Fonts

www.nicksfonts.com

The Qeehive

Nick's Fonts

Nick Curtis, founder of Nick's Fonts, has been fascinated with typography since he was a boy. He uses authentic historical forms pulled from sources such as the Library of Congress to develop his typefaces. His aesthetic inspiration spans designs from the Wild West to the gay nineties to the Jazz Age.

He began licensing his fonts in 2000. He first licensed Steppin' Out and Picayune Intelligence to Bitstream (124), then in 2001, licensed twelve designs to **International Typeface Corporation** (128) and three to what was then Agfa-Monotype (today **Monotype Imaging** [125]). After the launch of **MyFonts .com** (141), www.myfonts.com, in 1999, Curtis decided it was time to establish his own independent foundry. Today, Nick's Fonts library includes more than 500 type families.

Nick's Fonts

P22 Type Foundry

www.p22.com

Dada2

In 1995, Richard Kegler and Carima El-Behairy founded P22, a Buffalo, New York–based type foundry that specializes in creating computer typefaces derived from historical forms found in art, history, and natural science. With each font the foundry sells, it includes background information about the font's source and inspiration. P22 also works with museums and foundations to develop accurate historical typefaces suitable for computer use.

PampaType

www.pampatype.com

Argentinean information and type designer Alejandro Lo Celso founded the digital type foundry PampaType in 2001. The foundry, which recently moved back to Argentina from Mexico City, aims to produces high-quality fonts with "Latin flavor" inspired by the surrounding culture. Notable typefaces include the international award-winning Rayuela, Borges, and Arlt fonts.

Parkinson Type

www.typedesign.com

Jim Parkinson, founder of Parkinson Type, designed his first series of custom typefaces for *Rolling Stone* magazine. In 1990, while he was working for the *San Francisco Chronicle,* his designs became totally digital. Today, Parkinson Type consists of more than three-dozen retail fonts, including the popular Parkinson, Sutro, and Balboa. Parkinson also has created fonts for **Adobe** (124), **Monotype** (125), **Font Bureau** (127), and **International Typeface Corporation** (128), for whom he was one of the designers of ITC Bodoni. In addition to retail type, Parkinson also creates custom fonts and has drawn **display type** (213) for magazines including *Newsweek* and the *New York Times Magazine.*

PSY/OPS Type Foundry

www.psyops.com

Rod Cavazos founded PSY/OPS (short for Psychological Operations) in San Francisco in 1995. The small studio focuses on custom type development and has had dozens of clients since its founding. Currently, the foundry offers eighty retail fonts including Exemplar Pro, Eidetic Modern, and Armchair Modern from a variety of designers—from San Francisco and around the world—including Bob Aufuldish, Matthjs Van Leeuwen, and **Steve Mehallo** (133).

Storm Type Foundry

www.stormtype.com

Frantisek Storm founded Storm Type Foundry in Prague in 1993. The foundry's main objective is to revive classic type for digital use. When digitizing original Czech typefaces, Storm collaborates with designers including Otakar Karlas, Jan Solpera, and Josef Tyfa. Some of the foundry's more popular fonts include John Sans, Etelka, and Header.

Sudtipos

www.sudtipos.com

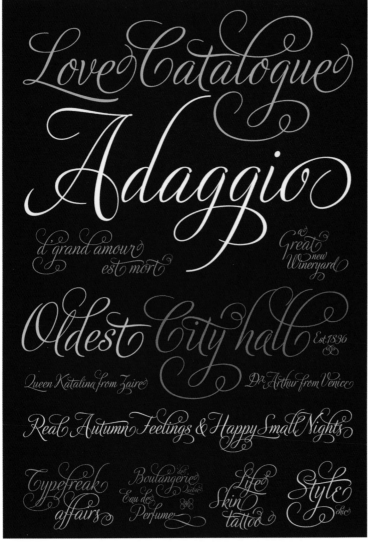

Adios

Designers **Alejandro Paul** (116), Diego Giaccone, Ariel Garofalo, and Claudio Pousada founded Sudtipos, the first Argentinean type foundry collective based in Buenos Aires. The foundry is a joint venture between design professionals whose expertise span from advertising and branding to television and new media. They see themselves as "graphic designers doing fonts for graphic designers." Some of their notable designs include Adios, Piel, and Burgues.

SuITCase Type Foundry

www.suitcasetype.com

SuITCase

Designer Tomas Brousil founded SuITCase, an independent digital type foundry based in Prague, Czech Republic, in 2003. The foundry currently offers more than 170 professional-quality retail typefaces and creates custom fonts for branding, corporations, and other clients. Some of SuITCase's more popular fonts include Tabac Sans, Fishmonger, and Kulturista.

Tour de Force Font Foundry

www.tourdefonts.com

THE ASTRONOMER hesitated. He said, "I will be truthful with you. They come from a denser planet. Ours is richer in **THE LIGHTER** atoms. "The principle remains. Said and forgotten. 94 times per day, 37 times per **YEAR, 25 TIMES PER HOUR. JUST MOMENT, RED.** I have a question to ask you? **The Industrialist** looked at the blue sky and the green-covered

Oblik2

Serbian designers Slobodan and Dusan Jelesijevic founded Tour de Force Font Foundry in 2009. The foundry is one of the Balkan Peninsula's major type foundries. Its best-selling typefaces include Passage, Oblik, and Belco.

Typerepublic

www.typerepublic.com

Andrew Balius is the founder and principal designer of the Barcelona-based independent type foundry Typerepublic. This foundry specializes in fonts with "local flavor" that draw on Spanish typographic history, influenced by the culture. The idea is to create fonts accessible to amateurs and professionals alike. Typerepublic also develops custom fonts, as well as fonts for retail such as its popular fonts Pradell, Carmen Fiesta, and Taüll.

TypeTogether

www.type-together.com

Veronika Burian (109) and **José Scaglione** (118) founded independent type foundry TypeTogether (TT) in 2006 by while they were both completing their master's degrees in type design at the **University of Reading** (348).

TT's fonts are cross-platform OpenType fonts with extended character sets and a focus on editorial use. TT provides custom modifications and specially tailored typefaces, in addition to font styles ready for immediate purchase. Some of TypeTogether's more notable fonts include Adelle, Skolar, and Bree.

Typodermic Fonts

www.typodermicfonts.com

Typodermic

In 2001, Ray Larabie, a Canadian font designer living in Nagoya, Japan, started Typodermic after designing fonts for five years. Larabie has created more than 1,000 fonts in 480-plus families for industrial and consumer use, including Junegull, Jillsville, Strenuous, and Tandelle. Currently, Typodermic's library offers more than 200 typefaces. Larabie's first 300 or so fonts, those created between 1996 and 2001, can still be acquired through Larabie's Fonts, a subfoundry operated through Typodermic.

Typofonderie

www.typofonderie.com

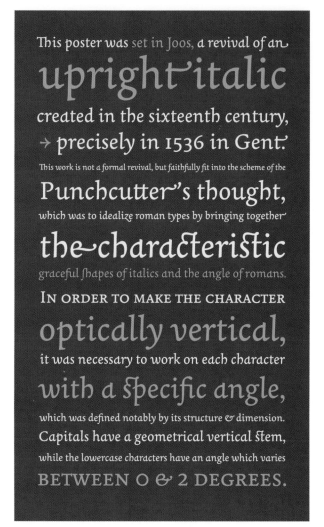

Joos

In 1994, Jean François Porchez founded France-based foundry, Typofonderie, as a way to distribute typefaces exclusively without the help of a retailer and to ensure he controlled the font sales and customer support. In 2006, the foundry moved to Sévres; today, Typofoundrie is located in Clamart, France, near Paris. Some of its most notable typefaces include Apolline, Angie Sans, and Anisette.

Die Typonauten

www.typonauten.de

Die Typonauten

Die Typonauten was founded in 2000 in Bremen, Germany. This small foundry specializes in **display types** (213) for corporate, editorial, publication, and information design, as well as for illustration. Notable fonts include Oklahoma, B-Movie Retro, and Newsletter.

Typotheque

www.typotheque.com

Typotheque, located in The Hague, The Netherlands, produces standard fonts that support all Latin-based European languages. In addition, it has created typefaces for Greek, Greek Polytonic, Cyrillic, Arabic, Armenian, and Devanagari scripts. The foundry, run by **Peter and Johanna Bilak** (83), characterizes itself as offering more complete fonts with more advanced features than other foundries. The Typotheque library includes Plan Grotesque, Irma Slab, and Fedra Serif.

Underware Type Foundry

www.underware.nl

Liza

Founded in 1999 by Akiem Helmling, Bas Jacobs, and Sami Kortemäki, Underware is based in Helsinki, Amsterdam, and The Hague. The foundry specializes in creating versatile fonts for both custom projects and retail. Some of its most popular retail fonts include Auto, Dolly, and Sauna. In addition to creating fonts, Underware also conducts type workshops, runs the radio station, **Typeradio** (377), and participates in numerous other activities.

Retailers/Distributors Foundries

This list represents a general collection of online font retailers, both large and small.

AscenderFonts

www.ascenderfonts.com

AscenderFonts is a retailer and distributor of TrueType and OpenType fonts for digital use. In addition to ready-to-buy fonts, the company also offers an extensive range of services including custom typeface development and font technology for developers, manufacturers, and enterprises.

Fonts.com

www.fonts.com

Fonts.com is an online font store owned by **Monotype Imaging** (125). The retailer offers more than 150,000 font products.

FontShop

www.fontshop.com

FontShop is an independent font retailer of digital type. It features fonts from FontFont, **Linotype** (129), **FontHaus** (131), **Exljbris** (131), and **PSY/OPS** (135), among many others.

HypeForType

www.hypefortype.com

Alex Haigh founded HypeForType in the early **2000s** (28). His goal for the online foundry was to create a "hotbed of typographic talent" and to showcase and supply to the creative masses the best high-quality, handcrafted fonts that the contemporary typographic talent could offer. HypeForType offers a variety of fonts from various independent type designers including Alex Trochut, SI Scott, and Craig Ward. Some of the most popular typefaces it offers include Now Deco, Hunter, and Killer.

Identifont

www.identifont.com

Identifont is a research-based typography website that specializes in cataloging and identifying popular typefaces. The site also acts as a liaison between buyer and retailer, allowing the customer to compare and contrast type specs before purchase.

MyFonts

www.myfonts.com

MyFonts.com is an online distributor of more than 62,000 fonts from more than 700 foundries including fonts from **Mark Simonson** (133), **Font Bureau** (127), Canada Type, and **Sudtipos** (136). It was founded in 1999 by Charles Ying, then **Bitstream's** (124) chairman of the board. MyFont has become more user-friendly with new systems for finding typefaces including WhatTheFont and More Fonts Like This.

Typographica

www.typographica.org

Founded in 2002 by Joshua Lurie-Terrell, Typographica is a review of typefaces and type books. Chris Hamamoto and Stephen Coles relaunched the site in 2009.

Veer

www.veer.com

Veer supplies stock photography, illustrations, fonts, and creative merchandise. The company also runs two blogs: The Skinny, a design news blog, and The Fat, a community blog.

Additional Online Retailers

www.daltonmaag.com

www.fontbros.com

www.fontdiner.com

www.fontfont.com

www.fontpool.com

www.fontsmith.com

www.foundrytypes.co.uk

www.fountaintype.com

www.macrhino.com

www.microsoft.com

www.mvbfonts.com

www.philsfonts.com

www.processtypefoundry.com

www.terminaldesign.com

www.typography.com

www.typography.net

www.vllg.com

www.waldenfont.com

Typefaces and Specimens

By Jason Tselentis

Johannes Gutenberg created the opportunity to mass-produce typography when he designed moveable type in the 1450s, and the technology spread throughout Europe. Printers—and later type foundries—crafted by hand individual letters that would become the typefaces used for producing printed material such as the *Gutenberg Bible*.

Many of those first typefaces stemmed from the **blackletter** (192) calligraphy so ingrained in Gutenberg's Germanic culture of the time. Venetian scripts, with their delicate and handcrafted qualities, were appropriated in later day Europe during the 1500s. Muscular, even angular strokes rose to prominence during the 1600s and 1700s, popularized by the Dutch. And **slab serif** (16) fonts used for advertising and promotion became a necessity in the 1800s, when large posters and signs shouted for attention.

But when William Caslon IV boldly obliterated the serifs from his 1816 type design, later called *sans syrruph* ("sans serif," or "without serifs") by English type founder Vincent Figgins in 1832, it paved the way for a new dawn in typeface design. Historically, technological developments such as the shift to **Linotype** (129) and **Monotype** (125) machines, and later to phototypesetting, shaped the how and why of a typeface's design. Today, differences in language, writing forms, marketing, and artistic vision sway look, feel, function, and trend. Many of today's typefaces are revivals (even re-revivals) or adaptations of original designs from centuries past. And unfortunately, some designers and foundries have rendered poor copies due to unreliable sources or too many variations from which to model their designs.

Letterlab typography specimen sh

Specimen Sheets

When it comes to selecting a typeface, a designer must consider many factors, but one tool continues to be helpful: a specification sheet, an example of every letter, symbol, and number in a typeface shown in different sizes and contexts. Type specimens have long enabled printers and designers to see an entire character set in a range of sizes. By looking at one or many typeface specimens, identifying the typeface (or typefaces) appropriate to a project should become clear.

In today's digital world, type specimens exist mostly on the Web in the form of simple character displays on websites. One of the newer specification tools is on-screen testing, during which websites allow users to view how the text of fonts—sometimes up to several dozen—will display. Those who intend to use the type in print are at a bit of a disadvantage looking at it on screen. Fortunately, many foundries and distributors offer a downloadable PDF for printing, testing, and comparing the specimens on paper—especially handy for instances of use with a colored or textured substrate that will modify the font's typographic color. Designers can also send away for specimens in printed catalogs.

During the past century, the number of available typefaces has moved in parallel with technological improvements. As technology for viewing and comparing typographic specimens increased, so too did the number of typefaces. Classification systems to help

Specimen sheets, such as these three from Monotype Imaging, have a similar layout and purpose as those printed during the predigital era, only they're available as downloadable PDF files from www.fonts .com. Whether found online or held as printed sheets, specimen sheets are vital tools for seeing how typefaces look and feel before committing them to a project.

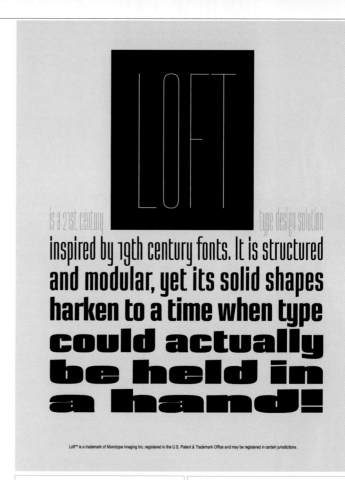

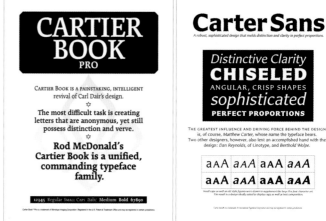

MAAR DIE POP WAAR GERRIT HET
OVER HAD. DAT IS NIET ZOO MAL
ALS HET LIJKT. JANS VAN DEN BOER
ZEGT: DA'S EEN FRAAIIGHEID DIE
ZE VAN DE REIS HEEFT MEEGE-
BRACHT. DA'S GEEN POPKE OM
MEE TE SPELEN, DAT IS ZOOVEEL
AS 'N ORNEMENT OP JE KASSIE,
OF VOOR JE MOOIE KAMER. ENNE,
ALS JE ALTIJD IN JE ALLEENIGHEID
BENT, GA JE IN JE EIGEN PRATEN.

POP!

NUMBER 5
THREE-D

P22 Pop Art Comic
ABCDEFGHIJKLMNOPQRSTUVWXYZ1234567890
P22 Pop Art Comic Bold Italic
ABCDEFGHIJKLMNOPQRSTUVWXYZ1234567890
P22 Pop Art Stencil
ABCDEFGHIJKLMNOPQRSTUVWXYZ1234567890
P22 Pop Art 3-D
ABCDEFGHIJKLMNOPQRSTUVWXYZ
P22 Pop Art Extras
[decorative symbols]

Pop Art Set

¶ The Pop Art font set was developed for the Albright-Knox Art Gallery in Buffalo, NY and is inspired by their exceptional collection of Pop Art. Artists such as Warhol, Lichtenstein, and Rauchenberg sought to blur the lines between high and low art as well as the boundaries between art and everyday life. The alphabets and Extras in this set reflect that spirit. All alphabet fonts in this set now contain lower case; they are all caps fonts.

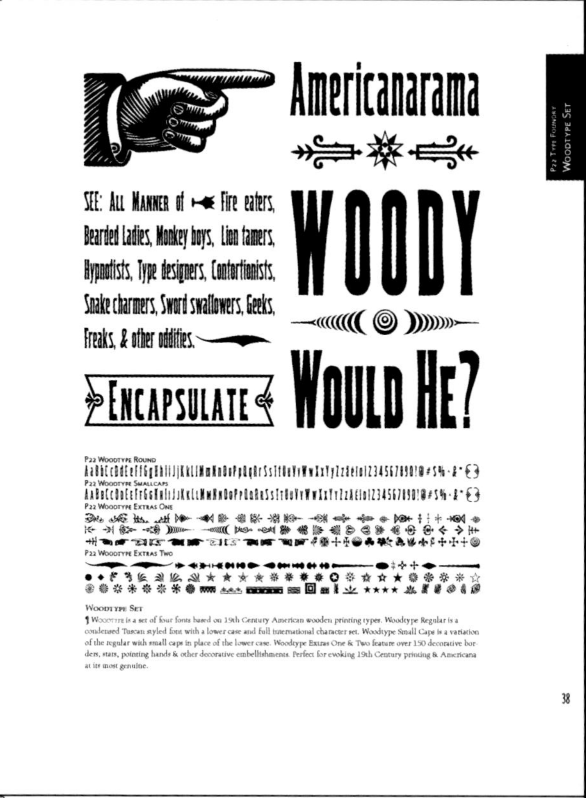

Americanarama

SEE: All Manner of Fire eaters,
Bearded Ladies, Monkey boys, Lion tamers,
Hypnotists, Type designers, Contortionists,
Snake charmers, Sword swallowers, Geeks,
Freaks, & other oddities.

WOODY

ENCAPSULATE

WOULD HE?

P22 Woodtype Round
AaBbCcDdEeFfGgHhIiJjKkLlMmNnOoPpQqRrSsTtUuVvWwXxYyZzŒœ1234567890!@*$%·£°€}
P22 Woodtype Smallcaps
AaBbCcDdEeFfGgHhIiJjKkLlMmNnOoPpQqRrSsTtUuVvWwXxYyZzŒœ1234567890!@*$%·£°€}
P22 Woodtype Extras One
[decorative ornaments]
P22 Woodtype Extras Two
[decorative ornaments]

Woodtype Set

¶ Woodtype is a set of four fonts based on 19th Century American wooden printing types. Woodtype Regular is a condensed Tuscan styled font with a lower case and full international character set. Woodtype Small Caps is a variation of the regular with small caps in place of the lower case. Woodtype Extras One & Two feature over 150 decorative borders, stars, pointing hands & other decorative embellishments. Perfect for evoking 19th Century printing & Americana at its most genuine.

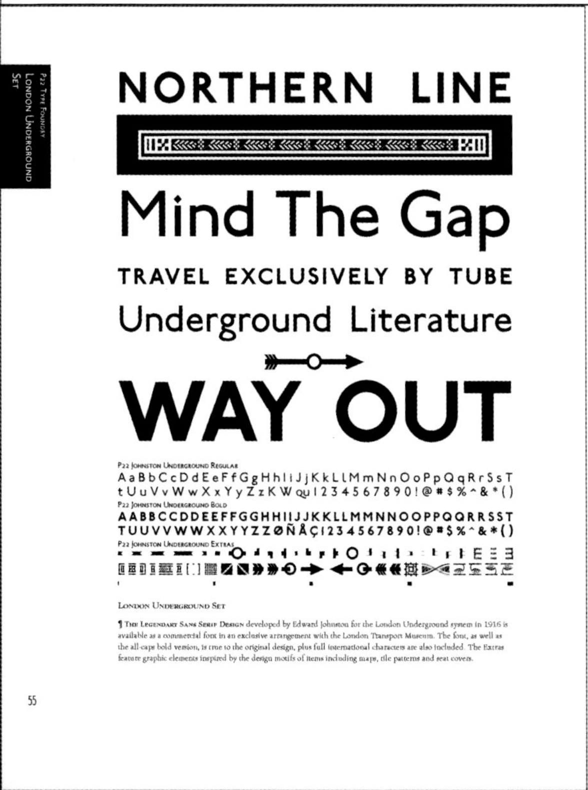

NORTHERN LINE

Mind The Gap

TRAVEL EXCLUSIVELY BY TUBE

Underground Literature

WAY OUT

P22 Johnston Underground Regular
AaBbCcDdEeFfGgHhIiJjKkLlMmNnOoPpQqRrSsTtUuVvWwXxYyZzKWqu1234567890!@#$%^&*()
P22 Johnston Underground Bold
AABBCCDDEEFFGGHHIIJJKKLLMMNNOOPPQQRRSSTTUUVVWWXXYYZZØÑÃÇ1234567890!@#$%^&*()
P22 Johnston Underground Extras
[decorative symbols]

London Underground Set

¶ The legendary Sans Serif design developed by Edward Johnston for the London Underground system in 1916 is available as a commercial font in an exclusive arrangement with the London Transport Museum. The font, as well as the all-caps bold version, is true to the original design, plus full international characters are also included. The Extras feature graphic elements inspired by the design motifs of items including maps, tile patterns and seat covers.

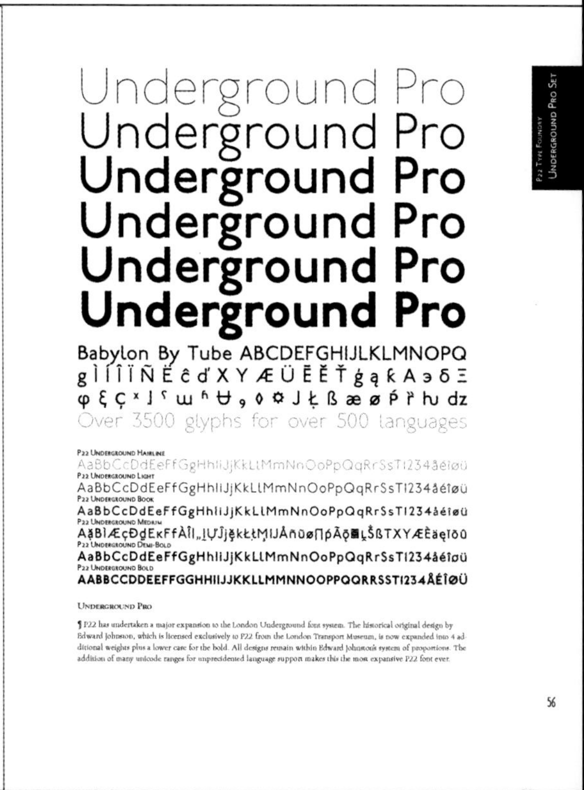

Underground Pro
Underground Pro
Underground Pro
Underground Pro
Underground Pro
Underground Pro

Babylon By Tube ABCDEFGHIJKLMNOPQ
gìlÎÍÑÉĉďXYÆÜĚĔŤ ǧąĸAәϬΞ
φξçˣʃˤɯʰ℧,ɷꝛʃŁßæøP̌þhu dz
Over 3500 glyphs for over 500 languages

P22 Underground Hairline
AaBbCcDdEeFfGgHhIiJjKkLlMmNnOoPpQqRrSsTt1234åéïøü
P22 Underground Light
AaBbCcDdEeFfGgHhIiJjKkLlMmNnOoPpQqRrSsTt1234åéïøü
P22 Underground Book
AaBbCcDdEeFfGgHhIiJjKkLlMmNnOoPpQqRrSsTt1234åéïøü
P22 Underground Medium
AaBbCcDdEeFfGgHhIiJjKkLtMlJAñoøПpÅǫⱮ ĻŠöTXYÆȅąęïöü
P22 Underground Demi-Bold
AaBbCcDdEeFfGgHhIiJjKkLlMmNnOoPpQqRrSsTt1234åéïøü
P22 Underground Bold
AABBCCDDEEFFGGHHIIJJKKLLMMNNOOPPQQRRSSTT1234ÅÉÏØÜ

Underground Pro

¶ P22 has undertaken a major expansion to the London Underground font system. The historical original design by Edward Johnston, which is licensed exclusively to P22 from the London Transport Museum, is now expanded into 4 additional weights plus a lower case for the bold. All designs remain within Edward Johnston's system of proportions. The addition of many unicode ranges for unprecedented language support makes this the most expansive P22 font ever.

The P22 foundry has its catalog available for purchase, and many of its specimen sheets show the type in use as a collection of phrases, and words in various weights.

designers sort and select type have come and gone, but sorting by history, features, tools used, usage classification, and the Vox system are the mainstays:

- Historical classifications position typefaces or their revivals within the time period during which their visual attributes were invented.
- Classifying by features such as shape, proportion, or use clusters typefaces into visual categories rather than within an historical canon.
- The tools used to create the typeface can also become a mode of classification. This is more prevalent for predigital typefaces, when myriad tools were used such as chisels, pens, geometric measuring devices, rulers, or brushes.
- Last, usage classification includes categories such as text or display, coated or uncoated paper, offset or digital printing, and—to fragment even further— digital as well as small screen.
- Of all the classification methods, the Vox system has the widest level of consensus. Maximillien Vox created it in 1954, and the **Association Typographique Internationale** (354) adopted it on the merits of its traditional terminology and historical criteria. The first four categories relate to early serif type forms including the Venetian Humanist, Garalde, **Transitional** (55), and **Didone** (56). The more familiar categories such as **slab serif** (59) and sans serif each have their own subcategories. And **Glyphic** (57), script, and graphic round out the list, helping to neatly position some of the typographic outliers.

Any of the above systems work under the proper circumstances, and depending on the piece at hand, designers still take liberties with the way they sort and view typefaces. But one constant remains: dispute. Many designers, typographers, artisans, and printers consider many of the new typographic breed weeds among the flowery time-tested faces included in this chapter. Everyone seems to have his or her own opinions about what is timeless and what is purely functional.

Put a graphic designer and a typographer in the same room and ask them to share with each other their list of top 100 fonts. Chances are good that that list would have as many similarities as differences. But those on which they agreed would likely have unique proportions, characteristics, shapes, or uses. After their voting, if they had to research the history of their chosen fonts, as well as those they left off of the list, chances are they would have a newfound perspective on those they selected and neglected.

Typefaces will continue to become popular or unpopular, but a broad, conceptual understanding of these time-tested typefaces can go a long way toward ensuring that designers have a springboard for the continued use and celebration of typography.

Web designers used to be limited to a mere dozen Web-safe fonts. But thanks to new tools such as Typekit, designers can browse through nearly any type specimen online. Typekit's online catalog allows the designer to see a range of styles and weights, along with how the font will appear in a variety of browsers and operating systems. This range of testing is akin to seeing how a font would appear on one type of paper versus another.

GILL SANS

ZAPF RENAISSANCE ITALIC

SABON

 ERIC GILL
{1882 – 1940}

 HERMANN ZAPF
{b. 1918}

 JAN TSCHICHOLD
{1902 – 1974}

Eric Gill was born in Brighton, Sussex in 1882. He began studying lettering under calligrapher Edward Johnston while attending classes at the Central School of Arts and Crafts in London. In 1924 Gill started a workshop in Wales where he created his best known typefaces: Perpetua, Joanna, and Gill Sans.

In 1927-30 Eric Gill designed the typeface Gill Sans, a humanist sans-serif inspired by Edward Johnston's Railroad Gothic. Gill Sans was an attempt to provide a legible sans serif typeface that would be suitable for both text and display.

Hermann Zapf is a prolific typeface designer who was born in Nuremberg, Germany in 1918. Zapf never received a formal education in the arts, but taught himself calligraphy from books and examples he found at the city library. In 1947 he was offered a position with the Stempel type foundry as head artist in their print shop. It was here that he designed his most legendary typefaces: Palatino, Optima, and Zapf Chancery.

Designed in 1979, Zapf Chancery is based on a style of handwriting developed during the Italian Renaissance by scribes in the papal offices.

Photo courtesy of The Society of Typographic Arts.

Jan Tschichold was born in Leipzig, Germany in 1902. His father, a provincial sign-writer, provided a strong artisan background that set Tschichold apart from other typographers. In 1923 he attended the first Weimar Bauhaus exhibition, inspiring his most noted work, *Die neue Typographie*. He is responsible for several typefaces that utilize both modern and classic design principles: Saskia, Transit, and Sabon.

In 1967 Tschichold designed Sabon, a typeface that enabled identical reproduction on both Monotype and Linotype systems.

LeTTRa™   100% COTTON FLUORESCENT WHITE

THIS BROADSIDE WAS PRINTED BY ONE HEART PRESS (LETTERPRESS) AND MOQUIN PRESS (LITHOGRAPHY) ON CRANE LETTRA // DESIGN BY MICHAEL OSBORNE DESIGN
WWW.CRANELETTRA.COM   1.800.613.4507

For its Crane Lettra poster, MOD/Michael Osborne Design
paired Gill Sans, Sabon, and Zapf Chancery with great effect.

Capítulo XXXVI

DEL GRANDE Y SOLEMNE RECIBIMIENTO

que hizo el gran Moctezuma a Cortés

GRAN CIUDAD DE TENOCHTITLÁN

La calzada toda iba llena de aquellas gentes que no cabían

ESTABAN LLENAS LAS TORRES Y CÚES

Y LAS CANOAS Y TODAS PARTES DE LA LAGUNA

✠ JAMÁS ✠

HABÍAN VISTO CABALLOS

ni hombres como nosotros

38 · TITLING

ESPINOSA NOVA REGULAR

ABCDEFGHIJKLMMNOPQ Q RSTUVWXYZ
abcdefghijklmnopqrsſtuvwxyz
ÁÀÂÃÄÅÇÉÈÊËÍÌÎÏŁŃÓÒÔÕÖØ
ŠÚÙÛÜÝŸŽÐÞÆŒß
áàâãäåçéèêëíìîïıłńóòôõöø
šúùûüýÿžðþæœß&@ªº
.,:;…""„''‚«»‹›"¡!¿?·--—_()[]{}
*·¶§†‡/\|¦+-×÷=≈≠±~<>≤≥^√%‰
#∞∫∂μΠΣΩ◊°$€£¢¥ƒ¤™©®✠

0123456789 0123456789
0123456789 0123456789
x0123456789 x0123456789
0123456789/0123456789 ½ ¼ ¾

ABCDEFGHIJKLMMNOPQRSTUVWXYZ
ÁÀÂÃÄÅÇÉÈÊËÍÌÎÏŁŃÓÒÔÕÖØ
ŠÚÙÛÜÝŸŽÐÞÆŒFIFLSS&

ß0123456789$€£¢¥ƒ¤

fb ff fh fi fj fk fl ff ft fb ff fh fi fj fk fl ff ft
ffb ffh ffi ffj ffk ffl fft ffb ffh ffi ffj ffk ffl fft
ffp ffh fft ffp ft

Sample pages from a specimen book for Espinosa Nova, an extensive revival of a typeface by Cristóbal Henestrosa.

ilustrissimos

iluſtrißimos

ilustrissimos

iluſtrißimos

Weiss Weiß

WEISS WEIß

WEISS WEIß

Weiss Weiß

WEISS WEIß

WEISS WEIß

51

In 1521, Hernán Cortés and his men, allied with other indigenous peoples, vanquished the Aztec empire. Only 18 years later, Juan Cromberger – head of a dynasty of German printers settled in Sevilla – sent the Italian Juan Pablos to Mexico in order for him to found the first printing office of the New World. ¶ Pablos bought the office from the Crombergers in 1548 and, in 1550, he hired Antonio de Espinosa, who moved to Mexico from Sevilla the next year. From this moment on, the quality of the press's works showed a remarkable increase and the repertoire of types was renewed: evidence points that some of them were made by the new employee, so he can be considered the first type designer of the continent. ¶ In 1559, Espinosa founded his own printing office, which he would hold until his death, in 1576. His books are considered the highest point in the history of Mexican ancient printing, and the few surviving copies are very appreciated treasures among bibliophiles. However, there wasn't a version that enabled a contemporary use, as opposed to other masters from the past, such as Garamond, Baskerville or Bodoni. ¶ To honor his skills, in Espinosa Nova I have invested many years of effort: the first sketches date from December 2001. I read about Mexican history, visited libraries and wrote a book about it (*Espinosa. Rescate de una tipografía novohispana*, Mexico, Designio, 2005). I drew, spaced, revised, and drew again. Nine years have passed, and so today I can declare myself satisfied with this digital interpretation, that has been fortunate enough to achieve awards at the most important type design competitions, both in the world (Type Directors Club) and in Latin America (Tipos Latinos).
Festina lente.

✠

CRISTÓBAL HENESTROSA
Mexico City, September 2010

Standard Ligatures · *Ligaduras estándar*

fi fl ffb ffj fi fl ffb ffj

Discretionary Ligatures · *Ligaduras discrecionales*

ch ch ct sp st ch ch ct sp st

Small Caps · *Versalitas*

a b c d & ß A B C D & SS

All Small Caps · *Todas versalitas*

Ç Ð $ 7 8 € Ç Ð $ 7 8 €

Stylistic Alternates · *Alternativas estilísticas*

M Q *h* & M Q *h* &

Lining Figures · *Números alineados*

0 1 2 3 4 0 1 2 3 4

Proportional Figures · *Números proporcionales*

1574 *1574* 1574 *1574*

Fractions · *Fracciones*

01234/56789 01234/56789

49

Type specimens have long enabled printers and designers to see an entire character set in a range of sizes.

Espinosa Nova Rotunda is a delicious interpretation of black-letter types from the first Mexican printed books. Robert Bringhurst's proposal of 𝔲𝔰𝔦𝔫𝔤 𝔦𝔫 𝔰𝔬𝔪𝔢 𝔠𝔞𝔰𝔢𝔰 𝔅𝔩𝔞𝔠𝔨𝔩𝔢𝔱𝔱𝔢𝔯 𝔯𝔞𝔱𝔥𝔢𝔯 𝔱𝔥𝔞𝔫 𝔅𝔬𝔩𝔡 may be considered extravagant, but it does not lack historic likelihood. ¶ *Espinosa Nova Rotunda es una deliciosa interpretación de las góticas con que se imprimieron los primeros libros mexicanos. La propuesta de Robert Bringhurst acerca de 𝔲𝔰𝔞𝔯 𝔢𝔫 𝔞𝔩𝔤𝔲𝔫𝔬𝔰 𝔠𝔞𝔰𝔬𝔰 𝔤ó𝔱𝔦𝔠𝔞𝔰 𝔢𝔫 𝔩𝔲𝔤𝔞𝔯 𝔡𝔢 𝔫𝔢𝔤𝔯𝔦𝔱𝔞𝔰 puede sonar extravagante, pero no carece de verosimilitud histórica.*

25

Serif

Since the 1400s, serifs have defined a generation of typefaces that evolved into what became known as Venetian, Garalde, and **Transitional** (55) classification. For simplicity's sake, contemporary historians and typographers tend to lump them all into one group. Classifications such as those within the serif lineage are convenient because they cluster fonts into schools, styles, or historical movements. But the job of classifying and subclassifying grows ever more difficult with the release of more and more typefaces, fragmenting each of the named classes into even smaller permutations.

In terms of popularity, many typefaces commonly used in print today are revivals of classics created centuries ago such as **Bembo** (155), **Baskerville** (154), and **Garamond** (162). Calligraphy strongly influenced Venetian typefaces such as those from the **fifteenth** (9) to **sixteenth century** (10), most evident in their sloped axis and low **contrast** (230). Old roman faces from the **seventeenth century** (10) share those traits, but are also low contrast, with more pronounced brackets and bigger serifs that make them appear heavier on close inspection. The Garalde forms possess the most variety (224), with both wide and narrow letterforms. **Transitional** (55) fonts earned that title because of where they sit in typographic chronology: between Garalde and **Didone** (56). Formally, Transitional typefaces have medium contrast and less stress than **Old Style** (54) faces.

Didone (56) (sometimes called Modern or New Roman) arrived in the **late eighteenth century** (10) and continued through much of the **nineteenth century** (12). Didone faces have vertical stress, but abrupt **contrast** (230) between their thick and thin strokes. **Bodoni** (156) was one of the earliest examples of this **formal** (64) trend that began in France and Italy. Hybridizations of these and other classifications continue to permeate the typographic landscape, with results that can look exquisite, garish, or conservative. But the specimens shown on the following pages set a standard that has influenced type designers for centuries, and their endurance has been difficult to match.

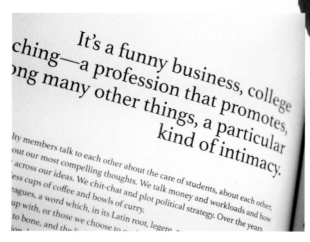

PNCA3 by
Veronika Burian

Typography	Typography	Typography	Typography
Humanist (set in Monotype Centaur): Calligraphic traits, high ascenders with low x-height, triangle-shaped serifs, pronounced stress of counters, small counters, longer descenders	Garalde (set in Hoefler Text): Medium contrast, large counters, medium x-height, inclined stress, flattened serifs, shorter descenders	Transitional (set in Times New Roman): High contrast, vertical serifs, downward-sloped ears, nearly flat serifs at stem bottoms, shorter descenders	Didone (set in Didot): Extremely high contrast between stroke widths, vertical stress, hairline serifs, some serifs with brackets, others without

Albin Polasek Museum Board of Trustees and International Assets Advisory Corporation

PRESENT

THE ARTIST IN ACTION *with*

ROBERTO SANTO

WINE & HOR D' OEUVRES
POLASEK MUSEUM
633 OSCEOLA AVENUE
WINTER PARK, FLORIDA 32789
RSVP 407 647 6294

MARCH 29TH, 2001
7:00PM – 10:00PM

A PORTION OF ALL SALES WILL GO
TO BENEFIT THE POLASEK MUSEUM'S
CAPITAL CAMPAIGN 2001

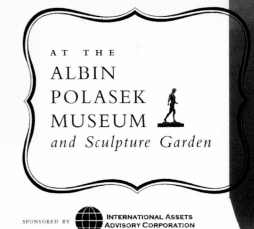

AT THE
ALBIN POLASEK MUSEUM
and Sculpture Garden

SPONSORED BY INTERNATIONAL ASSETS ADVISORY CORPORATION

An invitation by Jeff Matz of Lure design couples Bembo's graceful lines with subtle curves found in an artist's sculpture.

Bodoni Book and Bodoni Openface come together on the *The Eight Habits of Highly Successful Retailers* book cover. Designed by Cotton and Crown, United States.

This *RSA Design Directions* sketchbook cover by 2Creatives uses Adobe Bembo for its title. The interior spread incorporates it for subheads and body text.

The Allred Roof Systems identity collateral uses Adobe Garamond regular. Designed by Cotton and Crown, United States.

The Texas Children's Hospital Hand Hygiene Campaign by Principle combined Bodoni's grace with Gotham's force in a playful and complementary fashion.

CAN I GET A **HY5**?

⇨ ONLY IF THOSE HANDS ARE CLEAN!

Hand Hygiene is KEY in keeping our kids healthy and on the road to a speedy recovery here at Texas Children's Hospital. It's up to each of us to take responsibility for our own hand hygiene and clean our hands frequently.

Texas Children's Hospital®

Baskerville

ORIGINAL DESIGNERS	YEAR	CLASS
John Baskerville	circa 1754	Transitional

A B C D E F G H I J K L M N O P Q R S T U V W X Y Z
a b c d e f g h i j k l m n o p q r s t u v w x y z

Background

John Baskerville (70) took some of the biggest steps forward in letter design and printing. Using specially crafted paper and drying racks, he shortened the time ink remained moist on a paper's surface. This allowed Baskerville's foundry to print letters with a much higher **contrast** (230) between thick and thin, generating a light and delicate alphabet. In 1996, **Zuzana Licko** (94) based her font Mrs. Eaves on many of Baskerville's qualities and distributed it through the (126) foundry.

Traits

Baskerville's higher contrast between the thick and thin strokes makes for a lighter-looking letter. This makes Baskerville a safe choice for book designers who must set large volumes of **text type** (212) at sizes ranging from 9 to 12 point without overwhelming readers' eyes.

Like many of the **Transitional** (55) faces, the font has enough clarity for easy **readability** (330) without drawing much attention to itself. However, it possesses various widths throughout the alphabet that can make for unsightly **kerning** (334) pairs. For example, its **uppercase** (332) *E* has a noticeably longer beak (the bottom serif) that juts out oddly. Other unique characters include its *Q*, with an organic tail that sits below the baseline, an attribute that has prompted some designers to use Baskerville whenever they need a capital *Q*.

SELECTED BASKERVILLE ALPHABETS
Top to bottom: 12-point ITC New Baskerville roman, italic, and bold

EXAMPLE
10-point ITC New Baskerville

ABCDEFGHIJKLMNOPQRSTUVWXYZ 1234567890
abcdefghijklmnopqrstuvwxyz 1234567890
The quick brown fox jumped over the lazy dog.

ABCDEFGHIJKLMNOPQRSTUVWXYZ 1234567890
abcdefghijklmnopqrstuvwxyz 1234567890
The quick brown fox jumped over the lazy dog.

ABCDEFGHIJKLMNOPQRSTUVWXYZ 1234567890
abcdefghijklmnopqrstuvwxyz 1234567890
The quick brown fox jumped over the lazy dog.

A designer's job will become even more challenging as the quantity of information and noise **increases** during the twenty-first century. Those who possess a broad typographic understanding will best meet the communicative and creative challenge, especially during a time when people know the difference between one font and another—*and which ones read better or worse with software's default* **120-percent** *leading.*

Bembo

ORIGINAL DESIGNERS	YEAR	CLASS
Francesco Griffo	circa 1495	Old Style, Garalde

A B C D E F G H I J K L M N O P Q R S T U V W X Y Z

a b c d e f g h i j k l m n o p q r s t u v w x y z

Background

Francesco Griffo (76) originally designed Bembo for Cardinal Bembo for **Aldus Manutius** (78) to use to print the book *de Aetna*, written by Pietro Bembo. As a punchcutter, Griffo relied on his knowledge and expertise of metallurgy to arrive at more modeled letterforms than his contemporary letter designers could achieve using calligraphic methods. In 1929, **Stanley Morison** (97) based the Bembo typeface on Griffo and Manutius's printed work for Pietro Bembo.

Traits

Like Baskerville, Bembo works well for **text type** (212) not only because it was invented for uninterrupted reading, but also because of its crisp serifs and terminals. Those are traits that **Old Style** (54) fonts such as **Garamond** (162) lack; their blobby serifs have a more rounded appearance, which can create slightly heavier areas on a page.

SELECTED BEMBO ALPHABETS
12-point Monotype Bembo 1 book, book italic, and book bold

ABCDEFGHIJKLMNOPQRSTUVWXYZ 1234567890

abcdefghijklmnopqrstuvwxyz 1234567890

The quick brown fox jumped over the lazy dog.

ABCDEFGHIJKLMNOPQRSTUVWXYZ 1234567890

abcdefghijklmnopqrstuvwxyz 1234567890

The quick brown fox jumped over the lazy dog.

ABCDEFGHIJKLMNOPQRSTUVWXYZ 1234567890

abcdefghijklmnopqrstuvwxyz 1234567890

The quick brown fox jumped over the lazy dog.

EXAMPLE
10-point Monotype Bembo 1

A designer's job will become even *more* challenging as the quantity of information and noise **increases** during the twenty-first century. Those who possess a broad typographic understanding will best meet the communicative and creative challenge, especially during a time when people know the difference between one font and another— *and which ones read better or worse with software's default **120-percent** leading.*

ORIGINAL DESIGNERS	YEAR	CLASS
Giambattista Bodoni	circa 1785	Modern, Didone

A B C D E F G H I J K L M N O P Q R S T U V W X Y Z
a b c d e f g h i j k l m n o p q r s t u v w x y z

Background

Giambattista Bodoni (71) designed many of the Modern typefaces during the forty-five years he worked as the director of printing and publishing at the house of the Duke of Parma in Italy. In the late 1790s, he began experimenting with ways to use mathematics and geometry in his type designs. Combining those interests with his skill as a masterful engraver allowed Bodoni to render the sharp, hairline serifs that became his signature.

Traits

As body or **text type** (212), standard issues of Bodoni can appear faint with hard-to-see serifs. But both **Adobe** (124) and **ITC** (128) have book versions that make Bodoni an excellent choice for subheads or pull quotes, even text type.

SELECTED BODONI ALPHABETS
12-point Bodoni roman, italic, and bold

ABCDEFGHIJKLMNOPQRSTUVWXYZ 1234567890
abcdefghijklmnopqrstuvwxyz
The quick brown fox jumped over the lazy dog.

ABCDEFGHIJKLMNOPQRSTUVWXYZ 1234567890
abcdefghijklmnopqrstuvwxyz
The quick brown fox jumped over the lazy dog.

ABCDEFGHIJKLMNOPQRSTUVWXYZ 1234567890
abcdefghijklmnopqrstuvwxyz
The quick brown fox jumped over the lazy dog.

EXAMPLE
10-point Bodoni

A designer's job will become even *more* challenging as the quantity of information and noise **increases** during the twenty-first century. Those who possess a broad typographic understanding will best meet the communicative and creative challenge, especially during a time when people know the difference between one font and another—*and which ones read better or worse with software's* default **120-percent** *leading.*

Caslon

ORIGINAL DESIGNERS	YEAR	CLASS
William Caslon	1725	Old Style, Garalde

ABCDEFGHIJKLMNOPQRSTUVWXYZ

abcdefghijklmnopqrstuvwxyz

Background

Dutch foundries applied a more rigid and muscular shape to how they created letters, and Englishman **William Caslon I** (72) took this into consideration when he designed his Caslon type-face in 1734. It became the standard for many of the American colonies, eventually used in printed copies of the United States Declaration of Independence and the Constitution.

Traits

Caslon's short x-height makes its **lowercase** (332) ascenders appear statuesque compared to other serif typefaces. In terms of rendering, the italic *v, w,* and *y* appear handwritten compared to the rest of the lowercase letters.

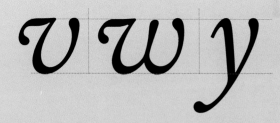

SELECTED CASLON ALPHABETS
Top to bottom: 12-point Adobe Caslon Pro roman, italic, and bold

ABCDEFGHIJKLMNOPQRSTUVWXYZ 1234567890

abcdefghijklmnopqrstuvwxyz 1234567890

The quick brown fox jumped over the lazy dog.

ABCDEFGHIJKLMNOPQRSTUVWXYZ 1234567890

abcdefghijklmnopqrstuvwxyz 1234567890

The quick brown fox jumped over the lazy dog.

ABCDEFGHIJKLMNOPQRSTUVWXYZ 1234567890

abcdefghijklmnopqrstuvwxyz 1234567890

The quick brown fox jumped over the lazy dog.

EXAMPLE
10-point Adobe Caslon

A designer's job will become even *more* challenging as the quantity of information and noise **increases** during the twenty-first century. Those who possess a broad typographic understanding will best meet the communicative and creative challenge, especially during a time when people know the difference between one font and another—*and which ones read better or worse with software's default* **120-percent** *leading.*

Centaur

	ORIGINAL DESIGNERS	YEAR	CLASS
	Bruce Rogers	1914	Humanist

ABCDEFGHIJKLMNOPQRSTUVWXYZ

abcdefghijklmnopqrstuvwxyz

Background

Bruce Rogers (99) based Centaur on **Nicolas Jenson's** (77) roman type from the **fifteenth century** (9) and designed it for New York's Metropolitan Museum Press. The typeface first appeared in Montague Press's *The Centaur* by Maurice de Guerin. In 1929, the **Monotype Company** (125) issued it for machine composition, bowing to requests to make the face available to the general public. Rogers worked with Frederic Warde to craft an italic face and used an italic version of Warde's Arrighi for Centaur italic.

Traits

Compared to Jenson's typeface, Centaur is lighter in color and has a crisp appearance when used for **text type** (212). Many of the **lowercase** (332) vertical strokes and stems appear curved, giving it a handcrafted feel.

SELECTED CENTAUR ALPHABETS
Top to bottom: 12-point Monotype Centaur regular, italic, and bold

EXAMPLE
10-point Monotype Centaur

ABCDEFGHIJKLMNOPQRSTUVWXYZ 1234567890

abcdefghijklmnopqrstuvwxyz 1234567890

The quick brown fox jumped over the lazy dog.

ABCDEFGHIJKLMNOPQRSTUVWXYZ 1234567890

abcdefghijklmnopqrstuvwxyz 1234567890

The quick brown fox jumped over the lazy dog.

ABCDEFGHIJKLMNOPQRSTUVWXYZ 1234567890

abcdefghijklmnopqrstuvwxyz 1234567890

The quick brown fox jumped over the lazy dog.

A designer's job will become even *more* challenging as the quantity of information and noise **increases** during the twenty-first century. Those who possess a broad typographic understanding will best meet the communicative and creative challenge, especially during a time when people know the difference between one font and another— *and which ones read better or worse with software's default **120-percent** leading.*

Century

	ORIGINAL DESIGNERS	YEAR	CLASS
	Linn Boyd Benton and T. L. de Vinne	1896	Old Style, Transitional

A B C D E F G H I J K L M N O P Q R S T U V W X Y Z
a b c d e f g h i j k l m n o p q r s t u v w x y z

Background

Linn Boyd Benton cut the first version of Century in 1894 with T. L de Vinne for *Century Magazine*. Century appeared darker than its contemporaries. Benton's son **Morris Fuller Benton** (81) created Century Expanded and other variants for American Type Founders. By 1915, the younger Benton had made further modifications, resulting in New Century Schoolbook.

Traits

Because of the added counterspaces in Century's **lowercase** (332) *a*, the letter looks airy compared to other **Old Style** (54) serifs. Both Century and New Century Schoolbook have tested well in **legibility** (330) studies, making it the de facto choice for setting children's reading primers and educational materials.

SELECTED CENTURY ALPHABETS
12-point Monotype Century Expanded roman, italic, and bold

ABCDEFGHIJKLMNOPQRSTUVWXYZ 1234567890
abcdefghijklmnopqrstuvwxyz
The quick brown fox jumped over the lazy dog.

ABCDEFGHIJKLMNOPQRSTUVWXYZ 1234567890
abcdefghijklmnopqrstuvwxyz
The quick brown fox jumped over the lazy dog.

ABCDEFGHIJKLMNOPQRSTUVWXYZ 1234567890
abcdefghijklmnopqrstuvwxyz
The quick brown fox jumped over the lazy dog.

EXAMPLE
10-point Monotype Century Expanded

A designer's job will become even *more* challenging as the quantity of information and noise **increases** during the twenty-first century. Those who possess a broad typographic understanding will best meet the communicative and creative challenge, especially during a time when people know the difference between one font and another—*and which ones read better or worse with software's default **120-percent** leading.*

Clearface

ORIGINAL DESIGNERS	YEAR	CLASS
Morris Fuller Benton	1907	Transitional

A B C D E F G H I J K L M N O P Q R S T U V W X Y Z

a b c d e f g h i j k l m n o p q r s t u v w x y z

Background

Morris Fuller Benton (81) designed Clearface in 1907, and it was recognized for its nuanced **lowercase** (332) letterforms. The rather small—almost **slab** (59)—serifs make it an understated **Old Style** (54) face. Due to Clearface's popularity, a majority of the major font foundries including **Linotype** (129), Intertype, **Monotype** (125), British Monotype, and Ludlow have licensed or copied it. Open-faced versions have been distributed under the names Clearface Open, Clearface Handtooled, and Dominus.

Traits

Clearface's lowercase *e*, *k*, *v*, *w*, and *y* all possess quirks that make the letters stand out when used for large bodies of **text type** (212). But it's the *a* that's the most significant because of its reduced curve from the ball terminal to the stem, creating more negative space than any other serif *a*. However, the condensed body enables many characters to be set in a paragraph measure compared with other, wider **Old Style** (54) typeface.

SELECTED CLEARFACE ALPHABETS
Top to bottom: 12-point ITC Clearface regular, italic, and heavy

ABCDEFGHIJKLMNOPQRSTUVWXYZ 1234567890

abcdefghijklmnopqrstuvwxyz

The quick brown fox jumped over the lazy dog.

ABCDEFGHIJKLMNOPQRSTUVWXYZ 1234567890

abcdefghijklmnopqrstuvwxyz

The quick brown fox jumped over the lazy dog.

ABCDEFGHIJKLMNOPQRSTUVWXYZ 1234567890

abcdefghijklmnopqrstuvwxyz

The quick brown fox jumped over the lazy dog.

EXAMPLE
10-point ITC Clearface

A designer's job will become even *more* challenging as the quantity of information and noise **increases** during the twenty-first century. Those who possess a broad typographic understanding will best meet the communicative and creative challenge, especially during a time when people know the difference between one font and another—*and which ones read better or worse with software's default* **120-percent** *leading.*

Didot

	ORIGINAL DESIGNERS	YEAR	CLASS
	Firmin Didot	1784	Modern, Didone

A B C D E F G H I J K L M N O P Q R S T U V W X Y Z
a b c d e f g h i j k l m n o p q r s t u v w x y z

Background

Firmin Didot (73) created his eponymous font during a search for clean and efficient letter rendering and did so with a high **contrast** (230) in strokes and minuscule hairline serifs. These traits epitomized the new Modern style, and Didot firmly established this standard in France. His work predates that by his Italian competitor, **Giambattista Bodoni** (71), but both are credited for laying the foundation for what's today known as Modern typeface.

Traits

Like Bodoni's, Didot's serifs contain no brackets. Other Modern features include a vertical stress and high contrast between strokes. The curved tail of the *Q* and curved leg of the *R* give Didot humanistic properties. Several revivals or newer versions look similar to the original, including those from Deberny & Peignot, Ludwig & Mayer, **Linotype** (129), and **Monotype** (125).

SELECTED DIDOT ALPHABETS
Top to bottom: 12-point Linotype Didot roman, italic, and bold

ABCDEFGHIJKLMNOPQRSTUVWXYZ 1234567890
abcdefghijklmnopqrstuvwxyz 1234567890
The quick brown fox jumped over the lazy dog.

ABCDEFGHIJKLMNOPQRSTUVWXYZ 1234567890
abcdefghijklmnopqrstuvwxyz 1234567890
The quick brown fox jumped over the lazy dog.

ABCDEFGHIJKLMNOPQRSTUVWXYZ 1234567890
abcdefghijklmnopqrstuvwxyz 1234567890
The quick brown fox jumped over the lazy dog.

EXAMPLE
10-point Linotype Didot

A designer's job will become even *more* challenging as the quantity of information and noise **increases** during the twenty-first century. Those who possess a broad typographic understanding will best meet the communicative and creative challenge, especially during a time when people know the difference between one font and another— *and which ones read better or worse with software's default 120-percent leading.*

Garamond

ORIGINAL DESIGNERS	YEAR	CLASS
Claude Garamond	1530	Old Style, Garalde

A B C D E F G H I J K L M N O P Q R S T U V W X Y Z
a b c d e f g h i j k l m n o p q r s t u v w x y z

Background

In the 1500s, French printers began to adopt the Venetian typographic traditions, and Frenchman **Claude Garamond** (74) took notice. Garamond moved away from designing type with calligraphic evidence and made advances to some of **Francesco Griffo's** (76) first italic letters. As a punchcutter, Garamond placed a priority on type design and casting, and he gained prominence as the founder of one of the first independent type foundries. Of the many Garamond revivals and variations, few come close to the exact specifications with which Garamond, the designer, created his initial typeface, making some designers skeptical of using this font.

Traits

Garamond has been called organic as a type family but labeled blobby because of the unrefined serifs. The subtle slant to the beaks of Garamond's *T* and *Z* give those letters a whimsical appearance.

SELECTED GARAMOND ALPHABETS
Top to bottom: 12-point Adobe Garamond Pro regular, italic, and bold

ABCDEFGHIJKLMNOPQRSTUVWXYZ 1234567890
abcdefghijklmnopqrstuvwxyz 1234567890
The quick brown fox jumped over the lazy dog.

ABCDEFGHIJKLMNOPQRSTUVWXYZ 1234567890
abcdefghijklmnopqrstuvwxyz 1234567890
The quick brown fox jumped over the lazy dog.

ABCDEFGHIJKLMNOPQRSTUVWXYZ 1234567890
abcdefghijklmnopqrstuvwxyz 1234567890
The quick brown fox jumped over the lazy dog.

EXAMPLE
10-point Adobe Garamond Pro

A designer's job will become even *more* challenging as the quantity of information and noise **increases** during the twenty-first century. Those who possess a broad typographic understanding will best meet the communicative and creative challenge, especially during a time when people know the difference between one font and another—*and which ones read better or worse with software's default **120-percent** leading.*

Goudy

ORIGINAL DESIGNERS	YEAR	CLASS
Frederic Goudy	1915	Old Style, Garalde

A B C D E F G H I J K L M N O P Q R S T U V W X Y Z
a b c d e f g h i j k l m n o p q r s t u v w x y z

Background

Frederic Goudy (90) designed Goudy for American Type Founders in 1915. In its lifetime, Goudy has gone through a number of revivals, thanks in part to the many versions and variations distributed by font foundries around the world.

Traits

Goudy has a gentle-on-the-eye appearance, due in part to its understated and small serifs. The *L*, *E*, and *Q* all have curvilinear shapes, and the *P* does not fully close at the stem, giving it an open quality. Because of the low x-height, Goudy sets best as **text type** (212) at sizes greater than 9 point, but even then, its italic can appear small and light.

SELECTED GOUDY ALPHABETS
Top to bottom: 12-point Adobe Goudy Old Style roman, italic, and bold

ABCDEFGHIJKLMNOPQRSTUVWXYZ 1234567890
abcdefghijklmnopqrstuvwxyz
The quick brown fox jumped over the lazy dog.

ABCDEFGHIJKLMNOPQRSTUVWXYZ 1234567890
abcdefghijklmnopqrstuvwxyz
The quick brown fox jumped over the lazy dog.

ABCDEFGHIJKLMNOPQRSTUVWXYZ 1234567890
abcdefghijklmnopqrstuvwxyz
The quick brown fox jumped over the lazy dog.

EXAMPLE
10-point Adobe Goudy Old Style

A designer's job will become even *more* challenging as the quantity of information and noise **increases** during the twenty-first century. Those who possess a broad typographic understanding will best meet the communicative and creative challenge, especially during a time when people know the difference between one font and another—*and which ones read better or worse with software's default* **120-percent** *leading.*

Sabon

	ORIGINAL DESIGNERS	YEAR	CLASS
	Jan Tschichold	1964	Old Style, Garalde

ABCDEFGHIJKLMNOPQRSTUVWXYZ

abcdefghijklmnopqrstuvwxyz

Background

Jan Tschichold (105) designed Sabon in 1964 for D. Stempel AG, **Linotype** (129), and **Monotype** (125) foundries for German printers who wanted a "Garamondesque" typeface. Tschichold based his design on a specimen sheet from the Egenolff-Berner foundry, and named the typeface after Jakob Sabon, a student of **Claude Garamond** (74). Sabon remains a mainstay in book design because of its **readability** (330) and what First Lady of Typography Beatrice Warde would call "transparent" properties.

Traits

The very open counters make Sabon airy, but the 5, 6, and 9 numerals are somewhat attention-grabbing because of their posture; they don't look like these same numerals from other typefaces. Like many **Old Style** (54) serifs, Sabon has been deemed reliable because of its time-tested usage and breadth of variations.

SELECTED SABON ALPHABETS
Top to bottom: 12-point Linotype Sabon roman, italic, and bold

ABCDEFGHIJKLMNOPQRSTUVWXYZ 1234567890

abcdefghijklmnopqrstuvwxyz 1234567890

The quick brown fox jumped over the lazy dog.

ABCDEFGHIJKLMNOPQRSTUVWXYZ 1234567890

abcdefghijklmnopqrstuvwxyz 1234567890

The quick brown fox jumped over the lazy dog.

ABCDEFGHIJKLMNOPQRSTUVWXYZ 1234567890

abcdefghijklmnopqrstuvwxyz 1234567890

The quick brown fox jumped over the lazy dog.

EXAMPLE
10-point Linotype Sabon

A designer's job will become even *more* challenging as the quantity of information and noise **increases** during the twenty-first century. Those who possess a broad typographic understanding will best meet the communicative and creative challenge, especially during a time when people know the difference between one font and another—*and which ones read better or worse with software's default* **120-percent** *leading.*

Times

ORIGINAL DESIGNERS	YEAR	CLASS
Stanley Morison and Victor Lardent	1932	Old Style, Garalde

A B C D E F G H I J K L M N O P Q R S T U V W X Y Z
a b c d e f g h i j k l m n o p q r s t u v w x y z

Background

The *Times* of London commissioned **Stanley Morison** (97) to direct production of a new typeface for the newspaper. Victor Lardent took the lead as draftsman, and based its formal qualities on Plantin by **Robert Granjon** (75). In 1932, Times made its debut, but the story of its origins remains a hotly debated topic to this day. Mike Parker, the type historian and director of typographic development at Mergenthaler Linotype Co. during the **1960s** (24) and **1970s** (25), found differing information. In the article "W. Starling Burgess, Type designer?" Parker reported that in 1903, Starling Burgess, a Boston aeronautical engineer and naval architect, designed for the Lanston Type Company the roman version that preceded Morison's design.

Burgess's renderings wound up in **Monotype's** (125) London archives. Frank Hinman Pierpont produced what later became known as Times New Roman.

Traits

Times New Roman has become a pervasive font thanks to its placement on both PCs and Macintosh computers, as well as in Microsoft's Office product suite. But this popularity can't overshadow the fact that Times is a highly **readable** (330) choice for **text type** (212), used in millions of educational, commercial, financial, and personal documents.

SELECTED TIMES NEW ROMAN ALPHABETS
Top to bottom: 12-point Times New Roman SF regular, italic, and bold

ABCDEFGHIJKLMNOPQRSTUVWXYZ 1234567890
abcdefghijklmnopqrstuvwxyz
The quick brown fox jumped over the lazy dog.

ABCDEFGHIJKLMNOPQRSTUVWXYZ 1234567890
abcdefghijklmnopqrstuvwxyz
The quick brown fox jumped over the lazy dog.

ABCDEFGHIJKLMNOPQRSTUVWXYZ 1234567890
abcdefghijklmnopqrstuvwxyz
The quick brown fox jumped over the lazy dog.

EXAMPLE
10-point Times New Roman SF

A designer's job will become even *more* challenging as the quantity of information and noise **increases** during the twenty-first century. Those who possess a broad typographic understanding will best meet the communicative and creative challenge, especially during a time when people know the difference between one font and another—*and which ones read better or worse with software's default **120-percent** leading.*

Sans Serif

Sans serif typefaces came about long after many serif fonts populated Eastern Europe, British colonies, and finally the United States. William Caslon IV has been credited with creating the first sans serif type, in 1816. Caslon called it an Egyptian typeface; its angular appearance was met with skepticism. It quickly became known as grotesque in Europe, gothic in the United States, and finally *sans syrruph* in 1832 by English typographer Vincent Figgins.

Besides the popular sans serif moniker, labels such as Gothic, Modernist, and Lineal persevere today. **Jan Tschichold** (105) championed the sole use of sans serif typefaces during the **1920s** (20), when most designers were focused on function instead of decoration. This preference continued into the **mid twentieth century** (18) when proponents of the Swiss International Style put more emphasis on strict composition with sans serif typefaces and **gridded** (220) layout systems.

Despite similarities in appearance, sans serif typefaces have subclassifications that include **Humanist** (61), **Grotesque** (60), Neo-Grotesque, and **Geometric** (62). **Akzidenz Grotesk** (170) and its mechanical structure exemplify the Neo-Grotesques in contrast to the Grotesques, which possess pen-drawn characteristics and rather slight **contrast** (230) of thick and thin strokes. Geometric sans serifs such as **Futura** (174) and **Kabel** (177) appear produced with merely a compass, ruler, and protractor. Humanist sans serifs owe as much to the calligraphic traits of fifteenth-century serifs as they do to their Grotesque and Neo-Grotesque brethren.

Kelly Salchow MacArthur's sustainable values poster "4 Decisions"

Typography

Humanist (set in Gill Sans): Classic proportions with serif influences, minimum contrast, some double-storey lowercase letters, medium x-height

Typography

Grotesque (set in News Gothic): Varying contrast, different stroke widths across lowercase letters, wider letterforms, no serifs

Typography

Neo-Grotesque (set in Helvetica): Nearly consistent stroke widths, more condensed letterforms compared to Grotesque faces, larger counters

Typography

Geometric (set in Futura): Geometric construction, monoline strokes, circular counters, single-storey lowercase forms

Think Big for Classic Graphics, designed by Cotton and Crown, uses Helvetica Neue juxtaposed with thirty other fonts.

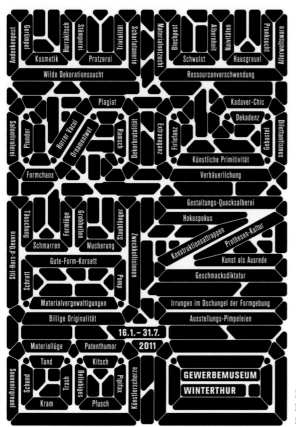

Boese Dinge poster by
Ralph Schraivogel set
in Akzidenz Grotesk

This still from Brent
Barson's *Typophile
5* video shows a staid
sans serif juxtaposed
against a slab serif
drinks and *taste* to
emphasize the sensations
individuals experience.

A large graphic printed on the wall of the Madison Square Garden Media offices uses the muscular Tungsten typeface to give the motivational quotes attitude and authority.

Ralph Schraivogel's 1995 poster for the *Cinemafrica* film series uses a textured Helvetica, making the popular typeface appear a little mysterious.

Akzidenz Grotesk

	ORIGINAL DESIGNERS	YEAR	CLASS
	Berthold Type Foundry	1898	Grotesque

A B C D E F G H I J K L M N O P Q R S T U V W X Y Z

a b c d e f g h i j k l m n o p q r s t u v w x y z

Background

Akzidenz Grotesk was known as Accidenz-Grotesk, but called Standard in the United Kingdom and the United States when first issued by Berlin's **H. Berthold AG** (126) foundry. Its design originated with Royal Grotesk light by Ferdinand Theinhardt, who was a royal type cutter. When the Theinhardt foundry merged with Berthold, the regular, medium, and bold weights were included. Günter Gerhard Lange, who was Berthold's art director, enlarged the typeface family in the **1950s** (22) but kept the unique properties inherent in the original.

Lange was also instrumental in expanding Akzidenz Grotesk to include other styles such as medium italic, extra bold, extra bold condensed, and extra bold condensed italic. He completed the series in 2001 with light italic, super italic, and light condensed, among others. Finally in 2006, Berthold released Akzidenz Grotesk Next, redrawn by Bernd Moellenstaedt and Dieter Hofrichter, as a single family with characteristics of the original.

Traits

Stroke weight varies slightly across the entire family, and its large x-height gives it a bigger appearance than other sans serif fonts. Its *G* has a spur and its *A* is flat at the top. In the **lowercase** (332) set, the *a* and *t* each has what looks like a curved serif on its foot.

SELECTED AKZIDENZ GROTESK ALPHABETS
Top to bottom: 12-point Akzidenz Grotesk Pro+ regular, italic, and bold

ABCDEFGHIJKLMNOPQRSTUVWXYZ 1234567890

abcdefghijklmnopqrstuvwxyz 1234567890

The quick brown fox jumped over the lazy dog.

ABCDEFGHIJKLMNOPQRSTUVWXYZ 1234567890

abcdefghijklmnopqrstuvwxyz

The quick brown fox jumped over the lazy dog.

ABCDEFGHIJKLMNOPQRSTUVWXYZ 1234567890

abcdefghijklmnopqrstuvwxyz

The quick brown fox jumped over the lazy dog.

EXAMPLE
11-point Akzidenz Grotesk Pro+

A designer's job will become even *more* challenging as the quantity of information and noise **increases** during the twenty-first century. Those who possess a broad typographic understanding will best meet the communicative and creative challenge, especially during a time when people know the difference between one font and another—*and which ones read better or worse with software's default* **120-percent** *leading.*

Folio

	ORIGINAL DESIGNERS	YEAR	CLASS
	Konrad Bauer and Walter Baum	1957	Neo-Grotesque

ABCDEFGHIJKLMNOPQRSTUVWXYZ

abcdefghijklmnopqrstuvwxyz

Background

Folio was released in Germany at the Bauer Foundry, adding to the already lengthy collection of sans serif fonts available to printers and designers. Folio has more in common with **Akzidenz Grotesk** (170) than more popular sans serif competitors such as **Helvetica** (176) and **Univers** (181). Folio gained more traction in the United States when it was released because of Bauer's strong sales and marketing channels.

Traits

As an alternative to the more popular **Grotesques** (60) to which designers default, Folio has a smaller x-height, making ascenders appear lengthy. Folio's *Q* has a unique tail that drops down vertically and juts to the side.

SELECTED FOLIO ALPHABETS
Top to bottom: 12-point Folio light, medium, and bold

ABCDEFGHIJKLMNOPQRSTUVWXYZ 1234567890

abcdefghijklmnopqrstuvwxyz

The quick brown fox jumped over the lazy dog.

ABCDEFGHIJKLMNOPQRSTUVWXYZ 1234567890

abcdefghijklmnopqrstuvwxyz

The quick brown fox jumped over the lazy dog.

ABCDEFGHIJKLMNOPQRSTUVWXYZ 1234567890

abcdefghijklmnopqrstuvwxyz

The quick brown fox jumped over the lazy dog.

EXAMPLE
11-point Folio

A designer's job will become even *more* challenging as the quantity of information and noise **increases** during the twenty-first century. Those who possess a broad typographic understanding will best meet the communicative and creative challenge, especially during a time when people know the difference between one font and another—*and which ones read better or worse with software's default* **120-percent** *leading.*

Franklin Gothic

ORIGINAL DESIGNERS	YEAR	CLASS
Morris Fuller Benton	1903	Grotesque

A B C D E F G H I J K L M N O P Q R S T U V W X Y Z
a b c d e f g h i j k l m n o p q r s t u v w x y z

Background

A popular choice in advertising, ITC expanded Franklin Gothic in 1980 when Victor Caruso added new weights. He also enlarged x-heights and condensed **lowercase** (332) forms. A decade later, **David Berlow** (82) developed condensed, compressed, and extra-compressed variations, further enhancing Franklin Gothic's versatility and popularity.

Traits

Franklin Gothic has rather subtle transitions from its thick to thin strokes, giving it a nearly monoline appearance at first glance. It possesses some humanistic touches too, such as a curved tail on the Q and a two-storey g, making the font appear more bookish than other sans serifs.

SELECTED FRANKLIN GOTHIC ALPHABETS
Top to bottom: 12-point ITC Franklin Gothic light, light italic, and bold

ABCDEFGHIJKLMNOPQRSTUVWXYZ 1234567890
abcdefghijklmnopqrstuvwxyz
The quick brown fox jumped over the lazy dog.

ABCDEFGHIJKLMNOPQRSTUVWXYZ 1234567890
abcdefghijklmnopqrstuvwxyz
The quick brown fox jumped over the lazy dog.

ABCDEFGHIJKLMNOPQRSTUVWXYZ 1234567890
abcdefghijklmnopqrstuvwxyz
The quick brown fox jumped over the lazy dog.

EXAMPLE
11-point ITC Franklin Gothic

A designer's job will become even *more* challenging as the quantity of information and noise **increases** during the twenty-first century. Those who possess a broad typographic understanding will best meet the communicative and creative challenge, especially during a time when people know the difference between one font and another—*and which ones read better or worse with software's default* **120-percent** *leading.*

Frutiger

ORIGINAL DESIGNERS	YEAR	CLASS
Adrian Frutiger	1976	Neo-Grotesque

A B C D E F G H I J K L M N O P Q R S T U V W X Y Z
a b c d e f g h i j k l m n o p q r s t u v w x y z

Background

Adrian Frutiger (88) originally designed his sans serif in 1975 for signage at the Charles de Gaulle Airport in Roissy, France. Designing during a time when sans serif faces such as **Helvetica** (176) and **Univers** (181) reached their peak popularity, Frutiger wanted to deliver a typeface with the mechanical properties of Univers coupled with subtle humanistic characteristics of a face like **Gill Sans** (175).

Traits

Because it was conceived first and foremost for distance viewing on signage, counterspaces such as those on the *c* and *e* are left open in an exaggerated fashion. Frutiger's tall x-height gives it extremely good **readability** (330) at small and large sizes. Like Univers, it uses a numerical coding system: odd numbers for romans, even numbers for italics.

SELECTED FRUTIGER ALPHABETS
Top to bottom: 12-point Frutiger Neue LT Pro book, book italic, and bold

ABCDEFGHIJKLMNOPQRSTUVWXYZ 1234567890
abcdefghijklmnopqrstuvwxyz
The quick brown fox jumped over the lazy dog.

ABCDEFGHIJKLMNOPQRSTUVWXYZ 1234567890
abcdefghijklmnopqrstuvwxyz
The quick brown fox jumped over the lazy dog.

ABCDEFGHIJKLMNOPQRSTUVWXYZ 1234567890
abcdefghijklmnopqrstuvwxyz
The quick brown fox jumped over the lazy dog.

EXAMPLE
11-point Frutiger Neue LT Pro

A designer's job will become even *more* challenging as the quantity of information and noise **increases** during the twenty-first century. Those who possess a broad typographic understanding will best meet the communicative and creative challenge, especially during a time when people know the difference between one font and another—*and which ones read better or worse with software's default **120-percent** leading.*

Futura

ORIGINAL DESIGNERS	YEAR	CLASS
Paul Renner	1927	Geometric

A B C D E F G H I J K L M N O P Q R S T U V W X Y Z
a b c d e f g h i j k l m n o p q r s t u v w x y z

Background

Paul Renner (98) created Futura during a time when designers emphasized geometry and engineering. Futura's even stroke widths and circular shapes mirror the look and feel of **Art Deco** (66) works from the same era.

Traits

Futura is not an ideal choice for body text because the *o* contains such a large counter and creates gaping white circles in running copy. Unlike most sans serif fonts, Futura has tall ascenders that creep above the capline. This requires greater leading for title case and **text type** (212) so ascenders do not hit descenders.

SELECTED FUTURA ALPHABETS
Top to bottom: 12-point Futura light, book, and bold

ABCDEFGHIJKLMNOPQRSTUVWXYZ 1234567890
abcdefghijklmnopqrstuvwxyz
The quick brown fox jumped over the lazy dog.

ABCDEFGHIJKLMNOPQRSTUVWXYZ 1234567890
abcdefghijklmnopqrstuvwxyz
The quick brown fox jumped over the lazy dog.

ABCDEFGHIJKLMNOPQRSTUVWXYZ 1234567890
abcdefghijklmnopqrstuvwxyz 1234567890
The quick brown fox jumped over the lazy dog.

EXAMPLE
11-point Futura

A designer's job will become even *more* challenging as the quantity of information and noise **increases** during the twenty-first century. Those who possess a broad typographic understanding will best meet the communicative and creative challenge, especially during a time when people know the difference between one font and another—*and which ones read better or worse with software's default* **120-percent** *leading.*

Gill Sans

	ORIGINAL DESIGNERS	YEAR	CLASS
	Eric Gill	1928	Humanist Sans Serif

A B C D E F G H I J K L M N O P Q R S T U V W X Y Z
a b c d e f g h i j k l m n o p q r s t u v w x y z

Background

Gill Sans is a hallmark of sans serif typeface design because it married the organic principles found in serif typography with the linear and mechanical simplicity of the sans serifs. Historians have debated whether **Eric Gill** (89) created his eponymous font as a tribute to Edward Johnston's London Railway font. The two typefaces share many formal attributes, and when viewed side by side, it's easy to see why that mythology holds up.

Traits

Gill Sans signature letters Q, R, a, g, and t demonstrate how it has more in common with serif fonts than sans serifs, especially those from Venetian-inspired foundries that created calligraphic letters during the **fifteenth century** (9).

SELECTED GILL SANS ALPHABETS
Top to bottom: 12-point Gill Sans regular, italic, and bold

ABCDEFGHIJKLMNOPQRSTUVWXYZ 1234567890
abcdefghijklmnopqrstuvwxyz
The quick brown fox jumped over the lazy dog.

ABCDEFGHIJKLMNOPQRSTUVWXYZ 1234567890
abcdefghijklmnopqrstuvwxyz
The quick brown fox jumped over the lazy dog.

ABCDEFGHIJKLMNOPQRSTUVWXYZ 1234567890
abcdefghijklmnopqrstuvwxyz
The quick brown fox jumped over the lazy dog.

EXAMPLE
11-point Gill Sans

A designer's job will become even *more* challenging as the quantity of information and noise **increases** during the twenty-first century. Those who possess a broad typographic understanding will best meet the communicative and creative challenge, especially during a time when people know the difference between one font and another—*and which ones read better or worse with software's default **120-percent** leading.*

Helvetica

ORIGINAL DESIGNERS	YEAR	CLASS
Max Miedinger and Eduoard Hoffman	1957	Neo-Grotesque

ABCDEFGHIJKLMNOPQRSTUVWXYZ

abcdefghijklmnopqrstuvwxyz

Background

While employed at the Haas Type Foundry, Edouard Hoffmann directed **Max Miedinger** (96) to render a competitor to **H. Berthold AG's** (126) popular **Akzidenz Grotesk** (170). They called their typeface Neue Haas Grotesk. In 1960, **Linotype** (129) and D. Stempel AG redrew it for the Linotype machine. This coincided with Neue Haas's renaming, first to Helvetia (Latin for "Switzerland") and then to Helvetica (Latin for "Swiss").

Traits

Helvetica is a time-tested, reliable choice for designers. It was released in the 1950s (22) and today is used so much that people don't even know what to call it. It has, in essence, become nameless.

SELECTED HELVETICA ALPHABETS
Top to bottom: 12-point Linotype Helvetica light, regular, and black

ABCDEFGHIJKLMNOPQRSTUVWXYZ 1234567890

abcdefghijklmnopqrstuvwxyz 1234567890

The quick brown fox jumped over the lazy dog.

ABCDEFGHIJKLMNOPQRSTUVWXYZ 1234567890

abcdefghijklmnopqrstuvwxyz 1234567890

The quick brown fox jumped over the lazy dog.

ABCDEFGHIJKLMNOPQRSTUVWXYZ 1234567890

abcdefghijklmnopqrstuvwxyz 1234567890

The quick brown fox jumped over the lazy dog.

EXAMPLE
11-point Linotype Helvetica

A designer's job will become even *more* challenging as the quantity of information and noise **increases** during the twenty-first century. Those who possess a broad typographic understanding will best meet the communicative and creative challenge, especially during a time when people know the difference between one font and another—*and which ones read better or worse with software's default **120-percent** leading.*

Kabel

ORIGINAL DESIGNERS	YEAR	CLASS
Rudolf Koch	1927	Geometric

A B C D E F G H I J K L M N O P Q R S T U V W X Y Z
a b c d e f g h i j k l m n o p q r s t u v w x y z

Background

Kabel first appeared in 1927, methodically drawn using many of the **geometric** (62) traits that **Futura** (174) possessed: circles, squares, and triangles. During the **1920s** (20), it became synonymous with the design aesthetic of the time, including **Art Deco** (66) ornamentation and extravagance. Victor Caruso redesigned Kabel for ITC; it became known as Cable in the United States.

Traits

Kabel's geometric properties get it easily confused with Futura. However, its **lowercase** (332) b does not have a spur. The original design of Kabel had a short x-height, making for long ascenders like Futura, but ITC Kabel's design possesses a larger x-height, making the ascenders look shorter. And unlike Futura, many of Kabel's **uppercase** (332) letters do not sit flush to the baseline or capline. Instead, there's an angular cut to the stems' tops and bottoms.

ABCDEFGHIJKLMNOPQRSTUVWXYZ 1234567890

abcdefghijklmnopqrstuvwxyz

The quick brown fox jumped over the lazy dog.

ABCDEFGHIJKLMNOPQRSTUVWXYZ 1234567890

abcdefghijklmnopqrstuvwxyz

The quick brown fox jumped over the lazy dog.

ABCDEFGHIJKLMNOPQRSTUVWXYZ 1234567890

abcdefghijklmnopqrstuvwxyz

The quick brown fox jumped over the lazy dog.

A designer's job will become even **more** challenging as the quantity of information and noise **increases** during the twenty-first century. Those who possess a broad typographic understanding will best meet the communicative and creative challenge, especially during a time when people know the difference between one font and another—**and which ones read better or worse with software's** default **120-percent** leading.

Monotype Grotesque

	ORIGINAL DESIGNERS	YEAR	CLASS
	Frank Hinman Pierpont	1926	Grotesque

A B C D E F G H I J K L M N O P Q R S T U V W X Y Z

a b c d e f g h i j k l m n o p q r s t u v w x y z

Background

Monotype Grotesque had been known as Grotesque 215 during its early release. For inspiration, Pierpont looked to other sans serif fonts popular at the time, including Berthold's Ideal. Monotype Grotesque was one of the earliest sans serifs cut for hot-metal machine typesetting.

Traits

Unlike **Helvetica** (176) and other **Grotesque** (60) sans serif fonts, Monotype Grotesque capitals do not contain some bookish features such as spurs. But it is light in color, making it suitable for setting as book text. Many of its heavier weights, such as bold and black, read well in display settings.

SELECTED MONOTYPE GROTESQUE ALPHABETS
Top to bottom: 12-point Monotype Grotesque regular, italic, and bold

ABCDEFGHIJKLMNOPQRSTUVWXYZ 1234567890

abcdefghijklmnopqrstuvwxyz

The quick brown fox jumped over the lazy dog.

ABCDEFGHIJKLMNOPQRSTUVWXYZ 1234567890

abcdefghijklmnopqrstuvwxyz

The quick brown fox jumped over the lazy dog.

ABCDEFGHIJKLMNOPQRSTUVWXYZ 1234567890

abcdefghijklmnopqrstuvwxyz

The quick brown fox jumped over the lazy dog.

EXAMPLE
11-point Monotype Grotesque

A designer's job will become even *more* challenging as the quantity of information and noise **increases** during the twenty-first century. Those who possess a broad typographic understanding will best meet the communicative and creative challenge, especially during a time when people know the difference between one font and another— *and which ones read better or worse with software's default 120-percent leading.*

News Gothic

ORIGINAL DESIGNERS	YEAR	CLASS
Morris Fuller Benton	1908	Grotesque

ABCDEFGHIJKLMNOPQRSTUVWXYZ
abcdefghijklmnopqrstuvwxyz

Background

Morris Fuller Benton (81) designed News Gothic for the American Type Founders, which issued regular, condensed, and extra condensed variations, but neither bold nor italic versions. It should come as no surprise that News Gothic was intended for use in newspapers and advertising, not only because of its name, but also because of its bold, strong appearance.

Traits

News Gothic owes a lot to **Akzidenz Grotesk** (170). Both have lighter stroke weights and a condensed appearance. But unlike Akzidenz Grotesk, News Gothic has a two-storey *g* and its *b*, *d*, *p*, and *q* use merely an oval with a straight line replacing one side of the curve.

SELECTED NEWS GOTHIC ALPHABETS
Top to bottom: 12-point News Gothic MT regular, italic, and bold

ABCDEFGHIJKLMNOPQRSTUVWXYZ 1234567890
abcdefghijklmnopqrstuvwxyz
The quick brown fox jumped over the lazy dog.

ABCDEFGHIJKLMNOPQRSTUVWXYZ 1234567890
abcdefghijklmnopqrstuvwxyz
The quick brown fox jumped over the lazy dog.

ABCDEFGHIJKLMNOPQRSTUVWXYZ 1234567890
abcdefghijklmnopqrstuvwxyz
The quick brown fox jumped over the lazy dog.

EXAMPLE
11-point News Gothic MT

A designer's job will become even *more* challenging as the quantity of information and noise **increases** during the twenty-first century. Those who possess a broad typographic understanding will best meet the communicative and creative challenge, especially during a time when people know the difference between one font and another—*and which ones read better or worse with software's default* **120-percent** *leading.*

Trade Gothic

	ORIGINAL DESIGNERS	YEAR	CLASS
	Jackson Burke	1948	Grotesque

A B C D E F G H I J K L M N O P Q R S T U V W X Y Z
a b c d e f g h i j k l m n o p q r s t u v w x y z

Background

As director of type development for Mergenthaler-Linotype in the United States, Jackson Burke designed some of the first iterations of Trade Gothic in 1948, and then developed alternate weights and styles until 1960. Unlike other sans serifs, it lacks unifying characteristics across the family.

Traits

Trade Gothic has narrower letterforms than other sans serifs, and this allows more text to be set across a measure. Like its cousin **News Gothic** (179), Trade Gothic has a staggered joint where the arm of the *K* meets the leg. And the lower portion of its *c* juts out slightly in front of the top terminal. Trade Gothic has been used in advertising and, more recently, website design along with serif text fonts, marrying classic with contemporary. The family isn't as unified as other **Grotesques** (60), and many of the differences between weight and width seem to make the font appealing to designers.

SELECTED TRADE GOTHIC ALPHABETS
Top to bottom: 12-point Trade Gothic Next Pro regular, italic, and bold

ABCDEFGHIJKLMNOPQRSTUVWXYZ 1234567890
abcdefghijklmnopqrstuvwxyz
The quick brown fox jumped over the lazy dog.

ABCDEFGHIJKLMNOPQRSTUVWXYZ 1234567890
abcdefghijklmnopqrstuvwxyz
The quick brown fox jumped over the lazy dog.

ABCDEFGHIJKLMNOPQRSTUVWXYZ 1234567890
abcdefghijklmnopqrstuvwxyz
The quick brown fox jumped over the lazy dog.

EXAMPLE
11-point Trade Gothic Next Pro

A designer's job will become even *more* challenging as the quantity of information and noise **increases** during the twenty-first century. Those who possess a broad typographic understanding will best meet the communicative and creative challenge, especially during a time when people know the difference between one font and another—*and which ones read better or worse with software's default **120-percent** leading.*

Univers

ORIGINAL DESIGNERS	YEAR	CLASS
Adrian Frutiger	1957	Neo-Grotesque

A B C D E F G H I J K L M N O P Q R S T U V W X Y Z
a b c d e f g h i j k l m n o p q r s t u v w x y z

Background

Adrian Frutiger (88) completed Univers—originally called Monde and predominantly known as a Swiss typeface—while he lived in France and worked for the Deberny & Peignot foundry. Frutiger employed a classification system so designers and composers could easily measure differences between one style and the next across light, regular, bold, and heavy weights, with odd numbers representing romans and even numbers denoting italics.

Traits

The larger x-height of Univers gives it a taller appearance in which **lowercase** (332) letters seem close in size to their **upper-case** (332) peers. The numeric classification system continues to work well for designers, and its wide breadth of weights and widths gives them a wealth of possibilities for setting **display** (213) or **text type** (212).

SELECTED UNIVERS ALPHABETS
Top to bottom: 12-point Univers 55 Roman, 55 roman oblique, and 65 bold

ABCDEFGHIJKLMNOPQRSTUVWXYZ 1234567890
abcdefghijklmnopqrstuvwxyz
The quick brown fox jumped over the lazy dog.

ABCDEFGHIJKLMNOPQRSTUVWXYZ 1234567890
abcdefghijklmnopqrstuvwxyz
The quick brown fox jumped over the lazy dog.

ABCDEFGHIJKLMNOPQRSTUVWXYZ 1234567890
abcdefghijklmnopqrstuvwxyz
The quick brown fox jumped over the lazy dog.

EXAMPLE
11-point Univers

A designer's job will become even *more* challenging as the quantity of information and noise **increases** during the twenty-first century. Those who possess a broad typographic understanding will best meet the communicative and creative challenge, especially during a time when people know the difference between one font and another—*and which ones read better or worse with software's default **120-percent** leading.*

Slab Serif

Also called Egyptian, square serif, or mechanistic, these nineteenth-century typefaces grew out of the Industrial Revolution and became prevalent in advertising campaigns that called for large, attention-getting slogans. Chronologically, slab serifs follow the **Didone** (56) era. They have been classified alongside serif typefaces, but have begun to receive their own classification system because of the cultural and functional milieu that brought about their creation.

Their medium **contrast** (230) and blocky serifs make them ideal for use at large sizes, as they were intended during the Industrial Revolution when posters and signs needed bigger, bolder type to successfully yell at passersby.

Clarendon (58) typifies this category, with enough weight and character for use in **display type** (213) such as headlines or subheads. Like serifs and sans serifs, **slab serifs** (59) have their own subclassifications known as Clarendons (or ionics) with their brackets and the unbracketed Egyptians. Slab serifs rarely get used for **text type** (212) because their bold forms weigh down the page with too much black, making for heavy passages in books, magazines, or newspapers.

Typography

Bracketed or Clarendon serif (set in Clarendon): Bracketed serifs, short descenders, pronounced drop forms and ball terminals, low contrast

Typography

Unbracketed or Egyptian serif (set in Rockwell): No brackets on serifs, short descenders, geometric properties

Typography

Geometric (set in ITC Lubalin Graph Book): No brackets on serifs, short descenders, predominantly geometric

Annenberg Community Beach House building facade done in Clarendon by AdamsMorioka, Inc., United States

Mohawk Via roll catalog by AdamsMorioka, Inc., United States

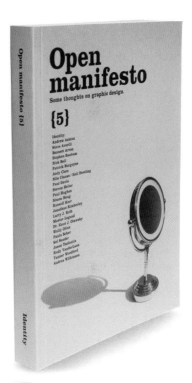

Open Manifesto book and interior done in Clarendon, Kevin Finn, Australia

American Typewriter

	ORIGINAL DESIGNERS	YEAR	CLASS
	Joel Kadan and Toni Stan	1974	Clarendon, Rounded Serif

ABCDEFGHIJKLMNOPQRSTUVWXYZ
abcdefghijklmnopqrstuvwxyz

Background

Original typewriter fonts from the **1970s** (25) and **1980s** (26) were monospaced; the letters all had a uniform width. Courier is a perfect example. Joel Kadan and Tony Stan designed ITC American Typewriter differently, where the letter rather than a universal measurement determined the width of the body. Despite these and other formal changes, American Typewriter still retains the rounded ball terminals that its typewriter kin— Remington, Underwood—possess.

Traits

The **uppercase** (332) *J*, *Q*, and *R* look organic, along with the *a*, *g*, and *r*. Like the original typewriter fonts, American Typewriter functions best at small sizes; when enlarged to display sizes above 15 point, many of its peculiarities become evident.

SELECTED AMERICAN TYPEWRITER ALPHABETS
Top to bottom: 12-point ITC American Typewriter light, medium, and bold

ABCDEFGHIJKLMNOPQRSTUVWXYZ 1234567890
abcdefghijklmnopqrstuvwxyz
The quick brown fox jumped over the lazy dog.

ABCDEFGHIJKLMNOPQRSTUVWXYZ 1234567890
abcdefghijklmnopqrstuvwxyz
The quick brown fox jumped over the lazy dog.

ABCDEFGHIJKLMNOPQRSTUVWXYZ 1234567890
abcdefghijklmnopqrstuvwxyz
The quick brown fox jumped over the lazy dog.

EXAMPLE
10-point ITC American Typewriter

A designer's job will become even *more* challenging as the quantity of information and noise **increases** during the twenty-first century. Those who possess a broad typographic understanding will best meet the communicative and creative challenge, especially during a time when people know the difference between one font and another— *and which ones read better or worse with software's default **120-percent** leading.*

Bookman

ORIGINAL DESIGNERS	YEAR	CLASS
Wadsworth A. Parker	circa 1900	Clarendon Serif

ABCDEFGHIJKLMNOPQRSTUVWXYZ
abcdefghijklmnopqrstuvwxyz

Background

Some versions and interpretations of Bookman date back to the late 1800s. It became a popular choice in the early 1900s because of its unique swash characters. After essentially disappearing from usage, it went through a revival in the late 1900s. Because so many versions existed without a complete family, **Ed Benguiat** (80) created a complete Bookman family for ITC in 1975.

Traits

Children's book designers have incorporated Bookman for decades because of its large x-height, which makes it easy to read even at small sizes. Because of this and its wide body, adding even a point or two of additional leading when setting **text type** (212) makes its paragraphs appear lighter, and in effect, easier for readers to digest because they see less weight optically. Bookman should be set at a wide enough measure to avoid too many hyphens.

SELECTED BOOKMAN ALPHABETS
Top to bottom: 12-point ITC Bookman light, medium, and bold

ABCDEFGHIJKLMNOPQRSTUVWXYZ 1234567890
abcdefghijklmnopqrstuvwxyz 1234567890
The quick brown fox jumped over the lazy dog.

ABCDEFGHIJKLMNOPQRSTUVWXYZ 1234567890
abcdefghijklmnopqrstuvwxyz 1234567890
The quick brown fox jumped over the lazy dog.

ABCDEFGHIJKLMNOPQRSTUVWXYZ 1234567890
abcdefghijklmnopqrstuvwxyz 1234567890
The quick brown fox jumped over the lazy dog.

EXAMPLE
10-point ITC Bookman

A designer's job will become even *more* challenging as the quantity of information and noise **increases** during the twenty-first century. Those who possess a broad typographic understanding will best meet the communicative and creative challenge, especially during a time when people know the difference between one font and another—*and which ones read better or worse with software's default* **120-percent** *leading.*

Cheltenham

ORIGINAL DESIGNERS	YEAR	CLASS
Bertram Goodhue	1896	Clarendon Serif

A B C D E F G H I J K L M N O P Q R S T U V W X Y Z
a b c d e f g h i j k l m n o p q r s t u v w x y z

Background

As a "classic" typeface, Cheltenham has undergone many revivals since its original design. The architect, Bertram Goodhue, originally designed Cheltenham, and in the 1900s, **Morris Fuller Benton** (81) expanded it for American Type Founders with various widths to make it a true type family. Tony Stan completed the design in 1975, giving it a larger x-height.

Traits

Goodhue infused Cheltenham with a sense of stability and structure that likely came from his training as an architect. Its short, stocky serifs make Cheltenham almost appear like a semi serif at smaller sizes. Because it is more condensed compared to its fellow **Old Style** (54) faces, Cheltenham fits more characters per measure. And its lack of distinct characters makes it a logical choice for **text type** (212) in books or magazines.

ABCDEFGHIJKLMNOPQRSTUVWXYZ 1234567890
abcdefghijklmnopqrstuvwxyz
The quick brown fox jumped over the lazy dog.

ABCDEFGHIJKLMNOPQRSTUVWXYZ 1234567890
abcdefghijklmnopqrstuvwxyz
The quick brown fox jumped over the lazy dog.

ABCDEFGHIJKLMNOPQRSTUVWXYZ 1234567890
abcdefghijklmnopqrstuvwxyz
The quick brown fox jumped over the lazy dog.

EXAMPLE
10-point ITC Cheltenham

A designer's job will become even *more* challenging as the quantity of information and noise **increases** during the twenty-first century. Those who possess a broad typographic understanding will best meet the communicative and creative challenge, especially during a time when people know the difference between one font and another— *and which ones read better or worse with software's default **120-percent** leading.*

Clarendon

ORIGINAL DESIGNERS	YEAR	CLASS
Robert Besley	1845	Clarendon Serif

ABCDEFGHIJKLMNOPQRSTUVWXYZ

abcdefghijklmnopqrstuvwxyz

Background

Clarendon (58) evolved during a time when large type graced large advertisements, signs, and posters in nineteenth-century Great Britian. Under the Ornamental Designs Act of 1842, Clarendon was protected, but this lasted only three years, after which others pirated Robert Besley's work.

Traits

As a bracketed **slab serif** (59), Clarendon lacks the geometric harshness of unbracketed Egyptian slab serifs such as **Rockwell** (190) or **Geometric** (62) slab serifs such as Lubalin Graph. Although classified as a serif, the Clarendon has enough weight and character to be used for **display type** (213) in headlines or subheads. The thick, rich, dense, and curvy large ball terminals become objects of affection when set in larger sizes.

SELECTED CLARENDON ALPHABETS
Top to bottom: 12-point Clarendon light, medium, and bold

ABCDEFGHIJKLMNOPQRSTUVWXYZ 1234567890

abcdefghijklmnopqrstuvwxyz

The quick brown fox jumped over the lazy dog.

ABCDEFGHIJKLMNOPQRSTUVWXYZ 1234567890

abcdefghijklmnopqrstuvwxyz

The quick brown fox jumped over the lazy dog.

ABCDEFGHIJKLMNOPQRSTUVWXYZ 1234567890

abcdefghijklmnopqrstuvwxyz

The quick brown fox jumped over the lazy dog.

EXAMPLE
10-point Clarendon

A designer's job will become even **more** challenging as the quantity of information and noise **increases** during the twenty-first century. Those who possess a broad typographic understanding will best meet the communicative and creative challenge, especially during a time when people know the difference between one font and another—and **which ones read better** or worse with software's default 120-percent leading.

Memphis

ORIGINAL DESIGNERS	YEAR	CLASS
Rudolf Wolf	1929	Egyptian

ABCDEFGHIJKLMNOPQRSTUVWXYZ

abcdefghijklmnopqrstuvwxyz

Background

Rudolf Wolf designed Memphis in 1929 for the D. Stempel AG foundry as the first Egyptian revival. The letter shapes are **geometric** (62), with stems and serifs having the same optical weight. Because of its demonstrative appearance, Memphis works well as a display face for posters, packaging, advertising, and headlines.

Traits

One of the most noticeable characters in the Memphis repertoire is the apex serif on the capital *A* (the serif at the very top). The extreme horizontal and unbracketed serif is characteristically **slab serif** (59). But it's the **uppercase** (332) *Q* that breaks form with the obtuse angle of its tail. Many of the round shapes in the Memphis lower- and uppercase letters appear perfectly round and circular.

ABCDEFGHIJKLMNOPQRSTUVWXYZ 1234567890

abcdefghijklmnopqrstuvwxyz

The quick brown fox jumped over the lazy dog.

ABCDEFGHIJKLMNOPQRSTUVWXYZ 1234567890

abcdefghijklmnopqrstuvwxyz

The quick brown fox jumped over the lazy dog.

ABCDEFGHIJKLMNOPQRSTUVWXYZ 1234567890

abcdefghijklmnopqrstuvwxyz

The quick brown fox jumped over the lazy dog.

A designer's job will become even *more* challenging as the quantity of information and noise **increases** during the twenty-first century. Those who possess a broad typographic understanding will best meet the communicative and creative challenge, especially during a time when people know the difference between one font and another— *and which ones read better or worse with software's default **120-percent** leading.*

Officina Serif

	ORIGINAL DESIGNERS	YEAR	CLASS
	Erik Spiekermann and Ole Schafer	1990 (with a 1998 revival)	Egyptian

A B C D E F G H I J K L M N O P Q R S T U V W X Y Z

a b c d e f g h i j k l m n o p q r s t u v w x y z

Background

During its initial release in 1990, Officina existed as a paired family of serif and sans serif faces in two weights with italics, promoted as a functional family for corporate and business correspondence such as stationery and annual reports. Over time, the typeface became popular for other uses, adopted for a slew of advertising and editorial purposes. Because Officina had been pushed beyond its original intentions, other weights were created including medium, extra bold, and black, each with matching italics.

Traits

Officina Serif sets narrower than other **slab serifs** (59), and therein lies its chief functional benefit. The near-monoline letters have unique subtleties such as a bar terminal on its *J* (at the top of the letter) and extended bar on the *G*. **Uppercase** (332) letters such as the *R* and many of the **lowercase** (332) letters such as the *h*, *m*, and *n* have half-serifs to help maintain an overall light color compared to other slab serifs. And friendly touches such as curved spurs on the lowercase *b* and *d* (at the bottom of the letters), as well as the curved foot of the *l* liken Officina Serif to **Humanist** (61) sans serifs such as **Gill Sans** (175) and Meta.

SELECTED OFFICINA SERIF ALPHABETS
Top to bottom: 12-point Officina Serif book, book italic, and bold

ABCDEFGHIJKLMNOPQRSTUVWXYZ 1234567890

abcdefghijklmnopqrstuvwxyz

The quick brown fox jumped over the lazy dog.

ABCDEFGHIJKLMNOPQRSTUVWXYZ 1234567890

abcdefghijklmnopqrstuvwxyz

The quick brown fox jumped over the lazy dog.

ABCDEFGHIJKLMNOPQRSTUVWXYZ 1234567890

abcdefghijklmnopqrstuvwxyz

The quick brown fox jumped over the lazy dog.

EXAMPLE
10-point Officina Serif

A designer's job will become even *more* challenging as the quantity of information and noise **increases** during the twenty-first century. Those who possess a broad typographic understanding will best meet the communicative and creative challenge, especially during a time when people know the difference between one font and another—*and which ones read better or worse with software's default **120-percent** leading.*

Rockwell

ORIGINAL DESIGNERS	YEAR	CLASS
Frank Pierpont	1934	Egyptian

A B C D E F G H I J K L M N O P Q R S T U V W X Y Z
a b c d e f g h i j k l m n o p q r s t u v w x y z

Background

Monotype (125) issued Frank Pierpont's Rockwell during a time when **slab serif** (59) typography was undergoing a revival. Although shown here in two weights, it also has a light version that further reinforces the typeface's linear qualities due to its thinner strokes. Like **Memphis** (188), Rockwell has undergone a revival on the Web, where designers use it for headlines and subheads because of its simplicity and easy-to-read geometric forms.

Traits

Like many **slab serifs** (59), Rockwell sets wide, making it less-than-ideal for large areas of **text type** (212). However, its large x-height makes it an optimal candidate for signage, wayfinding, and display uses. Designers set it with a standard 120-percent leading because of its short ascenders and descenders, but because of its dark typographic color, Rockwell benefits from more leading than that between each line.

SELECTED ROCKWELL ALPHABETS
Top to bottom: 12-point Rockwell roman, italic, and bold

ABCDEFGHIJKLMNOPQRSTUVWXYZ 1234567890
abcdefghijklmnopqrstuvwxyz
The quick brown fox jumped over the lazy dog.

ABCDEFGHIJKLMNOPQRSTUVWXYZ 1234567890
abcdefghijklmnopqrstuvwxyz
The quick brown fox jumped over the lazy dog.

ABCDEFGHIJKLMNOPQRSTUVWXYZ 1234567890
abcdefghijklmnopqrstuvwxyz
The quick brown fox jumped over the lazy dog.

EXAMPLE
10-point Rockwell

A designer's job will become even *more* challenging as the quantity of information and noise **increases** during the twenty-first century. Those who possess a broad typographic understanding will best meet the communicative and creative challenge, especially during a time when people know the difference between one font and another—*and which ones read better or worse with software's default 120-percent leading.*

Serifa

	ORIGINAL DESIGNERS	YEAR	CLASS
	Adrian Frutiger	1967	Egyptian

A B C D E F G H I J K L M N O P Q R S T U V W X Y Z
a b c d e f g h i j k l m n o p q r s t u v w x y z

Background

Serifa's frequent comparison to **Univers** (181) results from its similarities to Univers's wide breadth of variations. Also, updated versions of Serifa include a numbering system like its brethren. Often called "Univers with serifs," Serifa was designed to be as versatile as a sans serif, and it is suitable for text and display uses.

Traits

Serifa's serif and stroke weight are the same. It has a high x-height and eccentricities in its *C*, which does not have a bottom serif, its *G*, which has bottom spur, and the noticeable *Q*, with its horizontal tail. Some italic versions are merely slanted.

SELECTED SERIFA ALPHABETS
Top to bottom: 12-point Serifa 55 roman, 56 italic, and 65 bold

ABCDEFGHIJKLMNOPQRSTUVWXYZ 1234567890

abcdefghijklmnopqrstuvwxyz

The quick brown fox jumped over the lazy dog.

ABCDEFGHIJKLMNOPQRSTUVWXYZ 1234567890

abcdefghijklmnopqrstuvwxyz

The quick brown fox jumped over the lazy dog.

ABCDEFGHIJKLMNOPQRSTUVWXYZ 1234567890

abcdefghijklmnopqrstuvwxyz

The quick brown fox jumped over the lazy dog.

EXAMPLE
10-point Serifa

A designer's job will become even *more* challenging as the quantity of information and noise **increases** during the twenty-first century. Those who possess a broad typographic understanding will best meet the communicative and creative challenge, especially during a time when people know the difference between one font and another—*and which ones read better or worse with software's default* **120-percent** *leading.*

Blackletter

Blackletter has existed as a typographic style for centuries. It is a hybrid of both Carolingian and Old English writing, bearing resemblance to ancient scribes' handcrafted writing from ninth-century Italy and France, and as far east as Germany. Johannes Gutenberg's invention of movable type in the 1450s made blackletter popular throughout Germany, thanks mostly to Gutenberg's initial printing and distribution of the Bible.

Peter Schöffer took over Gutenberg's production facility when Schöffer's father-in-law, Johann Fust, foreclosed on Gutenberg, and the two of them finished the Bible production—leaving Gutenberg penniless. From then on, a long line of German type foundries and printers made names for themselves and distributed a wealth of printed goods set in blackletter. Notable among them were Conrad Sweynheym and Arnold Pannartz, who established a press in the Benedictine monastery of Subiaco in 1465. Over time, blackletter spread to northern Europe.

Centuries later, in the 1930s (21), Adolf Hitler and the Nazis plastered Germany with propaganda using blackletter Fraktur as the de facto type style. But by 1941, Hitler's secretary, Martin Bormann, decreed that blackletter—specifically Fraktur—was not to be used because of its supposed Jewish origins. Despite its use by the Nazis and Bormann's unusual ruling, blackletter remains a versatile typographic choice, and has enjoyed modern-day revivals by some of the industry's most celebrated type designers.

Today, it appears in newspapers, on beer labels, and in religious scriptures, connoting a sense of reverence, reliability, and timelessness. And in popular culture, blackletter has graced fleshy canvases as tattoos and has been used as wordmarks for heavy metal and hip-hop bands.

Editor's note: We do not recommend using these blackletter typefaces for long bodies of text.

BLACKLETTER SERIF CHARACTERISTICS

Typography	Typography	Typography	Typography
Bastarda (set in Lucida Blackletter): References to Carolingian minuscules, highly legible compared to other blackletters, angled ascenders and descenders, many curved strokes	Fraktur (set in Fette Fraktur): Dramatic and exaggerated strokes, descending feet and stems, swashed terminals, curved tails	Rotunda (set in San Marco): Highly legible, thick terminals, angled stress in counters, straight stems, and downstrokes	Textura (set in Old English): Hairline second strokes and flourishes, angular and narrow body width, split terminals, looped tails, various straight stems

Crane Lettra broadside, by MOD/Michael Osborne Design, United States

Memories in black-letter, by 2Creatives, United Kingdom

Clairvaux

ORIGINAL DESIGNERS	YEAR	CLASS
Herbert Maring	1990	Bastarda

A B C D E F G H I J K L M
N O P Q R S T U V W X Y Z
a b c d e f g h i j k l m n o p q r s t u v w x y z

Background

Clairvaux was part of a 1990 program that called on twelve font designers to represent styles from across the ages, for a series called "Type Before Gutenberg." Designer Herbert Maring was charged with developing Clairvaux, and he based his design on early Gothic typefaces.

Traits

Clairvaux's letters look more like those found in the Roman alphabet, and they are more **readable** (330) when set in the English language. Maring based many of its forms on those found in Carolingian manuscripts, especially the minuscule letters such as the **lowercase** (332) *a*.

SELECTED CLAIRVAUX ALPHABETS
24-point Clairvaux

A B C D E F G H I J
K L M N O P Q R
S T U V W X Y Z
1 2 3 4 5 6 7 8 9 0 abcdefghijk
lmnopqrstuvwxyz
The quick brown fox jumped
over the lazy dog.

EXAMPLE
16-point Clairvaux

A designer's job will become even more challenging as the quantity of information and noise increases during the twenty-first century. Those who possess a broad typographic understanding will best meet the communicative and creative challenge, especially during a time when people know the difference between one font and another—and which ones read better or worse with…

Duc de Berry

ORIGINAL DESIGNERS	YEAR	CLASS
Gottfried Pott	1991	Bastarda

Background

Linotype (129) issued Gottfried Pott's design in 1991 during a blackletter revival that celebrated many of the typographic styles and influences from the 1400s and 1500s. The typographic forms owe much to the French blackletter traditions, with more open counters and curvilinear strokes.

Traits

Duc de Berry's capital letters have a number of flourishes and hairline strokes, some with rectangular terminals that give the letters a rigid appearance. With its Romanesque qualities and lighter typographic color, Duc de Berry reads well when set as **text type** (212) compared to other blackletter typefaces.

SELECTED DUC DE BERRY ALPHABETS
24-point Duc de Berry

ABCDEFGHIJ
KLMNOPQR
STUVWXYZ
1234567890 abcdefghijk
lmnopqrstuvwxyz
The quick brown fox jumped
over the lazy dog.

EXAMPLE
16-point Duc de Berry

A designer's job will become even more challenging as the quantity of information and noise increases during the twenty-first century. Those who possess a broad typographic understanding will best meet the communicative and creative challenge, especially during a time when people know the difference between one font and another— and which ones read better or worse…

Fette Fraktur

ORIGINAL DESIGNERS	YEAR	CLASS
Johann Christian Bauer	1850	Fraktur

[Fette Fraktur uppercase and lowercase alphabet specimen displayed]

Background

Punchcutter Johann Christian Bauer designed Fette Fraktur in 1850, and the C. E. Weber Foundry later published a version in 1875. Other versions have been produced during the **twentieth century** (16), such as one in 1908 by the D. Stempel AG foundry.

Traits

Fette Fraktur has a vivid sense of **contrast** (230) thanks in part to its varied stroke widths and terminals. It possesses as many angular forms as it does curvilinear ones. With its fat, broken appearance, Fette Fraktur is best read in sizes larger than 16 point to ensure good **legibility** (330) and reproduction.

SELECTED FETTE FRAKTUR ALPHABETS
20-point Fette Fraktur

ABCDEFGHI
JKLMNOPQR
STUVWXYZ
1234567890 abcdefghijk
lmnopqrstuvwxyz
The quick brown fox jumped
over the lazy dog.

EXAMPLE
14-point Fette Fraktur

A designer's job will become even more challenging as the quantity of information and noise increases during the twenty-first century. Those who possess a broad typographic understanding will best meet the communicative and creative challenge, especially during a time when people know the difference between one font...

Wilhelm Klingspor Gotisch

ORIGINAL DESIGNERS	YEAR	CLASS
Rudolf Koch	1925	Fraktur

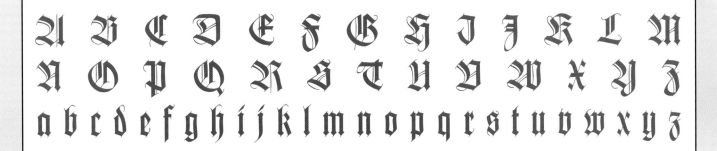

Background

Rudolf Koch (93), chief designer at the Klingspor Brothers Foundry in Offenbach, Germany, named his font in honor of the foundry's coowner. Koch employed his calligraphy skills to design Wilhelm Klingspor Gotisch, which some have deemed a leading Textura specimen.

Traits

Wilhelm Klingspor Gotisch has animated, vigorous, masterfully drawn letterforms with a generous amount of counterspace. Its narrow **lowercase** (332) letters are difficult to read at small sizes, making it preferable for display or titling.

SELECTED WILHELM KLINGSPOR GOTISCH ALPHABETS
24-point Wilhelm Klingspor Gotisch

ABCDEFGHI
JKLMNOPQR
STUVWXYZ
1234567890 abcdefghijk
lmnopqrstuvwxyz
The quick brown fox jumped
over the lazy dog.

EXAMPLE
16-point Wilhelm Klingspor Gotisch

A designer's job will become even more challenging as the quantity of information and noise increases during the twenty-first century. Those who possess a broad typographic understanding will best meet the communicative and creative challenge, especially during a time when people know the difference between one font and another—and which ones read better or worse with software's default 120-percent leading.

Scripts

Typography	**Typography**
Flowing Casual (set in Brush Script): Connected letters, suitable for nonformal uses such as signage or display text	Nonflowing Brush (set in Cascade Script): Unconnected letters, with thick strokes reminiscent of a round or chiseled brush

Scripts can be elegant in one font, funky in another. As with handwriting, they have a wide range of styles, weights, and widths, making them one of the more varied typographic categories.

Scripts owe more to the handwritten word than the commonly used serif and sans serif typefaces to which designers often default. Today's hand-lettering revival has turned more attention to scripts, especially when it comes to custom lettering, prompting many designers to leave behind the computer in favor of the brush or pen.

Scripts generally fall into two distinct categories: flowing (also called connected or linked) and nonflowing (also called disconnected or unlinked). Within those categories exist a morass of subcategories that each break down into further classes. Many of today's script faces come in a variety of alternate letters, custom ligatures, and swashes. Typographic standards such as letter shape and size have compromised some

Je T'aime Sutherland invite in Sudestada regular and Phaeton regular by The White Room Inc., Canada

Typography	*Typography*	*Typography*	**Typography**
Nonflowing Formal (set in Monotype Dorchester Script): Unconnected letters, suitable for formal uses that call for professionalism and elegance	Flowing Formal (set in Bickham Script): Connected letters, suitable for formal uses that call for professionalism and elegance, more angled posture	Handwritten (set in Texas Hero): Connected or unconnected, usually modeled closely after existing handwriting or penmanship	Casual Handwritten (set in Monoline Script): Connected or unconnected, modeled after handwriting or penmanship with many creative liberties taken

of the most unique handwritten characters digitized for mass distribution and digital use. But thanks to digitization and design software, producing a diverse range of letters has become more feasible.

Following the less-is-more principle comes in handy when designing with scripts. **Pairing** (232) script typefaces with sans serif letters delivers a balanced combination of elegance and mechanics, but pairing two scripts creates the sense that two handwritten words are competing for attention. Conscientious **kerning** (334) also comes in handy, especially with flowing scripts whose letters connect to one another to form words. Some scripts require delicate kerning to make sure the connections hit just right.

Editor's note: Most scripts are not for use in long bodies of text.

Letterlab exhibition poster
promotion, Strange Attractors
Design, The Netherlands

Still from *Typophile*
5 video from Studio
DVA, Brent Barson,
United States

Voice design studio
wordmark, Voice, Australia

Bickham

ORIGINAL DESIGNERS	YEAR	CLASS
Richard Lipton	1997	Flowing, Formal

A B C D E F G H I J K L M
N O P Q R S T U V W X Y Z
a b c d e f g h i j k l m n o p q r s t u v w x y z

Background

Bickham is based on eighteenth-century lettering such as the unparalleled engravings of George Bickham. The most recent version of Bickham, released in 2004, includes more than 1,700 glyphs per font thanks to the wizardry of OpenType.

Traits

The fluid typeface has been enhanced by a number of alternative characters, endings, ligatures, and ornaments available in Bickham Script Pro. Its exaggerated posture calls to mind romantic poetry and love letters from times past.

SELECTED BICKMAN ALPHABETS
30-point Bickham Script regular

A B C D E F G H I
J K L M N O P Q R
S T U V W X Y Z
1234567890 abcdefghijk
lmnopqrstuvwxyz
The quick brown fox jumped over the lazy dog.

EXAMPLE
24-point Bickham Script regular

A designer's job will become even more challenging as the quantity of information and noise increases during the twenty-first century. Those who possess a broad typographic understanding will best meet the communicative and creative challenge, especially during a time when...

Choc

	ORIGINAL DESIGNERS	YEAR	CLASS
	Roger Excoffon	1954	Nonflowing, Brush

A B C D E F G H I J K L M
N O P Q R S T U V W X Y Z
a b c d e f g h i j k l m n o p q r s t u v w x y z

Background

Roger Excoffon based Choc on Japanese brush calligraphy, with thick yet graceful strokes. Phil Grimshaw designed a light version, which maintains much of the same quirks evident in Excoffon's rendition.

Traits

As a **casual** (64) script, Choc looks quickly drawn, and this makes it less appropriate for business or professional documents.

SELECTED CHOC ALPHABETS
22-point Choc regular

A B C D E F G H I J
K L M N O P Q R
S T U V W X Y Z
1 2 3 4 5 6 7 8 9 0 a b c d e f g h i j k
l m n o p q r s t u v w x y z
The quick brown fox jumped over the lazy dog.

EXAMPLE
16-point Choc regular

A designer's job will become even more challenging as the quantity of information and noise increases during the twenty-first century. Those who possess a broad typographic understanding will best meet the communicative and creative challenge, especially during a time when people know the difference between one font and another—and which ones read better or worse...

French Script

	ORIGINAL DESIGNERS	YEAR	CLASS
	Morris Fuller Benton	1905	Flowing, Upright

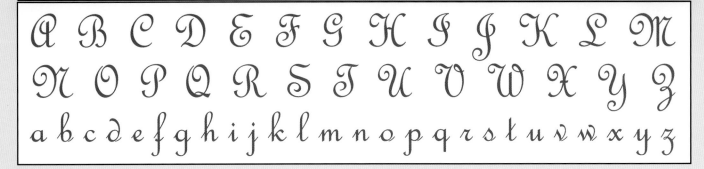

Background

Morris Fuller Benton (81) designed Typo Upright in 1905 for the American Type Founders, which became the basis for the 2003 version of **Monotype's** (125) French Script. Elegant in nature, French Script shares a stiff, upright posture prevalent in so many of the serif **Didones** (56).

Traits

French Script is ideal for formal announcements and invitations, but it lacks some of the animated qualities found in other scripts because it does not have as many flourishes and swashes.

SELECTED FRENCH SCRIPT ALPHABETS
30-point French Script regular

ABCDEFGHIJ
KLMNOPQR
STUVWXYZ
1234567890 abcdefghijk
lmnopqrstuvwxyz
The quick brown fox jumped
over the lazy dog.

EXAMPLE
19-point French Script regular

A designer's job will become even more challenging as the quantity of information and noise increases during the twenty-first century. Those who possess a broad typographic understanding will best meet the communicative and creative challenge, especially during a time when people know the difference between one font and another—and which ones read better or worse...

Snell Roundhand

	ORIGINAL DESIGNERS	YEAR	CLASS
	Matthew Carter	1966	Flowing, Formal

A B C D E F G H I J K L M
N O P Q R S T U V W X Y Z
a b c d e f g h i j k l m n o p q r s t u v w x y z

Background

Type designer **Matthew Carter** (85) translated Charles Snell's eighteenth-century writing mastery into this graceful, linked script. Like Snell's original writing, this typeface has a regularity of form and even typographic color across the entire character set.

Traits

Any deviation from the set tracking and **kerning** (334) would cause the links between the letters of Snell Roundhand to disconnect. It can be used to set small amounts of **text type** (212) due to its well-defined counters and clear differentiation between letters.

SELECTED SNELL ROUNDHAND ALPHABETS
20-point Snell Roundhand Script

A B C D E F G H I J
K L M N O P Q R
S T U V W X Y Z
1234567890 abcdefghijk
lmnopqrstuvwxyz
The quick brown fox jumped over the lazy dog.

EXAMPLE
16-point Snell Roundhand Script

A designer's job will become even more challenging as the quantity of information and noise increases during the twenty-first century. Those who possess a broad typographic understanding will best meet the communicative and creative challenge, especially during a time when people know the difference between one font and another—and which ones read better or worse…

Typographic Principles

By Jason Tselentis

Finbarr Fallon
Remote
Digitally enhanced
photograph

p3

Designing with type is as much a science as an art, requiring a delicate balance between all items in the format to deliver appropriate and functional solutions. Designers who rely "purely on instinct" often have the benefit of years of experience, and thanks to their training, can call on formal qualities and aesthetic conditions that have worked well for them in the past.

Contrasts (230) in size, shape, tone, placement, and color all factor into how elements placed in the format look. Being visually literate allows the designer to give words and images shape, bringing it all together as a composition created within the required format. Designing with type requires not only an understanding of what makes a serif and what makes a sans serif, but also a working knowledge of their use and even a small appreciation of the individual attributes that make one font different from another, as well as how they interact when placed together.

And what about style? Good typographic expression is an art, but it is also, without question, based on principles. Designers may use knowledge and experience to design works that evoke a particular period, place, person, or movement. Often, they will do so to further the communicative message required. Many intentionally take liberties and break the rules to create stylistic marvels for the client's interest, the audience's, and their own. But one of the most valued typographic principles deals with purpose, and more specifically function.

Designing a book requires a fair amount of restraint as well as respect for the divine principles that book designers have used for centuries. And **readability** (330) should take precedence. Creating a gigantic billboard, for example, calls for larger typography than a book designer employs. And then of course, there are the delicate niceties, much like stylistic guidelines that writers follow.

There's a saying that goes, "If all you have is a hammer, everything looks like a nail." This holds true for the designer. If all a designer knows is a handful of principles, then all a designer can create is a handful of solutions. This chapter may not include every rule, but knowing as many rules as possible helps designers expand their toolbox and decide what to use, and when.

Westminster School's *Vision* magazine, 2Creatives, United Kingdom

Design360 employed a dark contrast black type to make the lettering pop and read on the yellow background of the News Corporation Dow Jones office space.

This sign at Snoqualmie Falls by Lehrman Cameron Studio uses not just one type size, but many, to delineate information levels for the reader. Large sizes pull them in, medium sizes give deep information, and a third level provides map information.

2Creative's +81 T-shirt include a wealth of typographic information, but each typeface denotes designers by nationality—British, French, German, Dutch—using typefaces from the respected countries.

The office of MOD/Michael Osborne Design created a predominantly image-based poster, but gets the reader's attention by placing the headline in an off-angled element.

In her flattened "Elevate" poster, designer Kelly Salchow MacArthur willfully pulls the reader's gaze to the start of the word "elevate," and then back to the composition's top.

Format

Designers first take note of the size and proportion of the page or screen in which they will work. And although every format has edged boundaries that contain design elements, that shouldn't limit creative opportunities.

U.S. Page Sizes

The base size for printing in the United States is the broadsheet measuring 17 × 22 inches (43.18 × 55.88 cm). Half of a broadsheet is called tabloid size at 11 × 17 inches (27.94 × 43.18 cm). A quarter of a broadsheet is called letter size, which is 8.50 × 11 inches (21.59 × 27.94 cm). U.S. printers base many of their page sizes on the letter-sized proportion that sometimes measures 9 × 12 inches (22.86 × 30.48 cm). Smaller sizes derived from the letter sizes include:

- 5.50 × 8.50 inch (13.97 × 21.59 cm)
- 6 × 9 inch (15.24 × 22.86 cm)

Of the four listed above, the 5.50 × 8.50 inch (13.97 × 21.59 cm) sheet measures closest to the "divine proportions" found in the golden section of 1:1.618 (see "The Golden Section" at right for details).

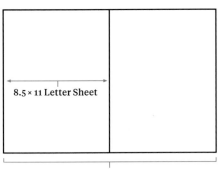

8.5 × 11 Letter Sheet

11 × 17 Tabloid Sheet

Many U.S. page sizes derive from the proportion of the letter-page size of 8.50 × 11 inches (21.59 × 27.94 cm), expandable to the tabloid size of 11 × 17 inches (27.94 × 43.18 cm).

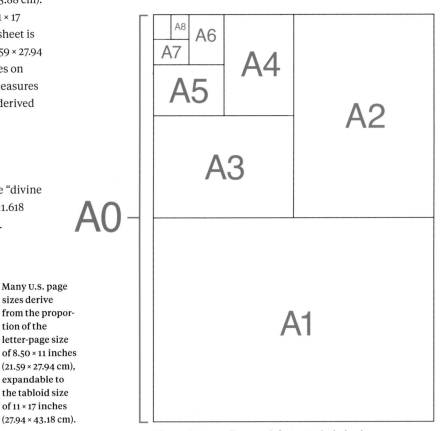

The ISO System allows each format to be halved, with the resulting format in the same proportion.

The Golden Section

In Western cultures, the golden section refers to this ratio between two numbers: 1:1.618. It has also been represented as a:b = b:(a+b). The proportion has been used since ancient times, even identified in ancient Greek architecture and art. It is said to create harmonious relationships between graphic elements placed on the page, and it has been used for the express purpose of generating printed formats for books, posters, and brochures.

Here's the process for building a golden section:

Begin by drawing a square of any size.

Bisect the square down the middle.

Draw a line from the bottom left corner of the bisection to the upper right corner (as indicated by the yellow line).

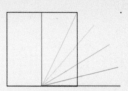

Rotate the line down to the square's baseline.

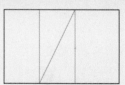

Draw a vertical line up from the new baseline to the top of the square, then left toward the square to close the new form. This is a golden section.

ISO Formats

Designers and printers outside of the United States use the International Standards Organization (ISO) format system. Nobel laureate Wilhelm Ostwald proposed a ratio of 1 to the square root of 2, yielding a 1:1.414 ratio across all paper sizes. When any sheet is halved, the resulting sheet remains the same ratio.

Unlike U.S. measuring systems, the ISO system relies on metric measurements. The A0 sheet is 33.11 × 46.81 inches (84.10 x 118.90 cm). Smaller sizes include:

- A1 sheet, 23.39 × 33.11 inches (59.41 × 84.10 cm)
- A2 sheet, 16.54 × 23.39 inches (42.01 × 59.41 cm)
- A3 sheet 11.69 × 16.54 inches (29.69 × 42.01 cm)
- A4 sheet 8.27 × 11.69 inches (21.01 × 29.69 cm)

It continues up to A10. Other series exist in the ISO system including the B0 sheet, 39.37 × 55.67 inches (100.00 × 141.40 cm), and C0 sheet, 36.10 × 51.06 inches (91.69 × 129.69 cm). Not only does the ISO system allow for reproduction of the 1:1.414 ratio when pages are halved, but it also relies on the mathematical nicety of the metric system based on tenths, hundredths, and thousandths, whereas the U.S. system uses inches, with difficult-to-delineate sixteenth proportions.

Typography Selection

One of the best methods to decide which typeface to use is to have a clear understanding of its application. Will the type be digital or in print? Will it require a range of weights and postures? If it requires a variety of fractions and numerals, does the typeface have a complete set of OpenType options for numbers? While every typeface has a distinct look and feel, its application ultimately dictates its usefulness.

Text Type

For text type, use typefaces designed for the purpose of uninterrupted reading such as **Caslon** (157), **Bembo** (155), and **Garamond** (162). These three work well for large areas of book text. **Times New Roman** (165) — though overused today—was designed in the **twentieth century** (16) to function as a newspaper typeface, and makes an adequate choice for book text as well. **Clearface** (160), **Centaur** (158), and **Sabon** (164) also have clear **readability** (330). Line length, word spacing, and leading all factor into a book text's readability, but choosing a time-tested typeface such as those listed in this chapter is as good a place as any to start.

The Adris Group's *Good Ideas Glow in the Dark* annual report uses a readable Minion Pro set in varying weights and styles to separate bodies of information. Bruketa&Žinić OM, Croatia

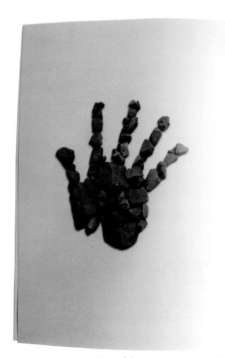

For continuous reading of the *Future, Country* book about Gelganyem, Kevin Finn used a standard two-column grid to deliver the book's text to the reader.

Display Type

Display type needs to quickly catch readers' attention, much like the messages on posters, advertisements, and promotions made popular during the **late nineteenth century** (16). Using typographic size to gain attention continues to this day, where assertiveness can help cut through the competitive visual noise. While **text type** (212) rarely relies on these measures to get attention, headlines and subheads in printed and digital matter must pull in readers, delineate levels of information, tell readers where they are, and keep their attention.

Display type must be **legible** (330), of course, but because the reader can decipher the small chunks of type rather quickly, legibility may not be as important as with text type. Also, the concept or message may call for something with more vigor and exuberance. **Slab serifs** (59) such as **Rockwell** (190), **Memphis** (188), and **Clarendon** (58) all have enough weight and character for use as display type in headlines or subheads. When enlarged, many of the raw visual forms become present for **Old Style** (54) and Garalde serif faces, so use these for display type with consideration. Finally, a variety of sans serifs and scripts can also do the job well.

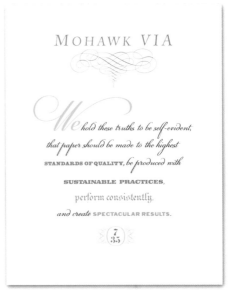

AdamsMorioka, Inc., paired a serif-faced headline that announces the Mohawk Via brand with a delicate, formal script for the quality assurance statement.

To enable distance reading and announce the place illustrated on Jennifer Beorkrem's poster, "The Great Lakes" is set in a large DIN typeface, while the smaller typographic elements mapped on the lakes identify each body of water.

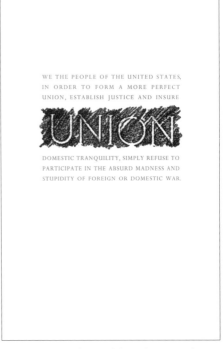

Even with just a glance of the Union poster by MOD/Michael Osborne Design, the reader knows that a patriotic message sits around the larger headline, not only because of the large type, but also because of the red, white, and blue color scheme.

Reading Direction and Scanning

Western cultures read the written language from left to right, which typically puts the reader's first glance at the upper left-hand corner of formats. From there, readers scan left to right, diagonally down to the next line, and back again from left to right. This Z-shaped scanning pattern often occurs when reading text type (212) in magazines or books, as well as with digital media such as content found on the Internet.

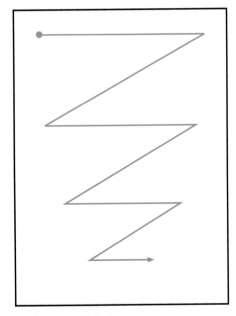

Readers typically begin at the top left (at the circle) and scan right and down, left and down, until finally reaching the composition's bottom. This is not a prescription but rather one of the many ways that readers approach and read graphic materials.

By positioning the letters *E*, *V*, *I*, and *L* vertically on this composition, this poster by Ralph Schraivogel reads "EVIL" one way and "LIVE" the other.

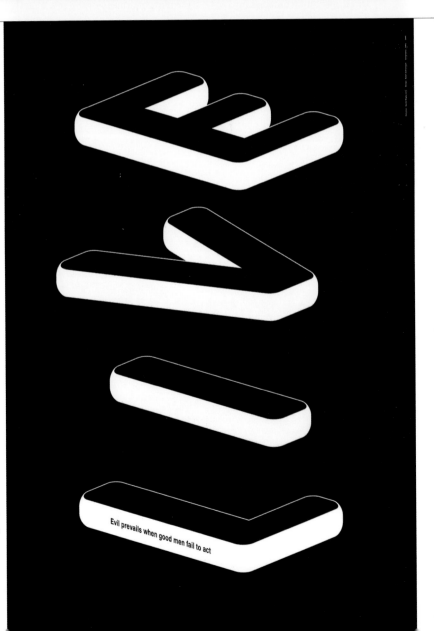

Evil prevails when good men fail to act

Focal Point

Dynamic compositions, especially those meant to attract a viewer's attention, often employ a focal point that does not allow a reader to scan starting with the top-left corner. In these compositions, the designer takes control, telling the reader what to read first on the format. This decisive communication method comes in handy for posters and advertisements, package design, and signage. **Contrasts** (230) in size, shape, typeface, color, and texture create these focal points.

Although economical in execution, Sara Cwynar's book cover isolates the title text amidst a textured background to effectively create a focal point. York University Department of Design, Canada.

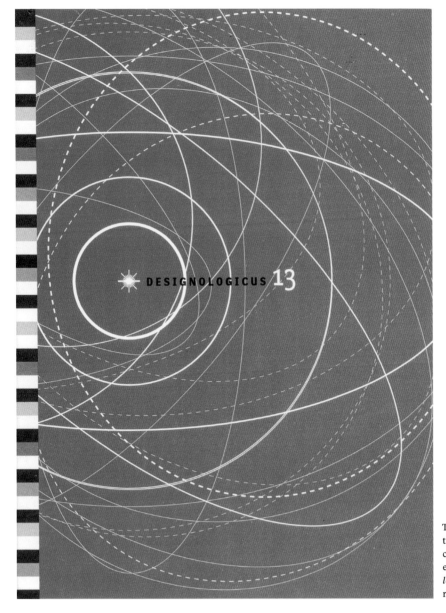

The straight line of black type serves as enough contrast against the circular elements in the *Designologicus* composition for readers to key in on the title.

This spread from
the book *Memories*
uses an extra-large
headline to announce
"Thanks." 2Creatives,
United Kingdom.

Center placement within a composition immediately grasps the reader's attention. Lure Design, United States.

Sometimes type works as a secondary visual component, as in this poster by MOD/Michael Osborne Design. Its flowery graphic element sits in the composition's center, offset by the smaller type headline in the lower-right corner. This composition would not have the same impact had the items been transposed, with the type large and the colorful graphic smaller.

Focal Point Enhancements

Other types of formal contrast that enhance focal point include, but are not limited to:

ACTIVE/STATIC
Anton Jeludkov's "Form Is Style" poster places hyperactive text on top of a static, solid color to help legibility. York University Department of Design, Canada.

GROUPING/SEPARATION
These colorful restaurant menus contain food dishes in separately boxed categories, but a friendly greeting sits isolated at the top to welcome patrons. AdamsMorioka, Inc., United States.

SEQUENCE/RANDOMNESS
As the letter *S* slowly disintegrates, new images appear on the reader's right, delivering the predicable and unpredictable. 2Creatives, United Kingdom.

FLAT/DEEP
Shayna Lauer's book cover places the title within a deep space setting, with the author's name sitting flatly and quietly as a line of white type. York University Department of Design, Canada.

ECONOMY/INTRICACY
Juxtaposing the linear titles amid a wash of ornamental and textured graphics and backgrounds helps maintain a sense of order for the reader to find and read each book's title. Jeff Domke, United States.

Large letters punch forth from an array of textures, radiations, and spatial illusions. In each case, the letterforms serve as the binding element that connects the graphics to the composition, gluing it all together logically. Anton Jeludkov, York University Department of Design, Canada.

Free Placement

If you ask several designers how they go about initiating the composition process of laying down an element or elements on a format, you'll likely receive a wealth of answers. This is especially true if you ask a cross-section of designers who work in a variety of media.

Most would likely say they begin by building a **grid** (220). Chances are, however, that some of them think image first, perhaps laying down the primary photograph or illustration upon which the rest of the typographic information delineates. Working in this manner can have its benefits, especially when a photograph or illustration has to be a primary element. But even when an all-typographic layout is necessary, freely positioning elements within the format can create exciting and dynamic compositions.

What this layout lacks in terms of gridded order it makes up for in the diagonal relationships created by the lines of type and collaged photographs. Kevin Paolozzi, York University Department of Design, Canada.

A mass of typography sits at the composition's top, intersecting the vertical image that demonstratively sits in the center. Kevin Paolozzi, York University Department of Design, Canada.

The Grid

Simply put, the grid is a tool that allows a designer to create compositions with some semblance of **unity** (224) and **variety** (224). Different grid structures already exist; designers can use these default settings imposed by software or create their own grid system using columns or modules. The number of modules, columns, and rows is not clearly or definitively set, but during a grid's creation, designers should consider at least these elements of the project:

- media
- format
- use
- image size
- typographic scope
- word count (or lack thereof)
- expandability

A traditional-looking and perfect-bound book could benefit from single left- and right-page columns to make text flow easily. With magazines, it's important to know where the gutter (the center margin) sits and how much the paper will creep toward the binding's center. And website grids often take on a flexible and dynamic nature, with their hierarchical structures allowing modules to morph in shape when viewed on screens of different sizes, for example, a large computer monitor or a phone's small screen.

Sara Cwynar's *Kitsch Encyclopedia* opens with large, heroic images filling the pages' single columns, as well as carrying over the entire spreads.

The bonus, full-color insert is a book within a book that uses its own grid structure. Sara Cwynar, York University Department of Design, Canada.

Later in the book, when headline and text content arrive, a two-column grid layout allows for more varied compositional play.

Teresa Yung designed these spreads from her book *Pills* with simple grid structure to bind imagery and text across each spread. This understated visual connection connotes a sense of sterility akin to the materials presented. Teresa Yung, York University Department of Design, Canada.

Anatomy of a Grid

The Cartesian grid system uses horizontal lines across an X-axis that intersects vertical lines on the Y-axis. These intersecting lines create individual modules that provide a framework in which designers can insert words and images. Each module becomes part of a larger system, such as columns and rows (for example, five modules makes up one column). That larger system becomes a tool—rather than a hindrance—for relating visual elements to each other. When used successfully, the tool can help designers achieve compositional unity and variety, as well as functionality.

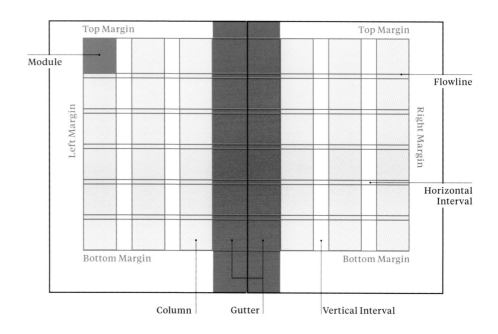

Grid Types

BOOK AND MANUSCRIPT GRID

Grids used for books and manuscripts typically have the fewest complexities, but constructing them takes time and forethought. Because books are usable, highly interactive pieces of design, proportional relationships should happen between the inside, outside, top, and bottom margins, such that readers can grasp the book's pages without obscuring the text they're reading.

Traditionally, book-length works have one text column per page and allow enough room at the top and bottom for page numbers, author name, and title. Giving readers enough room at the left and right sides to hold the book is also a functional measure to consider.

COLUMNAR GRID

Columnar grids can have any number of vertical divisions across the format, with as few as one per page. Though fewer flowlines (horizontal lines) across each page make columnar grids less flexible, the decision-making and layout processes become much easier for the designer. This example shows how the blocked tan-colored content could sit in a full-column length (I) or be broken into separate elements (II).

MODULAR GRID

A series of horizontally and vertically aligned modules create the structure on which text and image can reside.

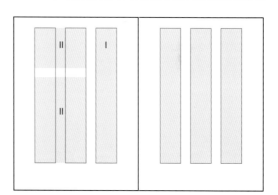

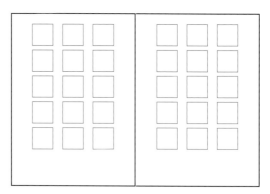

Hierarchy

Typographic hierarchy refers to the level of importance expressed by a piece of text in its environment, whether print-based or on screen. A variety of factors may indicate hierarchy: letterform size, letterform weight, letterform design characteristics, text color, text **contrast** (230) with the background, text position and orientation on the page or screen, and general mass.

These factors exist in relation to each other and also in relation to images, margin space, and space between lines on the page. For motion-based screen text, animation characteristics—how long the element is visible, how it moves into, off of, and around the screen—also affect hierarchy.

The viewers take cues from all of the above factors as they scan the text, making split-second decisions about what to read and in which order. Actually, "read" may not best describe what happens because viewers may actually be apprehending a variety of information at once rather than reading individual components. Indeed, as people become increasingly busy multitaskers, they make fewer hierarchically driven decisions about how much attention to divert to any single task. Designers must be cognizant of the scant amount of attention their designs may receive, making it increasingly important to create clear typographic hierarchy.

Each of these spreads from the *USC Law Viewbook* is an exemplar of the complex arrangement of hierarchical information. It is useful to observe how the format can be altered to suit the need of the subject matter, yet remain connected to the grid and typographic structure. Even though the pages include three typefaces—Adobe Caslon Pro, Century Expanded LT Std, and Avenir—a plethora of shifts in size, weight, case, slope, and tracking clearly direct the reader's attention to the text in order of its importance. The weight and size of the display type also serve as a kind of ballast for the pages, providing contrast and visual interest. AdamsMorioka, Inc., United States.

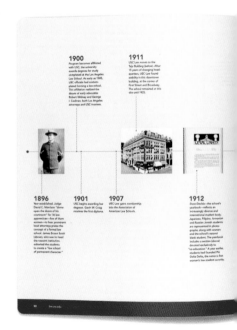

Hierarchy is especially important for environmental graphics, where the text guides the user through differing levels of information. In this The One Club Exhibition, the typeface Futura does the heavy lifting, announcing campaigns and catch phrases, among other text-based information. Varying the size demonstratively gives users enough visual cues from afar to pull them in. Design360, United States.

Unity and Variety

When differing elements on a format look like they belong together, designers call it unity. This togetherness across multiple documents, such as pages found in books or magazines or areas of a website, tells users that they are interacting with something whole and complete. Many designers use the term *Gestalt*—meaning an organized whole perceived as more than the sum of its parts—to explain unity in design compositions, whether printed, digital, or experiential. Repetition is one way to achieve unity through color, shape, size, placement, arrangement, order, or depth.

Typographic variety is one of the primary tools to create **hierarchy** (222) by varying, for example, the typeface's size, tone, color, texture, placement, weight, width, and position. Too much repetition isn't always necessary, and sometimes it can fragment a design's message or worse yet, frazzle the reader. Just enough variation between typographic elements can go a long way to differentiating levels of information at both large and small scales.

These three bottles for FdeC sherry each have different color contents and identification labels. However, the consistent visual treatment of the typography—in terms of size, weight, and placement—tells shoppers that the bottles come from the same product family. Design Bridge, United Kingdom.

As readers page through the Westminster School's *Vision* magazine, they encounter a range of weighted spreads that include photographic content, as well as all text. (These pages include the typefaces Akzidenz Grotesk, Garamond, and DIN.) One added feature in this design is the use of matte versus gloss inks, to give it a subtle but appreciative fourth level of variety. 2Creatives, United Kingdom.

THE DIRTY HOSTAGE

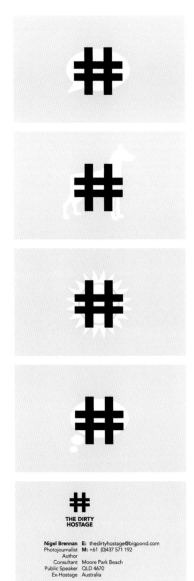

The Dirty Hostage Business card uses differing weights of Avenir typeface to identify the photo-journalist's name and contact information. Kevin Finn, Australia.

To convey a unified brand identity, Kevin Finn used a typographic and ruled system that ties together all of these business documents, despite each of their separate functions. From top to bottom: letterhead, invoice, label, business card. Globale Bold and Regular, Kevin Finn, Australia.

Symmetry and Asymmetry

Graphic designers can achieve balanced compositions through symmetrical or asymmetrical compositions. A symmetrical layout results when the left and right sides of a composition receive equal weight. This mirror-imaged layout often brings about less dynamic work than the contrasting option of asymmetry. An asymmetrical composition occurs when there is nothing similar between left and right. These tend to be less static than symmetrical work and less reliant on the center, where everything falls into a convenient and comfortable place. Neither compositional method is inherently better or worse; each is a tool to further a designer's intention, message, or concept.

A call-for-entries poster from the Australian Graphic Design Association situates centered lines of text that pull the reader down to the call to action, proving that a symmetrical layout can have purpose. Voice, Australia.

EAST EGG REALTY

This identity for East Egg Realty situates two opposing elephants on either side of an egg, denoting the harmonious, stable, reliable feeling that many of the realtor's clients hope to experience. Composing this with an asymmetrical, dynamic design would not give off the same sense of calmness. Spunk Design Machine, United States.

In its invitation for Sutherland Models, The White Room breaks up the format asymmetrically with a large photograph offset by a vertical headline that mirrors the statuesque model.

By placing the business card's typography off-axis, designer Kevin Finn not only creates a dynamic layout, but also uses each side of the divided card to separate contact information from name and title.

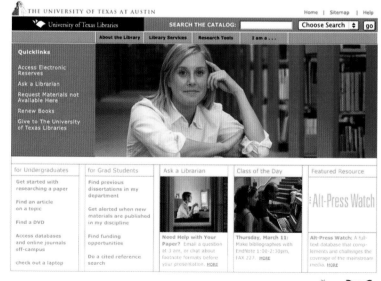

Matt Fangman's website for the University of Texas at Austin's library has distinct hierarchical levels of information, where typographic information and small photographs balance a large photograph above. This asymmetrical composition creates a sense of order and comfort for the viewer.

White Space

Designers call compositional areas that do not include text, image, or graphic elements white space or negative space. Some designers feel that using white space lends a degree of sophistication to layouts, in contrast to layouts with too many graphic elements.

Formally, white space allows the reader an opportunity to focus on the element or elements that demand the most attention. Conceptually, white space can further an underlying message the designer hopes to communicate to the viewer. Despite these issues, designers should use white space sparingly and functionally, as too much can make a composition look sterile.

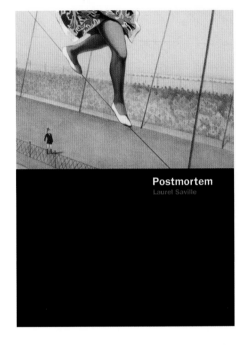

Postmortem
Laurel Saville

Although not technically white space, the black lower half of the *Postmortem* book cover interferes with the illustration to let flat typography (in Franklin Gothic) leap to the surface and identify both the title and author. This juxtaposition helps the reader zero in on the text, and the dark void doubles as a conceptual tool alluding to the book's content. AdamsMorioka, Inc., United States.

The "Faces" annual report for the Adris Group (done in Gotham Bold and Minion Pro) personifies the company with the jacket photographs, while the inside text layout calmly positions the past year's financial summary and future outlook amidst crisp areas of negative space. Bruketa&Žinić OM, Croatia.

The almost-blank lower-right side of this Crane Lettra swatch book compositionally balances out the more text-heavy left side (done in Trade Gothic). And the white strips of paper act as pull-tabs for designers and printers to tear and use during the specification process. MOD/Michael Osborne Design, United States.

THE PROOF IS ON THE PAGE

LET LETTRA TAKE A GREAT IMPRESSION FOR YOU

18

PAPER'S ROLE IS CHANGING IN THE VIRTUAL AGE. TELEPHONE BOOKS, ANNUAL REPORTS, AND A MYRIAD OF REFERENCE MATERIALS HAVE SPED TO THE WEB. YOU CAN PAY YOUR BILLS ON-LINE, LOOK UP ALMOST ANYTHING, CREATE ANIMATED E-CARDS, ALL IN CYBER-SECONDS.

ELECTRONIC MEDIA, MARVELOUS AS THEY ARE FOR SHARING INFORMATION, DO NOT DISPLACE THE APPEAL OF MATERIALS WE CAN HOLD. AT THE TACTILE END OF THE COMMUNICATION CONTINUUM, LETTERPRESS PRINTING IS ENJOYING A RENAISSANCE NOT ONLY OF POPULARITY BUT ALSO OF INGENUITY.

LET LETTRA DELIGHT YOUR EYE, INTRIGUE YOUR HAND, AND MASSAGE YOUR IMAGINATION.

FACING PAGE

FINAL PRESS PASS // LETTERPRESS (BLACK)
The black pass registers to the red and the blue. The image, and this demonstration on Lettra, are now complete. This fluffy, absorbent sheet, so soft to the touch, has shown itself to be a strong, silent type on press.

Federico Galindo's type-heavy book cover for *A Heartbreaking Work of Staggering Genius* has areas of repose, and these negative spaces on the cover, spine, and back side balance out the busy notes scrawled across the format. York University Department of Design, Canada.

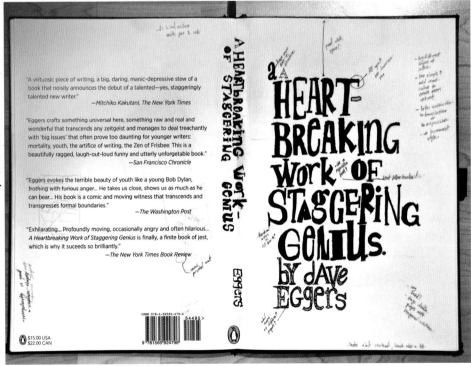

Contrast

Contrast is one of the best ways to create differentiation between graphic elements. With typography, contrasts in size, weight, width, color, position, and typeface are just some of the means to separate information or catch a viewer's glance. With typographic contrast, readers immediately see what matters most instead of being forced to read and make judgments on their own.

To create a new brand of premium rum for Banks Rum, Design Bridge paired sophisticated script type by Frederick Marns with the stability and stoicism of the typeface Gothic for the word "rum." The resulting typography works well together because of the noticeable differences between each letter treatment. Design Bridge, United Kingdom.

This wall at The One Club exhibition has a high level of contrast between the black typography on the white background, as well as the reversed typography on a black background. In both cases, the reader can easily read each line of copy. Design360, United States.

Setting information in italic white type contrasted against the black subject labels (in ITC Franklin Gothic and Bauer Bodoni) allows readers to quickly see which book is which when scanning the shelf. The White Room, Canada.

Despite the wealth of textures in each of Ralph Schraivogel's *Cinemafrica* posters, the letterforms are legible because their textures differ enough from the background elements.

A promotional card for the "Alphabetilately: An Alphabet of Philately" exhibition at the Smithsonian National Postal Museum positions a large and colorful typographic element at the composition's top in contrast with the black-and-white array of letters beneath it. MOD/Michael Osborne Design, United States.

Size, typeface, and weight all act as distinctly different pieces of typographic information to help the viewer discern between day of week, date, and month in this Mohawk Via paper calendar. AdamsMorioka, Inc., United States.

Typeface Pairing

Pairing typefaces should be more about **contrast** (230) than similarity. For example, using **Helvetica** (176) and Arial together in a composition does little to no good for the average viewer who won't notice the differences between the letterforms.

So how exactly do designers decide which typefaces work well together? Unfortunately, no prescription exists, no software can decide, and clients rarely offer creative suggestions. One of the most helpful tools is knowing of as many typefaces as possible. No matter the pairing, make sure the selected fonts honor the content, ensure **readability** (330), and speak to any conceptual undertones that need to come across.

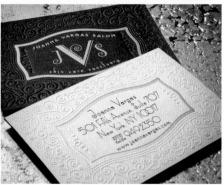

In these Joanna Vargas Salon identity elements, the modified and shadowed Sympathetique *V* between the *J* and *S* in the monogram elicits sophistication and highlights the proprietor's last name. DBD International, David Brier, United States.

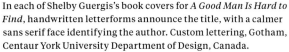

In each of Shelby Guergis's book covers for *A Good Man Is Hard to Find*, handwritten letterforms announce the title, with a calmer sans serif face identifying the author. Custom lettering, Gotham, Centaur York University Department of Design, Canada.

The Linneas Lights wordmark (in Burgues Script) looks delicate and classy on this business card, and the sans serif typography (Engravers' Gothic) calls out the business cardholder's name. Subtle changes in the serif typeface (Cordoba and Bodoni) used for the contact information also create different information levels. Eric Kass, United States.

Why pair just two typefaces when you can combine more than one flavor to deliver an array of looks and textures? Legacy Chocolate's identity sits at the mug's top (hand lettered and based on Bank Gothic), contrasted by a wealth of typographic identifiers such as "Connoisseur Grade" in Modesto, "Air-Roasted" in Serlio, and "Coffee" in QuigleyWiggly. DBD International, David Brier, United States.

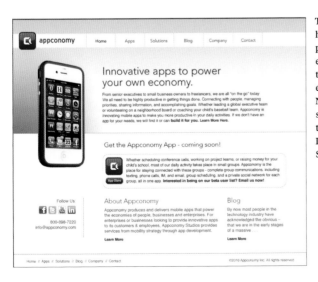

Designing this predominantly typographic poster required a combination of a sans serif (Trade Gothic), a serif (Engravers MT), and a wood typeface (Berkeley Oldstyle Book). Each typeface denotes a particular level of information, from the headline to the subhead down to the dates and events at the bottom. Tyler Blik (creative direction), Kaori Toda (design), Yuki Hayashi (design), Brian Pelayo (design), United States.

Thin, geometric headlines provide just enough oomph to headline each area of the Neo-Grosteque sans serif body text. Fangman Design, United States.

Contemporary Usage: Designing with Type

By Jason Tselentis, with Ina Saltz

"Obsessions make my life worse and my work better," custom typography, Sagmeister Inc., United States

A new generation of typographers continues to deliver fonts at an alarming pace. As a result, designers have a multiplicity from which to choose, and they take greater liberties with letterforms, modifying them often with abandon, yet sometimes with great care.

Technology has made type design—as well as type hybridization, layout, and destruction—accessible to almost anyone with a computer. Because graphic designers themselves understand the technologies and principles that type designers use, they sometimes envision themselves as potential type designers. On the fringes, a mass of type designers—in print and digital domains—has erupted around the world, many who consider their craft on par with typographers who slave over creating a single typeface.

So what makes a type designer? What makes a designer capable of desiging type? These questions have been hotly debated, and the fact that each dabbles in the other's trade further complicates matters.

Or perhaps this pluralism enlivens and expands an already-robust creative landscape. All of these disciplines continue to cross-pollinate, and despite the differences in perspective, practice, and style, one thing remains consistent: Anyone who designs type, designs with type, or hand letters type is involved in the world of type design.

For centuries, designers have used type for communicative, expressive, educational, and entertainment purposes. Contemporary designers continue those traditions, albeit through different approaches, technology, and aesthetics. Form may follow function. Type can become an image. No matter what, readers still seek out information and clarity, sometimes wanting merely visual entertainment, and in some cases, wanting a spectacle instead of a message.

In these pages are some examples of the inspirational ways that designers have used type as a primary means of design, an end unto itself: type as image, type as word, type as the ultimate communicator, form and function rolled into one.

"Wish You Were Here,"
Kelly Salchow MacArthur,
United States

Grand Prix,
Ralph Schraivogel,
Switzerland

Still from *Typophile 5* Studio DVA,
Brent Barson, United States

Posters

Black Point hand lettering, Voice, Australia

Florida Film
Festival done in
hand lettering and
with Kraftwerk
and Gill Sans,
Lure Design,
United States

The Appearance of Beauty with Helvetica in body text, Ralph Schraivogel, Switzerland

"Thinking Cap" poster in DIN 1451, Jennifer Beorkrem, United States

+81 cover in Univers, Meta, and Gridnik, 2Creatives, United Kingdom

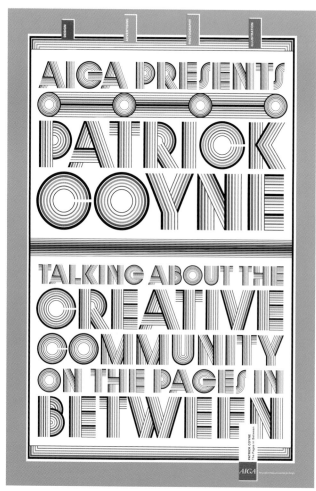

AIGA Charlotte Patrick Coyne Lecture in
Helvetica, Dazzle, A3 Design, United States

Soundvision triptych, Neil
Brown, United States

The words of his mouth were

smoother than butter,

but war was

in his

HEART

psalms 55:21

Vietnam heart
poster in Gill Sans,
MOD/Michael
Osborne Design,
United States

Black Angels
poster in
Knockout family,
Lure Design,
United States

Antalis Typography Poster, Eric Chan
Design Co. Ltd., Hong Kong

Dorkbot, Chalet New York 1960 + 1970, Jeff Domke, United States

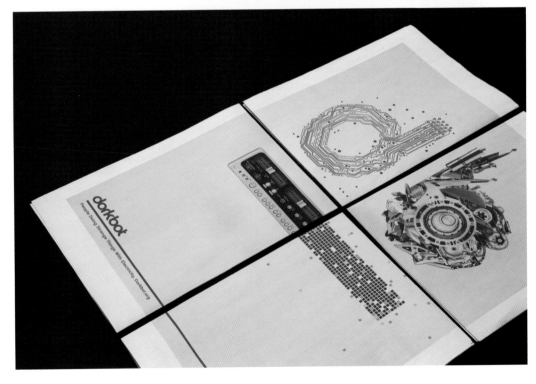

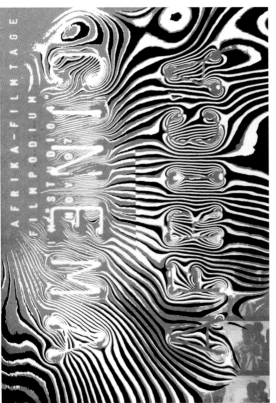

Cinemafrica posters, Ralph Schraivogel, Switzerland

Books

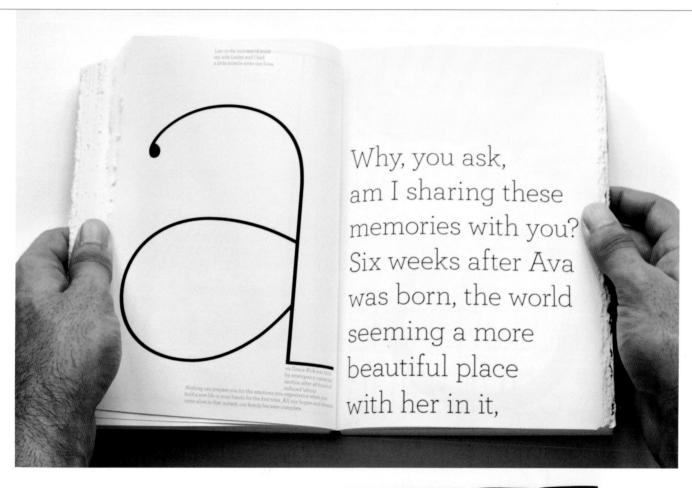

Memories in Trade Gothic bold condensed #20 and Archer, 2Creatives, United Kingdom

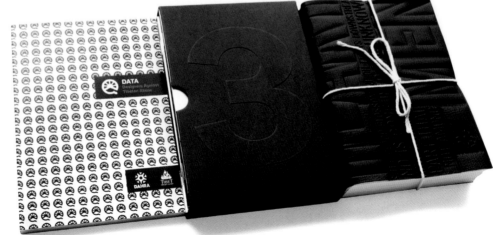

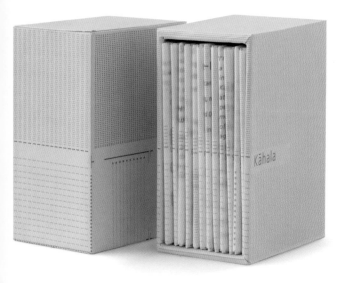

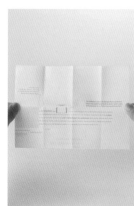

Kāhala as Place and Space in Frutiger, Hao In Kuan, United States

Polytrade Diary 2010, Eric Chan Design Co. Ltd., Hong Kong

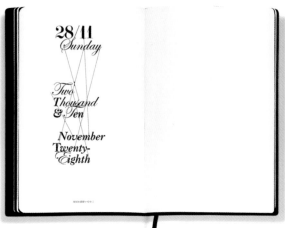

BMW book in Avant Garde and Baskerville, Expolab
advanced communication and design, Germany

*French General: Home Sewn:
30 Projects for Every Room
in the House* in Univers,
Grand Canyon, and Neutra,
Principle, United States

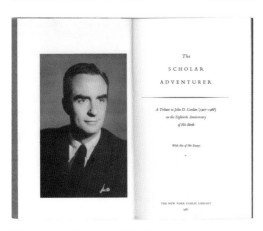

The Scholar Adventurer in Bembo,
AdamsMorioka, Inc., United States

Hamilton Press
booklet, David Harper,
United States

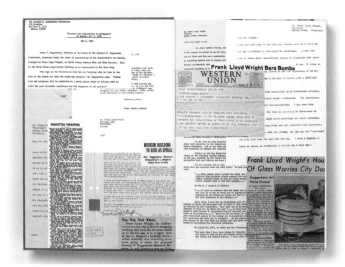

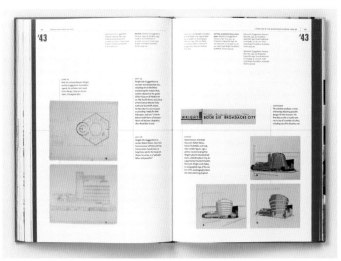

The Guggenheim in Verlag
and Nexus, Abbott Miller,
Pentagram, United States

Crane Lettra swatch book in Trade Gothic, MOD/Michael Osborne Design, United States

Grog War cover in Frutiger, Copperplate bold, and Swiss 721 BT bold condensed (for can label), Kevin Finn, Australia

The Fearless Baker: Scrumptious Cakes, Pies, Cobblers, Cookies, and Quick Breads that You Can Make to Impress Your Friends and Yourself in Pf Champion, Craw, CG Egiziano, Antique Central, Sentinel, Alternate Gothic, Century Expanded Lt Std, and Trade Gothic, AdamsMorioka, Inc., United States

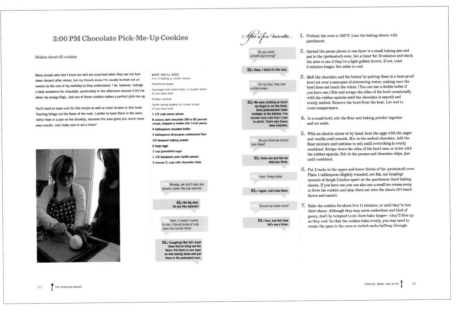

Future, Country in Gill Sans bold, Kevin Finn, Australia

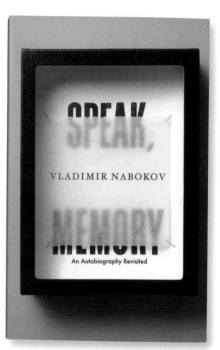

Speak, Memory in Garamond and Futura, Michael Bierut and Katie Barcelona, Pentagram, United States

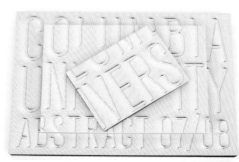

Columbia abstract book in Gravur, Sagmeister Inc., United States

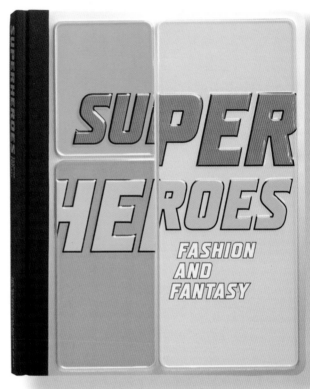

Superheroes in Teuton, Abbott
Miller, Pentagram, United States

Man Ray in Base Nine, The
White Room Inc., Canada

Publications/Magazines

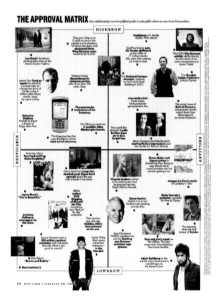

New York magazine in Elderkin, Miller, Franklin Gothic, Rockwell bold condensed, and Verlag, Luke Hayman, Pentagram, United States

The Guardian newspaper in Helvetica and Garamond, David Hillman, Pentagram, London

Khaleej Times newspaper in Freight and Retina, Luke Hayman and Paula Scher, Pentagram, United States

Step magazine cover in Didot, Adams-Morioka, Inc., United States

Circular 16, the magazine of the Typographic Circle in Courier, Domenic Lippa, Pentagram, London

Create magazine in Sauna and hand-drawn logotype, Adams-Morioka, Inc., United States

Collateral

Letterlab tattoos and T-shirts, Strange
Attractors Design, The Netherlands

Letterlab exhibition tickets and
promotion, Strange Attractors
Design, The Netherlands

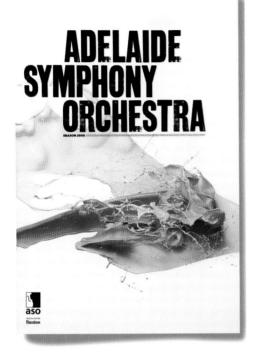
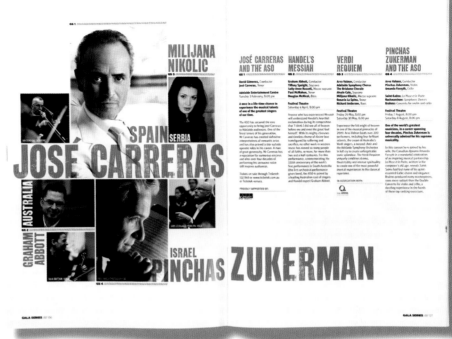

Adelaide Symphony Orchestra brochure, Voice, Australia

Family Service Power of Love fundraising invitation in customized typeface, MOD/Michael Osborne Design, United States

Think Creative brochures in Trade Gothic bold condensed and Trade Gothic bold condensed italic, Lure Design, United States

Tribeca Film Festival catalog in Gotham, Spunk Design Machine, United States

Document Solutions Collateral, in Interstate regular, Interstate right, Interstate bold, and Interstate light condensed, Fangman Design, United States

Ducati direct mailer in Univers, A3
Design, United States

ProTrader Securities direct mailer in News
Gothic light, News Gothic medium, and News
Gothic bold, Fangman Design, United States

Splice media labels in Alright Sans, Spunk
Design Machine, United States

Good Soles capabilities brochure in Copperplate
Gothic bold, Cotton and Crown, United States

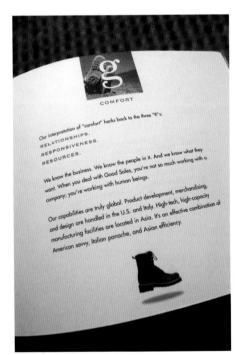

National Building Museum honor
award identity and collateral in
Mantinia, Neutra, and Acanthus,
Principle, United States

Emma Hack wallpaper design catalog in Liza, Poynter, and Verlag, Voice, Australia

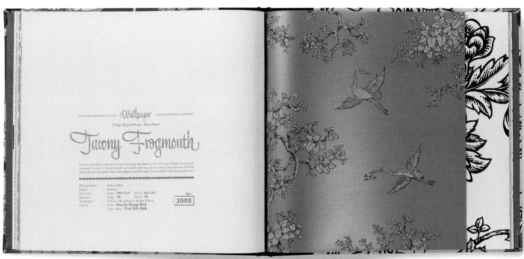

Lucky Shops VIP Party Invitation in Bodoni and Gotham, Jen Baker Brown, United States

Identity

The Oak Room, custom drawn, Michael Bierut and
Yve Ludwig, Pentagram, United States

Tecolote identity in Bullpen and Yearbook Solid, Tyler Blik (creative direction/design) Brian Pelayo (design), United States

John Bragg identity and stationery in Clarendon, Alternate Gothic No. 3, VAG Rounded, Berthold Bodoni Old Face, Embassy, and Antique Shaded, Eric Kass, United States

Naomi Finlay Photography identity in Gotham, The White Room Inc., Canada

Centigon Solutions business card, Chalet New York 1960 + 1970, Jeff Domke, United States

B1G

Big Ten Conference
collatoral, custom
drawn, Michael
Gericke, Pentagram,
United States

Cotton and Crown identity in Akzidenz Grotesk,
Cotton and Crown, United States

Splice logo in Alright Sans, Spunk Design
Machine, United States

Restoration Cleaners logo in Futura extra bold,
Fangman Design, United States

Wiremesh identity in Trade Gothic extended,
A3 Design, United States

appconomy

Appconomy logo in Interstate, Fangman
Design, United States

Adelaide identity, Voice, Australia

Every Youth has a Right to
Dignity, Humanity & Justice

Youth Justice Institute logo, MOD/Michael
Osborne Design, United States

Keito mark, Voice, Australia

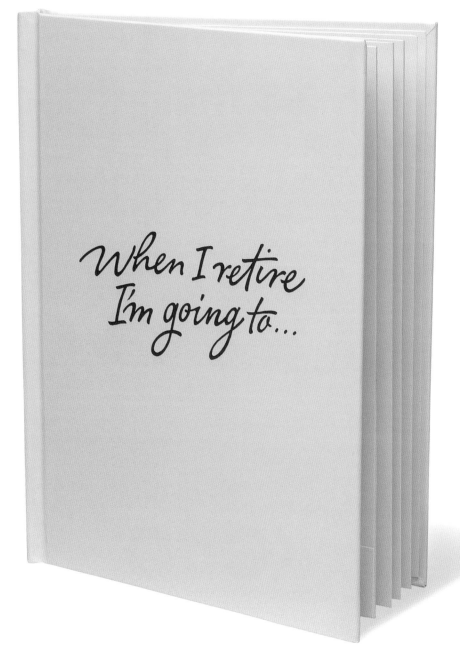

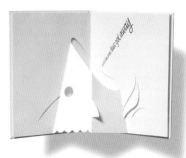

MAP Financial Strategies in hand
lettering, Voice, Australia

Adris Group "Good Ideas Glow in the Dark" annual report in Gotham bold and Minion Pro, Bruketa&Žinić OM, Croatia

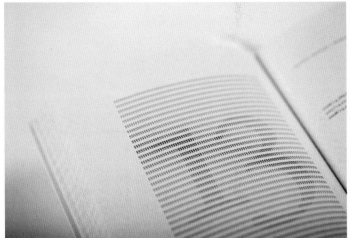

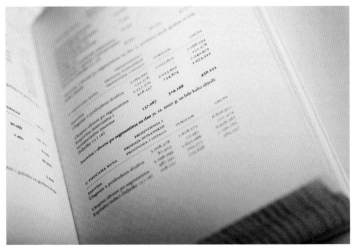

Bob Industries identity and stationery in Officina Sans, AdamsMorioka, Inc., United States

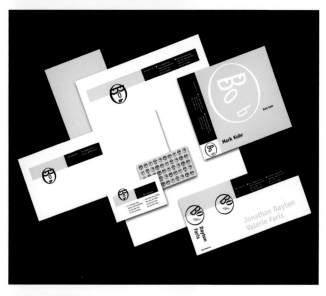

inVentiv Health 2009 annual report in News Gothic medium and bold, Jeff Domke, United States

P F AHL
CUSTOM BUILDERS

Pfahl identity and stationery in Futura, Cotton and Crown, United States

Eddie's Van for Hire communication system, hand-drawn wordmark loosely based on Home Run, Trade Gothic bold No. 2, Trade Gothic bold condensed No. 20, and Trade Gothic medium, Brian Pelayo, United States

The Bangle Business
identity, stationery,
invoices, and labels
in ITC Avant Garde
Gothic and Demi, Kevin
Finn, Australia

Spark House stationery in Clan
regular and extended, Spunk
Design Machine, United States

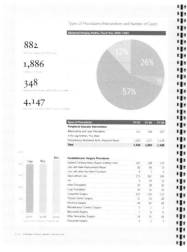

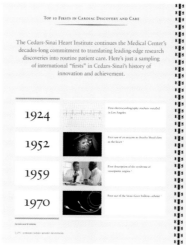
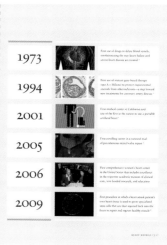

Cedars-Sinai Heart Institute in Franklin Gothic and
Sabon, AdamsMorioka, Inc., United States

Advertising/Promotion

...продукт ваших жеља

www.zitoproduktkg.com

Campaign for the Zitoprodukt bakery in Serbia, based on the
Bajka (Fairy Tale) Typeface, Dizjan Studio Box, Serbia

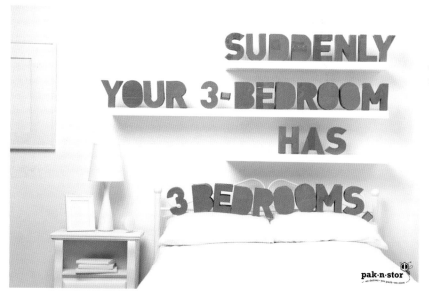

Calgary Paknstor ads in
DIN, Taxi, Canada

The Parks at Meadow View ads in Adobe Garamond, A3 Design, United States

Legacy Chocolates logo hand lettered and based on Bank Gothic, Kelmscott Roman, and Hoefler Text, DBD International, David Brier, United States

Caribou Coffee newspaper ad in hand lettering with Neutra Text Demi, Colle+McVoy, United States

Schell's Beer advertisements in Trade Gothic bold condensed, Colle+McVoy, United States

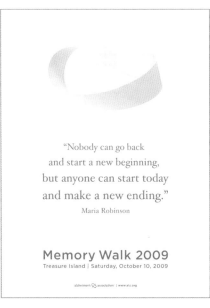

"Nobody can go back
and start a new beginning,
but anyone can start today
and make a new ending."
Maria Robinson

Memory Walk 2009
Treasure Island | Saturday, October 10, 2009

alzheimer's association: | www.alz.org

Walk on

Walk on

With hope
in your heart
—OSCAR HAMMERSTEIN III

MEMORY
WALK 2007
TREASURE ISLAND
SATURDAY, OCTOBER 6, 2007
❁❁❁❁WWW.ALZ.ORG❁❁❁❁

alzheimer's association®

A WALK TO REMEMBER

OCT
7TH
SATURDAY
9:30AM
2006

TREASURE
ISLAND
800-272-3900
www.alznorcal.org

alzheimer's association®

International
studies make it clear that
dementia occurs in every country of
the world. In the U.S., dementia affects
1 in 8 people over the age of 65 and nearly
1 in 2 over the age of 85. Worldwide there
are an estimated 30 million
people with dementia. By
2050, the number
will rise to over
100 million.

alzheimer's association®

Our destination is a world without Alzheimer's.

World Alzheimer's Day | September 21

Alzheimer's Association Memory
Walk banner, broadsides, and T-shirt
graphic in Gotham, Filosofia, Hoefler
Text, and Whitney, MOD/Michael
Osborne Design, United States

Gordon Brown general election campaign in Akkurat, 2Creatives, United Kingdom

Davis Co-Op brand identity
in DIN, Spunk Design
Machine, United States

Wrapping Paper

Label array in Trade Gothic, MOD/Michael Osborne Design, United States

Printed ephemera, MOD/Michael Osborne Design, United States

Typeface array, MOD/Michael Osborne Design, United States

Packaging

The Brown-Forman distillery's Jack Daniel's 160th birthday package and bottle in Chevalier, Gazette LH, and Engravers boldface LH, MOD/Michael Osborne Design, United States

Silverado Solo in Gotham and Adobe Jenson, MOD/Michael Osborne Design, United States

Black Label wine bottles in Helvetica Neue, Voice, Australia

Schell's Beer bottles and packaging in Trade Gothic bold condensed, Colle+McVoy, United States

Linneas Lights packaging in Burgues Script, Engravers' Gothic, Cordoba, and Bodoni, Eric Kass, United States

Wire Mesh packaging in Trade Gothic extended, A3 Design, United States

Bold for Men packaging in Helvetica bold, Bruketa&Žinić OM, Croatia

Williams-Sonoma soaps, bread mix,
drizzles, and pastes in Neutra, Mrs. Eaves,
Bodoni Old Face BQ, and Lucia, MOD/
Michael Osborne Design, United States

Legacy Chocolates packaging in Bank Gothic, Façade,
Modesto, Serlio, Kelmscott Roman, and Hoefler Text,
DBD International, David Brier, United States

Kettle Brand Potato Chips in Paragon and Typeka, MOD/Michael Osborne Design, United States

Wheaties box, Spunk Design Machine, United States

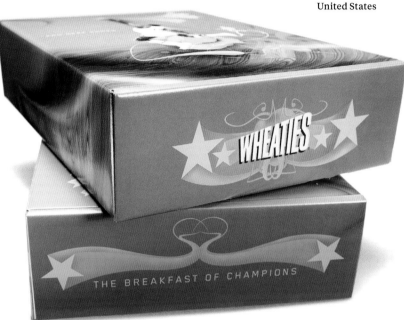

Love2Bake packaging in Clarendon LT light postscript Linotype AG, Clarendon LTRoman postscript Linotype AG, Clarendon LT bold postscript Linotype AG, and hand-drawn type by Frederick Marns, Design Bridge, United Kingdom

Botanical Bakery packaging in Concurso, Vogue, Pabst Oldstyle italic, and other custom typography for product names, DBD International, David Brier, United States

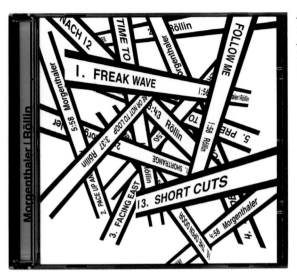

Aussen CD packaging in Akzidenz Grotesk, Ralph Schraivogel, Switzerland

Gwendolyn, The Brain Parade CD in Trade Gothic condensed No. 20, Lure Design, United States

DESIGNerd™ 100+ Trivia Games in Helvetica Neue, Kevin Finn, Steve Heller, and Stefan Sagmeister, Australia

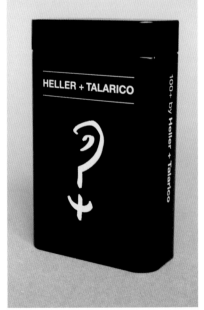

OFF ROAD

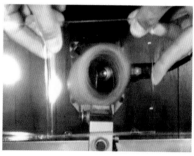

Off Road CD cover and process for machine-rendered *O*, Ralph Schraivogel, Switzerland

Lydia Lunch CD in Franklin Gothic condensed and Garamond 3, Lure Design, United States

Thinking Life billboard, custom typography, Sagmeister Inc., United States

POOL RULES

For the safety and enjoyment of all pool guests:

- Swimmers must shower before entering the water
- Swim suits or equivalent must be worn in the water
- Children under age 12 must be accompanied and supervised by an adult at all times
- Children under age 8 and under 4' in height must be accompanied by an adult in the water at all times
- Children requiring diapers must wear a swim diaper in the water

POOL RULES

The following are prohibited:

- Running, rough play, pushing or dunking of others
- Bikes, scooters, skates, skateboards
- Glass containers
- Masks, fins or snorkels during recreational swim
- Toys in the water, unless distributed by Beach House staff
- Flotation devices (except Coast Guard approved lifejackets)

Guests must abide by the decision of Beach House staff regarding the interpretation of any rules governing the use of this facility. Any behavior or activity determined by the staff to be unsafe, hazardous, inappropriate or a violation of the rules is prohibited.

MAXIMUM OCCUPANCY 113

WARNING: NO LIFEGUARD ON DUTY

Children under the age of 14 should not use pool without an adult in attendance.

NO DIVING ALLOWED

IN CASE OF EMERGENCY CALL 911

ARTIFICIAL RESPIRATION

1. Call 911
2. Tilt head, lift chin, check breathing
3. Give two breaths
4. Position hands on the center of chest
5. Firmly push down 2 inches on the chest 30 times
6. Continue with 2 breaths and 30 pumps until help arrives

Annenberg Community Beach House pool rules in Flama condensed and News Gothic, AdamsMorioka, Inc., United States

The Museum of Modern Art in MoMA Gothic, Paula Scher, Pentagram and Julia Hoffmann, MoMA's creative director for graphics and advertising, United States

Texas Children's Maternity Barricades in Gravur and DIN, Principle, United States

Letterlab Exhibition window signage, Strange Attractors Design, The Netherlands

Gough Street Festival posters, custom lettering from cloth, Eric Chan Design Co. Ltd., Hong Kong

Gordon Brown general election campaign in Akkurat, 2Creatives, United Kingdom

Signage/Wayfinding

New York University Department of Social
and Cultural Analysis, conference room
and detail of signage for each office in Trade
Gothic condensed, Design360, United States

Amway Center,
Orlando, Florida,
"Center" in
Trade Gothic,
RipBang Studios,
United States

News Corp Dow Jones in Helvetica,
Design360, United States

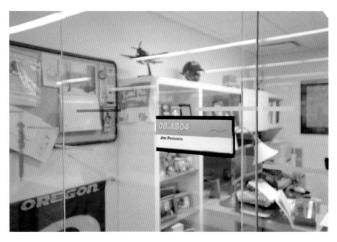

STAIR B
No Re-Entry
From This Stair
Except During
Fire Emergency

Snoqualmie Falls Interpretive Planning & Design signage in Adobe Garamond Pro and TheSans, Lehrman Cameron Studio (design/photography), United States

Ozone, Amway Center, Orlando, Florida, in Klavika, RipBang Studios, United States

Parking at 13-17 East 54th Street, New York, Verlag, Paula Scher, Pentagram, United States

Interiors and Environments

Bagby Office in Alternate Gothic, Trade Gothic, and Monterley, A3 Design, United States

S. I. Newhouse School of
Public Communications
Wall Mural in DIN, Poulin +
Morris Inc., United States

Oakland Museum of California Donor Wall in Benton Sans, Skidmore, Owings & Merrill LLP, United States Courtesy of SOM, ©Tim Griffith

Madison Square Garden Corporate Office Reception area in Tungsten, Poulin + Morris Inc., United States

Signage for "Alphabetilately" exhibit the Smithsonian National Postal Museum in Bodoni BT, Bodoni Old Face BQ, Avenir, and Gotham, MOD/Michael Osborne Design, United States

The One Club exhibition in Futura family, Design360, United States

Frank, Helms Workshop, Christian
Helms, United States

Queens Metropolitan Campus, hand drawn, Paula Scher, Pentagram, United States

Letterlab exhibition, Strange Attractors Design, The Netherlands

The Cooper Union in Foundry
Gridnik, Abbott Miller,
Pentagram, United States

Transportation

Connexxion buses, interiors, and uniforms in TheSans, TheMix, ITC Century, and Logotype based on Lesmore, Design Bridge, United Kingdom

Eddie's Van for Hire identity and van, hand-drawn wordmark loosely based on Home Run, Trade Gothic bold No. 2, Trade Gothic bold condensed No. 20, and Trade Gothic medium, Brian Pelayo, United States

VAN FOR HIRE

Motion

Letterlab exhibition commercial, Strange
Attractors Design, The Netherlands

"By the Force of Their Characters" in customized
Helvetica, David Harper, United States

Stills from *Typophile 5* video, Studio DVA Brent Barson, United States

"Veins of Life," David Harper, United States

Interactive

Gordon Brown general
election campaign in Akkurat,
2Creatives, United Kingdom

Rio Coffee website in customized Stealth and DIN, Voice, Australia

University of Texas Virtual Visitor Center website
in Tivoli Gothic regular, Tivoli Gothic bold, and
Helvetica, Fangman Design, United States

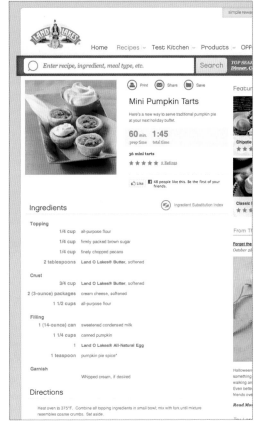

Land O'Lakes website in Chalet London
1960 + 1980, Colle+McVoy, United States

Kipps augmented reality in Gill
Sans, 2Creatives, United Kingdom

Website of architecture firm AVRP Studios in Perpetua
Small Caps & Old Figures and Perpetua regular, Tyler Blik
(creative direction), Brian Pelayo (design), United States

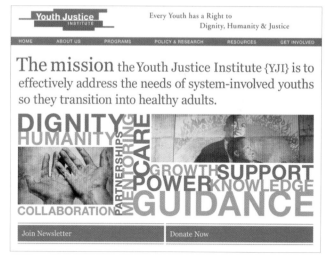

Youth Justice Institute, MOD/Michael
Osborne Design, United States

Typography Terminology and Language

By Tony Seddon, with Ina Saltz

Most professions develop their own terminology to facilitate communication of thoughts and ideas, and typography is no exception. It is important for all design practitioners to be well-versed in the language of type so they can communicate clearly with one another, especially with others who work with and design type or lettering.

Designers also often need to explain their creative choices to those who do not have an expertise in type, and being able to champion and explain their design choices is an important part of that process. Fluency in the language of typography indicates a knowledge of the field, an ability to educate clients, and a capacity to help others appreciate the work of a type designer.

For those reasons, here's a glossary of common typography terms and language.

A

Accent
See Diacritic

Adaptable fractions
Fractions made up of three separate characters, where the height of the diagonal equals the height of the numerals on either side. These are also known as built fractions. Some fonts contain adaptable fractions as glyphs, but these also can be created using a font's existing characters.

Alignment
The positioning of text within a text block, where the type lines up along an invisible axis, normally horizontal or vertical. Alignment can be flush left (all lines start at the same left-hand vertical axis, also referred to as left-justified or ragged right), flush right (all lines end at the same right-hand vertical axis, also called right-justified or ragged left), justified (aligned on left and right sides of the text block), centered (all lines have the same central vertical axis no matter their length) or **asymmetrical** (226) (free-form).

Alley
See Column gutter

Alphanumeric
A set of alphabetic characters or a run of text that consists of or uses numbers and letters.

Alternate characters
See Expert characters

Ampersand
The glyph representing the word "and," derived from the Latin word *et*.

Analphabetic forms
Characters that are part of an alphabet but do not appear in the alphabetical hierarchy, for example accents, the umlaut, or the asterisk.

Aperture
See Counter

Apex
The upper point at which the stems of a character meet to form a junction with an angle of less than ninety degrees, for example the top-most point of an **uppercase** (332) *A*. Apex points can be pointed, rounded, flat, or extended.

Arc
A curved stroke that extends from a straight stem but does not form a bowl; for example, the bottom of a **lowercase** (332) *j* or the top of a lowercase *f*.

Arm
A stroke that extends either horizontally from a vertical stroke or runs diagonally; for example, the top or bottom of an **uppercase** (332) *E* or the strokes of an uppercase *X*.

Ascender
The part of a **lowercase** (332) character that extends above the x-height of the other lowercase characters in a typeface; for example, the top of the lowercase *k, h,* and *d*.

Asymmetrical
See Alignment

B

Bad break
An incorrectly hyphenated word, a word break that does not make sense in terms of the structure of a sentence, or a line break that creates a widow or orphan. *See also* Widow; Orphan

Ball terminal
A circular termination at the end of an arm in characters such as lowercase (332) *a, c,* and *r*.

Base align
To align or position type on a common baseline across columns or pages.

Baseline
The invisible line on which the majority of characters in a typeface rest. A character's descender always dips below the baseline.

Baseline grid
An invisible **grid** (220) running across a page or spread based on a common baseline between separate blocks of text.

Beak
A sharp projection that most often appears at the end of the arc of a **lowercase** (332) *f*, as well as in the characters *c, j, r,* and y.

Bitmap font
A font made up of pixels set at a specific size that cannot be scaled up. Bitmap fonts work together with outline- or vector-based fonts, where the bitmap font produces the on-screen display of the outline font. Also commonly called screen fonts.

Blackletter
A typeface style based on early written forms that features elaborate thick-to-thin straight strokes and serifs, with narrow counterspaces and tight leading, thereby producing a heavy or "black" color on the page. The *Gutenberg Bible*, the first book ever printed with movable type, was set in a blackletter typeface to mimic the manuscript writing of the time. Blackletter, which has experienced a resurgence as a punk or Goth style of typeface, is also referred to as Old English.

Body size
The point size of a font. This originated from the height of the metal block on which a character sat in the days of hand composition.

Body text
Also referred to as body copy, body type, or **text type** (212), the paragraphs in a document that make up the bulk of its content. The body text should be set in a **legible** (330) style and size, typically between 8 and 12 points. All body text in any single document is commonly set in the same font and on the same leading.

Boldface
A font that has been drawn with a darker, thicker stroke such that it will stand out from the body text on a page. It shares common design characteristics with its "root" font but is heavier in appearance.

Bowl

The curved stroke enclosing the rounded or elliptical shape formed in characters such as *D*, *b*, and the top half of *g*. Bowls can be closed or open where the stroke does not meet with the stem completely, as in the **uppercase** (332) *P* of **Goudy** (163). Also sometimes referred to as an eye.

Bracketed serif

A serif transitioning from the stem of a character in one unbroken curve. The font **Century** (159), for example, has bracketed serifs.

Bullet

A dot or other character set to the left of listed items to show these as individual but related points that deserve particular attention.

C

Calligraphic

Roman or italic typefaces that appear hand-rendered with a flat-nibbed pen or brush. *See also* Uncial

Call out

A section of body copy pulled out from the main portion of text and emphasized using boldface or a larger point size.

Cap height

The height measured from the baseline to the top of **uppercase** (332) letters in a font. This may or may not equal the height of the ascenders. *See also* Ascender

Cedilla

An accent that appears primarily in French and is used to soften the letter *C*. It looks like this: Ç.

Centered

See Alignment

Character or character code

The word *character* is used differently in different contexts. Generally, it refers to a particular letterform or glyph. In the context of modern computing, it is often defined as a code with an attached meaning. In most operating systems today, 8-bit units of data known as a bytes represent character codes.

Cicero

A unit of measurement that expresses font size, used commonly in mainland Europe but not in the United Kingdom. A cicero equals 12 didot points and is slightly larger than a pica. *See also* Didot point

Color

The tonal value or visual weight of a block of text, expressed as a grayscale. Many factors influence typographic color, including letterform style, stroke width, weight, size, and leading of the text that makes up the text block.

Column gutter

The space between two columns of type. Also known as an alley.

Compressed

Typefaces that tend to be a little weightier than condensed fonts, better suiting them for use as display fonts than for body text. *See also* Condensed

Condensed

Narrow versions of characters designed to allow type to be set across a smaller measure. Correctly condensed fonts retain **readability** (330) despite a reduction in character width.

Counter

The space formed within characters such as *c*, *e*, and *g*. It can be open or closed. Do not confuse counters with bowls, which are strokes rather than areas.

Cross bar

The horizontal bar that connects two strokes in characters such as **uppercase** (332) *A* or *H*.

Cross stroke

The horizontal stroke that cuts across the stem of characters such as **lowercase** (332) *f* or *t*.

Crotch

The pointed spaced formed when an arm or an arc meets a stem, for example, in the inner top corner of an *E*. Crotches can be acute (less than ninety degrees) or obtuse (more than ninety degrees).

Curly quotes

See Typographer's quotes

D

Decorative

Decorative typefaces, also called ornamental, specialty, or novelty, do not fit easily into any other type classification. They can be highly stylized and may only have one weight or case. These typefaces are mainly used for display text such as titles or headlines, as they are not easily **legible** (330) at small sizes. Useful to evoke a particular subject, mood, or historical period. Rosewood is an example of a decorative font.

Descender

The part of a **lowercase** (332) character that extends below the baseline of the other lowercase characters in a typeface. For example the bottom portion of the lowercase *g*, *p*, and *y*.

Diacritic

A mark added to a character that gives it a specific phonetic value. For example, circumflex, acute and grave accents, cedilla, and umlaut. Often simply called accents.

Didot point

A unit of measurement that expresses font size, used commonly in mainland Europe but not in the United Kingdom. A didot point equals 0.0148 inches (0.0376 cm).

Dingbat

A typeface composed of decorative bullets, symbols, or illustrations. Zapf Dingbats is arguably the best-known example of a dingbat font. Dingbats are also called Pi Fonts and were known historically as printers' flowers.

Discretionary hyphen

A hyphen inserted into a word as a suggested point for division, should the need arise during text setting. This only appears in the text if the word is broken.

Display face

A slightly bolder version of a standard text font. More effective for use at larger sizes with headlines or signage.

Double-storey
A lowercase (332) *a* with a closed bowl and a stem with a finial arm above, or a lowercase *g* with a closed bowl and ear above a linked loop. For example, **Gill Sans** (175) features a double-storey *a* and *g*, while **Futura's** (174) are single-storey.

Drop cap
A character at the start of a paragraph. The letter is typically increased in size to a depth of two or more lines of body copy.

Dumb quotes
The term used to describe prime marks when used incorrectly as quotation marks or apostrophes instead of typographer's quotes. *See also* Typographer's quotes

Ear
The small projection that appears on some versions of lowercase (332) characters such as *g*. On the *g*, it typically sits on the top right side.

Egyptian
A typeface style that features slab or square serifs distinctly lacking in **contrast** (230) to the thickness of the stems. **Memphis** (188), named after the capital of ancient Egypt, is an example of an Egyptian style of typeface.

Em
A unit of measurement equal to the square of the font's point size. Traditionally the width of the font's widest letter, invariably the **uppercase** (332) *M*.

Em dash
A dash equal in width to one em for any given font. An em dash (—) indicates missing material or a break in a conversation or train of thought.

Em space
A nonbreaking space equal in width to one em, or the width of the font's point size. Also known historically as a mutton.

En
A unit of measurement equal to half the width of one em.

En dash
A dash equal in width to an en for any given font. An en dash (–) indicates a range of values, for example pages 8–24, and can sometimes be used in compound adjectives.

En space
A nonbreaking space equal in width to one en, or half the width of an em space. Also known historically as a nut.

Expanded
A typeface with characters made wider without adding weight, or thickness, to the stems.

Expert characters
A nonstandard letterform designed as part of a typeface but that may incorporate a swash, accent, or some other additional feature. Or it may simply be an alternative form of a standard character. Initially Type 1 Postscript expert sets were separated from standard weights in any given typeface and had to be installed separately. The advent of the OpenType format means all characters can now be incorporated into a single font file for each weight.

Extended
A typeface with characters expanded horizontally that retain their height.

Extenders
A common overarching name for ascenders and descenders. *See also* Ascender; Descender

Eye
See Bowl

F

Finial
A tapered, curved terminal at the end of a stroke, for example at the bottom of a *C*. Swashes and ornamental flourishes are also commonly called finials.

Flush left
See Alignment

Flush right
See Alignment

Font
All the characters, including numerals, punctuation, and symbols, for one typeface at one specific point size and weight. The terms "font" and "typeface" are often taken to have the same meaning, but there is a difference. This is best illustrated through the use of an example. Perpetua bold italic is a typeface; 10-point Perpetua bold italic is a font. *See also* Typeface

Font family
The collective point sizes, weights, and styles of one set of typefaces. A typical family contains at least four styles; the most common are roman, italic, bold, and bold italic. In practice, many families contain several additional styles such as light, demi, extra bold, heavy, and so on.

G

Geometric
A typeface style with characters designed around geometric shapes.

Glyph
The shape of each individual character in a font. Standard characters and symbols can both be called glyphs.

Gothic

A typeface style that in modern terms means something quite different from the **blackletter** (192) style popular in Gutenberg's time. Modern Gothic typefaces are sans serif with little **contrast** (230) between stems and other strokes and no ornamentation. The transposition of the name comes from the fact that modern gothics equal the bold presence of their predecessors. Gothic-style fonts often contain the word as part of their name, as in **Franklin Gothic** (172), **Trade Gothic** (180), and so on.

Greeking

The use of dummy text (often Latin) to indicate where real text will ultimately appear in a layout. It also can refer to the gray bars substituted for text too small to be displayed **legibly** (330) on a computer screen.

Grotesk

An alternative description for a sans serif typeface.

H

Hanging indent

Indented text that extends to the left of the rest of a paragraph's lines of text.

Hyphenation and justification

Often abbreviated to H&J, the settings that dictate the letter and word spacing across the measure of a line of justified text. Settings can be applied automatically or adjusted manually for lines that produce awkward spacing due to word lengths.

Hyphenation zone

The area at the end of a line of text within which it is acceptable to hyphenate a word.

I

Indent

A line of text set to a narrower measure than the full column width. Often indicates the beginning of a new paragraph in running text.

Initial cap

A large ornamental character at the beginning of a paragraph, usually more decorative than a simple drop cap.

Italic

A sloped version of a roman typeface always angled to the right and often used to indicate emphasis. A true italic has been completely redrawn with specific refinements in the design of the characters. The first italics, which date back to the beginning of the **sixteenth century** (10), were based on the handwriting style of the time. A true italic font never contains a double-storey **lowercase** (332) character.

J

Justified

See Alignment

K

Kerning

The adjustment of spacing between individual characters in a line of text. All page-layout software applies automatic kerning to text, but it is not always visually pleasing, especially at larger point sizes. Manual kerning improves the appearance and **legibility** (330) of text when the **white space** (228) between two characters appears visually awkward.

Kerning pairs

The pairs of characters in a font most likely to create visually displeasing typesetting, such as *Ty, Va,* or *YA*. A well-designed font contains embedded information that defines correct kerning for character pairings that need special attention.

L

Leading

The vertical distance, measured in points, from one baseline to the next in a body of text. Leading is also called **line spacing** (335) or line feed. The term originates from the days when typesetters inserted lead strips of varying thickness between lines of metal type to increase or decrease line spacing.

Legibility

The measure of how easy or difficult it is to distinguish one letter of a typeface from another. The responsibility for good **readability** (330) lies primarily with the typeface design rather than the typographic styling of a layout. Legible typefaces should not try too hard to draw attention to their design or style. *See also* Readability

Letter spacing

Not to be confused with **kerning** (334), letter spacing involves the average space between all characters in a block of text. *See also* Tracking

Ligature

A single character composed of two characters paired together in certain combinations that strongly depend on choice of typeface. The most common examples are *fi* and *fl*.

Line spacing

See Leading

Lining figures

See Old Style

Loop

A closed counter that extends below the baseline and connects to a bowl by a link. For example, a double-storey *g*.

Lowercase
The small letters of a typeface. Name derives from the fact that small letters were kept in the lower compartments of a type case when metal type was composed by hand. Historically, lowercase letters were known as minuscules.

Majuscule
See Uppercase

Minuscule
See Lowercase

Modern
A typeface style, developed in the **late eighteenth century** (10) and used throughout much of the **nineteenth century** (12), characterized by extreme **contrast** (230) between thick and thin strokes, as well as flat serifs. **Bodoni** (156) and Walbaum are classic examples of Modern style fonts.

Monospaced
A typeface in which all characters are allocated exactly the same width and so occupy equal space in a line of text.

Normal
See Roman

Oblique
A sloped version of a roman typeface in which the individual characters have not been radically redrawn. Do not confuse oblique with italic, in which a character often has different script qualities compared to its roman counterpart.

Old English
See Blackletter

Old Style
A typeface style based on early roman serif typefaces created between the late-fifteenth and **mid-eighteenth centuries** (10) generally characterized by low **contrast** (230) between thick and thin strokes and a left-leaning axis or stress. Serifs are almost always bracketed and head serifs are often angled. There are two groups of Old Style typefaces, Venetian and Garalde, which were influenced by the Renaissance and Baroque periods, respectively.

OpenType
A flexible new font format developed by **Adobe** (124) and Microsoft. Advantages over previous formats include its ability to include up to 65,536 glyphs in a single font, and the fact that because files are cross-platform, they can be installed on workstations running Mac OS and Windows.

Orphan or orphan line
At the end of a paragraph, a single word or line of text forced to the top of the next column or page.

Pica
A measurement equal to one-sixth of an inch (0.42 cm) or 12 points.

Point
A unit of measurement that expresses font size. A point equals 0.0139 inches (0.0353 cm).

Point size
The height of the body of a typeface. *See also* Body size

Prime marks
Mathematical symbols used to denote divisions. The most common typographical occurrence of prime marks indicate feet (') and inches (")—unless you count the incorrect use of prime marks in place of typographer's quotes or apostrophes.

Ragged left
See Alignment

Ragged right
See Alignment

Readability
Readability is the responsibility of the designer, not necessarily dependent on the **legibility** (330) of the chosen typeface. If reading a legible font proves difficult, it implies either an inappropriate font choice or a layout that does not utilize the font correctly. A well-designed font used badly in a layout will not display good characteristics of readability. *See also* Legibility

Regular
See Roman

Reverse type
Any occurrence of white characters printing on a dark background.

Roman
Type style that is upright rather than italicized or oblique and of a normal weight rather than light or bold. The roman weight of a typeface often gets dubbed as plain and is effectively the root style from which all other weights of a font family derive

S

Sans Serif
A typeface style that does not feature serifs (*sans* means "without" in French). The first sans serif typeface appeared shortly before 1900, but the Bauhaus design movement of the 1920s (20) first popularized the classification. Within sans serif fall four main classifications: Humanist (61), Grotesque (60), Geometric (62), and Square (63).

Screen font
See Bitmap font

Script
A typeface style that mirrors historical or modern handwriting styles. Typical scripts include connected or nearly connected flowing letterforms and slanted, rounded characters. Formal (64) script typefaces come from seventeenth-century writing styles and are generally neat, flowing, and regular in appearance. Casual (64) script typefaces may appear offbeat, playful, and look more like today's varied cursive and print handwriting styles. Calligraphic script typefaces mimic calligraphic handwriting and often appear written with a flat-tipped pen.

Serif
The small stroke that completes the arms, stems, tails, and descenders of characters in a serif typeface. Some groups of serif fonts include Transitional (55), Didone (56), and Clarendon (58).

Set solid
Type set without added leading between the lines. For example 10-point type on 10-point leading.

Set-width
The combined width of a character and the space that surrounds it. Tracking relies on the ability of page layout applications to tighten or loosen the set-widths around individual characters. *See also* Tracking

Single-storey
A lowercase (332) *a* with a closed bowl with no finial arm above or a lowercase *g* with a closed bowl, stem, and tail. For example, Futura (174) features a single-storey *a* and *g*.

Slab Serif
A serif font style that evolved from the Modern style, and became popular in the nineteenth century (12). Its serifs are large and square, generally bolder than serifs of previous typestyles with no bracketing. It is sometimes considered a subclassification of Modern.

Small caps
Uppercase (332) characters reduced to the same (or approximately the same) height as a typeface's x-height. True small caps are redrawn as a separate font and supplied as part of an expert set or as individual glyphs when using the OpenType format.

Smart quotes
See Typographer's quotes

Spur
The small projection that appears on some versions of characters such as uppercase (332) *S* or *G*.

Square serifs
See Slab serif

Stem
The main upright component of a character, such as the vertical strokes on either side of a capital *H*.

Stress
The horizontal, vertical, or diagonal emphasis suggested by a stroke.

Stroke
The main diagonal component of a character such as *N* or *Y*.

Subscript
Characters normally smaller than the point size of the body text and positioned on or slightly below the baseline.

Superscript
Characters normally smaller than the point size of the body text and positioned slightly above the cap height.

Swash
A flourish added to a standard character most commonly used in conjunction with italic typefaces. *See also* Finial

T

Tab stop
A horizontal marker set to indicate where the beginning of individual text lines should align.

Tail
The descending stroke on characters such as *Q* or *R*.

Terminal
See Finial

Thin
A space equivalent to one-fifth of an en space.

Tracking
The overall letter spacing (334) in any one line or full paragraph of text based on the characters' set width. A positive tracking value loosens the spacing between characters, while a negative value tightens spacing. Do not confuse this with kerning (334), which deals with spacing between individual pairs of characters. *See also* Letter spacing

Transitional
In the mid eighteenth century (10), Old Style typefaces evolved into the style known as Transitional largely because of improvements in printing techniques and paper quality. Primary characteristics are a medium contrast (230) between thick and thin strokes, less left-inclined stress than earlier Old Style faces, and a triangular or flat tip where diagonal strokes meet (such as at the base of a *W*).

TrueType
An outline font format first developed by Apple and later adopted by Microsoft. Its fonts are scalable and can therefore display on a computer screen and in print.

Type 1 Postscript font
A font format first developed by Adobe (124) that largely helped facilitate the Desktop Publishing Revolution. Individual fonts require two separate files to operate correctly, a screen font to allow accurate rendering on a computer screen, and a printer font for accurate rendering on a laser writer or other postscript-enabled device.

Typeface

A set of characters, independent of individual point size, but with common design characteristics such as width of strokes, use of serifs, and typographic classification. The terms "font" and "typeface" are often taken to have the same meaning, but there is a difference. This is best illustrated through the use of an example. Perpetua bold italic is a typeface; 10-point Perpetua bold italic is a font. *See also* Font

Typographer's quotes

The correct marks to use when typesetting quotation marks or apostrophes. These quotes resemble small raised 66s and 99s. The most common typographic error is arguably the incorrect use of prime marks (' and ") in place of typographer's quotes.

U

Uncial

A type style closely related to **calligraphic** (64) that combines elements of both **upper-** and **lowercase** (332) characters within a single typeface. *See also* Calligraphic

Uppercase

The capital letters of a typeface. Derives from the fact that capital letters were kept in the upper compartments of a type case when metal type was composed by hand. Historically, uppercase letters were known as majuscules.

Unbracketed serif

A serif that joins the stem of a character at a ninety-degree angle. Didot is a typeface featuring unbracketed serifs.

V

Vertex

The lower point at which the stems of a character meet to form a junction with an angle of less than ninety degrees, for example at the base of a capital *V*.

W

Wedge serif

A serif that transitions from the stem of a character at an angled slope without curves. **Adobe's** (124) versatile Warnock is an example of a font featuring wedge serifs.

Weight

The description, based on relative darkness, of various typefaces within a typeface family. Examples of type weights include light, roman or regular, book, demi or medium, heavy, extra bold, and black.

Widow or widow line

A single word or line of text at the beginning of a paragraph that appears at the bottom of a column or page.

Width

A term referring to whether a typeface has been either expanded or compressed. Examples of this typically include the word "condensed" or "extended" in a font's name.

Word spacing

Not to be confused with tracking, this is the space between words that can be adjusted without altering the standard **letter spacing** (334) across a line of type.

X

X-height

The height of a **lowercase** (332) *x. The x* is used to define this measurement because it has no ascenders or descenders and sits exactly on the baseline.

Anatomy of Type

What makes one typeface different from another? Many thousands of typefaces exist and in theory, they should all differ. Of course the differences are often extremely subtle and only distinguishable to a designer with an experienced eye. The details that provide a contrast (230) between one typeface or font and another are the visual characteristics of each glyph in the full character set. These characteristics center on the shape of the serifs, the angle of the strokes, the weight of the stems, the height and depth of the ascenders and descenders, and dozens of other small details.

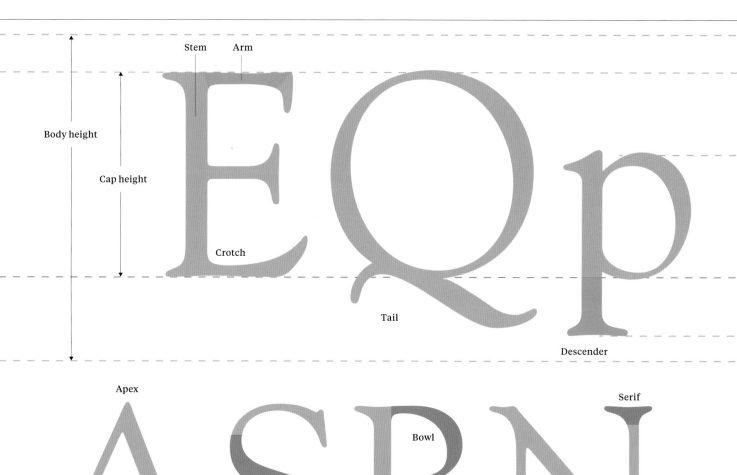

To talk with authority about the intricacies of type design, it is important to be familiar with the nomenclature applied to all the constituent parts of a letterform. The diagram here identifies the most important parts. Use it in conjunction with the glossary that appears on the preceding pages of this book.

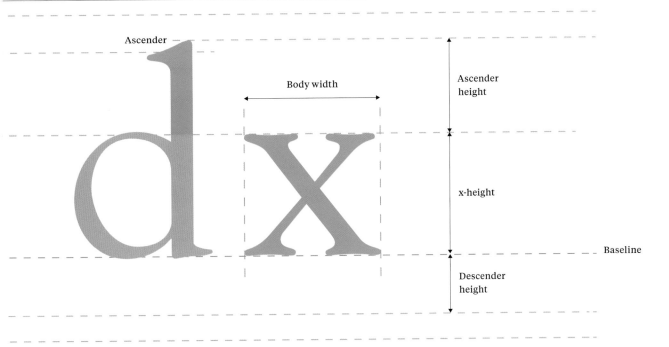

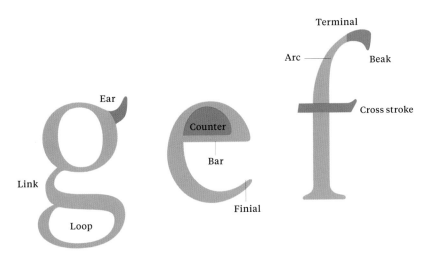

Legibility and Readability

Before we go any further it is important to point out that "legibility" and "readability" are not the same. Legibility is essentially the measure of how easy or difficult it is to distinguish one letter of a typeface from another. This makes it a typeface design issue rather than a typographic one, a subtle but important difference. Designers generally accept the technique that underpins the creation of legible typefaces: that they should not try too hard to draw attention to their design or style. A reader should see the words first and not get distracted by the typeface itself.

The most legible typefaces tend to have prominent features such as large x-height and large counters, along with individual character shapes clearly defined from one another and therefore easily recognizable. (X-height should not be too large, however, because too little **contrast** [230] between x-height and length of ascenders and descenders can compromise legibility.) For this reason—relative simplicity of character shapes—some argue that sans serif fonts are more legible than serif fonts.

It really depends on the individual typeface rather than the classification, and on the intended purpose of the typeface, whether for signage, display, text and so on. Weight plays an important part, too; ultra light or black/heavy faces are often not as legible as those with a roman or book weight, especially when set at smaller point sizes. Research has shown that the optimum stroke width for legibility is around 18 percent of the character's x-height.

It is also important to bear in mind that the vast majority of letters in running text are **lowercase** (332), so differences in lowercase character shapes and openness of counters have the greatest effect on legibility. Lowercase characters vary much more in shape between typefaces, not just because of proportions but also because of characters such as the double-storey *a* or *g*, which help distinguish those characters from the similarly shaped *o, e, q*, and so on.

In contrast to legibility, readability falls on the designer's shoulders and doesn't necessarily depend on typeface legibility. Reading should ideally take no additional effort beyond actually recognizing and comprehending what

A double-storey lowercase character such as an *a* or *g* helps to improve legibility between other similarly-proportioned characters.

Certain letterforms are more distinctive in serif typefaces. On the left, Garamond. On the right, Franklin Gothic.

Tiempos Text 24 point

Baskerville 24 point

Tiempos Text 24 point

Baskerville 32 point

How x-height effects legibility: Typefaces with large x-heights often appear larger set at the same size as typefaces with smaller x-heights.

the words say and mean. Once an individual has learned basic reading skills, the act of reading becomes a series of automated responses to the arrangement of the characters and words on the page or screen. It is up to the designer to make decisions that will create good readability.

It is not a given that a highly legible typeface will produce highly readable text. One of the more common mistakes made when selecting a typeface is choosing one designed for a purpose other than that which the designer has in mind. For example, typefaces designed specifically for signage will generally be highly legible, but this doesn't mean they work well as a text face. Take the time to find out about a typeface's origins and intended use, and experiment with dummy settings at various sizes to see how a face reads before making a committed choice.

Typeface choice aside, the combination of measure plus word-count-per-line is probably the dominant factor that affects readability.

A character count (including spaces) that falls somewhere between fifty-four and eighty per line of text tends to be the most satisfactory for readability. This range works for pretty much every typeface suitable for use as running text, with the typeface (and any restrictions imposed by the layout itself) influencing decisions about point size and measure.

Also, take into account subject matter of text when deciding how a measure will influence readability. For example, a long read such as a novel can support the use of a wider measure as the reader will relax into a "reading rhythm," allowing him or her to scan longer lines of text. In addition, longer measures allow **letter spacing** (334) to be set more evenly, further improving readability. On the flip side, text appearing in a reference book or newspaper benefits from being set over a shorter measure in a layout utilizing two or more columns for easy, quick scanning of bite-sized pieces of information.

A designer's job will become even more challenging as the quantity of information and noise increases during the twenty-first century. Those who possess a broad typographic understanding will best meet the communicative and creative challenge, especially during a time when people know the difference between one font and another—and which ones read better or worse with software's default 120-percent leading.

The short measure shown to the left is ideal for shorter sections of bite-sized information; it displays excellent readability properties and is perfect for newspapers or reference books. The longer measure below would work well in a novel, but readability is not as good over just four lines of text.

A designer's job will become even more challenging as the quantity of information and noise increases during the twenty-first century. Those who possess a broad typographic understanding will best meet the communicative and creative challenge, especially during a time when people know the difference between one font and another—and which ones read better or worse with software's default 120-percent leading.

Upper and Lowercase

Uppercase characters provide emphasis and stress importance, whether at the start of a sentence or when used in a headline. Caps are LOUDER than lowercase characters and can visually SHOUT to the reader. However, on the **readability** (330) front, uppercase text that extends beyond the length of the average headline is not as easy to scan, drastically reducing reading speed.

This is because a reader cannot recognize words set in uppercase as quickly; the word is read letter by letter rather than as a single image. This point does not apply to new readers, for example young children, but rather to seasoned readers who have learned to recognize word images in the same way a computer caches information. A word set in uppercase always appears as a rectangle with varying length depending on number of characters, while a mixture of upper- and lowercase gives every word its own unique shape. This ties in neatly with the notion that lowercase characters have the greater **legibility** (330).

Beyond this little snippet of typographic science, the use of upper- and lowercase characters simply comes down to style, limited only by a designer's skill and imagination.

Running text set in CAPS is harder to read because the shape of words set in lowercase appear as remembered word images to a seasoned reader. Words set in CAPS appear simply as rectangles.

A designer's job will become even more challenging as the quantity of information and noise increases during the twenty-first century. Those who possess a broad typographic understanding will best meet the communicative and creative challenge, especially during a time when people know the difference between one font and another—and which ones read

A DESIGNER'S JOB WILL BECOME EVEN MORE CHALLENGING AS THE QUANTITY OF INFORMATION AND NOISE INCREASES DURING THE TWENTY-FIRST CENTURY. THOSE WHO POSSESS A BROAD TYPOGRAPHIC UNDERSTANDING WILL BEST MEET THE COMMUNICATIVE AND CREATIVE CHALLENGE, ESPECIALLY DURING A TIME WHEN PEOPLE KNOW

"A designer's job will become even more challenging as the quantity of information...

Certain characters, such as the uppercase T appear slightly indented when positioned...

"A designer's job will become even more challenging as the quantity of information...

Certain characters, such as the uppercase T appear slightly indented when positioned...

Optical alignment allows certain characters that would otherwise appear as slightly indented to nudge into the margin, where they are referred to as "hung" characters.

Flush Left	Flush Right	Center
A designer's job will become even more challenging as the quantity of information and noise increases during the twenty-first century. Those who possess a broad typographic understanding will best meet the communicative and creative challenge, especially during a time when people know the difference between one font and another—and which ones read better or worse with software's default 120-percent leading.	A designer's job will become even more challenging as the quantity of information and noise increases during the twenty-first century. Those who possess a broad typographic understanding will best meet the communicative and creative challenge, especially during a time when people know the difference between one font and another—and which ones read better or worse with software's default 120-percent leading.	A designer's job will become even more challenging as the quantity of information and noise increases during the twenty-first century. Those who possess a broad typographic understanding will best meet the communicative and creative challenge, especially during a time when people know the difference between one font and another—and which ones read better or worse with software's default 120-percent leading.

Alignment

There are only four basic alignment choices—flush left, flush right, justified, and centered—and most people understand these terms regardless of their profession. However, good reasons exist for choosing one option over another, as well as for not mixing the options, all of which link back to **readability** (330) and aesthetics.

Flush-left text means a consistent vertical alignment down the left side of a column such that each new line of text starts from the same point. This helps improve readability. Flush-right text aligns at the right side of a column; this lessens readability for long passages of text, but can work for shorter paragraphs that range against the right side of an image or page edge in a layout. Beware of mixing flush-left and flush-right alignment in any given text chain. It never works and will ruin a professional layout.

Justified text, which aligns down both sides of a column, is better suited to text set over wider measures. To force the words in each line of text to justify, the word and **letter spacing** (334) gets adjusted across the full measure, occasionally introducing awkward spaces between longer words. It is sometimes possible to manually adjust the spacing to create aesthetically pleasing typography, but often editing the text results in the greatest improvement.

Centered text arguably provides the lowest level of readability, so it is best reserved for short, isolated paragraphs of text set over a fairly narrow column. Inappropriate use of centered text in a layout is a good indicator that a designer is not an experienced typographer. One of the most common mistakes is mixing centered headlines with flush-left text. On the other hand, a centered headline works with justified text as long as headline length and text measure balance well.

Optical alignment

Following from the basic points made above, aligning text along a vertical edge is not always as straightforward as it may seem. Certain characters, such as the **uppercase** (332) *T* or *W*, appear slightly indented when positioned at the start of a line. The same applies to punctuation, for example quotation marks. Adjusting these can achieve perfect optical alignment.

The offending characters must be "hung," meaning repositioned slightly to the left of the point of vertical alignment (if the text is flush left). The degree of adjustment varies from typeface to typeface and depends on the point size. The effect is less apparent at smaller point sizes, and the **kerning** (334) pairs built into a font deal with the problem in most circumstances. Page layout applications such as Adobe InDesign have built in functions such as optical margin alignment that get applied automatically.

Ave Aw Ay Ca Cl Ci Ey Ko Ky

Ma My Ov Ow Ox Oy Pa Pe Pi Pj Po Pr

Ra Re Ri Ro Ru Rw Ry n't i'l

Te Th Ti To Tr Ts Tu Tw Ty

Va Ve Vi Vo Wa We Wi Wo Wu Wy

Xa Xe Xi Xy Ya Ye Yi Yo Za Ze Zi Zo Zu

There are many kerning pairs that often require attention, especially when used at larger point sizes. Some may not seem familiar to you, but bear in mind that kerning pairs in your native language may differ from those commonly used in another language.

Letter spacing

This should effectively be invisible. The only spaces that should register in a reader's mind are those between words. The aim of kerning, the typographic term for letter spacing, is to achieve even visual spacing between all characters in all words of a text. No letter space should appear so large as to be mistaken for a word space or look larger than any of the neighboring spaces.

Type designers build into digital fonts what are called kerning pairs to alleviate the problem of unsightly letter spacing between pairs of characters that sit together awkwardly. The illustration below shows some of the more common problem-causing pairs. A well-designed typeface eliminates through the shape of its letterforms the need for an excessive number of kerning pairs, with the best letter spacing for optimum **readability** (330) between characters set automatically for any given font.

This auto-kerning works best for fonts within the 10- to 14-point range, known as the optimal size range. Type set below 10 point or above 14 point more likely will need some manual kerning. Point sizes below 10 may look like they are closing up and may need space added. Point sizes above 14 create the impression that the character spacing is too large, with the effect of increasing as point size increases.

Space can be added or subtracted uniformly for all lines of text in a layout by adjusting tracking, a facility built into Adobe InDesign, QuarkXPress, and other layout programs. Adjust kerning incrementally to achieve the best results, and watch out when ligatures (single characters composed of two characters paired together in certain combinations) are involved. If the kerning on either side of a ligature does not look right, choose between further kerning or replacing the ligatures with standard characters using the appropriate functionality of your design application.

Paragraphs and Line Spacing

An indent or a line space can indicate the start of a new paragraph. The width of the indent depends on designer preference and the measure being used. Narrow measures suit small indents, but wide measures likely require larger indents to be clearly visible. Although not compulsory, it is good practice to *not* indent the first line of a paragraph if it falls at the top of a new column in a multicolumn **grid** (220); the column break is enough to indicate the pause between paragraphs.

Make indents using the "first line indent" field in the Paragraph palette of your design application, or at the very least with a tab value, but never with typed spaces. If line spaces aim to separate paragraphs, indents are not required. It is usual to make the space between paragraphs a full line space equal to the value of the leading, enabling all lines of type to align to a baseline grid. Once again, this is not compulsory, and a baseline grid is not required. Line spaces can be judged visually. The decision to use indents or line spaces can derive from the nature of the text. A line space represents a bigger pause than an indent, so indents are best for flowing text and line spaces are more suited to text intended for reading in smaller, bite-sized chunks.

Another important consideration for paragraphs is the shape the line breaks form. Excessively jagged line endings look ugly, so it is best to eliminate them as much as possible by adding manual line breaks or editing the text to create a pleasing shape. Try this strategy: Attempt to set shorter lines at the start and end of a paragraph, with longer lines in the middle, giving each paragraph a curve outer shape at the right side.

Line spacing or leading is almost as important as measure and word count with regard to **readability** (330). A reader must be able to scan individual lines of text easily, moving his or her eyes from right to left to locate the beginning of each new line. Not enough leading makes this action difficult, particularly with a comparatively wide measure. Therefore, leading should theoretically increase for any given point size in relation to an increase in measure. There is no formula for this; it is a visual decision made in combination with other factors such as typeface and point size, but it does generally work. Take into account a typeface's x-height and length of ascenders and descenders, too. A face with a large x-height likely needs more leading than one with a small x-height, and short ascenders and descenders will less likely collide with adjacent lines if the leading is closed up.

There is a trend that exists among some designers to add leading to make text look more elegant. This can work in some circumstances but is not necessarily the best way to achieve stylish typography. Here's one rule of thumb to ensure that the leading does not generate **white space** (228) between lines: Leading wider than the word spaces of any given paragraph will decrease readability.

8.25 Tiempos text with appropriate letter, word and line sapcing

Looser word spacing and tighter line spacing (above), and a sample with looser letter spacing

Word spacing is too tight, line spacing too loose

A designer's job will become even more challenging as the quantity of information and noise increases during the twenty-first century. Those who possess a broad typographic understanding will best meet the communicative and creative challenge, especially during a time when people know the difference between one font and another—and which ones read better or worse with software's default 120-percent leading.

A designer's job will become even more challenging as the quantity of information and noise increases during the twenty-first century. Those who possess a broad typographic understanding will best meet

the communicative and creative challenge, especially during a time when people know the difference between one font and another—and which ones read better or worse with software's default 120-percent leading.

A designer's job will become even more challenging as the quantity of information and noise increases during the twenty-first century. Those who possess a broad typographic understanding will best meet the communicative and creative challenge, especially during a time when people know the difference between one font and another—and which ones read better or worse with software's default 120-percent leading.

Type
Management

By Ina Saltz, Jason Tselentis, and Tyler Alterman

Font management is a serious business for designers, especially with the number of digitally available typefaces soaring practically by the minute. Font management software is used for installing, uninstalling, activating, searching, comparing, and organizing fonts. Why do we need to manage fonts? Every active font in a system requires computing resources. Font management allows for activation of a font only when it's actually being used, which frees up computing resources so your system can function more efficiently.

While all computer platforms provide some basic form of font management, it is usually insufficient for professional designers, most who regularly use hundreds or thousands of fonts. Each font is composed of data, which take up storage space. Though fonts are typically not data-heavy files, the activation of many fonts simultaneously consumes processing and computing power and can significantly slow down efficiency and productivity.

For a single computer user, font management software greatly eases finding fonts and increases availability of computing power. In design, print, and publishing environments with multiple users linked into a network, administrators face additional font-management challenges that only a server-based font management can address. Administrators can control access rights across an entire work group from a centralized source, thus ensuring that members of the user group have the exact versions of fonts that they need and the appropriate permission to use the fonts without having to check and update each individual workstation.

In addition to technical reasons to use font-management software, it also allows the designer to organize and access fonts in an orderly fashion, like having tidy and logically arranged closets and storage areas. Besides peace of mind, good font organization helps designers focus their energies on the design process of the job at hand rather than getting bogged down sorting through a messy pile of fonts.

Although some designers (even some very well-known designers) profess to need only a few typefaces, most designers want and need a large selection (most of us can't get enough!), but we want to minimize the visual distraction of endless scrolling and increase our ability to locate what we need, when we need it. That's where good font management comes in. With a little investment of time up front, designers can save time when it matters—in the crunch of a deadline.

This chapter offers an overview of font-management tools to help any designer decide which features are most important and will work best for his or her font-management needs.

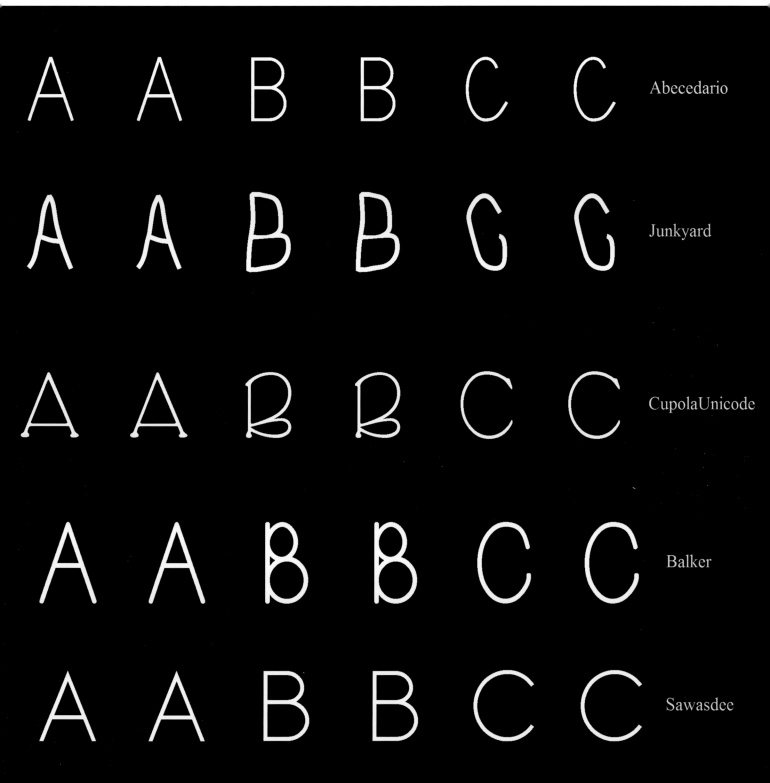

Abecedario

Junkyard

CupolaUnicode

Balker

Sawasdee

FontClustr by Ian Katz

Fontcase 2.0

www.bohemiancoding.com/fontcase

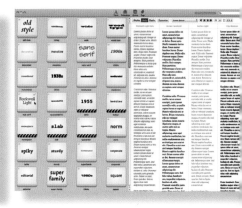

Fontcase provides an easy preview and iTunes-like user interface.

Fontcase is a relatively recent addition to the raft of font management solutions available, and it won an Apple design award in 2009 when it was dubbed "iTunes for your fonts" due to its elegant user interface. The UI has undergone a major overhaul for the 2011 release of v2.0 and retains one of the stand out features of this application—the ability to easily preview and compare your fonts as either display text, body text, or glyphs. It is also easy to select and compare fonts from different families and genres within the main application panel, saving you time spent previewing font choices in your page layout. If you work with websites, the brand new Typesetter panel is a winning addition as it allows you to view any website in a built-in browser and apply alternative font choices and sizes to see exactly how they will look online.

Another attractive feature is the way Fontcase uses metadata to organize your font collection by tag or genre. The application now integrates with Typedia, an online typography resource mentioned elsewhere in this book, to supply metadata information. You can also add your own metadata manually and create collections that are very useful if your workflow is project-based.

Other useful features include exportation of fonts as a single "vault" file, which can be shared with other members of a design team over a local network, automatic activation of fonts, duplicate font detection, and a very serviceable type specimen function for printed reference. For more information, go to www.bohemiancoding.com/fontcase.

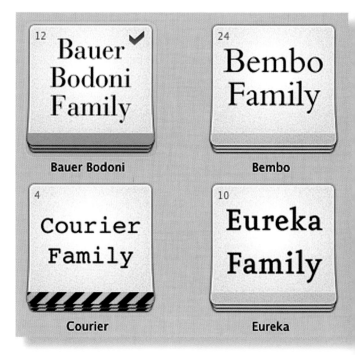

Compare fonts side by side.

FontExplorer X Pro

www.fontexplorerx.com/pro

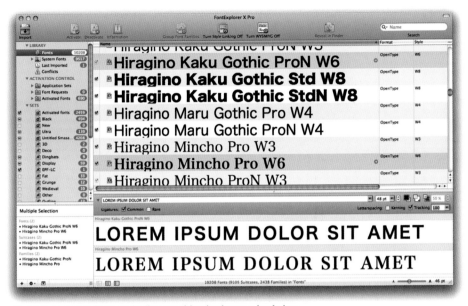

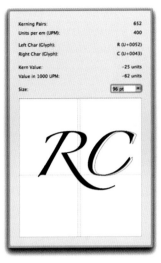

View kerning pairs
with this manager.

Quickly compare fonts and adjust tracking in the standard view.

Shop for type within the application
through Linotype's store.

This management solution from **Linotype** (129) leads the pack in striking a balance among usability, functionality, and aesthetic considerations. Not as pretty as **Fontcase** (338) or as feature-rich as some other managers, FontExplorer X Pro sports an intuitive interface with all of the most important basic functions quickly accessible.

FontExplorer also has some of the most useful preview options. The default preview pane allows for quickly examining **kerning** (334), viewing ligatures, and adjusting tracking, color, and opacity. For a more detailed glance, the app has a useful information overlay window. Here, unlike in other managers, **alignment** (333) and leading can be adjusted for running text previews and—best of all—you can examine kerning pairs.

For categorization purposes, FontExplorer's well-designed panel classifies fonts into usages, themes, and categories. The panel auto-classifies any font found in Linotype's catalog. A user can shop through this catalog right in the application, much like someone accesses the iTunes store in Apple's app. Finally, FontExplorer ships with built-in Spotlight support, so Apple users have the ability to quickly and easily search through their fonts. Another built-in feature is the font scanner that validates fonts to ensure proper functionality.

Extensis Suitcase

www.extensis.com

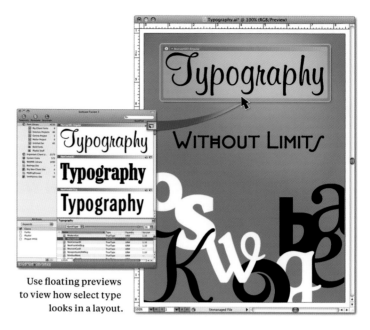

Use floating previews to view how select type looks in a layout.

Find visually similar fonts with QuickMatch.

With WebINK, preview Web headers like the one seen here in ITC Avant Garde.

Although one of the older font managers around, Extensis Suitcase 3 is the first to embrace the new age of Web typography. The newest version integrates with the site WebINK, which allows a user to look at any site rendered in fonts of his or her choice—without having to write code. Right inside Suitcase, test out WebINK's catalog of site-embeddable fonts, then pick ones to rent for website design.

Floating previews are another useful font-testing feature. By clicking an icon, a user can drag a text preview with a transparent background, for example, over to a layout in progress in Photoshop to see how it would look. Suitcase also has some of the best auto-activation capabilities due to Font Sense, a font-matching service useful when opening a document from a colleague that contains font substitution errors. For example, if one designer sends another a Photoshop document with Apple's version of **Helvetica** (176) and the designer on the receiving end only has the **Adobe** (124) version, Font Sense activates the right version of Helvetica accordingly to avoid nasty layout errors. Plus, Suitcase has a component called QuickMatch that finds visually similar type to any selected font.

FontAgent Pro

www.insidersoftware.com/FA_pro_osx.php

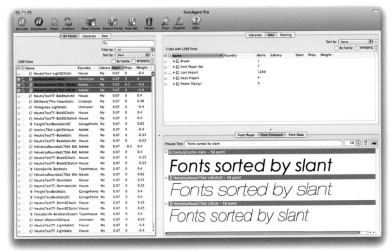

Sort fonts by slant, proportion, and weight attributes with FontAgent Pro

This app, which calls itself the world's smartest font "manager," does in fact have some pretty smart features, the smartest of which is the ability to sift through type by slant, proportion, and weight attributes all automatically detected by the software. Looking for an extra-compressed font to fit that narrow column? Sort by proportion to find the most condensed faces.

Equally useful for font filtering is the font classifier, which lets users browse and assign categories and styles such as Text Serif: Old Style preprogrammed into FontAgent. For additional organization options, Font Agent provides the standard set and smart set capabilities found in other management packages, but also allows for nested sets within sets. This is useful for grouping specific fonts, say 1970s (25) disco fonts, within broader ones, for example, period fonts, or for creating a poster project set within a larger branding project set.

Another unique perk is the Font Player. This component can "play" through a select set of fonts, allowing the user to mark those suitable for the project at hand. A final distinctive feature is Font-Agent Pro's ability to quickly print out a sheet comparing a selection of several fonts—a great plus because comparing fonts on a screen can sometimes be deceiving. And, as in other packages, FontAgent Pro allows users to share fonts over a local network and search for fonts to purchase.

Simpler Sorting

Alphabetically listing fonts helps designers who know the fonts by name, but sorting through a never-ending list can prove daunting. Just one of these fonts is serif. The rest are sans serif. Do you know which is the serif?

Baghdad
Bank Gothic
Barnhard MT Condensed
Baskerville
Baskerville Old Face
Batang
Bauhaus 93
Bell Centennial
Bell Gothic Std
Bell MT
Bembo
Big Caslon
Birth Std
Blackmoor LET
Blackoak Std
Blair
Bodoni
Book Antiqua
Bookman Old Style
Bookshelf
Bordeaux Roman
Bradley Hand

To find the handwritten font from the preceding list, users would need to sort through every font that comes before ITC's Bradley Hand. Only then would they see the handwritten font for which they were looking—and this all presupposes that they were using software that previews what the font looks like.

TypeDNA

www.typedna.com

TypeDNA, the newest font manager on the block, has debuted with a number of cutting-edge tools. Most compelling are its aut omated matching and filtering capabilities based in "sophisticated character analysis" technology. Here's how it works: Select any font and TypeDNA finds other similar options and others that harmonize. The latter function gives the user the ability to find compatible type by contrasting style within the given font family or for headline or body purposes.

Users also can activate SmartChoice, which compiles a list of headline, body, or mixed type from which to choose. Similarly interesting are the app's attribute filtering features that allow for font viewing by degrees of weight, width, slant, or optical size. Further, TypeDNA can filter fonts by serif or sans serif.

By combining an automatic selector with one of the aforementioned filters, users can browse through large libraries quickly and powerfully. The software's "card view" is useful for instantly comparing how large bodies of text would look rendering through different typefaces. The ability to go backward and forward through browsing history further enhances the browsing experience. Finally, TypeDNA has plug-ins for Adobe software, which can interact directly with text layout.

Using TypeDNA's sophisticated character analysis allows a user to harmonize headline type with Bembo regular body text.

Filtering fonts by "very heavy" and "very wide" attributes with TypeDNA

Type DNA integrates with Adobe software as an extension.

FontClustr

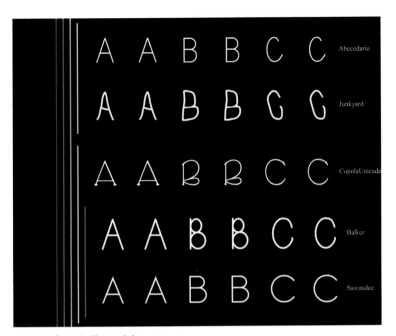

Viewing fonts by line weight

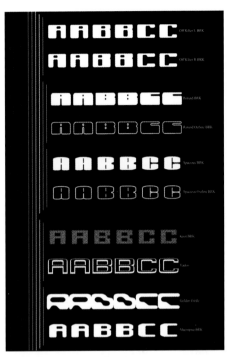

Various uncategorized styles

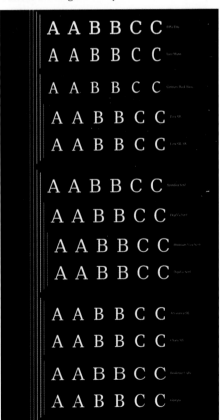

Viewing fonts by serifs

Customarily, computers display fonts through drop-down and fly-out menus built into software add-ons. External applications exist to help designers sort, enable, and disable fonts, but do not run on top of the program in which designers ultimately select, size, change, and edit the typography. Designer Ian Katz addressed that problem when he created the Font-Clustr sorting tool, which allows software to display fonts by formal properties instead of their alphabetical name.

FontClustr not only saves time with sorting and displaying, but it also aids designers by letting them see the visual style and group fonts into categories based on user preference instead of the standard—and often frustrating—alphabetical listing. Katz designed this tool to solve that exact problem: "FontClustr should be incorporated into font-selection tools to save time. It's customary to find fonts by name, but font names are meaningless. For example, serif fonts have names from A to Z—requiring you to cover the entire alphabet to decide which one you want even though only a fraction in my type library have serifs.

When we search for fonts, we are looking for shapes, and a good tool should allow us to drill down on the visual style we're after, not the name."

Type-Specific Resources

By Tony Seddon

Schools of Typography

Publications

Organizations

Conferences and Events

Films and Documentaries

Institutions and Collections

Online Resources

Bibliography

D ENTRIES FOR CAPITAL G

Newstype

SEARCH

Enter the query to search and hit ENTER.

CATEGORIES

Aetna
Aetna Condensed No. 1
Aldine Expanded
American Type Founders
American W.T. Co.
American Wood Type Mfg. Co.
Ampersand
Antique Double Outlined Shade
Antique Tuscan
Antique X Condensed
Antique XX Condensed
Arabian
Balloon Extra Bold
Berthold
Blackletter
Blair
border font
Broad-Stroke Cursive
Broadway Condensed
Brush
Calendar Set
capital A
capital B
capital C
capital D
capital E
capital F
capital G
capital H
capital I
capital J
capital K
capital L
capital M
capital N
capital O
capital P
capital Q
capital R
capital S
capital T
capital U
capital V
capital W
capital X
capital Y
capital Z
catchword
Chandler & Price Co.
Charles Tubbs
Clarendon
Clarendon Extended
Clarendon Extra Condensed Lightface
Cooper Black
Cooper Black Condensed
custom letterpress
De Vinne
die-cut type
Doric
eight
end grain
exclamation
five
Flash
foundry type
four
Free Stuff
French Clarendon
French Clarendon No. 2
French Clarendon XX Condensed
Futura Bold
Give Away
Gothic
Gothic Bold
Gothic Bold Condensed
Gothic Condensed Octagon Shade
Gothic Extended
Gothic No. 266
Gothic No. 4006
Gothic No. 5069
Gothic No. 81
Gothic Tuscan Condensed
Gothic Tuscan No. 3
Gothic X Condensed
Grecian Condensed
Hamilton Manufacturing Company
Hamilton Wood Type & Printing Museum
Howland
Index
Inland Type Foundry
Ionic
Jenson Old Style
Kabel
Keynote
Latin

Lydian Bold Condensed

LetterCult — CUSTOM LETTERS &c

LETTERSTREAM

INSPIRATION AND IMAGES collected from around the internet. If you know who created an image, or if you'd like to submit something, contact us.

SET 1

RECENT POSTS

ALPHABATTLE - Z
ALPHABATTLE - Y
BEST OF 2010 - CALL FOR SUBMISSIONS
ALPHABATTLE - X
ALPHABATTLE - W

TWITTER

[Best of 2010] is indeed coming! Next Friday or the following Monday. It'll be worth the wait. Thanks for your patience. /
days ago

[Artspotters] on the iPad? check out this Kickstarter project. key - h.k.it.MCRA/ / *days ago*

[AlphaBattle] Z is up. http://www.lettercult.com and/or/etc2111 after that? // *days ago*

follow us on Twitter

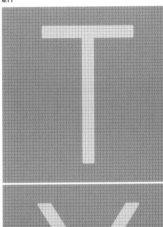

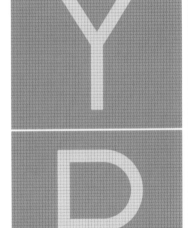

23 MARCH, 2010

Lettres à jour: public stencil lettering in France

Last edited 13 September 2010

Almost since my first visit to France I have been delighted by the look of the improvised public notices that are made with stencils, pochoirs, or (to use a more old-fashioned term) *lettres à jour* – letters pierced in metal that let the daylight show through them. Quite often the setting-out is irregular, even chaotic, but in France the roman letters are beautiful and formal. At their best, set out manually, one by one, they make notices that have authority but also a living quality.

Stencils were used in the 17th and 18th centuries in France and Germany to make the texts of big liturgical books. They were also used for marking playing cards. The first description of how the stencils themselves were made was written in the 1690s for the 'Description des Arts et Métiers' – the account of all trades that was prepared by a little group of specialists for the Academy of Sciences in Paris but most of which was not published at the time, leaving Diderot to carry out the idea in his *Encyclopédie*. In the 18th century you could buy your own alphabets, in plain but elegant roman letters or elaborate fancy script, or get labels or visiting cards cut to order. Some that Benjamin Franklin bought from a supplier called Bery in Paris are among his surviving possessions in Philadelphia.

Schools of Typography

It is very difficult to judge where to start (or end) when compiling a list of the best schools at which to study typography as a specialty or as part of a broader course of graphic subjects. Globally there are, of course, many good schools from which to choose. Some schools do have reputations that precede them and are undisputed as the cream of the crop, but that does not automatically make them optimal for everyone.

The study of any visual art is, by its nature, a personal journey that differs for every person who embarks on a career in the creative industries. Just ask a typographer for his favorite typeface and likely a different answer will come out every time. For this reason, here's the best advice this book can possibly give regarding schools: If you are looking for the right course to attend, spend as much time as possible researching as many schools as you can. For that matter, look at as many different geographical options as you can, too, drawing the line only at

schools in locations that present too many practical difficulties for you to attend. The influence of studying while immersed in a culture different from that to which you are accustomed can profoundly affect the way you approach your work.

The following list reflects schools that, at the time of this writing, offer specialist typographic courses or that contain a significant curricular element dedicated to the study of typography and type design. Wherever possible, we indicate specialty, but in all cases, we strongly recommend contacting any school of interest to ascertain whether it really is the best choice. Also, try to find out whether the school has an alumni group with graduates prepared to offer up opinions about how well the course worked for them.

The following list is organized alphabetically by country. Entries shown as a listing offer a course or courses during which typography is taught as part of a wider range of graphic design studies.

Argentina

Carrera de Diseño de Tipografía, Universidad de Buenos Aires, Buenos Aires
www.cdt-uba.org
The University of Buenos Aires runs a specialist course on type design through its department of design and typography. The course focuses on the cultural aspects of typography alongside practical tuition.

Belgium

De Koninklijke Academie voor Schone Kunsten, Antwerp
www.artesis.be
Typography is part of a wide range of graphic design studies.

La Cambre, École Nationale Supérieure des Arts Visuels, Brussels
www.lacambre.be
This school is regarded as the main Belgian location for the study of typography as a specialty. The course looks at a broad range of typographic applications including books, posters, signage, multimedia, and websites.

Chile

Information Design and Typographic UC, Santiago
www.det.cl
Information Design and Typographic UC (Diseño de Información & Estudios Tipográficos UC) runs a specialist typography course aimed at graduates who have already studied a related area of the visual arts. The course emphasizes the importance of typography as a central element of all graphic design and visual communication, and it promotes a wider typographic culture within the discipline of graphic design.

France

École Estienne, Paris
www.dsaatypo.info
This is the only French school offering a course focusing solely on type design, the DSAA Création Typographique. It is a municipal school so in theory free of tuition fees for full-time students, but verify this with the school based on individual circumstances. The school also offers general graphics courses closely related to the printing and publishing industries.

Germany

Hochschule für Grafik und Buchkunst (HGB), Leipzig
www.hgb-leipzig.de
The HGB is considered one of Germany's most exclusive design schools and runs bachelors and masters courses in typography and type design.

Italy

POLI.design, Consorzio del Politecnico, Milan
www.polidesign.net
This school runs a specialist and highly regarded advanced course in typeface design, taught by some of the foremost type designers working in Italy today. POLI.design, a consortium of departments within the Politecnico di Milano, prides itself on its particularly close links with industry.

Mexico

Centro de Estudios Gestalt, Veracruz
www.cegestalt.com
As well as typography modules within the graphic design and editorial design courses offered, students can study for a masters in typeface design at this college, regarded as one of the best places in Mexico to learn the subject.

The Netherlands

Royal Academy of Art, The Hague
www.kabk.nl
The Netherlands's Royal Academy of Art (Koninklijke Academie van Beeldende Kunsten) offers a full-time masters degree in type design and typography. The highly practical course requires students to work together in small groups, and the school maintains close relationships with industry. Students are encouraged to attend important conferences such as ATypI (Association Typographique Internationale) (354) and TYPO Berlin (358) as part of their study program.

Russia

British Higher School of Art and Design, Moscow
www.typoholic.ru/Type&Typography
A specialist practical course, "Type and Typography," aims at practicing designers who wish to raise their typographic skills to a new level. The scope of the course is wide-ranging and covers all the bases from typeface design and calligraphy to licensing. It approaches the topic from a global viewpoint rather than one that is strictly Russian.

Switzerland

Basel School of Design, Basel

www.basicsindesign.ch

This school runs a course dedicated to introducing the basic issues of typography and typography design. Typographic classification, **contrast** (230), and **hierarchy** (222) are studied in depth.

ECAL/University of Art and Design, Lausanne

www.ecal.ch

The University of Art and Design in Lausanne (École cantonale d'art de Lausanne), one of the world's most prestigious universities, offers a specialist typographic module within its master's degree in art direction. The course strongly focuses on emerging forms of editorial design, interactive media, and new technologies.

Zurich University of the Arts, Zurich

www.typetypo.ch

The Zurich University of the Arts (Zürcher Hochschule der Künste) offers a master's of advanced studies in type design and typography. The course is highly theoretical and experimental, with a great deal of practical content across all media forms. It offers a number of other specialist typography and type design courses on a part-time and evening-class basis.

United Kingdom

University of the Arts, London

www.arts.ac.uk

University of the Arts is the collective name for a conglomerate of five London colleges including the London College of Communication (formerly the London College of Printing), a school long regarded as a center of excellence for typographic study. It offers several bachelors- and masters-level courses with a strong emphasis on typography, including a masters of arts in contemporary graphic media, which focuses on the ambiguity and dynamism of visible language.

University of Plymouth, Plymouth

www.plymouth.ac.uk

Along with the **University of Reading** (see below), the University of Plymouth runs one of only two exclusively typographic degrees offered in the United Kingdom. The course, graphic communication with typography, places an emphasis on experimental exploration of the relationship between type and image and, of course, the achievement of typographic excellence. An extensive schedule of visiting lecturers and design practitioners supplements the course, which includes an international exchange program with schools throughout Europe.

University of Reading, Reading

www.reading.ac.uk

Reading's highly regarded masters of art in typeface design has produced many well-known type designers. The course includes a significant practical element and is split into three main components: practical typeface design, principles and applications, and a dissertation. Students design and produce their own original typeface as an integral part of the course, in the OpenType format and to commercial standards.

The University has a particularly good reputation for building strong relationships between students and industry, and maintains particularly close links with the St Bride Printing Library and Oxford University Press. It is also home to a number of outstanding typography and graphic communication works such as the national collection of archives of British publishing houses including The Bodley Head, Hogarth Press, Longman, Macmillan, Routledge, and Chatto & Windus.

United States

CalArts, California Institute of the Arts, Valencia, California
www.calarts.edu
Typography is part of a wide range of graphic design studies at CalArts.

The Cleveland Institute of Art (CIA), Cleveland
www.cia.edu
Typography is part of a wide range of graphic design studies at CIA.

The Cooper Union, New York
www.cooper.edu
The Cooper Union has a long-standing reputation for the teaching of typographic excellence, with alumni including such design greats as **Herb Lubalin** (95) and Milton Glaser. In conjuction with the **Type Director's Club** (355), the school recently introduced a postgraduate certificate in type design, Type@Cooper, the first of its kind offered in the United States. Visit www.coopertype.org for more information. This is truly a specialist typography and type design course, reflected by the fact that only those with an undergraduate qualification or professional experience are eligible. The school also incorporates the Herb Lubalin Study Center of Design and Typography.

Cranbrook Academy of Art, Bloomfield Hills, Michigan
www.cranbrookart.edu
Typography is part of a wide range of graphic design studies at Cranbrook.

Maryland Institute College of Art (MICA), Baltimore
www.mica.edu
Typography is part of a wide range of graphic design studies at MICA.

Montserrat College of Art, Beverly, Massachusetts
www.montserrat.edu
Montserrat College of Art offers an intensive course focusing on the fundamentals of typography and page layout. The school also provides in-house letterpress facilities for its students.

Parsons The New School for Design, New York
www.newschool.edu/parsons
Parsons offers a number of specialist typography courses, including an intensive program introducing students from other programs to the history, form, and use of typography. In addition there is typography studio, an advanced course aimed at students with an interest in developing more complex typographic projects.

Pratt Institute, School of Art & Design, New York
www.pratt.edu/academics/art_design
Typography is part of a wide range of graphic design studies at Pratt.

Rhode Island School of Design (RISD), Providence, Rhode Island
www.risd.edu
A specialist typography course open to graphics majors at RISD allows students to study letterforms, type design and classification, proportion, and **hierarchy** (222) to an advanced level. The course focuses on the details of page composition with particular emphasis on the relationship between space, **legibility** (330), and aesthetics.

Rochester Institute of Technology (RIT), Rochester, New York
www.rit.edu
Typography is part of a wide range of graphic design studies at RIT.

School of the Art Institute of Chicago, Chicago
www.saic.edu
Typography is part of a wide range of graphic design studies.

School of Visual Arts (SVA), New York
www.schoolofvisualarts.edu
Typography is part of a wide range of graphic design studies at SVA.

Yale University School of Art
www.art.yale.edu
Typography is part of a wide range of graphic design studies at the Yale University School of Art.

Type-Specific Publications

Many long-established magazines dedicated to graphic design subjects, and particularly to discussions about typography, have established good quality online portals in support of their printed product. Some sites act principally as marketing tools for their magazine, while others feature unique information threads that build on the printed content of each issue.

8 Faces

www.8faces.com

8 Faces is only at issue two at the time of this writing, but has already caused quite a stir in the design community. Its first issue, limited to 1,000 copies available by subscription through the website, sold out in less than two hours. The magazine is a biannual publication, printed on heavy stock with a foil-blocked cover, and will continue to be produced in limited print runs for future issues.

The premise for each issue is simple: Eight leading designers answer the question, "If you only had eight typefaces to use for the rest of your life, which would you choose?" Those who miss out on the printed edition can purchase the magazine online as a PDF download.

Codex: The Journal of Typography

www.codexmag.com

At the time of writing, this magazine has just published its first edition, and its pedigree indicates that it should be something to look forward to. The man behind ilovetypography.com, John Boardley, edits it, and it will publish quarterly and feature articles about type history and design, type reviews, essays, and interviews.

Computer Arts Projects

www.computerarts.co.uk

A spin-off of the successful United Kingdom–based monthly magazine *Computer Arts*, this is not strictly a specialist typography magazine. However, the concept behind *Computer Arts Projects* is that each month, the full magazine works around a specific theme, and periodically that theme is typography. Each edition includes relevant step-by-step tutorials and professional tips alongside profiles of key industry players and in-depth editorial features based around the monthly topic. Each issue also comes with a disk full of additional tutorials and resources exclusive to the magazine.

Creative Review

www.creativereview.co.uk

Like *Computer Arts Projects* (350), *Creative Review* includes topics covering all aspects of graphic design, but a large percentage of the articles cover type-related issues. Established in London in 1980 but with a global circulation, the print magazine is recognized as an authoritative barometer of what is happening in the world of graphics and typography. Furthermore, its extensive website features subject-driven tabs that filter all type-specific articles, although only subscribers can access much of the online content.

This cover shows detail from Roger Excoffon's original artwork for his Fonderie Olive typeface Calypso. See "Mr Mistral" by Sébastien Morlighem, *Eye* issue 79, volume 20, Spring 2011, pp. 76–83. Simon Esterson (*Eye* art director), Jay Prynne (art director), John L.Walters (editor).

Eye Magazine

www.eyemagazine.com

London-based *Eye* magazine is a quarterly graphic design journal with issues themed around specific design topics, including typography. The design standards and quality of the writing are extremely high, with a raft of knowledgeable industry commentators. It's a must read for professional designers, students, and indeed anyone with an interest in graphic design and visual culture. Subscriptions are available worldwide and collectors covet the back issues.

HOW Magazine

www.howdesign.com

HOW magazine covers all the bases with regard to its content, not just typography, but each of the six issues per year contains type-specific articles. There are occasionally special, combined, or expanded issues, and subscribers get a lot for their money.

Founded in 1985 and published by Cincinnati, Ohio–based F&W Publications, the magazine's goal is to give designers advice about how to be more creative, manage their workload and business, improve software skills, and so on. Profiles of influential and successful design professionals also make up a key portion of the magazine's content. The brand now extends beyond the print magazine through its program of annual events and conferences, its design competitions, and its book-publishing arm. Plus its website, which acts as a portal for the range of *HOW* activities, is also information-packed and a useful bookmark.

IdN

www.idnworld.com/mags

IdN magazine, with its six annual print issues, is just one product from this large collective of international designers. The designers' range of activities, reflected in the cutting edge and eclectic mix of content in the magazine, is difficult to pin down in one paragraph, so the best advice here is to look at the wealth of material showcased on the *IdN* website. This is another design publication that covers far more than simply typography, but issues periodically feature type-specific articles about the latest trends.

.net magazine

www.netmagazine.com

Good typography online is just as important as it is for print these days, especially now that technological advances make restrictions of the early Web design days a thing of the past. This magazine is the world's best-selling magazine for Web designers and developers and regularly features expert advice and step-by-step tutorials about typographic subjects. Anyone serious about Web design involving a lot of type should look at this magazine.

Print Magazine

www.printmag.com

Print Magazine, in circulation since 1940, is dedicated to showcasing the best work from the world of design. The bimonthly magazine has transcended its original title in that it is no longer restricted to that particular medium. It's another example of a magazine not specifically about typography but with regular content that focuses on type and the way today's designers use it. It's been the recipient of many publishing awards. *Print*'s online portal is also excellent, reflecting the high journalistic values of the magazine itself.

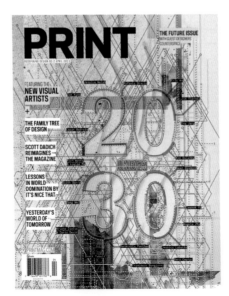

Smashing Magazine

www.smashingmagazine.com

Smashing Magazine is an online resource that aims to provide useful and innovative information for Web designers and developers in particular, although a brief trawl around the site reveals content useful for just about anyone involved in the graphic design industry. Founded in 2006 and put together by the team at Smashing Media, the magazine features articles from a large group of contributors who are independent—that is, likely to present unbiased views on current technology. A useful tagging system filters by subject, with typography listed as one of several main categories.

Typo

www.typo.cz/en

Based in the Czech Republic and set in both Czech and English, *Typo* is a quarterly print magazine devoted mainly to typography-related content. The audience is primarily professional typographers and font designers, but graphic design students and educators also find much to enjoy and inform in this publication.

It covers major events in the global graphic design calendar alongside articles about information graphics, showcases of up-and-coming designers' work, interviews with prominent figures from the world of typography, and reviews of important new font releases. Taking the view that typography and design are major components of overall culture, the magazine also publishes articles about architecture, photography, and even philosophy.

Unzipped

www.fontshop.be

Unzipped is the blog of the well-known type vendor FontShop (127; 140) and is therefore dedicated exclusively to type and typography. This is a great destination to check for announcements about new font releases and developments in Web fonts, which are revolutionizing the way readers view online typography. A visit to the site for a browse through the content reveals a wealth of informative articles on just about everything typographic. Even though it is linked to FontShop, it doesn't feel overly like a marketplace for the company.

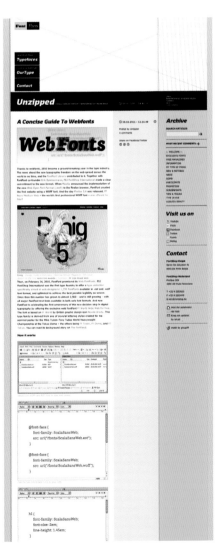

Voice: AIGA Journal of Design

www.journal.aiga.org

Voice is an exclusively online publication that acts as the AIGA's (354) discussion board for all things design, including interviews, essays, and criticism. The site encourages respectful comments from readers to expand on the subjects covered in the articles. With Steven Heller as editor and a raft of contributors drawn from the AIGA membership, the quality of the subject matter and writing is consistently high. Of course, the publication covers a wide range of design-related subjects, but a quick search for "typography" reveals dozens of articles with type-specific content.

Type-Specific Organizations

It is rare for any industry to operate without a supportive network of professional bodies and organizations, and the graphic design industry is no exception. There are numerous small organizations that work at a local level, but here we've listed the main players, some of which operate internationally.

American Institute of Graphic Arts (AIGA)

www.aiga.org

The AIGA, the professional association for design in the United States, was founded in 1914, making it the oldest and largest professional membership organization for designers. It aims to demonstrate and raise the value of design, to stimulate the way designers think about their work, and to help empower its members toward new challenges and successes at each stage of their careers. To quote from the AIGA website, "AIGA's mission is to advance designing as a professional craft, strategic tool, and vital cultural force."

This does not just extend to its members within the design profession, as the AIGA works hard to promote those important values to businesses and the general public as a whole. The association represents more than 20,000 design professionals, educators, and students, and it holds regular conferences, networking events, competitions, and exhibitions, many of which its numerous individual chapters and student groups organize. The excellent website offers information about membership, plus a wealth of additional content.

Association Typographique Internationale (ATypI)

www.atypi.org

ATypI is a global forum for designers, typographers, and anyone working in any profession that involves type. Founded in 1957, the association is a not-for-profit organization democratically run by an elected board with representatives drawn from a membership that spans more than forty countries (many of which have formed their own individual delegations).

ATypI provides a focal point through which the international type community can communicate, and its membership boasts many names instantly familiar to anyone working in the design industry. Among its many activities, ATypI seeks to preserve the tradition and cultural significance of type and typography, to promote contemporary digital fonts and protect original typeface designs, and to constantly encourage typographic excellence. ATypI's website provides details about how to become a member, along with information about the current board and delegation representatives.

The International Society of Typographic Designers (ISTD)

www.istd.org.uk

In line with other typographic societies and associations, ISTD aims to establish and maintain the standard of typography produced by typographers and graphic designers and to promote high-quality tutoring of typography among design educators. It also provides a forum for debate between members and within the greater design community.

Established in 1928 as the British Typographers Guild and based in the United Kingdom but with an ever-expanding international membership, the Society constantly strives to uphold its "real purpose" as described by its founder, Vincent Steer. As quoted on the ISTD website, this is "to bring together in friendship and mutual help, all those with a love of the printed word."

A key component of the ISTD calendar, recognized by any student of graphic design studying in the UK, is the annual Student Assessment Scheme. The assessment considers the holistic achievement of student projects rather than the final proposal, run not as a competition but rather entry into the Society for those students who manage to achieve the required standard. Find full details of membership and coming events on the ISTD website.

Type Directors Club (TDC)

www.tdc.org

Founded in 1946 by a group of the period's leading designers, the TDC centers around three annual competitions and the publication of its highly regarded *Typography Annual*. The first competition looks for outstanding examples of the use of type and the letterform in design; the second celebrates excellence in typeface design; and the third celebrates excellence in movie titles. The work of winners from all competitions gets published in the annual. The TDC also displays the work internationally as part of seven travelling exhibitions.

The collective resource established through this process forms an important historical archive of typographic trends—an important resource for both designers and educators. Indeed, education is very much at the fore of TDC activities, including the annual awarding of student scholarships, and a rolling series of lectures and seminars has happened since 1947, the second year of the Club's existence. **Cooper Union's** (349) postgraduate certificate in type design is offered in conjunction with the TDC. Find full details of the Club's activities and membership requirements on its excellent and well-populated website.

Society of Typographic Aficionados (SoTA)

www.typesociety.org

Rather like ATypI (354), the Society of Typographic Aficionados is run as a not-for-profit organization dedicated to the promotion and support of type and typography. The history and development of type and its use in both print and on today's digital platforms are key to its aims.

Quoting from SoTA's Charter from its website, the Society exists "for the affordable education of its members and participants; to further the development of type, typographical information, and typography; and to appreciate on multiple levels the attributes of type, typography, design, the book arts, and calligraphy. Furthermore, SoTA is committed to sponsoring relevant topics in pursuit of these goals." This is achieved partly through the Catalyst Award, an annual event open to typographers under age thirty. The award recipient receives an invitation to attend the Society's annual conference (see the chapter about Type-Specific Conferences and Events) and give a twenty-minute presentation based on his or her submitted project. As always, find full membership details and Society news on SoTA's website.

Type-Specific Conferences and Events

Typographic designers are, of course, passionate about their work, and a conference is the best way to share that passion with fellow designers. There are a number of excellent annual conferences that cover all aspects of graphic design; here we list only the conferences dedicated specifically to typography and type design.

ATypI Conference

www.atypi.org

The ATypI conference is an annual event organized by the **Association Typographique Internationale** (354). The conference, held internationally, moves to a different city each year. This gives local institutions and members of the society the chance to help organize events. The 2011 conference will be held in Reykjavik, Iceland. Spanning five days, the conference includes seminars and workshops covering developments in type technology, calligraphy, lettering, and type design. This important and highly regarded typographic event has run every year since 1957, ATypI's inaugural year.

TypeCon

www.typecon.com

TypeCon is an event organized by the **Society of Typographic Aficionados** (355) that has run annually since 1998. Like other conferences of its kind, TypeCon moves from city to city within the United States, with the thirteenth conference, in 2011, held in New Orleans.

Previous topics covered have included type design and font production, type for the screen and new media, the history of printing, book arts, Dutch design, type in motion, calligraphy and hand-lettering, the American Arts and Crafts Movement, experimental typography, and Web fonts. An exhibition of international typographic design accompanies the six-day conference.

International Conference on Typography and Visual Communication (ICTVC)

www.ictvc.org

The year 2010 marked the fourth occurrence of the International Conference on Typography and Visual Communication. The University of Macedonia in Thessaloniki hosted previous conferences—in 2002, 2004, and 2007—with the support of the department of typography and graphic communication at the **University of Reading** (348) in the United Kingdom and the **Association Typographique Internationale** (354), as well as a range of local sponsors. In 2010, a change of venue took the conference to the University of Nicosia on the island of Cyprus, though it still enjoyed the collaboration of its previous supporters.

A large number of international speakers and a selection of supporting workshops form an impressive program of events spanning five days, with details available through the conference website.

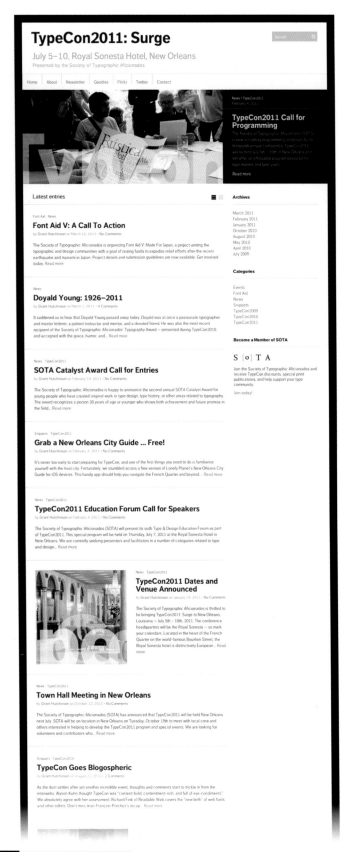

TYPO Berlin

www.typoberlin.de

At the time of this writing, the sixteenth TYPO Berlin conference is set to run during three days and feature the mix of international typographic stars that conference-goers have grown to expect. With previous speakers including **Neville Brody** (84), David Carson, Mario Garcia, David Linderman, Kurt Weidemann, Ken Garland, **Erik Spiekermann** (103), Jakob Trollbäck, Stefan Sagmeister, and Louis Rossetto, the credentials of this conference are clear.

The conference website, which can be viewed in English or German, clearly states the conference objectives: "To shift is to pick up speed, to push the envelope, to change your perspective. All three are useful strategies for TYPO 2011, in order to bring visual communications in line with the latest developments in technology."

Type-Specific Films and Documentaries

A visit to YouTube (www.youtube.com) reveals dozens of items about type and typography. For example, try entering "typography school" for a great short film about the London College of Printing, now the London College of Communication. In addition to those made by amateurs around the world, several more ambitious films about typography already exist or are in production at the time of this writing.

Helvetica

www.helveticafilm.com

Helevetica, a feature-length independent film produced and directed by Gary Hustwit, looks at typography, graphic design, and the effect of both these on global visual culture. It achieves its goal by focusing on how a single typeface, **Helvetica** (176), has managed through proliferation of use to populate so many of our urban spaces, and in doing so provokes a much larger conversation about the way that type affects our lives.

The cast of renowned typographers and type designers interviewed throughout the film reads like a who's who of typography and includes **Erik Spiekermann** (103), **Matthew Carter** (85), Massimo Vignelli, **Willem Hendrik Crouwel** (86), **Hermann Zapf** (107), **Neville Brody** (84), Stefan Sagmeister, Michael Bierut, David Carson, Paula Scher, **Jonathan Hoefler** (92), **Tobias Frere-Jones** (87), Experimental Jetset, Michael C. Place, Norm, Alfred Hoffmann, Mike Parker, Bruno Steinert, Otmar Hoefer, Leslie Savan, Rick Poynor, and Lars Müller.

The film premiered in March 2007 and subsequently toured film festivals and art house cinemas in more than 300 cities and 40 countries before receiving its television premiere on BBC1 in November 2007. It was shot in high-definition and in locations around the world including the United States, the United Kingdom, The Netherlands, Germany, Switzerland, France, and Belgium.

Danny van den Dungen from Amsterdam-based design company Experimental Jetset

Helvetica metal type shot at Manfred Schulz's letterpress in Frankfurt

The font Helvetica on the streets of New York

Typeface

www.typeface.kartemquin.com

This film is, in essence, a celebration of the perseverance and preservation of tradition alongside the convergence of traditional techniques with modern design sensibilities. It is set in Two Rivers, Wisconsin, a quiet Midwestern town struggling to survive amidst encroaching unemployment and the exodus of larger businesses from their rural roots. One local individual with entrepreneurial leanings, Jim Van Lanen, begins developing small museums to attract tourism and industry to the area. The most popular of these is the **Hamilton Wood Type and Print Museum** (363) housed in a section of the enormous old Hamilton print factory, now closed for business.

During the week, business is slow, with only the odd individual wandering in to greet the museum's lone employee. But come Friday, the scene changes dramatically. For one weekend each month, the old machines spring back to life when hoards of designers and artists congregate from all over the Midwest. People who count themselves among the region's top creative talent attend printmaking workshops led by some of the industry's leading practitioners.

This film documents a fascinating combination of the historical with the contemporary, illustrating how important the legacy of this disappearing craft is to the creative environment in which we work today. It is a film about people who believe that the future of their industry depends on the preservation of knowledge of the past.

Stills from the film *Typeface*

Linotype: The Film

www.linotypefilm.com

Linotype: The Film is a feature-length documentary that charts the efforts of a small group of people dedicated to saving from total extinction a piece of typographic history. The **Linotype** (129) typecasting machine, invented by Ottmar Mergenthaler in 1886, completely revolutionized type setting and printing. The machine cast an entire line of type at a time (hence the name "Line o' Type"), able to operate six times faster than the most skilled hand-compositor. This meant the printing of newspapers and books spiraled, dramatically changing writing, journalism, and society in the same way the Internet changed today's methods for distributing information.

The machine was an instant success and tens of thousands were manufactured and used all over the world. However, by the **1970s** (25), the technology was out of date and machines were routinely scrapped, leaving few intact and operational.

The film follows a group of former Linotype operators and enthusiasts in their quest to restore recovered machines to their former glory, and to keep the old skills alive to be passed down to future generations. What makes this film different is that it is not simply a sentimental journey lamenting the loss of a traditional technology. Rather, viewers are asked to look at the Linotype's place in our current age of new technology and why anyone should care about typography or the technology used to produce it. The film seeks to answer these far-reaching questions. Production began in August 2010 with film slated for release in late fall 2011. The film's website includes a trailer and details of ongoing production.

Jesse Marsolais talking about the Linotype machine

Matthew Carter showing a sign from his days at Mergenthaler Linotype

Guy Trower setting type on a Linotype

Making Faces: Metal Type in the 21st Century

www.makingfacesfilm.blogspot.com

Making Faces: Metal Type in the 21st Century documents the working methods of Jim Rimmer, a Canadian graphic artist and typeface designer, and follows the process of creating a new version of a font. The film began as a project to record the making of RTF Stern, the first-ever font issued simultaneously in digital and metal formats. Richard Kegler, who founded **P22 Type Foundry** (135), directed the film.

Metal type making is in danger of becoming a lost art as time passes, and few people still possess the skills required to cut and cast metal type. Even fewer makers are also type designers, but Rimmer did design many of his own faces. The film, which follows his technical working method, is interspersed with insights into his creative process and his inspirations. It is not a how-to film but rather an inspirational piece for anyone who admires and values the handmade skills and traditions that remain so important to typography despite massive technological advances. Sadly, Rimmer passed away in January 2010, so the film also stands as a testament to his work.

Type-Specific Institutions and Collections

Thanks to the dedication of enthusiastic curators and the generosity of numerous supporters, museums throughout Europe and the United States allow today's typographers a glimpse of the way the craft used to be done and the close link between typography and printing. The websites of each of the museums and institutions in this chapter include details of opening times and locations.

The Basel Paper Mill

BASEL

www.papiermuseum.ch

The Basel Paper Mill in Switzerland (Basler Papiermühle) is a working museum that brings together under one roof the arts of typography and printing and the manufacture of handmade paper. Original machinery dating from as far back as the Middle Ages demonstrates techniques to visitors, and the museum conducts a program of courses about typesetting, printing, and decorative paper manufacture. Central to the museum's inventory are the Swiss Historical Paper Collection and the collection of equipment and artifacts accumulated during the 400-year existence of the Haas Type Foundry of Munchenstein.

The Gutenberg Museum

MAINZ, GERMANY

www.gutenberg-museum.de

The Gutenberg Museum in Mainz, Germany, is one of the world's oldest museums of print. It was founded by a group of citizens in 1900, 500 years after Gutenberg's birth, to honor the inventor of movable type and showcase to a wider audience his technical and artistic achievements. Donations from various publishers and manufacturers of printing machines formed the original collection, which was part of the city library and included books dating back to the time of Gutenberg himself.

The museum possesses two of the *Gutenberg Bible*, the rarest and most valuable of books. The collection has now expanded to include sections about printing techniques, book art, graphics and posters, paper, and the history of writing. There is also a reconstruction of Gutenberg's workshop where type founding, typesetting, and printing can be demonstrated. Finally, the museum operates an educational unit called the Print Shop.

Hamilton Wood Type Museum

TWO RIVERS, WISCONSIN

www.woodtype.org

This museum is dedicated to the preservation, study, production, and printing of wood type, and it is operated by volunteers. The collection of this museum, located in Two Rivers, Wisconsin, contains more than 1.5 million pieces of wood type in more than 1,000 different styles and sizes, arguably the largest collection of its kind in the world.

Hamilton started producing type in 1880 and grew to become the main provider of wooden type in the United States until newer technologies forced its closure. The museum functions as an educational venue with regular monthly workshops, and it exhibits antique printing technologies that include the production of hot metal type and hand-operated printing alongside numerous tools of the trade and rare type-specimen catalogues. Local people who worked at Hamilton when it still operated play a large part in the workshops, passing on their skills to new generations of typographers. The museum is the subject of the new film *Typeface* (360).

Klingspor Museum, Offenbach

GERMANY

www.klingspor-museum.de

During the post–World War II years, a small institution dedicated to the art of modern book production and typography was established in the German city of Offenbach am Main. The private collection of Karl Klingspor formed the basis of the museum. Klingspor, together with his brother, Wilhelm, operated the Klingspor type foundry in the city in the first half of the **twentieth century** (16).

The museum opened to the public in November 1953. On Klingspor's death in 1950, his heirs donated the contents of his extensive library of more than 3,000 printed works, which includes rare examples of calligraphy, book illustration, book binding, and other fine examples of print and typography from the late 1800s and early 1900s. The museums website is also a useful source of historical typographic information, listing more than 3,000 type designers and the typefaces each has created.

The Bodoni Museum

PARMA, ITALY

www.museobodoni.beniculturali.it

The Bodoni Museum (Museo Bodoniano), the oldest established museum of printing in Italy, is located in the city of Parma. It opened its doors in 1963, coinciding with the 150th anniversary of the death of **Giambattista Bodoni** (71), the famous Italian engraver, publisher, printer, typographer, and designer of the **Bodoni** (156) family of typefaces. Bodoni lived and worked in Parma for an extended period of his life, and he died there in 1813. The museum was established to preserve the equipment and memorabilia saved from Bodoni's own workshop, and it promotes the study of graphic design and typography through its education program. The permanent collection includes more than 1,000 books printed by Bodoni, a unique set of punches, dies, and tools that belonged to him, and many miscellaneous printing tests and items of correspondence.

Museum Meermanno

THE HAGUE

www.meermanno.nl

Housed in the former residence of Baron van Westreenen of Tiellandt (1783–1848), the museum focuses on its unique collection of written and printed books. The collection is extensive, covering everything from hand-written medieval manuscripts to relatively modern nineteenth-century examples of book printing and binding. The collection also include examples of the oldest form of printed book, known in Latin as *incunabula*, which were printed using complete blocks of hand-carved text for each separate page.

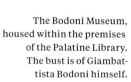

The Bodoni Museum, housed within the premises of the Palatine Library. The bust is of Giambattista Bodoni himself.

The Museum of Printing

NORTH ANDOVER, MASSACHUSETTS

www.museumofprinting.org

This establishment is dedicated to preserving the history of graphic arts and printing, which inevitably involve a great deal of typography. The museum holds in collection hundreds of antique printing, typesetting, and bindery machines, alongside an extensive library of books and print-related documents.

The museum was incorporated as a not-for-profit organization in 1978 to save for posterity the technologies that the printing and typesetting industries no longer use commercially. It also tells the story of the transition from letterpress printing through photographic processes to today's digital technology, using one of the world's largest collections of printing hardware. A principal exhibit comprises a timeline history of typography and typesetting reaching back 500 years and covering hand-setting, hot metal typesetting, photo typesetting, and of course, the digital technology in use today.

Museum of the Printing Arts

LEIPZIG, GERMANY

www.druckkunst-museum.de

The Museum of the Printing Arts in Leipzig, Germany, offers visitors the chance to experience what it was once like to work as a printer and typographer. It combines a working print shop with the more traditional aspects of a museum, covering 500 years of print and type history. Spread over four floors, the collection is composed of more than 200 fully working machines and presses demonstrating copperplate printing, lithography, and letterpress, with a particular focus on manual and mechanical typesetting. In addition, there is a fully working type foundry where lead type is cast by hand and by machine.

It is estimated that the museum's current collection includes approximately forty tons of lead type, matrices, and steel dies. If that isn't enough, it also has a fully operational bookbindery. The museum's motto is "See, smell and touch," which is great news for visitors who want to learn firsthand about the "black art" of printing. The museum holds regular workshops on a range of historic printing techniques including traditional typesetting and letterpress printing.

A set of blackletter type matrices from the vast collection held at the Museum of the Printing Arts in Leipzig, Germany

Leipzig's Museum of the Printing Arts houses more than 200 fully working machines and presses.

Museum of Printing History

HOUSTON

www.printingmuseum.org

Four printers who wanted to preserve and share with the community their own large collections founded the Museum of Printing History in 1979. The museum's goal, which it shares with many of the other museums listed in this book, is to preserve printing technology and skills, but it also is focused on the advancement of literacy.

The permanent exhibits narrate the story of written communication and the way in which printing and print technology have transformed our lives, with many galleries referencing the importance of the newspaper in this story. Other featured artifacts from the collection include Asian movable type, illuminated manuscripts, a 1450 Gutenberg press replica, a copy of Benjamin Franklin's *Pennsylvania Gazette*, an extensive letterpress and type collection, and antique bookbinding equipment.

Movable type samples from the collection of The National Print Museum in Dublin, Ireland

A "hands on" workshop experience at The National Print Museum in Dublin, Ireland

Museum of Typography

HANIA, CRETE

www.typography-museum.gr

This small museum on the Greek island of Crete is a relatively new project, made possible through the efforts of the local newspaper *Haniotika Nea* and opened in May 2005. At the time of this writing, visits happen by appointment only. (Unless you are a local resident, any visit is likely to be planned in advance anyway, so this shouldn't present a problem.) Exhibits include printing and typesetting equipment dating from the **nineteenth century** (12), rare books dating back to 1570, and items of local print ephemera including newspapers and banknotes. Arranged visits include demonstrations of the equipment.

National Print Museum

DUBLIN

www.nationalprintmuseum.ie

The National Print Museum, located in Ireland's capital city, aims to improve accessibility to the archival material of, and foster skills associated with, the Irish printing industry. The museum opened in 1996 and runs regular workshops that include both calligraphy and printing, providing a place for printers, typographers, historians, students, and the general public to see and hear how printing developed and brought information, in all its forms, to the world.

The permanent collection includes mechanical typesetting machines manufactured by **Linotype** (129) and Intertype and historical hand presses such as the famous Columbian and Albion. In addition, the museum maintains a rolling program of temporary exhibitions that showcase material from all over the world relating to the permanent collection. It also includes a reference library that visitors can use by appointment.

The Museum Plantin-Moretus

ANTWERP, BELGIUM

http://museum.antwerpen.be/plantin_moretus/index_eng.html

The origins of this Belgian museum stretch back to 1549 when Christoffel Plantin first settled in Antwerp. His shrewd business sense allowed him to build a huge printing operation, handling practically all officially sanctioned print contracts of the time, including the famous *Biblia Polyglotta* ("Bible in Five Languages"). His successor, son-in-law Jan I Moretus, took over the company on his death, and the family continued to run the business until its final collapse in 1876. The firm, along with its entire contents, was sold to the city of Antwerp and in 1877 the 300-year-old printing firm became the Museum Plantin-Moretus.

Of particular interest is the museum's remarkable collection of typographic material and equipment, which includes two of the oldest surviving printing presses in the world. Plantin traveled widely to acquire fonts for use by the firm, counting **Claude Garamond** (74) among his suppliers. The letters and dies he brought back to Antwerp still remain in the collection, and the museum possesses the only complete set of Garamond's letter dies remaining today. Another notable exhibit is the fully equipped type foundry where the Moretuses created their own typefaces.

The Type Museum

LONDON

www.typemuseum.org

At the time of this writing, The Type Museum, which was established in 1992, is undergoing a major period of redevelopment and so is closed to the general public. Limited access may be possible by appointment so check before planning a visit.

The museum's primary objective has always been to preserve the skills and methods used to make type, and with the help of the National Heritage Memorial Fund, it has managed to acquire collections that document the key chapters in Britain's history of type: traditional typefounding, woodletter type, and mechanical typecasting or hot-metal type. The various collections include material dating as far back as the **sixteenth century** (10) such as punches, matrices, and molds from principal London type foundries, as well as such diverse items as the complete business records of **Monotype** (125).

St Bride Foundation and Library

LONDON

www.stbride.org

St Bride Foundation was established in 1895 as a social, educational, and cultural center, and incorporated as a technical library and printing school. It eventually grew into what is now The London College of Communication, one of the foremost schools of its kind in the world.

With letterpress and the handmade experiencing a revival among graphic designers and typographers, the skills and techniques taught at St Bride are in demand once again, and the Foundation continues to strive to protect and promote the heritage of typography and printing through workshops, lectures, and conferences. In addition to having 50,000 specialist print, graphic design, and typography books, and 3,500 periodicals, the Library is the custodian of an unrivalled collection of printing artifacts. Type and typography is naturally a highlight of the collection with punches, matrices, and founders' type dating from the **seventeenth** (10) to the **twentieth centuries** (16). There are also roughly 200 special collections including, for example, 164 boxes of hand-scribed master letterforms for Letraset typefaces, and 2,600 woodblocks by Mary Byfield for the Chiswick Press. An ongoing series of workshops and specialist typographic courses runs alongside other print-related subjects, with details available through the website.

Blogs, Links, and Online Resources

Whether it's information about a particular typeface, the latest typographic developments and trends, or simply a bit of inspiration, typography blogs have it all. Some of the sites we list below are simply great portals for showcasing work the site owners have seen and liked. Others are vast depositories of invaluable typographic information.

AisleOne

www.aisleone.net

AisleOne is put together by New York–based designer Antonio Carusone, an associate creative director at Ogilvy, and displays a distinct fondness for what's sometimes called Swiss Style typography. The site introduces itself as an inspirational resource focused on graphic design, typography, **grid systems** (220), minimalism, and modernism, and it certainly lives up to its claim. There is a terrific selection of work on show ranging from brand-new projects to historical material from the **1960s** (24) and **1970s** (25). In keeping with the minimalist nature of the visual content, the captions for each article are generally succinct. However, this does not matter as the visuals really say it all.

BeautifulType

www.beautifultype.net

This typography blog, created by Web designers Francis Chouquet from Switzerland and Aurélien Foutoyet from France, intends to act as an inspirational showcase of their online work. What's interesting is that so much of the work is "handmade," especially given the fact that they are both Web designers. This lends credence to the idea that all good design, typographic or otherwise, starts with a pencil and a blank sheet of paper. The site is quite new with a limited number of posts as of this writing, but the selection of work showcased thus far is excellent. Keep logging on to see how the site develops.

Design Observer

www.designobserver.com

Design Observer is the real deal when it comes to high-end design-driven discussion, and it has developed from its earliest days into a group of connected sites. Observatory covers a vast range of general design topics including typography. Change Observer covers news about design and social innovation. Places is a forum of design for the public realm. Observer Media is home to audio and video content, and Observers Room is a straightforward design blog.

Michael Bierut, William Drenttel, Jessica Helfand, and Rick Poynor founded Design Observer in October 2003. The site now boasts a roster of contributors that reads like a who's who of the design world. Strictly speaking, it's slightly erroneous to include Design Observer in a directory of typography-specific sites, but the reality is that this site should appear on every directory relating to any sites connected to the design industry. For many, it's a daily read.

Easily Amused

http://johndberry.com/blog

John D. Berry is an editor and typographer, as well as the final editor of the venerable *U&lc* magazine and U&lc online, originally published by **International Typeface Corporation** (128). At the time of this writing, he is the president of the **Association Typographique Internationale** (354).

His blog, Easily Amused, exists as a subsection of his main portfolio website and contains an extensive archive of well-written and well-considered articles stretching back to May 2007. Though he does not post articles daily, he does go more in depth for individual posts than the average blog. It's rather like reading complete magazine articles. The site isn't over-populated with inspirational imagery, but at least one related image accompanies almost every article. However, this site is much more about the text. A useful tag cloud leads the viewer to groups of related articles by clicking on links such as book design, letters, or signage, and previous articles are accessible by month all the way back to the site's inception.

The End Grain

www.end-grain.net

This site is the work of Bethany Heck, a recent graduate of Auburn University in Alabama. It's a real labor of love in that Heck is obviously smitten with anything letterpress and wood type, so anyone who feels the same should make this a must-read.

The site revolves around Heck's collection of wood type letters, which are featured in her Daily Letters section, but also includes Character Studies, a blog charting her efforts to expand her collection. The site also lists some useful links to print shops working with letterpress and wood type, which provide inspiration. Plus, there's additional information for users wishing to get started with their own letterpress work and about where they can purchase letterpress work examples for themselves.

FontBook

www.fontbook.com

Hot of the press at the time of writing is a terrific new iPad app from the good people at **FontShop International** (127; 140), the publishers of that huge yellow type compendium that's been sitting on every graphic designer's book shelf since 1991. The new app features more than 620,000 typeface specimens, which is equivalent to more than twenty of the printed books, so this really is the ultimate typographic reference tool. Fonts can be viewed by name, style, typographic classification, designer, foundry, or year of publication. You can also cross reference faces that display similar design characteristics, very useful if you know what you like but can't find the right font for your next project. The app is primarily an online browser, so you'll need to stay connected to view all the content, but there is an offline mode that allows you to access a reduced content selection. The app will of course be continually updated as more typefaces become available, and there are some exciting additional features planned for future releases.

The FontFeed

www.fontfeed.com

The FontFeed has been around since September 2008 and is a spin-off site belonging to the well known and highly regarded online font vendor **FontShop International** (127; 140). Earlier in 2008, FontShop cofounder **Erik Spiekermann** (103) decided to create a standalone blog dedicated to all things typographic. The FontFeed is the result.

Once part of the main FontShop site (www.fontshop.com), FontFeed has now grown into a more independent voice free of any commercial restraints it felt from its inclusion on the parent site. Editor-in-chief Yves Peters maintains it and posts articles alongside former FontShop type director Stephen Coles, design writer Jürgen Siebert, and Spiekermann himself. A frequently updated general news section contains a wealth of international content including type events, new font releases, calls for entries, case studies, and more. There are also separate tabs filtering articles relating to specific areas of typographic interest. Handpicked typefaces highlights articles on both newly released and classic typefaces, Type Tips includes basic tips and more advanced tutorials about a range of typographic issues, and **Fonts in Use** (371) provides examples of typefaces in use in the real world, with accompanying commentary.

Fonts In Use

http://fontsinuse.com

Fonts In Use twists the inspirational typographic showcase blog on its head in the way it allows the viewer to search the content. As well as tags to search by industry or format, there is a tag for every typeface featured in each piece of work included on the site. Want to see how Eames Century Modern looks in a real life project? Just click on the typeface to head directly to those that use the face.

The site is an independent project run by Sam Berlow, Stephen Coles, and Nick Sherman. (Coles and Sherman both maintain additional sites, respectively **Typographica** (141; 378) and **Woodtyper** (380). The principal aim of the site is to provide a focused critique on typography in design, cataloging real-world projects from all areas and design disciplines.

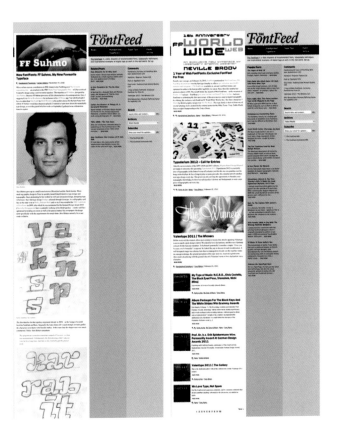

Grain Edit

http://grainedit.com

Although not strictly a dedicated typography site, California-based Grain Edit focuses on classic design work from the **1950s** (22) through the **1970s** (24) juxtaposed with contemporary work by designers and typographers influenced by the styles of those periods. As well as the usual mix of blogger articles and samples of inspirational work, the site includes interviews with leading design practitioners, type specimens, ephemera, posters, and vintage books from the collections of Dave C, Elizabeth Surya, Ethan Davis, and Grace Danico, the team members who put together the site. With archives dating back to September 2007, there is lot of excellent material to browse, with many articles reminding readers of the important influence typographic styling has on the look and feel of any given design genre.

I Love Typography

www.ilovetypography.com

I Love Typography is the brainchild of British-born graphic designer and writer John Boardley, who now resides in Japan. The site, launched in August 2007, strongly focuses on how letterforms originated and why type looks the way it does. It offers some great articles about font design, type terminology, font identification, and just about everything else type-related. Readers could easily spend many hours browsing the content, so avoid this site around deadline time.

That said, a well-organized search section is arranged chronologically, making browsing articles of particular interest a breeze. Boardley produces much of the content himself but also invites contributors to contact him with their own ideas for articles. That keeps the content nicely varied in terms of opinion and writing style. It is arguably one of the most up-to-date sites in terms of its reporting of current typographic trends, new font releases, and events, and its list of links to other typographic sites is vast.

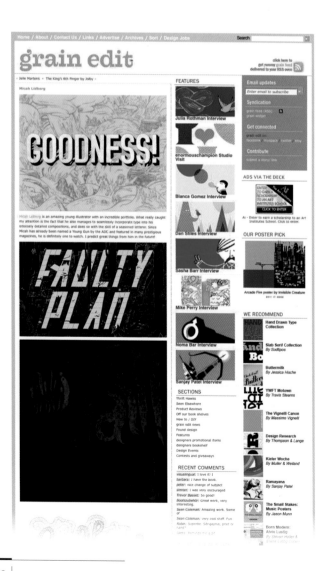

JON TANgerine

www.jontangerine.com

Jon Tan, who lives and works in Bristol, United Kingdom, is a founding member of the Analog cooperative with other members in San Francisco and New York. He is also the cofounder of Web fonts service Fontdeck. His site is dedicated mainly to the issues surrounding online typography and contains numerous articles that provide useful tips to achieve the best from fonts used within websites. There are also articles that discuss more general issues surrounding typography such as the correct use of quotation marks or the effects of reversing type out of black or a color.

However, the thing that stands out across all articles posted on the site is the level of cross-reference linking that Tan has included. Every piece links to other sites that contain additional information about the subjects being discussed or refer the viewer to the source material used to construct the original article. This is another site big on words rather than extensive imagery, and it is packed with useful content and some great insights into the technical aspects of font use online.

LetterCult

www.lettercult.com

This great site is a one-stop shop for anything related to custom lettering, and with its wealth of information, is a wonderful source of inspiration. Brian Jaramillo of Agency26 runs the site, which acts as a showcase for anyone working with custom letters: type designers, sign painters, graffiti artists, calligraphers, poster artists, and of course, typographers and graphic designers.

A principal feature of the site since March 2010 has been its regular Alphabattles during which Jaramillo invites contributors to post their custom letter designs for each alphabet letter. At the time of this writing, the alphabattle for *Z* just finished and the site was about to start on numbers. The results are fascinating and incredibly diverse, and every contributor provides a link to his or her own site, creating a practically endless trail to more lettering inspiration. Other tabbed sections include Letterstream, a collection of cherry-picked letterforms, Custom Logos, Custom Movie Titles, and Custom-Other, which contains some of the most interesting content on the whole site. It's a real gem for custom-lettering fans.

Letterpress Daily

www.letterpress.dwolske.com

For those who like everything wood type, this site is heaven. David Wolske, cofounder of design company and letterpress printer Smart & Wiley, lovingly puts together Letterpress Daily. The premise is simple: Each day, Wolske posts a large photographic image of a block of wood type selected from his expanding collection, with the printed image from the block beneath. He adds a short identifier caption and occasionally a little more information about the history of the typeface.

Viewers can access every individual post archived on the site by using the list of tags. Search either by name of typeface or by letter shown, for example all capital *A*'s; numbers *3*'s, and so on. He also includes an extensive list of links to other letterpress and wood type–related sites.

Ralf Herrmann: Wayfinding and Typography

www.opentype.info/blog

The blog of German designer and author Ralf Herrmann has much to say about signage and wayfinding, which undoubtedly has much to do with the fact that as of this writing, Herrmann is writing a P.h.D. dissertation that covers his investigation into the implications of cognitive map research applied to the design of maps and wayfinding systems.

The result is useful pointers for anyone involved or interested in typography for traffic signage and wayfinding signage for public spaces such as airports or shopping malls. He also includes informative content discussing the differences between font formats, font design in general, and the increasingly important topic of Web fonts and Web font services; for example, a well-constructed article explaining the myths surrounding the OpenType format.

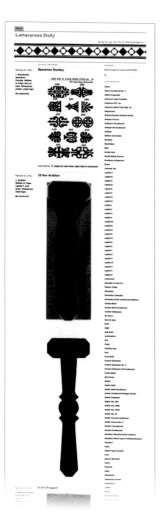

RockPaperInk

rockpaperink.com

The people behind this new design blog are also the people behind this book. Rockport has been in the business of publishing books about design for many years so know a thing or two about the subject. The site is billed as a place for "inspiration, ideas, and opinions from design fanatics" and, despite the short timespan since the site launched, it certainly promises to fulfill this criteria. Much is covered by the regular columnists drawn from the ranks of Rockport's authors, and whilst the content isn't typography specific, Jason Tselentis's "Points, Pixels, Paper" column does focus on all things typographic. The emphasis throughout the site is on interaction, with numerous opportunities to add your own comments or even contribute material.

Type Directors Club Online

ww.tdc.org

This site provides an online presence for the **Type Directors Club** (TDC) (355), a New York–based organization that operates internationally to encourage and support typographic excellence in print and on screen. The TDC, founded in 1946 by a group formed from the leading typographers of the day, boasts a venerable history. The group offers membership and its benefits via an annual paid subscription. It also holds two competitions per year, one for use of typography in design, the other for typeface design.

The site itself is designed to promote the Club's activities, but also carries a range of articles and book reviews covering all things typographic. Anyone can access this material. For anyone interested in becoming a member of the Club, the site is obviously a must-read. If not, it's likely still well worth bookmarking as the articles offer a good insight into industry opinions of the moment's best typographic practices.

Typedia

www.typedia.com

Typedia is like Wikipedia for typography. Several individuals act as moderators for the site, but essentially it is a community site for typographers that anyone can join and to which anyone can contribute. The aim is to provide a facility for designers to use to classify, identify, and discover typefaces. It also aims to educate people about how a typeface originated, who designed it, when and where it was designed, and why it looks the way it does.

Apart from the typeface browser, which uses common typographic terms to facilitate easy searches for groups of typefaces with similar attributes, there is a learning section with a glossary of typographic terms, plus a section explaining the anatomy of type. There is also a lively forum and a blog updated regularly with all manner of type-related articles. The site is growing all the time as new users sign up and add their own material. There are inevitably gaps in the content (just like with Wikipedia), but the site is already so richly populated with information that one can easily forgive this.

Typefoundry

www.typefoundry.blogspot.com

The first thing a reader finds on this blog is its author, James Mosley, owning up to the fact that, at the time of writing at least, the blog contains just thirty-five posts. However, each post already on the site takes the form of a well-written illustrated essay.

The posts cover a wide range of subjects, from an extensive guide to the present location of typographical punches, matrices, drawings, type specimens, and archives, to an examination of the various lettering styles used to paint the "10" on the front door of 10 Downing Street, home of the United Kingdom's Prime Minister. Despite being engagingly personal in their approach, the posts are well-researched and packed with historical points of reference of interest to anyone who enjoys reading about the history of type and letterforms.

Typeradio

www.typeradio.org

Visually, this site has little to offer. But the URL gives away the fact that visuals are not the site's forte. Typeradio is a specialist radio channel about type and typographic design. It's is a Micro FM broadcast, an MP3 Internet radio stream, and a podcast station that has been on air regularly since 2004. The individuals behind the site, Donald Beekman, Liza Enebeis (a.k.a. LoveLiza), and pan-European design collective **Underware** (139), are based in The Netherlands and Finland.

To collect material for their broadcasts, these three attend various design events around the world to meet and talk to designers and typographers. New material appears with surprising regularity considering the obvious challenges the team faces to get it. For those who do happen to work their way through all the recent broadcasts, the channel also keeps an extensive archive of material in which the big names of design (Stefan Sagmeister, Paula Scher, Bruno Maag, to name a few) rub shoulders with some new names.

typo/graphic posters

www.typographicposters.com

This site is pure inspiration, and there is plenty of it to go around, with more than 450 directories containing multiple examples of each contributing designer's work. The site aims to provide a "timeless source for studies, inspiration, and promotion of good design through poster culture and cultivation of typography and pure forms of graphic design," according to the site's creator André Felipe. It really does deliver quality visuals that are a feast for the eyes.

The site is nicely put together with a variety of viewing options such as grid or list view, plus the ability to change the background color. (This is surprisingly useful when looking at posters with dark or light backgrounds.) Also, using the free navigation option, a viewer can use the mouse to scroll freely around each profile window rather than having to constantly click a button to move between posters.

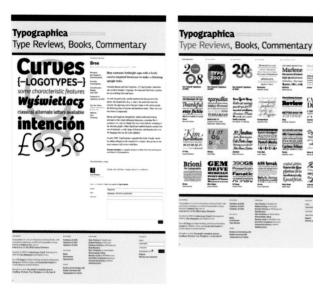

Typographica

www.typographica.org

Typographica is dedicated to reviewing typefaces and type-related books and is maintained by Stephen Coles, former **FontShop** (127; 140) type director, also one of the main contributors to **The FontFeed** (371). Joshua Lurie-Terrell founded the site in 2002, but it underwent a redesign by Chris Hamamoto and Coles in 2009.

The type reviews are a particularly useful feature of this site because a user can simply scroll through the large selection of samples to discover a new typeface. There is also a neat feature that allows users to view fonts by designer, foundry, or classification—a nice touch given the number of faces to peruse. Each typeface appears against a large sample setting with an impartial review, details of the typeface's designer, and purchasing information. At the time of this writing, the book review and commentary sections are comparatively small, but the reviews are in-depth and informative, and the articles are particularly well written. They include some recorded interviews with well-known figures from the design world. To cap all that, the overall design of the site is really excellent.

Typography Served

www.typographyserved.com

Unlike most other sites listed in this book, Typography Served is a collection of sites that showcases category-specific content selected from the well-known online platform Behance Network where creative pros can showcase their work. The dedicated team that curates the site is always on the lookout for work that features good quality type design, lettering, illustrated typography, plus work that utilizes a strong typographic treatment.

Any designer interested in getting his or her work featured must first create a portfolio with the Behance Network. Membership to Typography Served is free and by invitation only, but there is a link that designers can use to request that invitation. This seems like a slightly curious arrangement, but someone is obviously busy accepting new applicants on a regular basis because the site contains a huge amount of content to plough through. It also lists job ads with a good international mix, too, for anyone looking for a fresh career start.

Typophile

www.typophile.com

A firm favorite among designers and typographers, Typophile has been around for more than ten years and enjoys a large membership of registered users. Registration is free and allows the user to contribute to the thousands of separate threads split between three categories on the home page—hottest, newest, and hand-picked. A click on the Forums tab reveals a more specific division of the forums: general discussion, design, critique, build, release, type ID, and special interest groups. It is rare not to find a lively debate on the merits of a particular font or the suitability of a typeface for a particular application. In addition, it includes a well-populated typowiki created by the site's users, and a Projects section with regular type battles open to anyone who wishes to contribute ideas. Overall, it's a very useful site that every designer should bookmark.

Typoretum

www.blog.typoretum.co.uk

Typoretum is a private press based in rural Essex, United Kingdom, run by Justin Knopp. Launched in 2008, the site is a must-see for letterpress aficionados interested in the mechanics of letterpress, as well as the way it looks once printed. Knopp has documented much of the work he has done to restore his equipment to its former glory, allowing viewers to read about (and see in high-quality photographs and video) everything from the ornamentation on the famous Columbian Press to the difficulties in moving an 1888 Wharfedale cylinder press into a workshop. The numerous links embedded in the articles cover just about every letterpress-related site and article on the Internet. This is a well-researched and informative site from someone who plainly lives for letterpress.

We Love Typography

www.welovetypography.com

The man behind We Love Typography is John Boardley, who also runs the site **I Love Typography** (372). This site differs in that it is a bookmarking site given over completely to type-related content. The intention is simply to inspire, and the collection Boardley has put together is vast. An invitation-only membership arrangement allows contributors to submit images they deem worthy of inclusion. The arrangement ensures content that is both appropriate and high quality. All images are intelligently tagged so the search facility allows easy access to groups of images; users can even search by predominant color.

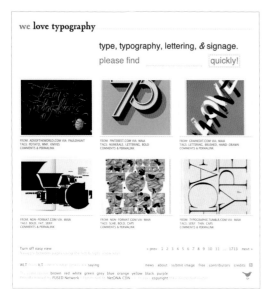

Woodtyper

www.woodtyper.com

Edited by Nick Sherman (also of **Fonts In Use** (371), Woodtyper is a journal site focusing on wood type and any related topics, with subjects ranging from large-scale lettering and sign painting to poster work and engraving. The site is pretty straightforward and is not overly expansive in terms of amount of content, but what is there is well worth a look. The site appears to have taken a hiatus around June 2010, though we hope this does not signal the end of the site. Fingers crossed that Sherman has simply been too busy to post recently.

Under Consideration

www.underconsideration.com

An ever-expanding network of sites dedicated to, in the words of
its founders, "the progress of the graphic design profession and
its practitioners, students, and enthusiasts. At times intangible,
its purpose is to question, push, analyze, and agitate graphic
design and those involved in the profession."

Under Consideration, begun in 2002, is the considerable
undertaking of Bryony Gomez-Palacio and Armin Vit. The site
was the first dedicated design blog of its kind to catch the industry's attention with the nature of its articles on anything and
everything design; it has continued to deliver since day one.
There are six separate sites to date living under the Under Consideration roof: Speak Up (now closed to new posts), Brand New,
Quipsologies, The Design Encyclopedia, Word It, and FPO, for
PRINT only. There is far too much in the collection of sites to
begin to describe it here. Rather, just go take a look, but set aside
plenty of time. Once again, this is not strictly a dedicated typography site, but it is far too important to omit.

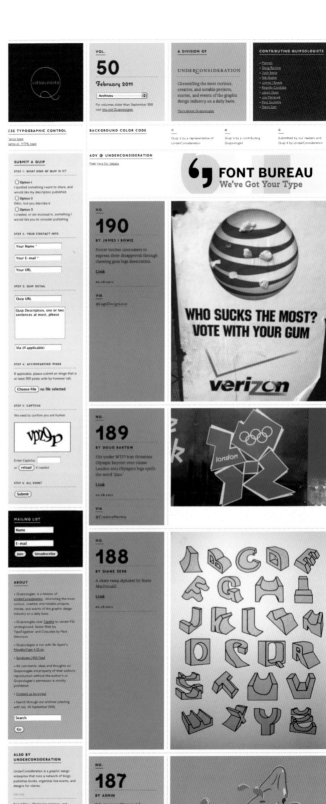

Bibliography

Abbink, Jeanette and Emily C. M. Anderson. *3D Typography*. New York: Mark Batty, 2010.

Abe, Kazuo, Kaori Shibata, and Toru Hachiga. *New Typo Graphics: The New Faces of Contemporary Typography*. Tokyo: P.I.E. Books, 1993.

AbiFarès, Huda Smitshuijzen. *Arabic Typography: A Comprehensive Sourcebook*. London: Saqi, 2001.

AbiFarès, Huda Smitshuijzen. *Typographic Matchmaking: Building Cultural Bridges with Typeface Design*. Amsterdam: BIS Publishers & Khatt Foundation, 2007.

Ambrose, Gavin and Paul Harris. *The Fundamentals of Typography*. Lausanne, Switzerland: Ava Academia, 2007.

Apicella, Vincent F., Joanna V. Pomeranz, and Nancy G. Wiatt. *The Concise Guide to Type Identification*. New York: Design Press, 1990.

Atkins, Kathryn A. *Masters of the Italic Letter*. Boston, MA: David R. Godine, 1988.

Bain, Peter, Paul Shaw, et al. *Blackletter: Type and National Identity*. New York: Princeton Architectural Press, 1998.

Baines, Phil and Andrew Haslam. *Type & Typography*. London: Laurence King, 2005.

Balius, Andreu. *Type At Work: The Use of Type in Editorial Design*. Amsterdam: Enfield BIS, 2003.

Bartram, Alan. *Five Hundred Years of Book Design*. New Haven, CT: Yale University Press, 2001.

Bartram, Alan. *Futurist Typography and the Liberated Text*. New Haven, CT: Yale University Press, 2005.

Baumann, Gerd, Barbara Baumann, Baumann & Baumann, and Musashino Bijutsu Daigaku. Pictowords: *Semantic Typography/ Wortbilder: Semantische Typografie/Imironteki Taipogurafi*. Zürich: Niggli, 2005.

Beaumont, Michael. Type: Design, Color, Character & Use. Cincinnati, OH: North Light Books, 1987.

Bellantoni, Jeff and Matt Woolman. *Type in Motion: Innovations in Digital Graphics*. New York: Rizzoli, 1999.

Berry, Edward D. *The Fundamentals of Typographic Art: A Discussion of Page Arrangement and Its Elemental Factors*. Chicago, IL: Edward D. Berry, 1930.

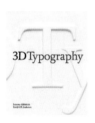

Berry, John D. (ed.). *Language Culture Type: International Type Design in the Age of Unicode*. New York: Graphis Press, 2002.

Berry, John D. *U&Lc: Influencing Design & Typography*. New York: Mark Batty, 2003.

Berry, John D. *Dot-Font: Talking About Design*. New York: Mark Batty Publisher, 2006.

Berry, John D. *Dot-Font: Talking About Fonts*. New York: Mark Batty Publisher, 2006.

Berry, John D. *Talking About Matthew Carter*. New York: Mark Batty, 2008.

Berry, John D. *Talking About Typography*. New York: Mark Batty, 2008.

Bigeleisen, J. I. *Classic Type Faces and How to Use Them: Including 91 Complete Fonts*. New York: Dover Publications, 1995.

Biggs, John R. *An Approach to Type*. London: Blandford Press, 1949.

Biggs, John R. *The Use of Type: The Practice of Typography*. London: Blandford Press, 1954.

Binns, Betty. *Better Type*. New York: Watson-Guptill, 1989.

Blackwell, Lewis. *20th-Century Type*. New Haven, CT: Yale University Press, 2004.

Bringhurst, Robert. *The Elements of Typographic Style*. Point Roberts, WA: Hartley & Marks, 2004.

Brown, Bruce. *Browns Index To Photocomposition Typography: A Compendium of Terminologies, Procedures, and Constraints for the Guidance of Designers, Editors, and Publishers*. Minehead, UK: Greenwood Pub, 1983.

Burke, Christopher. *Paul Renner: The Art of Typography*. London: The Hyphen Press, 1998.

Carter, Harry and James Mosley. *A View of Early Typography: Up to About 1600*. London: Hyphen Press, 2002.

Carter, Rob. *Experimental Typography*. East Sussex, UK: RotoVision, 1997.

Carter, Rob, Ben Day, and Philip B. Meggs. *Typographic Design: Form and Communication*. New York: Van Nostrand Reinhold, 1993.

Carter, Sebastian. *20th Century Type Designers*. Farnham, UK: Lund Humphries Publishers, 2002.

Case, Lockwood, and Company. *Typographic Specimens and Advertisements*. Hartford, CT: Case, ca. 1940.

Cheng, Karen. *Designing Type*. New Haven, CT: Yale University Press, 2006.

Chermayeff, Ivan and Thomas H. Geismar. *Watching Words Move*. San Francisco, CA: Chronicle Books, 2006.

Chizlett, Clive and David Jury. *Typography: The Perfect Setting in the Desktop Age*. Bristol, UK: Intellect, 2003.

Clair, Kate. *A Typographic Workbook: A Primer to History, Techniques, and Artistry*. New York: Wiley, 1999.

Cliff, Stafford. *The Best in Cutting Edge Typography*. East Sussex, UK: RotoVision, 1994.

Craig, James. *Basic Typography: A Design Manual*. New York: Watson-Guptill Publications, 1990.

Craig, James, Irene Scala, and William Bevington. *Designing with Type: The Essential Guide to Typography*. New York: Watson-Guptill Publications, 2006.

Crawford, Don. *Logical Lettering & Layout*. Belmont, CA: Logi-Cal Art Equipment Manufacturing Co., 1978.

Dachy, Marc. *Kurt Schwitters: Typography and Graphic Design*. New York: Greenidge, 2003.

Dair, Carl. *Design with Type*. Toronto: University of Toronto Press, 1967.

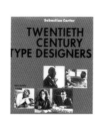

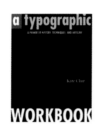

Davis, Graham, Robin Dodd, Keith Martin, and Bob Gordon (designer). *1000 Fonts: An Illustrated Guide to Finding the Right Typeface.* San Francisco, CA: Chronicle Books, 2009.

De Jong, Cees, Alston W. Purvis, and Friedrich Friedl. *Creative Type: A Sourcebook of Classic and Contemporary Letterforms.* London: Thames & Hudson, 2005.

De Vicq de Cumptich, Roberto and Francine Prose. *Men of Letters & People of Substance.* Boston, MA: David R. Godine, 2008.

De Vinne, Theodore Low. *The Practice of Typography: A Treatise on the Processes of Type-Making, the Point System, the Names, Sizes, Styles and Prices of Plain Printing Types.* New York: Century Co., 1900.

De Vinne, Theodore Low. *The Practice of Typography: A Treatise on Title-Pages, with Numerous Illustrations in Facsimile and Some Observations on the Early and Recent Printing of Books.* New York: Century Co., 1902.

Denastas, Anne, Camille Gallet, and Miriam Seifert-Waibel. *Einfuhrung in die Typographie/An Initiation in Typography/ Une initiation à la typographie.* Zürich: Niggli, 2006.

Dodd, Robin. *From Gutenberg to Opentype: An Illustrated History of Type from the Earliest Letterforms to the Latest Digital Fonts.* Vancouver, Canada: Hartley & Marks, 2006.

Dowding, Geoffrey. *Finer Points in the Spacing & Arrangement of Type.* London: Wace, 1966.

Dowding, Geoffrey. *An Introduction to the History of Printing Types: An Illustrated Summary of the Main Stages in the Development of Type Design From 1440 Up to the Present Day: An Aid to Type Face Identification.* London: Oak Knoll Press, 1998.

Drucker, Johanna. *The Alphabetic Labyrinth: The Letters in History and Imagination.* New York: Thames & Hudson, 1995.

Earls, David. *Designing Typefaces.* East Sussex, UK: RotoVision, 2002.

Eckersley, Richard, et al. *Glossary of Typesetting Terms.* Chicago, IL: University of Chicago Press, 1994.

Elam, Kimberly. *Grid Systems: Principles of Organizing Type.* New York: Princeton Architectural Press, 2004.

Elam, Kimberly. *Typographic Systems.* New York: Princeton Architectural Press, 2007.

Ellison, Andy. *The Complete Guide to Digital Type.* London: Laurence King, 2006.

Evolution Graphics. International Typographic Almanac 2. London: Internos Books, 1994.

Fawcett-Tang, Roger and David Jury. *New Typographic Design.* New Haven, CT: Yale University Press, 2007.

Felici, James. *The Complete Manual of Typography: A Guide to Setting Perfect Type.* Berkeley, CA: Peachpit Press, 2003.

Fredes, Andrés. *Font Family: Get Familiar with Fonts!.* Barcelona: Indexbook, 2009.

Friedl, Friedrich, Nicolaus Ott, and Bernard Stein. *Typography: An Encyclopedic Survey of Type Design and Techniques Throughout History.* New York: Black Dog & Leventhal, 1998.

Friedman, Mildred S., et al. *The Evolution of American Typography.* Cambridge, MA: MIT Press, 1990.

Gandl, Stefan, Victor Cheung, Victionary (Firm), et al. *Type Addicted: The New Trend of A to Z Typo-Graphics.* Hong Kong: Victionary, 2007.

Garrett, Malcolm and Catherine McDermott. *New Typographies.* London: Batsford, 1993.

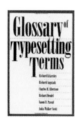

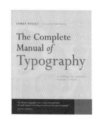

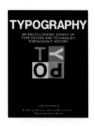

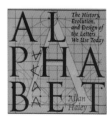

Gill, Eric. *An Essay on Typography*. Boston, MA: David R. Godine, 1993.

Gomez-Palacio, Bryony and Armin Vit. *Graphic Design, Referenced*. Beverly, MA: Rockport Publishers, 2009.

Gordon, Maggie and Eugenie Dodd. *Decorative Typography*. Oxford: Phaidon, 1990.

Gottschall, Edward M. and International Typeface Corporation (ITC). *Typographic Communications Today*. New York: International Typeface Corporation, 1989.

Gray, Nicolete. *Nineteenth Century Ornamented Typefaces*. Berkeley, CA: University of California Press, 1976.

Gray, Nicolete. *A History of Lettering: Creative Experiment and Letter Identity*. Boston, MA: Cambridge, MA David R. Godine, 1986.

Gutjahr, Paul C. and Megan Benton. *Illuminating Letters: Typography and Literary Interpretation*. Amherst, MA: Oak Knoll Press, 2001.

Haley, Allan. *Typographic Milestones*. New York: Van Nostrand Reinhold, 1992.

Haley, Allan. *Alphabet: The History, Evolution, and Design of the Letters We Use Today*. New York: Watson-Guptill Publications, 1995.

Heller, Steven. *The Education of a Typographer*. New York: Allworth Press, 2004.

Heller, Steven and Christine Thompson. *Letterforms, Bawdy, Bad & Beautiful: The Evolution of Hand-Drawn, Humorous, Vernacular, and Experimental Type*. New York: Watson-Guptill Publications, 2000.

Heller, Steven and Philip B. Meggs. Texts On Type: *Critical Writings on Typography*. New York: Allworth Press, 2001.

Heller, Steven and Gail Anderson. *New Ornamental Type: Decorative Lettering in the Digital Age*. New York: Thames & Hudson, 2010.

Hill, Will and Christopher Perfect. *The Complete Typographer: A Manual for Designing with Type*. Upper Saddle River, NJ: Prentice Hall, 2005.

Hinrichs, Kit and Delphine Hirasuna. *Typewise*. Cincinnati, OH: North Light Books, 1990.

Hochuli, Jost. *Detail in Typography*. London: Hyphen Press, 2008.

Hochuli, Jost and Robin Kinross. *Designing Books: Practice and Theory*. London: Hyphen Press, 1996.

Hutt, Allen. Fournier: *The Compleat Typographer*. Totowa, NJ: Rowman and Littlefield, 1972.

Jardí, Enric. *Twenty-Two Tips on Typography*. Barcelona: Actar, 2007.

Jaspert, Berry and Johnson Jaspert. *Encyclopaedia of Typefaces*. London: Cassell, 2009.

Johnston, Alastair. Alphabets to Order: *The Literature of Nineteenth-Century Typefounders' Specimens*. New Castle, DE: Oak Knoll Press, 2000.

Jubert, Roxane. *Typography and Graphic Design: From Antiquity to the Present*. Paris: Flammarion, 2006.

Jury, David. About Face: *Reviving the Rules of Typography*. East Sussex, UK: RotoVision, 2002.

Jury, David. Letterpress: *New Applications for Traditional Skills*. East Sussex, UK: RotoVision, 2006.

Kane, John. *A Type Primer*. Upper Saddle River, NJ: Prentice Hall, 2003.

Kegler, Richard. *Indie Fonts*. Beverly, MA: Rockport Publishers, 2002.

Kegler, Richard, James Grieshaber, and Tamye Riggs. *Indie Fonts 2*. Beverly, MA: Rockport Publishers, 2003.

Kegler, Richard, James Grieshaber, and Tamye Riggs. *Indie Fonts 3*. Beverly, MA: Rockport Publishers, 2007.

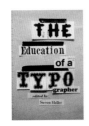

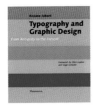

Kelly, Jerry, Alice Koeth, *American Institute of Graphic Arts, and Society of Scribes. Artist & Alphabet: 20th Century Calligraphy & Letter Art in America*. Boston, MA: David R. Godine, 2000.

Kelly, Rob Roy. *American Wood Type, 1828-1900: Notes on the Evolution of Decorated and Large Types and Comments on Related Trades of the Period*. New York: Van Nostrand Reinhold Co., 1969.

Kelly, Rob Roy. *Wood Type Alphabets: 100 Fonts*. New York: Dover Publications, 1977.

King, Emily and Robert Brownjohn. *Robert Brownjohn, Sex And Typography, 1925-1970: Life and Work*. New York: Princeton Architectural Press, 2005.

King, Jean Callan and Tony Esposito. *The Designer's Guide to Text Type: Leaded Showings of Fifty-One Popular Text Typefaces in 6 Point through 12 Point Plus 14 Point*. New York: Van Nostrand Reinhold, 1980.

Kinross, Robin. *Modern Typography, 2nd Edition*. London: Hyphen Press, 2004.

Knuth, Donald Ervin. *Digital Typography*. Stanford, CA: CSLI Publications, 1999.

Krantz, Steven G. Handbook of *Typography for the Mathematical Sciences*. Boca Raton, FL: Chapman & Hall/CRC, 2001.

Kunz, Willi. *Typography: Macro- and Microaesthetics*. Sulgen: Niggli, 2000.

Kunz, Willi. *Typography: Formation + Transformation*. Sulgen: Niggli, 2003.

Larcher, Jean. *Fantastic Alphabets*. New York: Dover Publications, 1976.

Lawson, Alexander S. *Anatomy of a Typeface*. Boston, MA: David R. Godine, 1990.

Loxley, Simon. *Type: The Secret History of Letters*. London: I.B. Tauris, 2004.

Loy, William E. *Nineteenth-Century American Designers and Engravers of Type*. New Castle, DE: Oak Knoll Press, 2009.

Lupton, Ellen. *Thinking with Type: A Critical Guide for Designers, Writers, Editors, & Students*. New York: Princeton Architectural Press, 2010.

McLean, Ruari. *The Thames and Hudson Manual of Typography*. London: Thames & Hudson, 1980.

McLean, Ruari. *Typographers on Type: An Illustrated Anthology from William Morris to the Present Day*. New York: Norton, 1995.

McLean, Ruari. *How Typography Happens*. London: New Castle, 2000.

MacLean, Ruari and Jan Tschichold. Jan Tschichold: *A Life in Typography*. New York: Princeton Architectural Press, 1999.

Macmillan, Neil. *An A-Z of Type Designers*. London: Laurence King Publishing, 2006.

McMurtrie, Douglas C. *Modern Typography & Layout*. Chicago, IL: Eyncourt Press, 1929.

McMurtrie, Douglas C. *Active-Age Typography*. Chicago, IL, 1930.

McMurtrie, Douglas C. Contemporary *European Typography*. Cincinnati, OH, 1933.

McMurtrie, Douglas C., South Dakota State University Dept. of Journalism and Mass Communication. *Newspaper Typography That Sells Merchandise: Proofs Showing Alternative Settings of Identical Copy*. Brookings, SD: South Dakota State College, 1939.

Meggs, Philip B. *Type & Image: The Language of Graphic Design*. New York: Van Nostrand Reinhold, 1989.

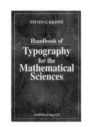

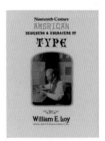

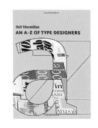

Meggs, Philip B. and Rob Carter. *Typographic Specimens: The Great Typefaces*. New York: Van Nostrand Reinhold, 1993.

Meggs, Philip and Alston Purvis. *Meggs' History of Graphic Design*. Hoboken, NJ: Wiley & Sons, 2006.

Menten, Theodore and Roman Scherer. *Art Nouveau and Early Art Deco Type and Design: From the Roman Scherer Catalogue*. New York: Dover Publications, 1972.

Meynell, Francis. *The Typography of Newspaper Advertisements*. New York: Frederick A. Stokes Company, 1929.

Middendorp, Jan and Erik Spiekermann. *Made With Fontfont: Type for Independent Minds*. New York: Mark Batty Publisher, 2007.

Morgan, Margaret. *The Bible of Illuminated Letters: A Treasury of Decorative Calligraphy*. Hauppauge, NY: Barron's Educational Series, 2006.

Morison, Stanley and Brooke Crutchley. *A Tally of Types: With Additions by Several Hands; And with a New Introduction by Mike Parker*. Boston, MA: David R. Godine, 1999.

Neuenschwander, Brody, Leonard Currie, and David Quay. *Letterwork: Creative Letterforms in Graphic Design*. London: Phaidon Press, 1993.

Noordzij, Gerrit. *Letterletter: An Inconsistent Collection of Tentative Theories That Do Not Claim Any Other Authority Than That of Common Sense*. Point Roberts, WA: Hartley & Marks, 2000.

Noordzij, Gerrit. *The Stroke: Theory of Writing*. London: Hyphen Press, 2005.

Norton, David M. and Berton Braley. *Progressive Typography*. Syracuse, NY: Spare Moments Press, 1961.

Ogg, Oscar, Ludovico degli Arrighi, Giovanni Antonio Tagliente, and Giovanni Battista Palatino. *Three Classics of Italian Calligraphy*. New York: Dover Publications, 1953.

Paoli, Cristina. *Mexican Blackletter*. New York: Mark Batty, 2007.

Paterson, Donald Gildersleeve and Miles A. Tinker. *How to Make Type Readable: A Manual for Typographers, Printers and Advertisers, Based on Twelve Years of Research Involving Speed of Reading Tests Given to 33,031 Persons*. New York and London: Harper & Brothers, 1940.

Peace, David. *Eric Gill, The Inscriptions: A Descriptive Catalogue; Based On The Inscriptional Work of Eric Gill*. London: Herbert Press, 1994.

Perfect, Christopher, Gordon Rookledge, and Phil Baines. *Rookledge's Classic International Typefinder: The Essential Handbook of Typeface Recognition and Selection*. London: Laurence King, 2004.

Perry, Michael. *Hand Job: A Catalog of Type*. New York: Princeton Architectural Press, 2007.

Poulin, Richard. *The Language of Graphic Design*. Beverly, MA: Rockport Publishers, 2011.

Poynor, Rick. *Typographica*. New York: Princeton Architectural Press, 2002.

Poynor, Rick and Edward Booth-Clibborn. *Typography Now: The Next Wave*. Berkeley, CA: Ginko Press, 1998.

Rafaeli, Ari. *Book Typography*. New Castle, DE: Oak Knoll Press, 2005.

Rand, Paul (ed.). *Typ Mundus 20: A Project of the International Center for the Typographic Arts (Icta)*. New York: Reinhold, 1966.

Re, Margaret, Matthew Carter, Johanna Drucker, James Mosley, and Albin O. Kuhn Library & Gallery. *Typographically Speaking: The Art of Matthew Carter*. New York: Princeton Architectural Press, 2003.

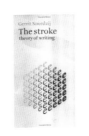

Rehe, Rolf F. *Typography and Design for Newspapers.* Indianapolis, IN: Design Research International, 1985.

Reyes, Fabiola and Josep Maria Minguet. *Typo: The Beautiful World of Fonts.* Barcelona, Spain: Maidstone Monsa, 2008.

Roberts, Caroline, Matilda Saxow, and A. Young Kim. *Letterform Collected: A Typographic Compendium 2005-2009.* London: Grafik Magazine/Adventures in Publishing, 2009.

Rosen, Ben. *Type and Typography: The Designer's Type Book: Hot Metal Type.* New York: Van Nostrand Reinhold, 1989.

Rosendorf, Theodore. *The Typographic Desk Reference.* New Castle, DE: Oak Knoll Press, 2009.

Rosentswieg, Gerry. *Type Faces.* New York: Madison Square Press, 1995.

Rosentswieg, Gerry. *The New Typographic Logo.* New York: Madison Square Press, 1996.

Rummonds, Richard-Gabriel. *Printing on the Iron Handpress.* New Castle, DE: Oak Knoll Press & The British Library, 1998.

Saltz, Ina. *Body Type: Intimate Messages Etched in Flesh.* New York: Abrams Image, 2006.

Saltz, Ina. *Typography Essentials: 100 Design Principles For Working With Type.* Beverly, MA: Rockport Publishers, 2009.

Samara, Timothy. *Type Style Finder: The Busy Designer's Guide to Choosing Type.* Beverly, MA: Rockport Publishers, 2006.

Samara, Timothy. *Typography Workbook: A Real-World Guide to Using Type in Graphic Design.* Beverly, MA: Rockport Publishers, 2006.

Sassoon, Rosemary. *A Practical Guide to Lettering & Applied Calligraphy.* New York: Thames & Hudson, 1985.

School of Visual Arts. *Uncommon Characters by Uncommon Characters.* New York: The School of Visual Arts, 1980.

Sherbow, Benjamin. *Effective Type-Use for Advertising.* New York: B. Sherbow, 1922.

Siegfried, Laurance Benjamin. *Typographic Design in Advertising.* Washington, D.C.: United Typothetae of America, 1930.

Simon, Oliver and David Bland. *Introduction to Typography.* London: Faber & Faber, 1963.

Smeijers, Fred. *Counterpunch: Making Type in the 16th Century, Designing Typefaces Now.* London: Hyphen Press, 1997.

Smeijers, Fred. *Type Now: A Manifesto; Plus, Work So Far.* London: Hyphen Press, 2003.

Smith, Virginia. *Forms in Modernism: A Visual Set: The Unity of Typography, Architecture and the Design Arts.* New York: Garsington Watson-Guptill, 2005.

Spencer, Herbert. *Pioneers of Modern Typography.* London: Lund Humphries, 1990.

Spiekermann, Erik and E. M. Ginger. *Stop Stealing Sheep & Find Out How Type Works.* Berkeley, CA: Adobe Press, 2003.

Spiekermann, Erik, Jürgen Siebert, and Mai-Linh Thi Truong. *Fontbook.* Berlin, Germany: FSI FontShop International, 2006.

Strizver, Ilene. *Type Rules!: The Designer's Guide to Professional Typography.* Hoboken, NJ: Wiley, 2006.

Stuart, Edwin Hamilton and Grace Stuart Gardner. *Typography, Layout & Advertising Production; Handbook For Newcomers to the Advertising Profession.* Pittsburgh, PA: Stuart, 1947.

Sutton, James, Alan Bartram, and British Library. *Typefaces for Books.* London: British Library, 1990.

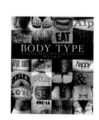

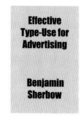

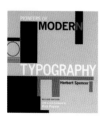

Swann, Cal. *Techniques of Typography.* New York: Watson-Guptill Publications, 1969.

Tracy, Walter. *Letters of Credit: A View of Type Design.* Boston, MA: David R. Godine, 2003.

Triggs, Teal. *Type Design: Radical Innovations and Experimentation.* New York: Harper Design International, 2003.

Tschichold, Jan. *Treasury of Alphabets and Lettering.* New York: W. W. Norton & Company, 1995.

Tschichold, Jan. *The New Typography.* Berkeley, CA: University of California Press, 2006.

Tschichold, Jan, Cees de Jong, et al. *Jan Tschichold: Master Typographer: His Life, Work & Legacy.* London: Thames & Hudson, 2008.

Tselentis, Jason. *Type Form & Function.* Beverly, MA: Rockport Publishers, 2011.

Unger, Gerard. *While You're Reading.* New York: Mark Batty, 2007.

Updike, Daniel Berkeley. *Printing Types: Their History, Forms and Use.* New Castle, DE: Oak Knoll Press, 2001.

Van Krimpen, Jan. *On Designing and Devising Type.* New York: The Typophiles, 1957.

Vervliet, Hendrik D. L. *Sixteenth Century Printing Types of the Low Countries.* Amsterdam: Menno Hertzberger, 1968.

Vervliet, Hendrik D. L., Harry Carter, and John Dreyfus. *Type Specimen Facsimiles.* London: The Bodley Head Ltd, 1972.

Wales, Hugh G. *Advertising Copy, Layout, and Typography.* New York: Ronald Press Co., 1958.

Wallis, L. W. *A Concise Chronology of Typesetting Developments, 1886-1986.* London: Wynkyn de Worde Society in association with Lund Humphries, 1988.

Walter, Roy. *A-Z of Typography.* Windsor, VA: Virginia Brook Pub., 1991.

Walton, Roger. *Big Type.* New York: HBI, 2002.

Walton, Roger. *Type: No Borders, No Boundaries, No Limits.* New York: HBI, 2002.

Walton, Roger. *The Big Book of Typographics 1 & 2.* New York: Collins Design, 2004.

Walton, Roger. *The Big Book of Typographics 3 & 4.* New York: Collins Design, 2004.

Wheildon, Colin and Mal Warwick. *Type & Layout: How Typography and Design Can Get Your Message Across—or Get in the Way.* Berkeley, CA: Strathmoor Press, 1995.

White, Alex. *Type in Use: Effective Typography for Electronic Publishing.* New York: W.W. Norton, 1999.

White, Alex. *Advertising Design and Typography.* New York: Allworth Press, 2007.

Willen, Bruce and Nolen Strals. *Lettering & Type: Creating Letters and Designing Typefaces.* New York: Princeton Architectural Press, 2009.

Woolman, Matt. *Type in Motion 2.* London: Thames & Hudson, 2005.

Woolman, Matthew. *A Type Detective Story. Episode One: The Crime Scene.* East Sussex, UK: RotoVision, 1997.

Zapf, Hermann, Gudrun Zapf von Hesse, John Prestianni, Friends of Calligraphy (San Francisco, Calif.), and San Francisco Public Library. *Calligraphic Type Design in the Digital Age: An Exhibition in Honor of the Contributions of Hermann and Gudrun Zapf: Selected Type Designs and Calligraphy by Sixteen Designers.* Corte Madera: Gingko Press, 2001.

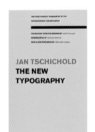

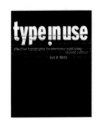

Allan Haley

Allan Haley is director of words and letters at Monotype Imaging, where he is responsible for strategic planning and creative implementation of just about everything related to typeface designs, as well as editorial content for the company's type libraries and websites.

Haley is also a past president of the board of the Society of Typographic Aficionados and the New York Type Directors Club. A prolific writer, he has written five books about type and graphic communication and hundreds of articles for graphic design publications.

Richard Poulin

Richard Poulin is cofounder, design director, and principal of Poulin + Morris Inc., an internationally recognized, multidisciplinary design consultancy in New York City. His work has been published in periodicals and books, is in the permanent collection of the Library of Congress, and has received awards from organizations worldwide. Poulin is a fellow of the Society for Environmental Graphic Design, past president and board member of the New York chapter of AIGA, and a recipient of a research grant from the Graham Foundation for Advanced Studies in the Fine Arts. Since 1992, he has been a faculty member of the School of Visual Arts in New York City and was formerly an adjunct professor at The Cooper Union. He is the author of *The Language of Graphic Design: An Illustrated Handbook for Understanding Fundamental Design Principles* published by Rockport in 2011. Poulin lives in New York City and Clinton Corners, New York, with his partner of twenty-two years

Jason Tselentis

Jason Tselentis teaches typography and design at Winthrop University in Rock Hill, South Carolina. He has worked in branding, information design, and Web design since 1996 for commercial, nonprofit, and academic clients. His writings about design and visual culture have appeared in *Arcade*, *Emigre*, *Eye*, *How*, and *Mental Floss* magazines. Rockport Publishers produced his first book, *Type, Form & Function*, in 2011.

Tony Seddon

Tony Seddon studied graphic design in his native Cornwall and at Bournemouth College of Art before graduating in 1987. During the following twelve-year period, Seddon lived and worked in London, first for a multidisciplinary design consultancy, then as a senior art editor for an illustrated book publisher. In 1999, he relocated to the south coast and has continued to specialize in book design and art direction while working for several publishing companies in Lewes and Brighton.

In January 2011, Seddon began a new career as a freelance designer and writer. He has authored three books: *Images: A Creative Digital Workflow for Graphic Designers*, *Graphic Design for Nondesigners*, and *Art Directing Projects for Print*. He currently lives in Alfriston, East Sussex.

Gerry Leonidas

Gerry Leonidas is a Senior Lecturer in Typography at the University of Reading, UK. He teaches typographic design and typeface design at under- and postgraduate levels. His research interests include Greek typography and the development of typeface design as a field of study.

Ina Saltz

Ina Saltz is an art director, designer, author, photographer, and professor of art at The City College of New York. Her areas of expertise are typography and magazine design; she is also chairperson of the art department at CCNY.

Saltz has authored more than fifty articles on typography and design for design publications. She is a board member and program director of the Type Directors Club. She is on the design faculty of the Stanford Publishing Course, and she frequently lectures on topics related to magazine design and typography, including, most recently, in Toronto, Atlanta, Denver, Moscow, Calgary, and Amsterdam.

Saltz is the author of three books: *Body Type: Intimate Messages Etched in Flesh*, 2006, and *Body Type 2: More Typography Tattoos*, 2010, published by Abrams, and *Typography Essentials: 100 Design Principles for Working with Type*, 2009, published by Rockport Publishers. She had solo exhibitions of her photographs from Body Type at Cooper Union's Herb Lubalin Study Center of Design and Typography and at the Snug Harbor Cultural Center's Newhouse Center for Contemporary Art. She is currently working on a third volume of Body Type. She lives in New York City with her husband, Steven Beispel.

Kathryn Henderson

Kathryn Henderson is a writer, editor, and designer interested in the convergence between design and pop culture. After obtaining her BFA in Graphic Design from the Rochester Institute of Technology, Henderson switched gears from creating to observing, graduating in 2010 with an MFA in Design Criticism from the School of the Visual Arts. She has since applied her skills to projects with The Noguchi Museum, The Century Association Archives Foundation, and various sites including Complex.com. Currently, you can find her at Pentagram Design obsessing over new design work and assisting with daily communications as deputy editor of Content Development for Pentagram.com.

Tyler Alterman

Tyler Alterman is a fourth-year student in The City University of New York's Macaulay Honors College studying creative behavior change. His obsessions include the science of persuasion, cognitive neuroscience, graphic design, cinnamon pita chips, and any fine type with high contrast, ball terminals, or geometric forms.

About the Designer

Donald Partyka is an educator and award-winning editorial designer. He is the Creative Director of the journal *Americas Quarterly* and teaches typography and design at The City College of New York. Partyka has launched, redesigned, and art directed numerous consumer, trade, and educational publications over the past 18 years. A graduate of The Rhode Island School of Design, he recently completed his first semester as a student in Cooper Union's Postgraduate Certificate Program in Type Design.

Contributors

2Creatives
Harrow Weald, UK
www.2creatives.com
ISTD, Gordon Brown design team:
creative director and designer:
Rishi Sodha
+81, Vision design team:
creative directors: Rishi Sodha,
Anton Webb
**Orion [augmented reality with
Gill Sans] design team:** creative
directors: Rishi Sodha, Anton
Webb; design and typography:
Rishi Sodha; developer: Anton
Webb
Memories Limited Edition:
DAHRA, 2Creatives, OneTenEleven
Media, Subism and Garrick Webster
http://dahra.org
2Creatives design team:
creative directors: Rishi Sodha,
Stuart Boyd, Antony Kitson, Gar-
rick Webster; design, cover, and
typography: Rishi Sodha; chief edi-
tor: Garrick Webster; editors: Stuart
Boyd, Antony Kitson; Rishi Sodha

A3 Design
Webster, New York
www.a3-design.com
Ducati Mailer team:
designers: Alan Altman, Arrick
Maurice; photography: Ducati, Italy.

Rui Abreu
Lisbon, Portugal
www.r-typography.com

AdamsMorioka, Inc.
Beverly Hills, California
www.adamsmorioka.com
Creative directors: Sean Adams and
Noreen Morioka; designers: Monica
Schlaug, Nathan Stock, Nichelle
Barnes, Chris Taillon

Brent Barson
Studio DVA
Provo, Utah
www.visualarts.byu.edu
Typophile 5 project team:
Brent Barson, creative director,
producer, and animator.
Designers/animators: Jessica
Blackham, Brian Christensen,
Analisa Estrada, Meg Gallagher,
John Jensen, Regan Fred
Johnson, Colin "The Pin" Pinegar,
Wynn Burton, Olivia Juarez
Knudsen, Casey Lewis, Reeding
Roberts, and Deven Stephens.

Ed Benguiat
Hasbrouck Heights, New Jersey
Jennifer Beorkrem
www.orkposters.com
John Berry
Peter Bilak
Typotheque
The Hague, The Netherlands
www.typotheque.com
Tomáš Brousil
Suitcase Type Foundry
www.suitcasetype.com
Jen Baker Brown
www.nomadicbydesign.com/jen
Neil Brown
www.nomadicbydesign.com
**Bruketa&Žinić OM
Zagreb**
Zagreb, Croatia
www.bruketa-zinic.com
Adris Group Annual Report:
creative directors: Bruketa&Žinić
OM / Davor Bruketa, Nikola
Žinić; art director: Tomislav
Jurica Kaćunić; copywriter: Daniel
Vuković, Ivan Čadež; designer:
Igor Miletić; production manager:
Vesna Đurašin; desktop publishing:
Radovan Radičević; account direc-
tor: Ivanka Mabić; Adris Group,
editor: Predrag Grubić
**Faces, Adris Group Annual
Report:** creative directors:
Bruketa&Žinić OM / Moe Minkara;
art directors/designers: Imelda
Ramović, Mirel Hadžijusufović;
desktop publishing: Radovan
Radičević; account director: Helena
Rosandić; photographer: Dorijan
Kljun; book photos: Domagoj Kunić
Bold for Men packaging:
senior brand consultant: Brandoc-
tor / Anja Bauer Minkara; junior
brand consultant: Maja Benčić;
creative director: Moe Minkara; art
director/designer: Jurana Puljić;
account director: Helena Rosandić

Jos Buiveriga
Exljbris Font Foundry
www.exljbris.com

Veronika Burian
TypeTogether
Prague, Czech Republic
www.type-together.com

David Cabianca
York University/Department of
Design
Toronto, Canada
www.design.yorku.ca

Margaret Calvert
London, United Kingdom

Pilar Cano
Barcelona, Spain
www.pilarcano.com

Rod Cavazos
Jim Chambers
Eric Chan
Eric Chan Design Co.
Hong Kong, China
www.ericchandesign.com
**Gough Street Festival design
team:** design director: Eric Chan;
art directors: Eric Chan, Iris Yu;
designer: Eric Chan; photogra-
pher: Tim Lau of Tim Photography.
**Antalis - Typography Poster
design team:** design director:
Eric Chan; art director: Eric Chan;
designer: Sandi Lee.
**Everything Has Two Sides Poster
design team:** design director: Eric
Chan; art directors: Eric Chan, Iris
Yu; designers: Iris Yu, Andries Lee,
Sandi Lee; illustrators: Miva Tsang,
Iris Yu.
Polytrade Diary 2010 design team:
creative director: Eric Chan; art directors: Eric Chan, Iris Yu; design-
ers: Eric Chan, Jim Wong; logotype:
Iris Yu, Jim Wong, Manson Chan.

Colle + McVoy
Minneapolis, Minnesota
www.collemcvoy.com

Cotton and Crown
Charlotte, North Carolina
www.cottonandcrown.com

Nick Curtis
www.nicksfonts.com

Joshua Darden
Darden Studio
Brooklyn, New York
www.dardenstudio.com

DBD International, Ltd.
Menomonie, Wisconsin
www.risingabovethenoise.com

Design360
New York, New York
www.design360inc.com

**News Corp Dow Jones project
team:** designers: Jill Ayers
(creative director), Rachel
Einsidler (senior designer), and
Christine Giberson (designer);
architect: Studios Architecture; fabricator: Xibitz (static),
XL Video/AV Services/Pod
Design (dynamic); photog-
rapher: Jeffrey Kilmer.
**New York University Department
of Social and Cultural Analysis
project team:** designers: Jill
Ayers (creative director), Rachel
Einsidler (designer); architect:
LTL Architects; fabricator: Xibitz;
photographer: Michael Moran.
**The One Club Exhibit project
team:** designers: Jill Ayers
(creative director), Rachel
Einsidler (senior designer),
Christine Giberson (designer);
fabricator: VGS: Visual Graphic
Systems Inc.

Design Bridge
London, UK
www.designbridge.com

Dizajn Studio Box
Kragujevac, Serbia
www.dizajnstudiobox.com

Jeff Domke
www.jeffdomke.com

Experimental Jetset
www.experimentaljetset.nl

**Expolab advanced
communication and
design**
Munich, Germany
www.expolab.eu

Fangman Design
Austin, Texas
www.fangmandesign.com

Kevin Finn
Finn Creative
Brisbane, Australia
www.finncreative.com.au
www.openmanifesto.net
DESIGNerd 100+ Trivia Games
typefaces: handwriting: Kevin Finn,
Steven Heller, Stefan Sagmeister

Contributors

Ryan Pescatore Frisk & Catelijne van Middelkoop
Strange Attractors Design
Rotterdam, The Netherlands
www.strangeattractors.com

Luc(as) de Groot
Lucas Fonts GmbH
Berlin, Germany
www.lucasfonts.com

Tomi Haaparanta
Suomi Type Foundry
Helsinki, Finland
www.type.fi/suomihome/html

Hao In Kuan

David Harper
Evansville, Indiana
www.daveharperdesign.com

Stefan Hattenbach
MAC Rhino Fonts (MRF)
Stockholm, Sweden
www.macrhino.com

Akiem Helmling

Christian Helms
Helms Workshop
Austin, Texas
www.helmsworkshop.com

Cristóbal Henestrosa
www.estudio-ch.com

Jessica Hische
Brooklyn, New York
jessicahische.is/awesome

Dusan Jelesijevic
www.dusanjelesijevic.com

Eric Kass
Funnel
Indianapolis, Indiana
www.funnel.tv

Ian Katz
www.tinylittlelife.org

Stefan Krömer

Ray Larabie
www.larabiefonts.com

Lehrman Cameron Studio
Seattle, Washington
www.lehrmancameron.com

Snoqualmie Falls project team:
design: Lehrman Cameron Studio;
photos: Lehrman Cameron Studio;
LCS lead designer: Mindy Lehrman
Cameron; LCS project manager:
Maxwell Cameron; LCS graphic
designers: Faith Haney, Fran Terry;
LCS designer: Roma Shah.

Zuzana Licko
Emigre, Inc.
Berkeley, California
www.emigre.com

Lure Design
Orlando, Florida
www.luredesigninc.com

Kelly Salchow MacArthur
thrive design
Ann Arbor, Michigan
www.elevatedesign.org
Elevate project team: Kelly
Salchow MacArthur, Asya
Palatova, and Richard Sweeney.

Ulga Marekowa

Steve Matteson
Ascender Corporation

MOD / Michael Osborne Design
San Francisco, California
www.modsf.com

Monotype Imaging
Woburn, Massachusetts
www.fonts.com

James Montalbano
Terminal Design, Inc.
Brooklyn, New York
www.terminaldesign.com

German Olaya
Bogota, Colombia
www.typo5.com

Eric Olson
Process Type Foundry
Golden Valley, California
www.processtypefoundry.com

P22 type foundry, Inc.
Buffalo, New York
www.p22.com

Alejandro Paul
Sudtipos
Buenos Aires, Argentina
www.sudtipos.com/home

Brian Pelayo
www.bpelayo.com
AVRP Studios website:
creative direction: Tyler Blik;
design: Brian Pelayo
City of National City poster:
creative direction: Tyler Blik;
design: Kaori Toda, Yuki Hayashi,
Brian Pelayo
Tecolote Youth Baseball:
creative direction: Tyler Blik; design: Tyler Blik, Brian Pelayo
Eddie's Van For Hire:
design: Brian Pelayo

Pentagram
www.pentagram.com

Poulin + Morris, Inc.
New York, New York
www.poulinmorris.com

Principle
www.designbyprinciple.com

Vikki Quick
Monotype Imaging

RipBang Studios
Venice, California
www.ripbangstudios.com

Sagmeister Inc.
www.sagmeister.com
Columbia Abstract team:
art direction: Stefan Sagmeister,
Joe Shouldice; design: Joe Shouldice, Richard The, Daniel Harding;
editor: Scott Marble
Obsessions Make My Life Worse
and My Work Better team:
design: Richard The, Joe Shouldice,
Stefan Sagmeister

José Scaglione
TypeTogether
Rosario, Santa Fe, Argentina
www.type-together.com

Ralph Schraivogel
Zurich, Switzerland
www.ralphschraivogel.com

Mark Simonson
www.marksimonson.com

Skidmore, Owings & Merrill LLP
San Francisco, California
www.som.com
Oakland Museum of California
Donor Wall photographs courtesy
of SOM, ©Tim Griffith and ©Skidmore, Owings & Merrill LLP

Fred Smeijers
OurType
De Pinte, Belgium
www.ourtype.com

Mark Solsburg
www.typobrand.com/experience/solsburg.html

Kris Sowersby
Klim Type Foundry
Wellington, New Zealand
www.klim.co.nz

Spunk Design Machine
Minneapolis, Minnesota
www.spkdm.com

Sumner Stone
Stone Type Foundry
Gunida, California
www.stonetypefoundry.com

Taxi
www.taxi.ca
Pak-n-stor design team:
art director & illustrator: Kelsey
Horne; copywriter: Nick Asik; photography: Jason Stang.

Typekit
www.typekit.com

Voice
Adelaide, Australia
www.voicedesign.net

Jürgen Weltin
Type Matters
Pullach, Germany
www.typematters.com

The White Room Inc.
Toronto, Canada
www.thewhiteroom.ca

Fabian Widmer
Letterwerk Type & Media
Zurich, Switzerland
www.letterwerk.ch

Stefan Willerstorfer
Willerstorfer Font Foundry
Vienna, Austria
www.willerstorfer.com

Luke Williams
Luke Williams Graphic Design
Chicago, Illinois
www.lukelukeluke.com

Image Credits

Index